POSTWAR ECONOMIC TRENDS
IN THE UNITED STATES

☆

EDITED BY

RALPH E. FREEMAN

HARPER & BROTHERS   PUBLISHERS   NEW YORK

POSTWAR ECONOMIC TRENDS
IN THE UNITED STATES

AMERICAN PROJECT SERIES
Center for International Studies

MASSACHUSETTS INSTITUTE OF TECHNOLOGY

Books from the Center for International Studies

PUBLISHED BY HARPER & BROTHERS

A Proposal: Key to an Effective Foreign Policy
by M. F. Millikan and W. W. Rostow, 1957

Forging a New Sword: A Study of the Department of Defense
by William R. Kintner, with Joseph I. Coffey and Raymond J.
Albright, 1958

The American Style: Essays in Value and Performance
edited by Elting E. Morison, 1958

Postwar Economic Trends in the United States
edited by Ralph E. Freeman, 1960

The United States in the World Arena: An Essay in Recent History
by W. W. Rostow, 1960

The Question of Government Spending: Private Wants and Public
Needs, 1960
by Francis M. Bator

OTHER BOOKS FROM THE CENTER FOR INTERNATIONAL STUDIES

The Dynamics of Soviet Society
by W. W. Rostow, Alfred Levin, and Others, Norton, 1953; Mentor
Books, 1954

Soviet Education for Science and Technology
by Alexander G. Korol, Technology Press of MIT and Wiley, 1957

The Economics of Communist Eastern Europe
by Nicolas Spulber, Technology Press of MIT and Wiley, 1957

The Structure of the East German Economy
by Wolfgang F. Stolper, Harvard, 1959

The Prospects for Communist China
by W. W. Rostow and Others, Technology Press of MIT and Wiley,
1954

China's Gross National Product and Social Accounts: 1950-1957
    by William W. Hollister, Free Press, 1958

The Chinese Family in the Communist Revolution and A Chinese Village
in Early Communist Transition
    by C. K. Yang, Technology Press of MIT and Harvard, 1959

Scratches on Our Minds: American Images of China and India
    by Harold R. Isaacs, John Day, 1958

Changing Images of America: A Study of Indian Students' Perceptions
    by George V. Coelho, Free Press, 1958

Moscow and the Communist Party of India
    by John H. Kautsky, Technology Press of MIT and Wiley, 1956

Industrial Change in India: Industrial Growth, Capital Requirements,
and Technological Change, 1937-1955
    by George Rosen, Free Press, 1958

Industrial Growth in South India: Case Studies in Economic Development
    by George B. Baldwin, Free Press, 1959

Indonesia's Economic Stabilization and Development
    by Benjamin Higgins, Institute of Pacific Relations, 1957

Financing Economic Development: The Indonesian Case
    by Douglas S. Paauw, Free Press, 1959

Overseas Chinese Nationalism: The Genesis of the Pan-Chinese Movement in Indonesia, 1900-1916
    by Lea Everard Williams, Free Press, 1959

The Religion of Java
    by Clifford Geertz, Free Press, 1959

Handbook for Industry Studies
    by Everett E. Hagen, Free Press, 1958

The Japanese Factory: Aspects of Its Social Organization
    by James C. Abegglen, Free Press, 1958

Bloc Politics in the United Nations
    by Thomas Hovet, Jr., Harvard, 1959

The Passing of Traditional Society: Modernizing the Middle East
    by Daniel Lerner, with Lucille W. Pevsner. Co-sponsored by the
    Bureau of Applied Social Research, Columbia University. Free Press,
    1958

CONTENTS

CONTRIBUTORS' FOREWORD

These papers have been extracted from us by Ralph E. Freeman. They represent more, however, than the fruit of his entrepreneurial skill. From our viewpoint they are simultaneously a tribute to his wise and gentle leadership of the Department of Economics and Social Science at the Massachusetts Institute of Technology over twenty-five years and to him as colleague and friend. This is not a *Festschrift*, edited by the object of the celebration. But we cannot let this occasion pass without indicating, unknown to him, how much it has meant to each of us to work with Professor Freeman in scholarly endeavor.

EDITOR'S FOREWORD

This volume is a product of the American Studies Project at the Center for International Studies, Massachusetts Institute of Technology, an undertaking made possible by the Carnegie Corporation.

The only link between these essays is that they all relate to economic trends in the United States since the end of World War II. Each author was asked to write on a subject in which he was especially interested. No attempt was made to set a uniform pattern as to length, style, or method of approach. Though the emphasis is on the past decade, some of the writers found it desirable to give considerable attention to prewar events as background for more recent developments.

The absence of a central theme and the diversity of treatment made the task of the editor relatively simple. He was also greatly helped by the fact that all the authors are members of the staff of M.I.T., and the fact that he had at hand the invaluable assistance of Miss Beatrice A. Rogers of the M.I.T. Department of Economics in preparing this volume for publication.

RALPH E. FREEMAN
Cambridge, Massachusetts

ONE

☆

THE DYNAMICS OF
AMERICAN SOCIETY

☆

W. W. ROSTOW

Between 1940 and 1958 two processes which for more than half a century had posed the central questions for American social and political life came to a stage of at least interim resolution—suburbanization, based on the spread of the automobile; and the evolution of the welfare state.

There was a resumption in the first decade after World War II of the pattern of economic and social evolution which had taken shape in the 1920's and an acceptance of the political adaptation of the 1930's. The set of institutions and public attitudes crystallized in the first phase of the New Deal were consolidated; and, in the end, they were accepted by both political parties and by a substantial majority of the public as the appropriate matrix of mid-twentieth-century American life. The rise of real income and the progressive diffusion of durable consumers' goods and services did not cease as the postwar decade came to an end; nor were the problems and contours of the welfare state once and for all settled. But, just as the forces on the world scene were moving away from prevailing American images during the early 1950's, something of the same appears to have been taking place at home; and by 1956–1958 a relatively new set of issues for American economic and social life, and for politics as well, began to define and assert themselves.

Changes in Domestic Life

The changes in domestic life during the postwar decade, and in the patterns of action of individual American citizens, raised a fundamental question: Had the emergence of American society to a stage of tightly organized urban life, accompanied by high and secure levels of consumption, brought with it a change in American values?

This is not an easy matter to sort out; for human action, being a choice among perceived alternatives, is determined by the interplay between human values and aspirations on the one hand and, on the other, by the setting in which men and women seek to make these values and aspirations effective. The setting determines the range of choice available.

3

Changes in the setting of a society result, however, from the flow of past action; that is, they reflect the past interplay between values and the environment in which those values expressed themselves. At any particular period, therefore, the setting of a society is not simply a material, objective fact determined merely by external circumstance; it reflects the prior interplay between both sides of the equation, both sides of the market.[a] It is thus difficult to establish for any society the extent to which changes in its setting are the product of objective factors external to human values and aspirations as opposed to the cumulative (if partial) influence of values on past action; and it is equally difficult to establish whether changes in human action are due to shifts in values or due to shifts in the choices which the setting of a society allows its citizens.

Despite the inherent complexity of this interaction, it is nevertheless useful to consider first the changes in the setting of American society as it evolved from 1940 down to the mid–1950's and then to explore changes in action and performance which may reflect an authentic change in values, a change in the alternatives open to Americans, or a combination of both.

THE ECONOMIC SETTING

The major changes in the economic setting of American life in the recent past are familiar and may be briskly summarized.

The heavy unemployment of the 1930's was dissipated during the war years; and although there were postwar recessions at roughly three-year intervals, following a rhythm of inventory fluctuation at least a century and a half old, an environment of relatively full employment was maintained, imparting to the postwar years a gradually gathering sense of security with respect to employment.

The rise in employment and the more or less regular increase in productivity built into American economic institutions yielded a rise in real income per head and per family. Real income thus defined rose sharply during the war years and continued to rise slowly in the postwar decade. Average (mean) personal income per family or unattached individual after taxes, at 1956 prices, increased from $4,520

---

[a] In economics, demand and supply can be regarded as independent variables only in the short period; but in the long period they emerge as interdependent, thus posing almost insuperable obstacles for long-period economic analysis by classical, equilibrium methods. For further discussion, see the author's *Process of Economic Growth* (New York: W. W. Norton & Company, Inc., 1952), pp. 4–7 and pp. 38–48.

in 1947 to $5,050 in 1955.¹ Changes in the structure of the working force and the nation's progressive tax structure combined to shift an expanding proportion of the population into middle-class income levels, where the ownership of a single-family house and an automobile was the normal expectation. In 1955, 59 per cent of American families or unattached individuals had annual incomes (before income tax) of more than $4,000.²

The movement from rural to urban life proceeded; and within urban life there was a surge to the more distant suburbs, a shift which moderated during depression and wartime years but then resumed at an accelerated pace. By the mid–1950's about half the population of metropolitan areas were living in suburban areas, as opposed to about one-third in 1940.

How did Americans dispose of their rising real incomes? With respect to consumption, in periods of peace and full employment the pattern of relative expenditures followed a path of change reasonably consistent with the previous four decades. Increasing relative amounts were spent on transportation, recreation, medical care, and insurance. Outlays on household equipment and operation fell away slowly; the percentages expended on clothing, housing, private education, religion, and private welfare fell away somewhat more sharply. The proportion spent on food, liquor, and tobacco, although falling in the post–1945 years, remained higher than in the prosperous 1920's. And within the universal human categories—food, shelter, and clothing—there was a shift toward more expensive and various forms of consumption away, as it were, from the old staples.

The changing level and pattern of American expenditures yielded a relative shift in the working force into services and government, as opposed to manufacturing and the older related activities. (See table below.)

In a sense, the most important change in the pattern of consumption was the remarkable rise in the birth rate, which began about 1940. Americans gave a decreasing priority to what they took for granted and elevated what they did not have. Specifically, Americans began to behave as if they preferred the extra baby to the extra unit of consumption. During the war years the birth rate rose from 18 per 1,000 to about 22. This was judged at the time—and, to a large degree, it certainly was—a phenomenon of resumed full employment and of early wartime marriages. In the postwar years, however, the level of births moved up and stayed at about 25 per 1,000, yielding a

NUMBER OF WAGE AND SALARY WORKERS IN
NONAGRICULTURAL ESTABLISHMENTS, 1940, 1956*
(IN MILLIONS)

	1940	%	1956	%
Manufacturing, mining construction, transport, and public utilities	16.0	50	24.9	48
Trade, finance, and service	11.9	37	19.8	38
Government	4.2	13	7.2	14
Total	32.1	100	51.9	100

* *Economic Report of the President,* January 1958, (Washington, D.C.: Government Printing Office), p. 140, Table F–22.

rise in the population, as well as changes in the age structure of the population, with implications reaching far into the future.

As real income rose and full employment was maintained, the availability of personal service declined; and services tended to become commercialized where they were not thrown back on the family itself. Although the American housewife, with more children, more gadgets, and less service, led an extremely hard-working life, the decline of the average work week yielded some increase in leisure—for men, at least—reflected in a sharp expansion of outlays on recreation: from horse and dog racing and pinball machines to motorboats, paper-bound books, long-playing records, and do-it-yourself workshop equipment.

The pillars of the postwar boom lay in housing, automobiles, durable consumers goods, and in the industries and services related to them. In resuming in the post–1945 decade a prosperity based on the rapid spread of the automobile and the suburban one-family house, which had marked the 1920's, the economy was strongly supported by the backlog of housing and durable-goods demand unfilled during the war years. The filling of the wartime gap, however, concealed some natural deceleration in these categories as higher proportions of the American population achieved a middle-class level of life and the amenities that went with it. The output of refrigerators, washing machines, vacuum cleaners, and electric toasters, for example, began to decline in the early 1950's; and, although air conditioners, dryers, and home freezers were at an early stage of their diffusion, the extent to which full employment and growth could continue to be built on the regular expansion in the older categories of consumption came into question.[b]

The diffusion of certain major durable consumer goods is reflected in the following table.[3]

As the impulses from the housing, automobile, and durable consumers' goods industries waned somewhat after 1955, a surge in commercial construction and in outlays by state and local governments carried the economy forward until the recession of 1957–1958.

THE SOCIAL SETTING

Three other slow-moving but powerful forces were meanwhile altering the social setting of American life: a spread of bureaucratic experience, a rise in the educational level, and an increase in social homogeneity.

The proportion of the total working force employed within large-scale units increased. So far as the economy as a whole was concerned, this phenomenon turned out to be a consequence mainly of the shift of labor out of agriculture rather than of any marked tendency toward increased concentration in American business. Since 1929 the proportion of agricultural to nonagricultural employment has

[b] A similar question underlies S. H. Slichter's view, expressed in an address at the annual meeting of the Associated Industries, March 3, 1958: . . . "The automobile industry will be meeting increasingly severe competition from many sources during the next several years. The growing competition being met by automobiles is shown by the fact that between 1953 and 1957 personal consumption expenditures increased by 21.6 per cent, but outlays for new cars, used cars, and parts increased by 18.9 per cent. Between 1953 and 1956 (the latest date for which detailed figures are available), when spending for new and used automobiles increased by 11 per cent, many important kinds of personal expenditures increased far faster:

Elementary and secondary education	55.1 per cent
Higher education	47.7
Barber shops and beauty parlors	47.7
Interest on personal debt	37.2
Boats and pleasure aircraft	35.0
Privately controlled hospitals and sanatoriums	31.0
Telephone and telegraph	29.2
Foreign travel	28.4
Medical care and hospitalization insurance	21.8
Electricity	21.4
Physician's fees	16.1

. . . Probably the greatest competitor of the automobile industry (and of many industries) will be children."

TABLE I
DISTRIBUTION OF DURABLE CONSUMER GOODS IN AMERICAN FAMILIES

Year	Families owning automobiles* (percentage of all families)	Percentage of all wired homes with†						
		Television	Refrigerators	Freezers	Vacuum cleaners (floor)	Electric washers	Dryers (electric and gas)	Air conditioners
1946	n.a.	—	69.1	—	48.8	50.5	—	0.2
1947	n.a.	—	71.2	—	49.5	63.0	—	.2
1948	54	2.9	76.6	4.3	51.7	67.4	0.4	.3
1949	56	10.1	79.2	5.2	52.8	68.6	.7	.4
1950	60	26.4	86.4	7.2	56.5	71.9	1.4	.6
1951	65	38.5	86.7	9.3	57.7	73.5	2.4	.8
1952	65	50.2	89.2	11.5	59.4	76.2	3.7	1.4
1953	65	63.5	90.4	13.4	60.5	78.5	5.1	2.6
1954	70	74.1	92.5	15.1	62.2	81.3	6.6	4.0
1955	71	76.1	94.1	16.8	64.3	84.1	9.2	5.6
1956	73	81.0	96.0	18.0	66.7	86.8	11.9	7.6

* Source: Board of Governors of the Federal Reserve System. Note: data relate to ownership of an automobile by some member of the family early in each year. Data are not available prior to 1948.
† Source: Electrical Merchandising, McGraw-Hill Publishing Company.

fallen from more than 25 per cent to less than 10 per cent.

Within industry such comparable statistics as are available indicate that the proportion of wage earners in the largest 5 per cent of manufacturing establishments rose modestly: from 55 per cent in 1914 to 62 per cent in 1947.[4] But the trend in manufacturing does not apply to business as a whole because of the vitality of small business units in other sectors, notably retail trade and services. The independence of these small units is, however, often compromised by their links to the great corporations, as in the case of automobile dealers.

Government greatly expanded. The civil service rolls of the federal government rose from about 600,000 in 1930 to about 2,400,000 in 1955; and the armed forces have remained mobilized at something like ten times their level of the 1930's. Cumulatively, about 20,000,-000 American men have known the round of military life.

More than that, important branches of American industry as well as university and intellectual life became partially linked to the government's military programs, pressing the framework of federal bureaucracy far out into the society. By and large the experience of life and work within a large-scale organization became increasingly typical of American society.

The dynamics of the national commitment to popular education extended rapidly toward the end of the nineteenth century into secondary and higher education. Its broad consequence can be seen in the relative educational status of enlisted men in World War I and World War II.[5]

Percentage Distribution of Education in World War I and World War II

Years of Schooling	World War I	World War II
Grade school	76.7	30.9
High school		
4 years	4.1	23.3
3 years	2.7	11.2
2 years	4.8	10.9
1 year	6.3	7.8
College		
4 years	1.2	3.6
3 years	0.9	2.0
2 years	1.5	4.0
1 year	1.8	6.3
Total	100.0	100.0

S. Stouffer[6] presents the following data on education by age group
in a more recent national sample:

Percentage Distribution of Education within Each Age Group

National Cross Section	21–29	30–39	40–49	50–59	60 and over
College graduates	8	10	9	7	4
Some college	14	10	9	9	6
High school graduates	40	33	20	14	13
Some high school	24	23	24	20	13
Grade school	14	24	38	50	64

Veterans' benefits and the high level of postwar incomes have carried this process forward with wide-ranging consequences covering
the whole realm of public taste, opinion, and manners.

There has been a parallel maturing of American intellectual life,
marked, for example, by a sharp increase in the American contribution
to theoretical concepts in both the physical and the social sciences.
This trend toward virtuosity in theory was accelerated by the immigration of European intellectuals from the Continent in the 1930's
and probably by the intrusion into American academic life of certain
war and postwar problems of public policy. But the development appears to have been implicit in the aspirations and intellectual values
of the generation of American scientists which came of age between
the wars and which reacted along a broad front against the extreme
empirical bias of its elders.

In the pre–1914 years immigration to the United States was running
at the rate of about one million per year. It decreased in the 1920's and
became a thin trickle in the 1930's. The process of adjustment to the
predominant goals of American life and culture steadily proceeded,
generation by generation; and it broke down or strongly diluted
those groupings in American life based on racial or national origin
which for a time formed enclaves of non-American cultures. To this
process was added the industrial revolution in the South of the past
two decades, which also produced changes in the direction of national uniformity.

There was, then, a marked increase in the socal homogeneity of
the American population. However, this broad trend left the problem
of the social status of the Negro in a special category, felt, perhaps,
with peculiar acuteness as other minority problems became less sharp

and as the average economic and educational level of the Negro rose and with it his level of aspiration.

To summarize, abstracting, from the Second World War and international involvements of the post–1945 years, American society appeared to have found in the early 1950's a distinctive moving equilibrium in which certain of the old processes—notably the open frontier and a large flow of immigration—were supplanted by the dynamics of an industrial growth oriented increasingly to durable consumer goods and services and to the migration to the suburbs. Having gradually thrashed out a resolution which narrowed the conflicts between industrial private capitalism and the other values of political and social democracy, Americans found themselves a suburbanizing nation, increasingly at work in large bureaucracies, with a new security of employment, rising levels of welfare, rising standards of education and of intellectual sophistication, and an increased social and political homogeneity.

CONFLICT AND CONVERGENCE OF EXTERNAL INFLUENCE

The setting of post–1945 American society is a product not only of forces arising from the sweep of domestic history but also of their interplay with forces arising from protracted engagement in the world arena of power since 1941.

Basically, the nation's new international status set in motion forces which ran counter to the directions decreed by the dynamics of the domestic society. The nation emerged from the Second World War in a position (and with the evident desire) to cultivate a rather attractive domestic garden. And it had reached a stage of economic, social, and political development where a uniquely comfortable life under conditions of relatively low political and social tension was probably possible. At just this stage, American society was required to take active measures to protect the security of the nation against forces and methods for which it was not well prepared; and it has lived since 1945 under a foreseeable threat of direct, catastrophic assault from nuclear weapons, a threat made increasingly real after September 1949. It has had to allocate not only large resources but also a substantial proportion of its energy and talents to maintain minimum national security. An America come to terms with the welfare state at high and rising levels of real income and an America as the fortress base of the West in an intense cold war shadowed by nuclear destruction have made, indeed, a curious mixture.

Nevertheless, in its impact on American society the cold war has converged with many of the trends built into the nation's domestic dynamics at the same time that it has set up important counter-trends and tensions.

The scale of the military budget has made it easier to maintain full employment but has posed more sharply than would otherwise have been the case the problem of inflation control in a political and social democracy of diffused authority.

The scale and ramified industrial and intellectual activities of the military establishment have accentuated the trend toward bureau-cratization.

The workings of the Selective Service, combined with the social values built into the military establishments and veterans' benefit legislation, have accelerated the trend toward social homogeneity, toward higher average levels of education, and (via veterans' housing) toward suburbanization.

The imperatives of the arms race in new weapons and, to a degree, the problems of policy-making in relation to societies which do not share American values and institutions have stimulated the development of both the natural and the social sciences, encouraging the practical application of abstractions of a higher order than would have been demanded if American science had continued to be oriented toward the concerns of a more isolated domestic society.

The cumulative effect of overseas experience during the Second World War, of occupation duties, and of the Korean War, and the narrower but powerful experience of work by Americans in overseas aid and information programs have radically increased knowledge and awareness of the world outside the United States; and the flow of international news, punctuated by a series of major crises, has carried this awareness deep into the society in all regions of the country. Although knowledge and awareness are by no means to be equated with sympathy and a sense of common interest, isolationism has been considerably weakened by these intrusions of the world on American life.

The existence of chronic national emergency has led to the development of an elaborate system of personnel security by the federal government. Given the scale of the national security effort and the administrative techniques of the personnel security program, the lives of millions of Americans have been touched in one way or another by this dimension of national policy, quite aside from that phase of

the postwar experience when personnel security issues became em-
broiled with national policies.

The drawn-out and intractable nature of the struggle with the
Soviet Union—including the frustrations of the Communist take-
over in China, the indecisive outcome of the Korean War, the
nation's impotence in the face of the Hungarian revolt, the Soviet lead
in missiles—has imposed a sense of limitation on the nation's old
image of itself, a limitation which has been accented with greater
or less maturity and which has touched the nation's domestic life
at many points with elements of escapism, with a tendency to search
for scapegoats, with simple worry, and with much thoughtful, re-
sponsive effort as well.

HAVE VALUES CHANGED?

Against the background of these changes in the setting of
domestic life, there appeared in the early 1950's an extensive literature
focused upon this question: Have fundamental American values
and aspirations been undergoing important change?[7] There emerged
a wide range of agreement that Americans were making choices
among the alternatives they perceived to be open to them in terms
of objectives which differed from the prevailing concept of what
American objectives had hitherto been; and many thoughtful observers noted a definitive shift of American society away from the values
of the Puritan ethic. A useful summary of the believed shift in values
is that of George Spindler.

It came to be widely believed, then, that Americans were adapting
themselves to the new setting of their society in ways which diminished the pursuit by individuals of the goals of personal material
success in favor of conformity to organizational and group objectives
on the one hand and, on the other, to the cultivation of the immediate
satisfactions and private values offered by a rich society.

Something of the same judgment about American society was
reflected in the work of American novelists who treated World
War II not primarily as a clash betwen humane civil values and the
brutal facts of organized violence but as a problem of the individual's
relation to a massive bureaucracy. In different ways, this was true, for
example, of *From Here to Eternity, Mr. Roberts, The Caine Mutiny,*
and *Guard of Honor.* Each of these works dramatizes the clash
between the individual personality and the unfeeling requirements of
a massive military organization which, in a higher interest, must deal

TRADITIONAL VALUES	EMERGENT VALUES
Puritan morality (Respectability, thrift, self-denial, sexual constraint; a puritan is someone who can have anything he wants, as long as he doesn't enjoy it!)	*Sociability* (One should like people and get along well with them. Suspicion of solitary activities is characteristic.)
Work-success ethic (Successful people worked hard to become so. Anyone can get to the top if he tries hard enough. So people who are not successful are lazy, or stupid, or both. People must work desperately and continuously to convince themselves of their worth.)	*Relativistic moral attitude* (Absolutes in right and wrong are questionable. Morality is what the group thinks is right. Shame, rather than guilt-oriented personality is appropriate.)
Individualism (The individual is sacred, and always more important than the group. In one extreme form, the value sanctions egocentricity, expediency, and disregard for other people's rights. In its healthier form the value sanctions independence and originality.)	*Consideration for others* (Everything one does should be done with regard for others and their feelings. The individual has a built-in radar that alerts him to others' feelings. Tolerance for the other person's point of view and behavior is regarded as desirable, so long as the harmony of the group is not disrupted.)
Achievement orientation (Success is a constant goal. There is no resting on past glories. If one makes $9,000 this year he must make $10,000 next year. Coupled with the work-success ethic, this value keeps people moving, and tense.)	*Hedonistic, present-time, orientation* (No one can tell what the future will hold, therefore, one should enjoy the present—but within the limits of the well-rounded balanced personality and group.)
Future-time orientation (The future, not the past, or even the present, is most important. There is a "pot of gold at the end of the rainbow." Time is valuable, and cannot be wasted. Present needs must be denied for satisfactions to be gained in the future.)	*Conformity to the group* (Implied in the other emergent values. Everything is relative to the group. Group harmony is the ultimate goal. Leadership consists of group-machinery lubrication.)[8]

with the individual virtually as a statistical unit; and each, in its way, made the case for the primacy of the organization and its communal purposes. And as the novelists turned to the issues of the postwar world, once again the theme of the individual personality in relation to bureaucracy emerged—often in relation to the bureaucratized structure of modern American business. Even where the hero withdraws, to a degree, from the imperatives of successful organizational activity —as in Sloan Wilson's *The Man in the Grey Flannel Suit*—the case for the individual expressing his creativeness through his role in a group, and within the terms set by a large institution, is strongly made.

This recurrent contemporary theme, which identifies the central issue of American society as the individual's relation to bureaucracy and which counsels a high degree of respect for the imperatives of bureaucratic order and continuity, was indeed new to the national literature, in which the classic heroes had for the most part a strong touch of defiant anarchism about them. It differed radically from both the protest of the individual against the values of the market place, which dominated so much of American writing in the prosperous 1920's and from the wider ranging protests against the values and institutions of capitalism, which characterized much creative writing of the depressed 1930's.

The question has been raised as to whether the shifts in the objectives pursued by Americans can be correctly identified with a change in basic American values, notably if those values are defined at a high level of generality. Some commentators would argue the possibility that fundamental American values have not altered but the setting of American life has altered the objectives open to Americans in such ways as to make the pursuit of the old values in terms of the old objectives impossible. Winston White, for example, following leads from Talcott Parsons, points to the institutionalization of business management, of risk taking, and of innovation as having eliminated some of the classical areas in which the lonely purposeful individual might find effective expression.[9] He thus poses the problem of distinguishing the extent to which a change in action is determined by a change in the available alternatives on the one hand or by a change in values on the other. Moreover, much depends on the level of abstraction at which values are defined.

Fundamental values become deeply embedded in a society only over very long periods of time, over which they appear to gather legitimacy by yielding a flow of acceptable solutions to individual and community problems;[10] and it is, perhaps, too soon to know whether in some long-run sense the context of American life will be such as to alter permanently the old emphasis on the optimistic individual pursuit of goals and achievements external to the private sphere of life.

What would happen to the quality of American society if hedonism and security were to supplant individual striving and adventure in a challenging physical environment as the norms? Put another way, are Americans (and human beings in general) capable of maintaining a life consistent with the oldest values out of the Western past if that life does not require that men work hard? Are human beings, in the large, capable of building an ordered and satisfying life centered upon the pursuits of leisure and the cultivation of peace of mind? Could a large population live within the kind of environment that was emerging in the United States in the early 1950's, where the challenges and possibilities to the individual were reduced—or altered out of the traditional context of frontier, farming, and the market place—without the nation's becoming a bore to itself and to the world?[11]

The Domestic Crisis of 1956–1958

At just the time when these issues were being defined with increasing clarity and were receiving a kind of official reality in the conduct of President Eisenhower's first term—when, to many, peace and prosperity seemed to have been successfully institutionalized—the setting of American life began to change. The problems of what might be defined as secular stagnation of the spirit (as opposed to the economy) appeared to be at least postponed.[c]

SCHOOL INTEGRATION

The national mood was altered in 1956–1958 by a specific series of independent events: the crisis over school integration, and, notably,

---

[c] The parallelism between spiritual and economic secular stagnation is, for an economist, legitimate. The assumptions of diminishing relative marginal utility and of diminishing marginal productivity are the twin pillars of formal economics. The concept of secular economic stagnation is simply an extension of the classical economist's prognosis of diminishing marginal productivity; while the concept of spiritual secular stagnation implies that, as real income rises, the value of additional increments falls, relative to leisure—and that man fails to fashion a spiritually satisfying life with so high a proportion of his time uncommitted to the pursuit of income.

the events of Little Rock in the autumn of 1957; the severity of the recession of 1957–1958; the reappraisal of the purposes and values of the American educational system, induced by both the competition of young people for placement in college and the emergent Soviet lead in missile technology; and, finally, the increasing evidence that the nation had been living off its social-overhead capital not only with respect to schools but also with respect to its urban areas, roads, railroads, water supply, and in other directions as well. In combination with the running crisis in the nation's international position, these factors yielded—perhaps only for an interval—an atmosphere markedly different in the spring and summer of 1958 from what it had been two years earlier.

With respect to segregation, Americans except in the South had generally welcomed the Supreme Court's decision of 1954. The decision may have been received, however, as the measure of progress already made in the nation's long evolutionary struggle with the Negro problem rather than as the opening of a complex and difficult new phase. The nation as a whole only gradually became aware of the depth of feeling stirred in the South by the desegregation decision and by the expectations of further social change to which it gave life. In the limited areas where the decision was executed, there was nothing automatic about the result; local organization and local leadership at the highest levels of good sense and statesmanship were required. And where desegregation was postponed or frustrated, the primitive strength of the emotions which still surrounded the Negro problem were revealed with uncomfortable clarity to the nation and to the world.

THE RECESSION OF 1957–1958

If Little Rock gave a generation of Americans a moment of apparent second sight into the emotional setting of the Civil War, the recession of 1957–1958 faintly evoked the moods of the Great Depression of a quarter of a century earlier. A depression which raises unemployment to five million directly touches the lives of about eighteen million persons; and it shadows the lives of those placed on short time as well as those who feel that they too may be laid off.[12]

Fundamentaly, however, the situation was vastly different from that of the 1930's. Built-in stabliizers strongly cushioned the downswing—a tax system which automatically cut tax payments with the fall of income, and substantial unemployment benefits and farm income supports. Unlike the situation in 1929–1933, there was virtually unanimous agreement that an unbalanced federal budget was a necessary and proper instrument for bringing the country back to full employment. Differences concerned the method by which the federal budget should be unbalanced, the scale of an appropriate deficit, and the optimum timing of a tax cut, if any.[d]

REVALUATION OF EDUCATION

The launching of the Soviet earth satellites crystallized and heightened a controversy which had been building up for some years, posed by the rising pressure of population of school age, the rise in education costs, and the shortage of teachers, to which was now added the shock of competitive failure in the missiles race, which became widely (but inaccurately) associated with a failure of the nation's educational system.[e]

The main elements in the position which emerged in opposition to the educational *status quo* could be summarized in some such terms as these:[13]

1. The intellectual life would have to be accorded a higher prestige and be more truly cherished by society. In particular, it would be necessary to allocate disproportionate educational resources to students of first quality.

2. Basic education as a whole should be given a greater rigor and should be less diluted with courses of an empirical character designed to give the student merely enlarged factual knowledge about the workings of his society.

3. The nation would have to offer its teachers both more money

[d] There were three schools of thought on how the recession of 1957–1958 should be handled. One advocated an expansion in government outlays—including those for social-overhead capital. It was claimed that such outlays had been unnaturally restrained in recent years. Another group came out in favor of a tax cut, which was taken to be the most prompt, sure, and administratively simple method for increasing employment. A third position was taken by the Administration, which believed it made sense to await the possibility that an upswing might begin without a tax cut, accepting the consequences in resources wasted by prolonged unemployment.

[e] In fact the American lag in missile development can be traced not to failures in the American educational system—yielding relatively too few scientists and engineers—but to a method of administering military research and development in the post–1945 years, and notably in the period 1953–1957, which grossly misused and misallocated the existing available pool of creative talent in science and engineering. This judgment would not exclude the possibility that continued rapid pace in Soviet education accompanied by continued failure to solve the problems in American education might in time yield results costly to the national interest.

and higher social status; and it would have to invest vastly increased resources in school buildings and other physical facilities for education.[14]

The open emphasis on quality and the affirmation that it was legitimate in American society to allocate unequal amounts of public resources to the children of equal citizens ran counter to the strong egalitarian strand in the nation's tradition. Yet there was something familiarly American about the new emphasis on intellect. The nation behaved a little like a business firm confronted by competition from an unexpected source and in an unexpected dimension: if brains were the payoff, then it would be necessary to cultivate brains. Thus, Eisenhower elevated the President of M. I. T. to a high post in the White House, as his principal response to the launching of the first Soviet sputnik.

New Forces at Work

SHIFTS IN POPULATION

However transient the mood of 1956–1958 turns out to be, two forces were at work in American society, generated from the dynamics of the war and postwar years, which were not to be denied. The first of these forces was the rise in population brought about primarily by the sharp increase in the birth rate since 1940; the second was the increasing claims on the nation's resources for social-overhead capital. Between them they promise to alter the setting of American society significantly for a decade at least, quite aside from the possibility that other domestic or international forces might press in the same direction.

During the early 1960's the rise in the birth rate will yield a rising rate of family formation certain to increase the demand for housing, the standard household package of durable consumer goods, and social-overhead capital. The expansion of the working force which will come about as the children of the 1940's go to work will temporarily be outpaced, however, by the expansion of the population as a whole. From the mid-nineteenth century to about 1940 the proportion of the working force to the population regularly increased. The reversed trend of recent years is likely to continue for a time, with each worker supporting, as it were, an increased number of both older and younger dependents, as suggested in Chart I.[15]

The presence of these changes at the heart of American society

Chart I

Percentage Distribution of Population by Dependent and Working Age Groups, 1850-1950, with Estimates for 1960.

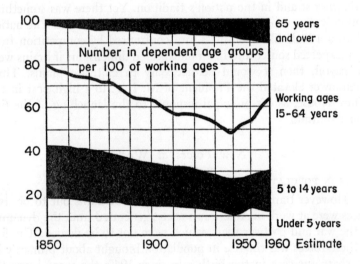

is likely to alter at least for the time being the notion that hours of work are bound progressively to decline, that retirement at sixty-five is an overriding objective, and that a regular rise in private consumption per head is somehow automatic and a necessary condition for a decent national life.

CLAIMS FOR SOCIAL-OVERHEAD CAPITAL

The suffusion of national life with a touch of austerity in the private sector will be strengthened to the extent that the nation faces and meets its accumulating bill for social-overhead capital. The post-1946 decade saw a remarkable rise in outlays for housing and automobiles. Meanwhile, however, roads, schools, and the urban areas (whose taxable revenue was drained away by the flow to suburbia) were grossly neglected. In a vivid chart, the Report of Panel IV of the Rockefeller Special Studies Project caught and measured roughly the extent to which the nation had been living off its previously accumulated social capital in certain major directions.

"In the period 1915–1940 per capita expenditures in constant dollars on schools, roads, waterworks, and other public works rose at an average annual rate of 4.5 per cent. In this manner, federal, state, and local governments provided the public assets needed by a growing economy.

"Expenditures dropped sharply in 1932 and 1933 and, despite a massive effort by the federal government, did not

Chart II

Per Capita Expenditures on Public Works[16]

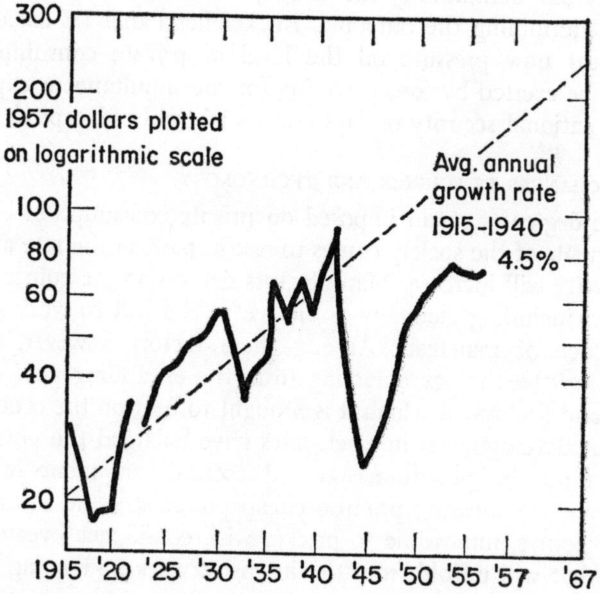

regain their previous rate until 1936. This experience shows that public works programs are slow to get under way.

"Despite the sharp increase during the past decade, per capita expenditures on public works are no higher than they were two decades ago. Moreover, they have leveled out in the past few years. And total public works expenditures have lagged behind the growth of total national output—the ratio to GNP declined from 4.5 per cent in the late 1930's to 3 per cent now."

If the nation is to correct this lack of balance, a shift in resources in favor of social-overhead capital is required. And this, too, could put pressure on the level of private consumption per head. Rockefeller Report IV estimated that the nation's minimum bill for social-overhead capital (given the likely rate of increase in national security expenditures over the next decade) would permit only a 2 per cent per capita increase in consumption to be maintained if the growth of GNP were increased regularly at 4 per cent per annum. A 5 per cent growth rate in GNP will be required if social-overhead capital is to be built up to high levels and the nation's "normal" 2 per cent increase in consumption per capita is to be maintained.[17]

Aside from dramatizing the strategic importance of the growth rate in determining the outcome, Rockefeller Panel IV calculations make clear how pressure on the level of private consumption is likely to be exerted by forces making for the simultaneous expansion of both national security outlays and social-overhead capital.

RECENT CHANGES IN SCIENCE AND TECHNOLOGY

The degree of strain imposed on private consumption by other requirements of the society comes to rest in part on the rate at which productivity will increase. Many factors determine the course of productivity, including elements as elusive as the will to work and the competence of managers. Among these factors however, are the flow of new technology emerging from the expanding pool of basic science and the rate at which it is brought to bear on the economy.

Recent developments in electronics have enlarged the possibilities of what is now called automation; and recent developments in nuclear science and engineering promise cheap power at some future stage. It is, of course, impossible to predict with confidence over the long future what will unfold from the intensive work now going forward in electronics and nuclear engineering. Over a shorter span—of, say, ten years—automation will certainly be extended, shifting the proportions between men and capital and, especially, increasing the requirements for skilled workers in factory and office. Automation should contribute to the maintenance of recent productivity increases of, say, 3 per cent per annum.[f]

---

[f] The average rate of increase in American productivity has risen from 1.25 per cent in 1910–20 to 3.00 per cent in 1946–53, averaging over the whole period 2.14 per cent.—Raymond H. Ewell, "Role of Research in Economic Growth," *Chemical and Engineering News*, July 18, 1955, p. 2982.

For the United States, with its still relatively cheap supplies of coal, gas, and oil, nuclear power based on fission is likely to supply over the next decade only a small proportion of total energy. If and when the problem of fusion power is solved, the United States and the world may well have a cheap and inexhaustible source of energy. But even then, given the global pressure of expansion in energy requirements on natural resources, fusion power is not likely to be enough cheaper than other sources of power to bring about in itself an economic millennium.[g]

The expansion of research and development is proceeding, of course, on a much wider front than these two areas. Between 1920 and the mid–1950's the nation's research and development expenditures had regularly risen from something like 0.1 per cent of the gross national product to about 1 per cent, the latter figure representing outlays of about $4 billion a year.[h] The industries which had led the way in industrial research earlier in the century retained their leadership: chemicals, electricity, and aircraft (including missiles). But the conception that industry must systematically organize the innovational process was becoming generally applied. A continuation of this trend, increasing the outlay on research and development at a rate of about 10 per cent per annum, will almost certainly be required to maintain the post–1945 rate of increase in American productivity.

Despite the accelerating development of science and technology, the nation will have to run hard to stay where it is. This speculative judgment flows from the following considerations: consumers are spending increasing amounts on services, where research and development can make only a limited contribution. Similarly, the construc-

[g] Although it would not in itself bring about the millennium, John von Neumann's vision of energy as free as "unmetered air" would indeed be a radical contribution to productivity: ". . . Fission is not nature's normal way of releasing nuclear energy. In the long run, systematic industrial exploitation of nuclear energy may shift reliance into other and still more abundant modes. Again, reactors have been bound thus far to the traditional heat-steam-generator-electricity cycle, just as automobiles were at first constructed to look like buggies. It is likely that we shall gradually develop procedures more naturally and effectively adjusted to the new source of energy, abandoning the conventional kinks and detours inherited from chemical-fuel processes. Consequently, a few decades hence energy may be free—just like the unmetered air—with coal and oil used mainly as raw materials for organic chemical synthesis, to which, as experience has shown, their properties are best suited."—Fortune, June 1955, p. 107.

[h] Ibid., pp. 2981–2982. By 1956 the figure had leaped to $6.4 billion, reflecting a rise in the costs of research and development combined with a radical increase in government outlays, notably for the missile program.—National Science Foundation, Review of Data on Research and Development, No. 10, May 1958.

tion industries, mainly involved in the expansion of social-overhead capital, are not among those which have exhibited a capacity to develop rapid increases in productivity.[1] And, finally, large resources (including research and development resources) will continue to be allocated to military purposes.

Some Future Problems of Austerity and Affluence

The dynamics of American society in the period 1940–1956 has yielded two situations likely to impose a somewhat more austere environment for private consumption in the decade or so to follow. First, the quiet, unexpected choice of postwar Americans for enlarged families over enlarged stocks of durable consumer goods and services is having and will have profound material consequences. Second, an unbalanced extension of private consumption since 1940 has left the society with an enormous backlog of social-overhead requirements at precisely the period when increases in population and family formation are about to enlarge requirements for social-overhead capital. Political economy will remain the art of dealing with scarcity. The four-day week can wait.

Although the acceptance of the essentials of the New Deal and Fair Deal by the Eisenhower administration brought a phase of American political history to a close, the recurrent national debate over the appropriate balance between the interests of private property and the interests of the private citizen was by no means ended. The heirs of Cotton Mather, Alexander Hamilton, William McKinley, and Calvin Coolidge are still likely to be identifiable, as well as the heirs of Roger Williams, Thomas Jefferson, Andrew Jackson, Woodrow Wilson, and Franklin Roosevelt. Nevertheless, the nation's life is likely to be dominated by a clash between elements in the individualist-utilitarian creed somewhat different from the debate in the decades since the Civil War. Decade after decade the nation debated the extent to which the state was a legitimate instrument for re-

[1] There is no reason, of course, why concerted and imaginative efforts might not yield radical increases in productivity in the generally sluggish construction industries. For further elaboration of the author's views on the American productivity problem see *Comparisons of the United States and Soviet Economics*, Joint Economic Committee, Part III. Washington: Government Printing Office, 1954, pp. 604–606; and "The Problem of Achieving and Maintaining a High Rate of Economic Growth: An Historian's View," *American Economic Review*. Proceedings, May 1960.

distributing income and providing increased equality of opportunity. While these issues had by no means become irrelevant, they were being superseded as a matter of urgency by the question of how much of the community's resources should be allocated to the public sector in order to improve the balance and quality (as well as to increase the security) of the common life.

The great affairs of domestic policy—education, health, water supply, the rebuilding of the cities, the control of inflation, the provision of adequate social-overhead capital for a bulging population— are, in a curious way, community rather than special interest or regional issues. The problems of allocating resources between private and public sectors, which have traditionally dominated state and local politics, appear likely to be elevated to the national level. In its politics as in its social life and communications, the nation is likely to become increasingly a continental township. Desegregation is, in one sense, a special case—a stage in a long, slow, familiar, painful, ongoing process. But the solution to the problem—like the solution to the other major domestic issues—requires an extraordinary concert of effort by the majority in each community, an effort which could not be conceived of as realistic until quite recent times.

At some stage, the level of armaments expenditures will have to decline as a result of mutual satiety or as a result of an effective arms-control agreement. The resources available for nonmilitary outlays will then increase. As Gerhard Colm has said: ". . . Demobilization would not create an entirely new problem but would add to the problem which we have to meet anyway in an economy of increasing productivity."[18] It can be demonstrated that, let us say, a halving of military outlays over the next decade would pose problems in maintaining full employment of a relatively limited kind. Put another way, there can be envisaged reasonable increases in personal consumption, private domestic investment, foreign net investment, and government outlays for purposes other than security adequate to maintain full employment in the less armaments-ridden world of, say, 1965. Colm exhibits the possible consequences of a 50 per cent decline in security outlays as follows:

The arithmetic of some such transition suggests that, while the nation might be forced to shift resources sharply into social-overhead capital to maintain full employment (and/or cut the work week), the ending of the arms race in its present form would, in itself, pose only a modest problem of adjustment for American society.

TABLE II

GROSS NATIONAL PRODUCT
CALENDAR YEAR 1956 AND ALTERNATIVE PROJECTIONS FOR 1965
(BILLIONS OF 1956 DOLLARS)

Item	1956	1965	Change between 1956 and 1965
Gross national product	412.4	584.0	+171.6
National security expenditures	41.6	20.0	−21.6
Personal consumption	265.8	395.0	+129.2
Private domestic investment	65.3	91.0	+25.7
Foreign net investment	1.4	4.0	+2.6
Government purchases, other than for national security	38.3	74.0	+35.7

These calculations—dramatizing the power of compound interest—also suggest, however, that in the sufficiently long run the problem of increasing wealth and leisure—the threat of secular spiritual stagnation—surely will become central to organized societies. Will the devil make work for idle hands, and men find ways of destroying sufficient capital, while not destroying the planet, so that they can continue to build their lives on active material striving? Will human beings regularly reimpose Malthusianism; that is, create a sufficient rise in the birth rate to avoid the horrors of universal plenty and excessive leisure? Will men find in outer space a frontier sufficiently expensive and rewarding to put off the day when the relative marginal utility of real income becomes dangerously low? Or will the human race, placed *en masse* in the material status of an aristocracy within a traditional society, find in a life of expanding sport, leisure, and repose, combined with the irreducible challenges and drama of carrying forward the species, sufficient inner frontiers to maintain a tolerable life?

The state of society in the United States and in parts of western Europe during the 1950's was such as to justify the posing of these questions; and, to a degree, they are likely to continue to lurk as a real element in the lives of portions of the population in the advanced societies. But with American society under increasing pressure and challenge from forces arising out of both the world arena and its own dynamics, the question of secular spiritual stagnation seemed, for the time span most relevant to current decision, among the less urgent of the nation's problems. American society was not yet quite as affluent as it looked.[j]

Notes

[1] *Economic Report of the President*, January 1957 (Washington, D.C.: Government Printing Office, 1957), p. 106, Table D–7.

[2] *Ibid.*, Table D–8.

[3] *Ibid.*, pp. 110–111.

[4] See A. D. H. Kaplan, *Big Enterprise in a Competitive System* (Washington, D.C.: Brookings Institution, 1954), p. 70; and, in general, Chap. III, for a survey of evidence on changing business scale. See also E. S. Mason, "The Apologetics of 'Managerialism,' " *The Journal of Business of the University of Chicago*, January 1958, pp. 1–2.

[5] J. F. Dewhurst, *America's Needs and Resources* (New York: Twentieth Century Fund, 1947 ed.), p. 302.

[6] S. Stouffer, *Communism, Conformity, and Civil Liberties* (New York: Doubleday & Company, Inc., 1955), p. 92. On the correlation between "tolerance" and level of education, see especially Chap. 4 (pp. 89–108) and the conclusion summarized on p. 236.

[7] For an excellent analytic summary of this literature, as well as perceptive judgments on the problem of changing values, see Clyde Kluckhohn, "Have There Been Discernible Shifts in American Values during the Past Generation?" and a chapter in E. E. Morison (ed.), *The American Style: Essays in Values and Performance* (New York: Harper & Brothers, 1958).

[8] George Spindler, "Education in a Transforming American Culture," *Harvard Educational Review*, summer 1955, quoted by Clyde Kluckhohn, *loc. cit.*

[j] The argument presented here shares with that in J. K. Galbraith's *The Affluent Society* (Boston: Houghton Mifflin Company, 1958) an emphasis on the lack of balance between private consumption and social-overhead capital in contemporary American society. It differs, however, in its assessment of the likely claim on American resources of military and foreign policy over the coming decade and in its assessment of the implications of changes in population and the working force. While sharing the judgment that it is necessary to examine the composition of the nation's output—not merely the rate of increase of GNP— it is the author's view that a rapid and steady rise in GNP will, in fact, be necessary if the nation is to meet the multiple claims of security and the good society at home. There is nothing in the present argument which would justify, for example, the complacent acceptance of protracted periods of substantial unemployment, no matter how comfortably cushioned by increased benefit payments.

[9] Winston White, "Are American Values Changing?"—an unpublished paper. Also Talcott Parsons, "A Tentative Outline of American Values," an unpublished paper.

[10] For further discussion of this conception, see the author's *British Economy of the Nineteenth Century* (Oxford: Clarendon Press, 1948), Chap. VI, especially pp. 133–137.

[11] See, notably, David Reisman, "Consumption for What?" *Bulletin of Atomic Scientists*, April 1958. For the author's evocation of this issue, in a foreign policy context, see M. F. Millikan and W. W. Rostow, *A Proposal: Key to an Effective Foreign Policy* (New York: Harper & Brothers, 1957), pp. 149–151.

[12] A Roper poll (*Boston Sunday Globe*, July 20, 1958) found that about one-third of American families were directly affected by the slump of 1957–1958: 10 per cent had members of the immediate family out of work; 22 per cent suffered a decline of income.

[13] See, notably, "The Pursuit of Excellence," *Education and the Future of America*, Special Studies Project Report V, Rockefeller Brothers Fund (New York: Doubleday & Company, Inc., 1958).

[14] The Rockefeller panel on education suggested that the proportion of national product going to education would have to rise from 3.6 per cent to 5 per cent over the coming decade, which would more than double outlays (at constant prices) as between 1955 and 1967.—*Ibid.*, p. 34.

[15] Quoted in Dewhurst, *America's Needs and Resources*, p. 64.

[16] Quoted in *The Challenge to America: Its Economic and Social Aspects*, Special Studies Project IV, Rockefeller Brothers Fund (New York: Doubleday & Company, Inc., 1958).

[17] *Ibid.*, pp. 68, 71, 72.

PROJECTIONS OF FEDERAL, STATE AND LOCAL GOVERNMENT EXPENDITURES
(*billions of 1957 dollars*)

	1957 Actual	Range of Estimates for 1967	
		Low	High
National security	$46.0	$60.0	$70.0
Education (including school construction)	13.0	24.0	30.0
Welfare	20.0	38.5	45.0
Public works (except schools and hospitals)	9.5	20.5	27.0
Other	25.5	27.9	31.0
Total government cash expenditures	$114.0	$170.9	$203.0

PROJECTIONS OF GOVERNMENT PURCHASES OF GOODS AND SERVICES
(billions of 1957 dollars)

| | 1957 | 1967 | | | |
| | | Low Estimate for 1967 | | High Estimate for 1967 | |
		Growth Rate at 3%	Growth Rate at 4%	Growth Rate at 4%	Growth Rate at 5%
Gross national product	$434	$583	$642	$642	$707
Less government purchases	86	127	127	153	153
Less gross private investment	67	100	112	112	123
Available for consumption	281	356	403	377	431
Annual growth rate of per capita consumption		0.8%	2.1%	1.4%	2.8%

[18] Gerhard Colm, "The Economic Implications of Disarmament," *Illinois Business Review*, July 1957, p. 7.

TWO

☆

AMERICAN
ECONOMICS

☆

PAUL A. SAMUELSON

Earlier American Economics

While I am here primarily interested in the current status of economics in America, I ought first to go a little into its history. This for two reasons: the subject has its intrinsic interest, and a survey of history and development may possibly throw some light on the current status of economics.

Every textbook on the history of economic doctrines includes a separate section on American thought. Invariably the same names appear: Benjamin Franklin, Alexander Hamilton, Henry C. Carey, Henry George, Francis Walker, and John Bates Clark. Certain clichés and stereotypes about the character of American economics are repeated in every discussion. What are some of these?

American economics is first and foremost supposed to be "optimistic." Men living on a bounteous and yet unsettled continent during a time of rapid progress in population and real national product per capita could hardly be expected to take much stock in a gloomy Malthusian vision of diminishing returns and subsistence wages. And they did not. Henry C. Carey, writing just before the middle of the nineteenth century, rebelled against the dismal aspects of classical economics. His logic was often bad and his prolix style atrocious. But his fundamental empirical inferences seem correct for his time and place.

By virtue of technological developments in transportation the effective supply of land and natural resources, far from declining relative to labor and capital, was actually increasing.[a] Most important, real wages were rising as a result of technological change and capital formation, and in addition could confidently be expected to continue to rise. No wonder Henry C. Carey saw social harmony everywhere— and before Bastiat, as he himself bitterly pointed out. It is instructive that the economic theories which Carey used to deduce those glowing trends were not unlike the labor-theory-of-value models. Yet they were

[a] David Ricardo, Thomas Malthus, and the classical economists generally can be criticized for failing to stress the really important aspect of the nineteenth century—namely, the industrial revolution, which was going on and which, by shifting the schedules of their theoretical system, dwarfed the less important movements along the schedules on which they chose to concentrate.

used to deduce predictions about real wages quite opposite from those of Karl Marx—predictions which we now know are more nearly in accordance with the historical record than Marx's expectation of an absolute or relative impoverishment of labor.

A second characteristic of nineteenth century economics is its "theological" character. The typical textbook writer seems to have been an ordained clergyman teaching as an amateur economist in a college. As Cliffe Leslie pointed out in his essay, *Political Economy in the United States* (1881), anyone looking over the leaves of American treatises would be tempted to classify them as "Sunday" rather than "weekday" books: they take for granted that God designed the competitive economic system in a harmonious way, regarding this as an axiom rather than as a theorem proved by Adam Smith.[b]

A third characteristic commented on by most writers is the "protectionist" leanings of American economists. Since this seems hardly consistent with a belief in the harmonious nature of free private enterprise, most chroniclers have tried to explain protectionism in terms of aberrations of logic.

A better explanation of protectionist leanings will be found, I suspect, in a fourth characteristic of American economics, its "nationalistic" nature. Thus to the array of important American economists I would add the name of Friedrich List. Of course List would usually be considered the arch exponent of German nationalism; but Joseph Dorfman, in his monumental study *The Economic Mind in American Civilization*, has convincingly argued that List's theories had already jelled prior to his returning to Germany from the United States, and that it was in the nature of an accident that he wrote his *National System of Political Economy* in German.[c] Native writers, such as Harvard's Francis Bowen, produced textbooks with such titles as *American Political Economy*; and as late as the First World War Thomas Nixon Carver was writing elementary textbooks of an unashamedly nationalistic character.

As an ethical end, Carey and his followers wanted a diversified

---

[b] Optimism and theology were in fact related, but they are logically distinguishable. Thus Malthus used religion to argue for the inevitability and rightness of poverty and the struggle against it.

[c] While the thesis that List was an "exporter of the American system" stands up well when one looks at the additions to his thought after he left America, it is weakened somewhat by the consideration that he had already acquired some of his convictions *prior* to arriving in America at the age of thirty-six.—Joseph Dorfman, *The Economic Mind in American Civilization* (New York: The Viking Press, Inc., 1946), Vol. 2, pp. 575–84.

America. I suspect they were willing to pay an economic price for this,[d] but they were poor enough reasoners to be able to convince themselves that no price would be exacted. Instead of presenting their many specious arguments in favor of a tariff, they would have done better to concentrate on the "infant industry" argument. In retrospect, knowing as we do that America has developed a comparative advantage in many lines of manufacture, it seems to me a legitimate hypothesis that tariffs which speeded up their introduction and *initiated early experimentation* may have had some helpful role in accelerating the pace of American development.

Undoubtedly, however, the most powerful forces pushing economists toward arguments for protection were not the interests of industries yet unborn but the established coal and iron interests. Little wonder that Pennsylvania was a hotbed of protectionism and that no free trader could teach at the University of Pennsylvania.[e]

This brings me to a fifth characteristic of nineteenth century American economics—its "pro-business, conservative" character. The harmonies of the economic system were the harmonies of ruthless competition. Whereas at the beginning of the century many writers thought that the result would be an equalitarian society, by the end of the century economists observed that the outcome did involve great disparities of wealth. Many followed Herbert Spencer in embracing a crude form of "social Darwinism," in which the poor were blamed for their misfortune and the rich praised for their success. One such "forgotten man," who enthralled several generations of Yale men with this stern philosophy, was William Graham Sumner.

The final characteristic of earlier American economics that most writers have agreed on is its "untheoretical," even "anti-theoretical,"

---

[d] If the citizens of a country desire such a goal, a good technical case can be made for protective tariffs. Certainly we cannot expect each consumer voluntarily to spend his money in such a way as to pull production into a diversified pattern —for the same reasons that we cannot expect individuals voluntarily to pay for the optimal pattern of "public goods" that they really want. And if the state is going to interfere with the pattern of production so as to protect domestic industry, it seems to me that a tariff (particularly an ad valorem tariff on a broad variety of similar products) is an even-handed, not-too-inefficient way of granting a subsidy.

[e] Academic freedom was notably absent in nineteenth-century America. Not only could one be excluded from employment in Pennsylvania for preaching free trade, but in the Harvard of the 1870's one could be switched from the teaching of economics to the teaching of history—a dire fate?—for *not* preaching free trade. At least that is what President Charles Eliot is alleged to have done to Francis Bowen as a result of his advocacy of protective tariffs.

nature. This is summed up in the much-quoted view of Harvard's C. F. Dunbar, who said in his essay "Economic Science in America, 1776–1876": ". . . The United States has done nothing towards developing the theory of political economy . . . ." There is much to this, but two reservations must be made.

First, there is the fact that Dunbar was pretty much satisfied with theoretical economics as laid down by the classical economists. (He was the person Eliot picked to teach sound free-trade economics in place of Bowen.) So he could hardly be regarded as an unbiased judge of the newer doctrines of Carey and other Americans.

Second, there is the neglected American theorist John Rae. Rae developed a sophisticated theory of capital and interest and put forth many interesting notions concerning invention and progress.[*] Not only was Rae a theorist of international caliber, but in addition it can be argued that most of what is valid in Carey he might have found in his reading of Rae.

But, all in all, we must accept the charge that early American economics was on the primitive side where economic theory was concerned. Perhaps nothing more could have been expected of amateurs writing in a provincial backwater. The tendency of American thought to be derivative and doctrinaire—as seen by the popularity and repeated imitation of the textbooks of Jean Baptiste Say and John Ramsay McCulloch—fits in with such a pattern too. There may be something also in the notion that Americans are peculiarly pragmatic, content to stay close to the facts and untempted toward long chains of deductive reasoning.[1]

A more flattering interpretation of this untheoretical trait may be found in the nature of the subjects in which American economics excelled. Around the turn of the century Americans did a great deal of work on business cycles, which culminated in Wesley C. Mitchell's magnificent book published in 1913. The fact that American fluctuations were always so much bigger than those abroad led naturally to an interest in this subject. Even those of us who are fondest of economic theory will not argue that cultivating the economic theories

[*] Though John Rae wrote in 1833, his book, as John Stuart Mill ruefully pointed out, was too little known in Europe. Not until 1905, when C. W. Mixter edited a version of the book under the title *The Sociological Theory of Capital*, was Rae's work readily accessible. At this point I might mention that Albert Gallatin's *Free Trade Memorial* (1831) gives an analysis of the tariff burden that contains many analytically sophisticated points—as e.g. that the revenue collected is a "transfer" and that its dead-weight loss comes from the adjustments made to the new price.

of the classical and neoclassical writers would have been an optimal way of then advancing knowledge of business fluctuations.

The second subject that American economists can be said to have been studying with special vigor comprises what would today be called "growth and development economics." Thus the early writers were interested in promoting thrift and capital formation, were stressing progress and technological change, and were emphasizing the economies of large-scale production. It is true that they did not succeed in formulating a simple and comprehensive theory to cover growth and development. But modern economists of the 1960's are least likely to blame them—since in our own day the philosopher's stone that would unify and illuminate this area has long been sought, but the search has as yet produced only a catalogue of important but not unobvious tendencies and countertendencies.

The Transition to Modern Economics

Does this survey of American economics throw much light on the present position of the subject? I am not sure.

From it one would hardly be prepared for the fact that abstract mathematical economics and statistics are being avidly studied today here in the United States. (That economists should be busily engaged in operations research and programing for large corporations and the armed services fits in a little better with the earlier pattern.)

Nor would reading a survey of the nature of early American economics lead one to guess that today large parts of the business community look on economists with suspicion—as impractical "eggheads" bent on criticizing private enterprise and putting it in fetters. The intervening years of trust formation at the turn of the century and of mass depression in the 1930's substantially changed characteristic patterns of the earlier economics.

The evolution of American economic thought would, however, have prepared one for the emergence in the first part of this century of the *institutionalist* school of economics. This was associated with the names of Thorstein Veblen, John R. Commons, and Wesley C. Mitchell. For the most part this school has not succeeded in reproducing itself and today it seems to be almost extinct. But at the University of Wisconsin and the New School for Social Research in New York in the years after the First World War, this school did appear to be the wave of the future.

It is hard today to see what such diverse men really had in common, that is, aside from their all being critical of the deductive economics promulgated by complacent classical and neoclassical theorists. Veblen—the American Karl Marx—was primarily an iconoclast and social critic, debunking in murky but brilliant prose the cherished beliefs and institutions of his time. The lasting achievements of Commons and Mitchell would not seem to reside in anything that they had particularly in common with Veblen or with each other but rather with the important work in applied economics that each was motivated to do—Commons in the field of labor economics and Mitchell in the field of business cycles.

Prior to the institutionalists, America was not without its critics of the existing order. About Henry George and his single-tax movement I shall say little, since so forceful a speaker and stylist was able to command for himself an amount of attention disproportionate to his intrinsic importance. The imputation of land income is unlikely to be considered by the economic historian of the future as a problem of the first magnitude, and the expectation by George's followers that the single tax would cure most of the ills of society seems merely crankish.[g]

One would have expected the deflationary decades at the end of the nineteenth century to have created a group of radical economists. In the political field itself we had the era of Populist agitation, and this did have its counterpart in the realm of thought.[2] The young John Bates Clark was a kind of Christian socialist; and Francis Walker at the threshold of his career as an economist felt himself to be a militant critic of the harmonies of laissez faire. As is well known, the American Economic Association was founded in the 1880's by the younger economists—many of whom had studied in Germany under so-called "socialists of the chair" and exponents of the historical method—as a protest movement against the older conservative economists. It may not seem remarkable today but it was then a use of strong language for them to have put in their platform

---

[g] I used to have the vague notion that George was a good expositor of the Hume-Ricardian theory that land rent, being the return to a factor in inelastic supply, was not so much price determining as price determined and hence provided a good object for taxation in the sense of creating little dead-weight loss. But when a few years ago I looked for passages in *Progress and Poverty* to include in an anthology of readings in economics for beginning students, I was astonished not to be able to find any connected passages with a firm analytical structure.

the assertion: "We regard the State as an educational and ethical agency whose positive aid is an indispensable condition of human progress." How different this was from the Jeffersonian notion that the best government is the least government!

In time the American Economic Association lost its radical tinge and embraced almost all the leading American economists. And it is interesting to observe how many of the men associated with its founding became less radical with advancing age and prestige. In the nineties Richard T. Ely, one of the leading spirits in the founding of the Association, was formally accused at the University of Wisconsin of being a socialist. Not only did he clear himself of this charge, but, what is more remarkable, he agreed that if the charge had been true, it would have been good grounds for disqualifying him from teaching. And Clark ended by formulating in his classic *Distribution of Wealth* the doctrine that the imputation of functional wages and interests by the specific productivity laws that prevail under free competition is *ethically* optimal.

Perhaps the pressures of what was on the whole an intolerant society can explain the increasing conservatism of the transitional generation of economists. Certainly some explanation for the relative unimportance of socialism in modern American thought is called for. As far as the changing ideas of economists themselves are concerned, I have this hypothesis to put forward. By the turn of the century economists were ceasing to be amateurs and were making their livelihoods as college professors. This professionalization of economics may have had as one of its by-products a toning down of radical feelings, for the university environment and the full-time study of economics may make for a reduction of Utopian ardor. (It is interesting to note that Alfred Marshall in England and Léon Walras in France and Switzerland went through similar developments, each starting and ending with warm social sympathies but in the course of time becoming more and more skeptical about proposals for the radical remaking of society.)

The professionalization of American economics greatly improved its analytical quality. Now articles and books were being written by men who had been taught by other economists, not by themselves. What was lost in originality was more than compensated for in cogency. The two great figures from the standpoint of analytic contribution undoubtedly were John Bates Clark and Irving Fisher.

It is not of much moment that Clark should have rediscovered a decade later the Jevons-Menger-Walras doctrines of marginal utility, since if he had chosen to he could easily have read these contributions. But what is significant is the fact that by the end of the 1880's he had fully developed the marginal-productivity theory. I judge that he had a complete outline of this doctrine before Wicksteed or Léon Walras, even though its full statement was not published until his *Distribution of Wealth* appeared in 1899.[h]

Yale's Irving Fisher did important original work in many fields. His doctoral dissertation, A *Mathematical Investigation into the Theory of Price* (1892), can be regarded even today as a rewarding discussion of general equilibrium. His many statistical researches and his work in connection with the quantity theory of money are well known. But most important of all in my judgment is Fisher's contribution to the theory of capital. Here for the first and last time we have a definitive statement of the equilibrium conditions determining the rate of interest along with all other prices. While Fisher laid himself open at times to the interpretation that his was merely an "impatience" theory of interest, careful examination of his work shows that his is indeed a general model into which any of the special theories of capital and interest can be easily fitted. What Eugen von Böhm-Bawerk attempted but was technically unable ever to finish, Irving Fisher brought to a successful completion.[1]

After World War I this transitional period culminated in such world-famous economists as Frank H. Knight, John Maurice Clark,

[h] Stuart Wood, to whom Harvard gave the first American Ph.D. degree in economics, seems to have arrived simultaneously at similar ideas. Alfred Marshall's *Principles* (1890) contains suggestions of marginal-productivity notions but never completely worked out; and, of course, von Thünen had long since discovered the general notion of marginal productivity.

[1] A long list of important economic scholars could easily be drawn up. It would contain such names as Frank W. Taussig, who in addition to making significant contributions to international economics was also a brilliant teacher and editor; H. J. Davenport, a formulator of rigorous economics, who was at the same time a man of strong social sympathies and the best friend Thorstein Veblen ever had; Allyn A. Young, whom we know from oral tradition to have been a keen and creative thinker but who, alas, has left in written form only a few suggestive fragments. His being called to an English chair was in 1927 a remarkable event— more remarkable than it would be today. Something of Young's caliber as a theorist can be judged from the fact that it was he who, in his original review of A. C. Pigou's *Wealth and Welfare* (1912), pointed out that the bidding up of factor prices in a so-called "increasing cost industry" was a transfer item that in no way entailed the Marshall-Pigou notion that it would be optimal for society to interfere and tax such industries so that they would contract relative to other industries.

and Jacob Viner. These men, the sons of our grandfathers, belonged to the first generation of topnotch economists to have been completely reared by American graduate schools. They provide a fitting bridge to the modern generation of American economists.

The Modern Scene

In giving a survey of present-day American economics and American economists, I must not make the mistake of the patriotic Greek who insisted that the moon of Athens was different from the moon of Sparta. American economics is plainly in the tradition of Western economics generally. Indeed, to a Russian it would be indistinguishable from French or German economics. To a Latin American it would not seem different from English economics. (And even we American economists have our private little joke concerning our great advantage over the English. They read only their own writings, whereas we can get the benefit from reading their papers and our own too!)

Furthermore, by American economics one cannot mean economics as taught and discussed by persons *born* in this country. Scarcely one French professor in twenty was born outside of France. But of twenty outstanding American economists at the time of World War II, perhaps two came here from England and six to eight from Europe. (I do not even distinguish Canadian from American economists. Another of our jokes is that we are all Canadians!) An American university that tried to recruit its economics department from Mayflower descendants would, I fear, have a tough time of it.

These and other characteristics of the American economic profession would also be quite typical of other disciplines: mathematics, physics, chemistry, classics, sociology, medicine—and in some degree law and history. Many of my remarks then, though couched in terms of the concrete detail of economics, will be applicable to American academic life generally; and this essay can be considered a contribution to the general subject of *comparative academics*.

For about a quarter of a century now, American economics has been first-rate. What does this mean? It means what any competent observer means when he says that a particular university or person is in the forefront in creative research in the field of mathematics, physics, or medicine. Naturally there is an inevitable subjective element in any such appraisal. And there is an inevitable bias that predisposes any observer to magnify the accomplishments of his own town, province, and country. When I state that the *quantity* of economic thought in Cambridge, Massachusetts, is second to none anywhere in the world, I might be able to back this up by a count of the pages of articles published in learned journals, by measurement of the total inches of our theoretical and statistical curves, by the decibel count of the seminars at Harvard and further down the river. But when I go on to state that the *quality* of this thought is second to none, you must make allowance for the fact that Cambridge is where I sip my morning coffee.

In saying that American economics has been first-rate for a quarter of a century, I seem to be implying that prior to that time it was not. One can never be sure about such judgments, but I am inclined to risk the hypothesis that the scholarly research done by Americans in economics prior to, say, 1932 was generally not quite of the first rank. And I suspect this is a judgment that could be risked about mathematics, physics, and chemistry, too.

Let me illustrate by the case of mathematics and physics. Toward the end of the Second World War, when President Roosevelt set up the Bush Committee to survey science, I recall hearing I. I. Rabi, himself an American Nobel prize winner in physics, point out that in our history we had produced only one truly outstanding theoretical physicist (presumably Willard Gibbs). And the story is told that when the young G. D. Birkhoff proved in 1910 a famous conjecture of the dying J. H. Poincaré, the French mathematician C. E. Picard refused to believe that an American could have done it.[k]

It was not purely for reasons of fashion that at the turn of the century Americans went to Germany to do their graduate work. In the natural sciences the best work was being done there, and many Americans who studied abroad were frank to report that they found themselves less well prepared and creative than many of the fellow students they met in Europe.

Returning to economics, can we explain the earlier trek to Germany purely in terms of the world superiority of German *economic*

---

[k] This is not to deny that prior to World War I America had many eminent mathematicians: Bôcher, Osgood, Moore, Bliss, and many others; and such eminent physicists as R. A. Millikan, A. A. Michelson, and many others. But it does assert that Germany, England, and France may have had an even greater number of luminaries. I believe I. I. Rabi is the source, too, for the story that up to the early 1920's the Göttingen library was content to take America's leading physics journal, *Physical Review*, in bound form *at the end of the year*. Contrast this with the present world status of the journal.

scholarship? I think not. If American economics was years ago clearly inferior to some other economics, one would have to point to English economics as the clearly front-rank effort. So, I suppose, we must invoke the institutional factor that German universities were set up to give graduate instruction whereas Cambridge (and Oxford) were not. If an economist like J. B. Clark could have gained anything from his teachers—and there is little evidence that so self-oriented and original a man could—one would have thought that a W. S. Jevons might have given him more than could a Karl Knies or any other less theoretically oriented German scholar. But Jevons taught undergraduates in a university that was not yet even red brick. And even after the nineties, when Alfred Marshall was widely regarded as the world-leading economist, there was really no way for anyone to do graduate study in his Cambridge classroom—much less at his knee.[1] Had a young American been venturesome enough to break away from the German pattern, how could he get into an English college? And outside the college commons room, whom would he have found to talk to? Worst of all, to cap his folly he would have had to return to our shores unanointed by the all-important Ph.D. degree, which was the necessary passport for a successful teaching career.

Demand creates its supply. We have seen that American universities increasingly began to process their own graduate students and to award domestic Ph.D. degrees. And yet, as we have seen, it was perhaps still not true that American economics was first-rate. This led many observers by the familiar *post-hoc-ergo-propter-hoc* reasoning to the inference that our second-rateness must be due to our horrible propensity to insist on doctor's degrees. Even today this view will take one a long way in many a commons room of the British Isles, and there are *Gelehrten* here at home who think that the mere *absence* of a degree will convert a mediocre son of the Middle Border into a sparkling and omniscient don.

I must confess my own original predilections were against our Ph.D. until, under the impact of direct empirical observation, I was forced to the view that the absence of a comprehensive Ph.D. program may be the curse of economics abroad. This is not at all because our average doctoral dissertation is a substantial contribution to scholarship, a work of art, or even a literate document. To look at

[1] After 1904 the Rhodes scholarships did provide a bridge between American students and English university life. But they were intended for leaders, not scholars, and they served to give a taste of undergraduate life rather than of graduate study.

the thesis is to miss the point; it is only the exposed peak of a sub-merged iceberg. If the Ph.D. program had never existed, we should now have to invent it—for the simple reason that *it gives us the excuse to carry on advanced instruction in economics.*

For, make no mistake about it, modern economics has become a complicated subject—one which takes a long time to learn. Gone are the days when one could give a bright undergraduate a copy of Marshall to take along with him on his vacation trip to the mountains and expect him to end his undergraduate days as an accomplished economist. True, such a system may generate clever essays about Marshall's use of the representative firm or his concept of quasi rent. But that is not the sort of thing that economists today regard as important work—nor would similar clever essays by Marshall on Mill's use of "derived demand" have earned him *his* world reputation.

GRADUATE SCHOOL AND OTHER TRENDS

Since the graduate schools are all-important as the producers of economists and as the places where much research takes place, the trends in their development are worth reviewing. Such early graduate centers as Johns Hopkins and Clark University lost out, for reasons that are not too clear but which probably involved a shortage of financial sustenance. Harvard, Chicago, Columbia, and Wisconsin would probably be recognized as our strong graduate institutions around the time of the First World War but with many other universities not far below in size and prestige.

By the time of the Second World War the degree of concentration of American graduate study, if one could measure it, would probably have shown a centripetal growth. In the early 1930's Chicago—like the London School of Economics—enjoyed, under Frank H. Knight, Henry Schultz, and Jacob Viner, a position of great prestige. Toward the end of the decade Harvard, covering the field of microeconomics with J. A. Schumpeter, E. H. Chamberlin, and W. W. Leontief, and macroeconomics with Alvin Hansen and J. H. Williams, had reached a degree of ascendancy which gave rise to much comment and talk about "the old school tie" and mutual back scratching.

Economists played an important role in World War II.[m] Washing-

---

[m] The next few paragraphs are adapted from my paper "What Economists Know," which appeared in French in the 1959 *Esprit* symposium on the social sciences, edited by Daniel Lerner. Also in paper bound Meridian Press, April, 1959, pp. 183–213.

ton became in a real sense *the* center of economic science. In some numbers economists joined the government to help solve military and civilian policy problems. So did numerous businessmen.

What were the batting averages of the two groups? If one can hazard a guess, I would suggest that the decisions followed tended usually to be those framed primarily by people from the universities and that these were on the whole the better decisions. What were the reasons for this? Certainly not differences in articulateness. Aside from the fact that it is the economists' business to be thinking about social decision making, I think there was also the factor that a considerable payoff exists just to the exercise of the ordinary precautions of loose scientific method—a wish to dig up relevant evidence, and a respect for such factual data once they have been collected and analyzed.

In the realm of decision making itself, there seemed to be a military role for persons trained in the discipline of economics. In one military agency, units of historians and economists worked side by side; and I think disinterested third parties would agree that the economists seem ablest at making the important policy decisions. It is as if the repeated study of the imponderables of economic life— where the data are never complete and where calculated guesses have to be made—was a valuable preparation for wartime problems.

It is such considerations that fortify the teacher of graduate economics. As he puts each generation through the paces of advanced economics, he is a rare man if he does not sometimes ask himself what the connection is between these rarefied concepts and the concrete realities of economic life. But it seems to be a brute fact of experience that somehow going through such training does alert the economist to an important way of looking at things—to a concentration on relevant alternatives and a predisposition to question their relative costs and advantages. Perhaps there ought to be some cheaper way of producing this degree of economic sophistication, but no one seems yet to have found it.

As an outsider, I can testify to the high quality of the technical wartime economics in Washington. Committee meetings were then carried on at a level that would do credit to advanced university seminars. This is in interesting contrast to what our postwar bombing surveys learned from the German records about the caliber of wartime planning in that country. Apparently all calculations had been made for a short war, and the national income and other information needed to coordinate an intense and prolonged war effort were simply not to be had in the Third Reich. In Washington, on the other hand, the general predictions of wartime economic magnitudes were vindicated by the subsequent facts—so much so in fact that the economics profession as a whole was becoming a little cocky. Whom the gods would destroy they first raise up. It is an ironical fact worth pondering that the best brains from our best universities using the best economic tools known to our discipline and having at their command the statistical resources of a great nation went significantly haywire in making the famous 1945 prediction that the immediate aftermath of the war would involve mass unemployment. When the facts proved otherwise, this constituted a chastening experience—one which has rightfully increased the humility of a generation of economists.[n]

After the war there was a great exodus of economists out of Washington back to the universities. One of the interesting postwar trends seems to have been a decrease in the concentration ratio of American economic graduate study: I mean by this that in addition to the few traditionally strong graduate schools, which continued strong and indeed were engulfed by a torrent of returning servicemen, there emerged a number of vigorously competing centers for graduate study in economics. It would be invidious to attempt a comprehensive list but the names of Stanford, M.I.T., Yale, Michigan, Johns Hopkins, and California will be recognized by anyone familiar with the American scene as providing keen competition to the established centers. (I have named half a dozen schools but I could easily name others of equal or superior quality.)

The reasons for this postwar decentralization seem to be obscure. On the one hand by this time America had more topnotch economists than could be hired by only a few graduate schools; and thus there was a willing and eager supply of teachers to man the new programs. On the demand side, there remained the fact that a venerable institution of learning has the tremendous advantage of inertia working in its favor. It is well known in subjects other than economics that long after a particular department has receded from its peak, it continues to have applicants sent to it by its former students and continues to attract applicants from the public at large. Working

---

[n] Careful study of forecasting throughout the postwar years suggests to me that professional economists generally do do better at this chancy game than nonprofessionals. But this is not to deny that there still remains a great deal of unreliability in the predictions of the best of forecasters.

against this centralizing factor of inertia, there was perhaps an accumulated realization that the slightly smaller institutions might have certain advantages on the research side and in connection with the important problem of being placed in a good job after graduation.

WHERE WE STAND

The early American economist would be astonished to look at a present-day learned journal. The professionalization of the subject has been carried to the point where much of it might seem incomprehensible. The most visible manifestation of this is of course the use of mathematical symbolism. But even if all mathematical expressions were replaced by their verbal equivalents, there would still remain the increased technical character of modern economics. An economist who recently retired was heard to say: "I'm glad I'm not thirty-five years old, for I'd then feel I had to learn a lot of mathematics." In a way he was right, yet in two ways wrong. First, there are notable examples to prove that a man can do first-class creative work in the field of modern American economic analysis even if he has but a primitive training in mathematics. Second, the intricacies of current discussions are such that mere knowledge of mathematics will not suffice to carry one very far. It cannot be restated too often that mastery of mathematics textbooks is neither a necessary nor sufficient condition for mastery of economics. This is not to deny that it may be a highly useful tool in meeting the miscellaneous statistical and theoretical problems that turn up in the course of a modern economist's year—as students of Harold Hotelling and Henry Schultz learned just a generation ago.

There are many things that a modern economist feels he must know: statistics, economic history, sociology and interdisciplinary subjects, mathematics, foreign languages—and I have seen lists which even included public speaking and the ability to write clear English. In recent years we have been turning out graduates who could pass comprehensive examinations—particularly those of the objective-type format—in a vast range of subjects. (When an international civil service gives such examinations to students from the various countries of the world, there is some evidence which suggests that American students score high grades on the average.) It has sometimes been suggested that our most advanced students know everything except common sense. To this I have heard the reply that that is something which will come with age, whereas if you do not learn the other things in youth you never will.

One of the notable features of modern American economics is the sheer number of economists. Back in the days of Alfred Marshall one could count on two hands the economists who mattered in England. They were a small group, writing for each other. The time is now here when the members of the American Economic Association will have to be reckoned in five digits. With the individual propensity to write articles the same at all times, it is little wonder that it is harder today to get a marginal article published than it was even a generation ago. With the individual propensity to read articles no greater, mere multiplication of journals cannot restore the old proportion without at the same time creating a feeling of frustration on the part of those who feel guilty when they are not keeping up with the literature. The only solution would seem to be a specialization of function: a journal for econometricians, one for operations researchers, one for linear-programing operations researchers, and so on. And something like this has actually come to pass as new subdisciplines have formed new associations and new official organs.

The number of American economists can itself have an overwhelming impact on the foreigner. Imagine his feeling when he attends for the first time the Christmas meetings of the AEA! I remember Lionel Robins once commenting on the great number of American economists, telling how he had been brought by Harry D. White during the war to meet some American economists in the Treasury—only to learn that they were merely the economists in White's division of the Treasury!

This problem of magnitude leads to an optical illusion, which we must guard against. When a country goes from a few economists to many, there will almost certainly have to be a lowering of *average* quality. Such a move is therefore sometimes deemed a bad thing— as if average quality were what is to be maximized (a goal which would entail there being only one best economist left). Actually, if we are interested in the general advance of a scholarly subject, it is the *total* contribution that counts. So long as we do not lose any of the best men at the top, their work will be supplemented by the contributions made all up and down the line.°

° It has occasionally been suggested that all contributions come from a few great men, but I do not think this Carlylean thesis will stand up under a careful examination of the evolution of a science. To be sure, there is a social cost of maintaining more men in a science, which has to be measured against their scholarly and teaching contributions; and there is even a cost, involved in the drain

I would not dare to attempt a catalogue of names of topnotch economists today working in America, but they obviously constitute a great number. Within the realm of analytical economics itself, notable progress has been made in such diverse topics as the following: linear programing, welfare economics, game theory, operations research, national income and fiscal policy, subjective probability and decision making under uncertainty, and many others. The National Bureau of Economic Research, the Cowles Foundation for Economic Research, and other research groups continue to add to our knowledge of business cycles and how to moderate them. The study of economic growth and development is today all the rage, and its voluminous literature testifies that the world's demand for treatment of the subject is met by a copious supply.

Throughout all this, as has been true characteristically of American economics, the applied areas flourish. These applied fields provide an outlet for sublimating what in earlier times and other places would have been an antipathy for pure theory and a liking for historicity. The ancient battle between prosaic Baconian description and brilliant Newtonian synthesis still goes on, but it now takes place within the framework of an understanding and respect for economic analysis.

Some Problems

I must not, however, end on a complacent note. There is always plenty to worry about in connection with the development of a live discipline. We certainly have our share of problems. Let me briefly mention a few.

First, we have seen that the present generation of American economists was greatly improved by the importing of able scholars from abroad. Are we now self-perpetuating? Or, in the absence of political uneasiness abroad of sufficient magnitude to keep up the flow of migrants to our shores, will we revert to a lower level of

---

on other people's attention, whenever someone issues a paper of little scholarly merit. One solution to the problem of the plethora of publication, but not one that I would personally favor, has been approached in some countries: a lottery that involves talent, articulateness, and luck manages to pick a few leading scholars who occupy the best posts at the few best universities; they then publish for each other's edification and for the edification of a larger group of scholars who follow their work closely. This makes for more interesting personalities and makes the reading problem more manageable; but it also makes for flurries of fashion and raises questions of fairness and efficiency.

quality?ᵖ Nobody can yet know the answer to this question, which obviously involves questions about the whole American educational system at the collegiate and precollegiate level.

A second major concern also has to do with the question of quality. During the depression decade of the thirties a great many able minds were attracted to the study of economics. There is some evidence that the economist, in helping to cure the business-cycle ills of the world, has to some degree worked himself out of an exciting job. He may be a little like the children's undertaker or the mastoid surgeon, who have become technologically obsolete in consequence of the discovery of antibiotics. There has been noted in recent years some tendency away from economics as a field of concentration on American campuses. More of the best minds these days go into the fields of physics, law, and medicine. There is even some competition felt now from business management as a career.

Finally, it may be argued that modern society is becoming so affluent as to cause a euthanasia of the economic problem—and with it the euthanasia of challenging problems for the economist. This brings us back to an argument often used a century ago to explain the backwardness of American economics. America, it was said, had no economic problems and therefore could not generate a vital science of economics. Like the rumor of Mark Twain's death, any declaration of the end of economic problems is somewhat premature. But, since political economy is not an end in and of itself, its devoted practitioners can be counted on to help hasten that happy day.

Notes

[1] See J. A. Schumpeter, *History of Economic Analysis* (New York: Oxford University Press, 1954), pp. 514-519 and 863-877 for a good discussion of early American economics and for references to other writers.

[2] See Joseph Dorfman, *The Economic Mind in American Civilization* (New York: The Viking Press, Inc., 1949), Vol. 3, for a full treatment of this era.

[p] This raises the economic problem of the mobility of highly-skilled factors of production. Being the richest country in the world, America has some pull on artists, musicians, and scholars. Even in the absence of political disorder, we may find that our living conditions and conditions of research assistance will be such as to attract many of the best users of such resources. Certainly many have expressed some concern in the last decade that international agencies such as the United Nations and the International Fund and Bank should have drawn off to our shores some of the better trained foreign economists who might have been put to very good use at home.

THREE

☆

POSTWAR MONETARY POLICY

☆

RALPH E. FREEMAN

POST-WAR MONETARY
POLICY

BY

RALPH E. FREEMAN

Heritage of War and Depression

Monetary policy, for which high hopes had been held during the twenties, fell into disfavor in the following decade. Reserve bankers had to contend with the disintegrating forces which in the early thirties shattered the banking system. Despite a policy of easy money, the economy did not fully recover till World War II. Though the Gross National Product (GNP) rose from $56 billion in 1933 to over $91 billion in 1939, unemployment did not drop below 7.7 million.[1] A series of laws culminating in the Banking Act of 1935 strengthened the hands of the newly reconstituted Federal Reserve Board. These improvements, however, did little to make monetary policy effective during the depression years.

Partly as the result of a reduction in the gold content of the dollar in 1934, and partly because of a flight of capital from abroad, large quantities of gold poured into the country and took control of credit out of the hands of the Federal Reserve authorities. From $4 billion at the end of 1933 the gold stock increased rapidly to reach a total of $23 billion in 1941. Huge excess reserves were created in the member banks, the interest rate on Treasury bills was driven down below 0.25 per cent, and the yield on long-term government bonds went to less than 3 per cent. Indeed, in the late thirties the bill rate fell below zero and the long-term yield went under 2.5 per cent.[2] It is hard to understand why the Treasury did not try to strengthen the Federal Reserve Board by a bold policy of gold sterilization.

During 1936 and early 1937, when commodity prices advanced rather sharply, the Board became alarmed at the mounting excess reserves and raised reserve requirements to the legal maxima. Excess reserves were cut back to $750 million, and there followed a serious decline in business activity. As to the causes of this recession, opinion is divided. There was inventory liquidation following a too rapid build-up of stocks. The Treasury sterilized some gold. There was a shift in the federal budget from deficit to near balance. Though the Board insisted that its action was designed to lower the inflation potential rather than to slow down economic expansion, many people put the blame for the recession on the raising of reserve requirements.

53

That deflation set in while unemployment was still high was taken by some as evidence of the incompetence of our central bankers and the impotence of monetary policy.

It is generally conceded that, as a stimulant to recovery from a slump, monetary policy is weak. The central bank can make loans cheap and easy to get but cannot induce the public to borrow. During the depression of the thirties there was little demand for credit because borrowed money could not be put to profitable use. The fact that credit control might be effective as a check on inflation was regarded as of little consequence. The problem was one of deflation, not inflation. As the depression dragged on, the conviction grew that unemployment had become chronic and that there was slight prospect of monetary policy being called upon to do the work for which it was adapted.

This conviction was provided with a theoretical basis in the writings of the followers of J. M. Keynes.[3] They pointed out that investment was a key factor in determining the national income, and that if there were insufficient opportunities for investment, income would remain below the full-employment level. Because these writers were pessimistic about the investment outlook and more pessimistic than Keynes as to the effect on investment of changes in money and interest rates, they visualized a future of economic stagnation. In their view the chief hope for full recovery lay in greater outlays by government to make up for an expected deficiency in private investment spending.

Though most businessmen and bankers, and some economists, refused to follow the Keynesian line, the new ideas apparently made some impression in Washington. There was a shift of emphasis from monetary to fiscal policy. It was contended that such recovery as was achieved during the thirties owed more to the federal government than to the Federal Reserve Board. From 1933 to 1939 the national debt increased from $24 billion to $47 billion. The advocates of fiscal policy argued that the budget deficits of the period gave a stimulus to recovery by pumping new funds into the income stream.

Interest rates, which increased slightly during the 1936-1937 period of credit restraint, continued to edge downward till the end of the decade. Uncertainty as to how long money would continue to be cheap created a preference among investors for short-term securities. The thirties were characterized by a wide spread between long-term and short-term rates. The Treasury contributed to this disparity by concentrating on long-term issues, thus creating a scarcity of bills that were suited to the investment needs of commercial banks.

When the United States became involved in World War II and it became clear that large government borrowings would be required, the Treasury decided that the level of interest rates should be kept low in order to minimize the money cost of the war. Moreover, when it was realized that commercial banks would be called upon to furnish a large part of the borrowed money, the Treasury determined to maintain the exceptionally low interest rates on short-term issues which had special appeal for banks.

During the war the Treasury was the dominating influence in monetary policy. The Federal Reserve Board fell in with the financing plans of the government. In its *Annual Report* for 1941 the Board announced:

> The System is prepared to use its powers to assure that an ample supply of funds is available at all times for financing the war effort and to exert its influence toward maintaining conditions in the United States Government security market that are satisfactory from the standpoint of the Government requirements.[4]

In April 1942 Federal Reserve banks guaranteed to buy all Treasury bills offered to them on the basis of 0.375 per cent for those of ninety-day maturity. They gave sellers the option of repurchase at the same price. A preferential discount rate was established on government securities maturing within one year. Issues with longer maturities than bills carried higher rates, ranging from 0.875 per cent for one-year certificates to 2.5 per cent for twenty-five to thirty-year bonds.

The Treasury made liberal use of bills which carried the lowest rate, most of which were taken up by commercial banks. As the banks needed additional reserves to support growing deposits and expanding currency, they sold bills to the Federal Reserve System. By the end of the war over 85 per cent of the security holdings of the System consisted of government issues maturing in less than one year. By this time the demand for securities of longer maturity had forced their yield below 2.5 per cent.

The total gross debt of the federal government increased from $64 billion in December 1941 to $279 billion in the same month of 1945. During this period the Reserve banks raised their holdings of government securities from $2.3 billion to $24.3 billion. Commercial bank holdings went up from $21 billion to $91 billion. Since the other assets of these banks increased but little, government securities as a percentage of total assets increased from 30 per cent to 58 per cent. Commercial banks purchased the bonds by setting up new deposits for the government; and, as the Treasury drew checks to meet payrolls and purchases of war supplies and equipment, private demand deposits increased. These rose from $41 billion to $80 billion between 1941 and 1945; and time deposits from $16 billion to $30 billion. Meanwhile there was a large increase in circulating currency.

The additional reserves needed to support the expansion of currency and deposits were obtained by commercial banks, as indicated above, largely through the sale of government securities to Reserve banks. But there were other sources of increased reserves. An amendment to the Federal Reserve Act exempted from reserve requirements (and from assessments for deposit insurance) government deposits maintained at commercial banks (war loan accounts). This provision released reserves which otherwise would have been tied up. Moreover, in 1942 the reserve requirements of central reserve city banks were lowered from 26 per cent to 20 per cent, where they remained throughout the war.

The volume of government bonds in the hands of the public increased along with their money balances. From December 1941 to December 1945 individual holdings of government securities went up from $13.6 billion to $64.1 billion, and those of nonfinancial corporations from $4 billion to $22 billion; while insurance companies and savings banks expanded their portfolios of government bonds from $11.9 billion to $34.7 billion. These increases reflect the high level which savings attained during the war years. Personal savings as a percentage of disposable income rose from 5.5 per cent in 1940 to 25.2 per cent in 1944. This rise was attributable mainly to the apparatus of wartime regulations—wage and price controls, allocations and rationing—which reduced the volume of goods available for consumption and helped to curtail civilian spending. In 1941 the Board, having been given authority to regulate consumer credit, established minimum down payments and maximum maturities for consumer loans. In the following year the terms were tightened. Yet the decline in outstanding consumer credit which occurred thereafter was caused more by the lack of durable goods than by consumer-credit restraint.

The high volume of wartime savings helped to keep inflation in check. Disposable income doubled between 1940 and 1945. Since this income encouraged spending in excess of the volume of goods and services available at existing prices, there was a strong upward pressure on the price level. If a considerable percentage of the income had not been saved and thus withheld from consumption, the rise in prices would have been much greater than it was. The wholesale price index rose 20 per cent and the consumer price index about 22 per cent during the war years. However, because of the development of black markets where higher prices prevailed, the official indexes underestimated the degree of inflation which actually occurred and did not fully register the unavailability of many goods.

As the result of heavy wartime imports of raw materials and the restrictions imposed on exports, large dollar balances were built up in favor of many countries in Latin America and elsewhere. Some of these balances were converted into gold; and the monetary gold stocks of the United States declined from $22.7 billion at the end of 1941 to about $20 billion at the end of 1945. This loss of gold, together with large increases in the notes and deposits of Reserve banks, reduced the gold certificate reserve ratios of the banks to nearly their legal minima—40 per cent against notes and 35 per cent against deposits. In June 1945 legislation was passed establishing a minimum of 25 per cent against both notes and deposits. Since then the Reserve banks have had gold reserves well in excess of the legal requirements.

The war left the economy in a highly liquid condition. Individuals, business enterprises, and financial institutions had stored up a vast quantity of quick assets in the form of money and near-money. Because of the bond-support policy, the government securities in the hands of commercial banks were readily convertible into reserves upon which additional loans and deposits could be erected. Before Pearl Harbor, private debts were about double the liabilities of government—local, state, and federal. By the time Japan surrendered in August 1945 the proportion had been reversed. The federal debt alone was around 60 per cent of total obligations—public and private. It dominated the postwar economy, profoundly affecting the behavior of consumers and producers and changing the character of commodity and security markets. The pervading liquidity was a source of uneasiness and perplexity for those who were charged with responsibility for managing the money supply. They were worried about the possibility of a stampede to convert liquid assets into goods.

There were indeed strong reasons to expect a surge of buying. Consumers had been starved of many things—especially housing, automobiles, household appliances, and other durables. Business concerns had built up heavy arrears of maintenance and were in need of new plant and equipment for replacement and modernization. The huge backlog of demand and the tremendous supply of assets readily convertible into cash were an explosive mixture. The economy was ripe for inflation.

Monetary Policy in Eclipse

THREE YEARS OF INFLATION

As the war in Europe ended, other inflationary forces came into play. There was an urgent demand for American products from nations whose economies had been disrupted during the fighting. Large grants and loans were made, at first through the United Nations and the Export-Import Bank, and later through the Marshall Plan. A big export surplus was built up which put an additional inflationary strain on the American economy.

Pressure came also from organized labor. In the fall of 1945 unions in the automobile, steel, and other leading industries demanded a 30 per cent increase in wages; and a wave of strikes broke over the economy. The increases actually obtained in mass-production industries centered upon 17 per cent. The unions argued that the cost of living had risen faster than wages during the war period and that take-home pay had declined following the discontinuance of high-paid war jobs and reductions in overtime. Nevertheless, these wage concessions and others that followed had some inflationary impact. The Office of Price Administration in early 1946 was instructed to approve price advances consistent with increasing labor costs.

The heated controversy over the fate of the OPA reflected the doubts and disagreements that existed concerning the outlook for prices and employment.[5] In the summer of 1945 union leaders and government officials predicted that reconversion unemployment would rise to around eight million. Some economists, clinging to the thesis of secular stagnation, contended that as soon as the economy got back to normal, chronic underemployment tendencies would reassert themselves. The strength of the inflationary potential was underestimated by many people who expected a deflationary movement like that of 1920–1921 after the First World War. Price controls were finally abandoned in November 1946.

In that year Congress passed the Employment Act, which declared it to be "the continuing policy and responsibility of the Federal Government to use all practicable means . . . to promote maximum production and purchasing power." It was apparent that Congress conceived the problem then confronting the nation to be one of deflation rather than inflation. The main significance of the act, however, was that responsibility for maximum production was placed squarely on the shoulders of the federal government. It came to have a profound influence on the attitude of the public toward the future of the economy. The conviction grew that another depression was unlikely because the government "would not let it happen again."

That inflation was the real postwar threat was soon to be demonstrated. Unemployment, which rose to 2.7 million by March 1946, dropped back to 2.3 million in July and remained near that level till January 1949. The economy could not deliver all the goods and services that were in demand. The wholesale price index (based on the 1947–1949 average of prices) went up from an average of 68.8 in 1945 to 104.4 in 1948. The consumer price index (based on the same period), which averaged 76.9 in 1945, increased in each of the following three years, reaching 102.8 for 1948. Inflation was on the march.

A rising price level was responsible for about three-quarters of the $50 billion increase in GNP which occurred between 1946 and 1948. Since outstanding currency, plus the demand deposits of commercial banks, went up by only about $1.5 billion during this period, most of the dollar expansion was financed by an increase in the velocity of circulation of money. The ratio of GNP to the money supply went up from 1.9 to 2.3. The turnover of demand deposits in banks outside New York City rose from 16.5 in 1946 to 19.2 in 1948. The counterpart of the rise in the velocity was, of course, a decline in idle-money balances. Though this process resulted in some reduction of liquidity, the volume of quick assets in the hands of individuals, business concerns, and financial institutions, swollen during the war, remained more than adequate for all liquidity requirements.

The Reserve banks could have checked this inflationary movement by cutting down the reserves of member banks, but their hands were tied. The Treasury was determined that a level and pattern of interest rates similar to those which prevailed during the war should be continued. The purposes were to keep down the charges on the federal debt and to facilitate prospective large refunding operations. Moreover, there was widespread apprehension that a decline in bond prices, or the threat of a decline, would precipitate selling and thus "demoralize" the bond market and make it difficult for industries to finance their reconversion operations.

In the circumstances it is not surprising that the Federal Reserve Board concurred—though somewhat reluctantly—in maintaining the low level of interest rates inherited from the depression and the war. Early in 1946 the Open Market Committee announced that the existing pattern would be followed—0.875 per cent for one-year certificates, and 2.5 per cent for long-term bonds.

As will be observed from Table I, most of the additional reserves acquired by the member banks during the first three postwar years came as the result of an inflow of gold. The authorities, it is true, did something to offset the effects of this gold movement. Reserve credit was curtailed by about $1 billion. In 1948 reserve requirements for demand deposits were raised from 20 per cent to 26 per cent for central reserve city banks, from 20 per cent to 22 per cent for reserve city banks, and from 14 per cent to 16 per cent for county banks. Reserves against time deposits were lifted from 6 per cent to 7.5 per cent. Yet despite these moves the free reserves of member banks (excess reserves minus borrowings) showed only a slight decline.

Reserve requirements were raised to these levels under authority granted by Congress called in special session by President Harry S. Truman in the summer of 1948 to deal with the problem of inflation. The Federal Reserve System was given the power to increase the requirements above previous maximum limits, by 4 points for demand deposits and 1.5 points for time deposits. This power, however, was limited to one year and was not renewed.

During the spring and summer of 1948, following a relatively stable first quarter, there was an increase in the pace of inflation. Both consumer and wholesale prices advanced to new peaks. There continued to be a tremendous demand for funds to finance business expansion and the purchase of durable consumer goods. A third round of wage increases was being negotiated. The Federal Reserve System was providing funds for these inflationary activities by

TABLE I*
CHANGES IN MEMBER BANK RESERVES
DECEMBER 28, 1945, TO DECEMBER 30, 1948
(*in billions of dollars*)

Factors Causing Change	Effect on Reserves
Federal Reserve credit	
Security holdings	−0.7
Discounts and advances	−0.1
Other factors affecting federal reserve credit†	−0.1
Gold holdings	+4.2
Currency in circulation‡	+0.3
Other factors (net)§	+1.0
Reserve balances of member banks	+4.6
Required reserves	+4.9
Excess reserves	−0.3
Free Reserves (excess reserves less borrowings)	
December 28, 1945	.88
December 30, 1948	.64

* This Table and similar ones which follow indicate only the end results of changes occurring between two specific dates.

† Mainly float.

‡ A decrease in this item causes an increase in reserves and vice versa.

§ Treasury currency outstanding, Treasury cash holdings, and all deposits other than those of member banks.

permitting lending institutions to turn their government securities into cash on advantageous terms.

When Congress adjourned in August 1948, the Treasury announced an increase in the rate paid on one-year certificates from 1 to 1.25 per cent—the first such change since January. In September higher reserve requirements went into effect. These measures precipitated a liquidation of government securities, especially by banks. But then the System intervened with bond purchases amounting to over $2 billion, thus giving back with one hand what it took away with the other. These operations afforded a striking demonstration of the way in which the bond-support policy precluded attempts to control prices. Neither open-market operations nor alterations in the discount rate nor changes in reserve requirements could be used effectively to check inflation.

The federal government during these early postwar years added to inflationary pressure by encouraging home building. In addition to direct lending by government agencies, mortgage-loan insurance was introduced by the Federal Housing Administration (FHA) and loan guarantees by the Veterans Administration (VA). During the years 1946–1950 the annual volume of these government-backed mortgages increased steadily, reaching over $20 billion by the end of the period. They constituted about 40 per cent of total outstanding mortgage loans. These activities profoundly affected the character of conventional mortgages and thus brought the entire structure of housing credit under government influence. They exerted a downward pressure on mortgage rates and stimulated residential construction. Nonfarm-housing starts increased from 209,300 in 1945 to 931,600 in 1948.[6]

ANTI-INFLATIONARY MOVES

Being barred from effective use of their traditional powers, the Reserve authorities had to rely on other means of inflation control—means that did not require abandonment of par support for 2.5 per cent government bonds.

1. Moral suasion was frequently employed. In the latter part of 1947, for example, a special effort was made to persuade commercial banks and other credit agencies to adopt more conservative lending policies.

2. Though fiscal policy is discussed elsewhere in this volume, something should be said here about the debt-retirement program. About $23 billion of federal government bonds were retired in 1946 and $7.5 billion in 1947. The redemptions of 1946 were financed mainly out of the excess funds available from the Victory Loan floated in the latter part of 1945. This operation had virtually no anti-inflationary impact. Most of the bonds retired were held by commercial banks and were paid off by checks against the war loan accounts of these banks. Since these accounts were exempt from reserve requirements, there was no reduction in excess reserves. The redemptions of 1947 were accomplished mainly by utilizing the budget surplus. In this case the retirement of bonds held by commercial banks reduced the volume of deposits subject to reserve requirements. Some of the securities held by Reserve banks were also retired—a process that resulted in a decrease in the reserves of member banks.

Except to the degree that tax collections reduced current spending, none of these operations had much influence in checking the rise of prices. The monetary authorities could not engage in any tightening of credit which would raise interest rates and depress the prices of government bonds below par. However, the bond-retirement program, by reducing the volume of government securities in portfolios of commercial banks, did reduce somewhat the liquidity of these institutions.[7]

3. To the disappointment of the Reserve authorities, their request for retention of their wartime power to regulate consumer credit was turned down. After the war ended, this form of credit became a source of inflation, rising from $5.6 billion in 1945 to $11.5 billion in 1947. Congress felt that such control discriminated against consumers—especially veterans—and objected to the administrative complications involved in regulating the many thousands of lending agencies. Authority to prescribe the terms of consumer loans was later restored to the Board on a temporary basis, once in the summer of 1948 and again in September 1950.

4. In its report for 1945 the Reserve Board asked for authority to raise the required reserve ratios of member banks beyond the existing legal maximum limits. Such authority was not granted till 1948, and then, as we have seen, only for one year. No effective tightening of credit resulted because the member banks continued to hold substantial amounts of government securities, which could be converted into reserves at prices guaranteed by the Reserve System.

The Board also asked for authority to require member banks to hold, in addition to their existing primary reserves, secondary reserves of short-term government securities up to a maximum of 25 per cent of demand deposits and 10 per cent of time deposits. The aim was to enable the Board to immobilize a considerable part of the short-term holdings of member banks and thus restrict their power to obtain additional reserves for credit expansion.[8] This recommendation got nowhere.

5. Although the Reserve authorities apparently concurred in the policy of supporting long-term governments, they objected to the continuance of the wide differential between short- and long-term rates. They kept advocating an unfreezing of the rates on bills and certificates. They argued that this abnormal pattern inherited from the war was not essential to the maintenance of order in the capital market and that more flexibility in the prices of bills and certificates would lower their "monetary quality" and reduce the liquidity of the commercial banks.[9]

The proposal to unfreeze the short-term rates was accepted by the Treasury after some hesitation and delay. The first halting step was taken in April 1946, with the discontinuance of the preferential discount rate of 0.5 per cent on government securities maturing within twelve months. But this had little meaning because banks were not then availing themselves of the preference. The second step was not taken till July 1947, when the Open Market Committee voted to terminate the 0.375 per cent fixed buying rate on Treasury bills, as well as the repurchase option. The bill rates then moved up to 0.75 per cent. The Treasury cooperated in this unfreezing operation. Early in 1948 the certificate rate reached 1.125 per cent and the bill rate 0.95 per cent.

These moves injected an element of uncertainty into the bond market. Institutions and individuals holding government bonds became uneasy. They feared that the lowering of support levels for short-term issues might be followed by similar action for issues of longer maturity. Insurance companies and other institutional investors, therefore, began to sell. From October 1947 to February 1948 they sold nearly $7 billion of long-term government bonds, whose prices dropped from several points above par to near par levels.

Though the Reserve System finally had to step in and protect the parity level, the unfreezing of the short-term rates must be regarded as a step toward more flexible rates for all government securities. It gave some indication of what monetary policy could do if allowed to operate uninhibited by the Treasury.

RECESSION, RECOVERY, AND KOREA: 1948–1951

The recession which began in the late fall of 1948 can hardly be attributed to the anti-inflationary gestures of the preceding summer; for, as pointed out above, the market-support program ruled out any effective tightening of credit. The first signs of a downturn appeared in a slackening of retail trade, which led to a slowdown in the rate of inventory accumulation. This was soon followed by a shift from accumulation to liquidation. Though the business setback of 1948–1949 is usually regarded as an "inventory recession," declines occurred also in outlays for private construction and foreign investment.

As inflation gave way to a mild deflation, the Reserve authorities took steps to promote easier credit conditions. Consumer-credit regulations were relaxed and allowed to expire on June 30, 1949. The margin requirement for security loans was reduced from 75 per cent to 50 per cent. Reserve requirements for member banks were cut back in three stages by a total of 4 percentage points for demand deposits and 2.5 points for time deposits. These reductions, together with a decline in commercial and industrial loans, made it possible for member banks to add to their holdings of government securities, whose prices advanced.

The securities purchased by member banks were supplied by the Reserve System, which cut down its holdings by $4.6 billion during

TABLE II

CHANGES IN MEMBER BANK RESERVES
DECEMBER 29, 1948, TO DECEMBER 28, 1949
(*in billions of dollars*)

Factors Causing Change*	Effect on Reserves
Federal Reserve credit	
Security holdings	−4.6
Discounts and advances	−0.1
Other factors affecting reserve-bank credit	−0.1
Gold holdings	+0.2
Currency in circulation	+0.6
Other factors (net)	+0.1
Reserve balances of member banks	−3.9
Required reserves	−3.7
Excess reserves	−0.2
Free reserves (excess reserves less borrowings)	
December 29, 1948	.64
December 28, 1949	.72

* See footnotes to Table I, p. 61.

1949. This is shown in Table II. It will be seen that reserve balances declined by slightly more than the required reserves. Excess reserves at the end of 1949 amounted to $857 million—about $200 million below the level at the beginning of the year; but free reserves increased. The turnover of money went down during that year for the first time since the end of the war.

On June 29, 1949, the following statement appeared in the press:

The Federal Open Market Committee, after consultation with the Treasury, announced today that with a view to increasing the supply of funds available on the market to meet the needs of consumers, business and agriculture, it will be the policy of the Committee to direct purchases, sales and exchanges of government securities by the Reserve Banks with primary regard to the general business and credit situation. The policy of maintaining orderly conditions in the Government security market and the confidence of investors in Government bonds will be continued. Under present conditions the maintenance of a relatively fixed pattern of rates has the undesirable effect of absorbing reserves from the market at a time when the availability of credit should be increased.[10]

This statement was taken to mean that the Reserve System had shifted from a policy of pegging government-bond prices to one of flexibility. It turned out, however, that the "fixed pattern" was to be abandoned only in the sense that bond prices would be allowed to rise. There was no intention of permitting long-term governments to fall below the parity level. It was one-way flexibility.

Signs of recovery began to appear in the late summer of 1949; and by the end of the year it was apparent that the recession was at an end. Unemployment, however, did not begin to decline until March 1950. Thereafter the price level advanced and increases were registered in inventories, new construction, personal income, industrial production, and most of the other economic indicators. Expansion and inflation were gaining momentum when, in June, the United States entered the Korean War.

Just how much the easing of credit contributed to this recovery cannot, of course, be measured. It may have helped business to avoid excessive inventory liquidation and may have done a little something to encourage the expansion forces to reassert themselves. The Administration claimed that the easing of terms on government-backed mortgages was a factor in the early recuperation of economic activity. Housing starts increased from 931,600 in 1948, to 1,025,100 in 1949.

The mildness of the recession can be explained largely in terms of consumer spending. While industrial production declined and unemployment increased, there was only a slight drop in personal income, and total consumption expenditures actually rose. These expenditures were supported by increased unemployment benefits paid out of government trust funds. There were also reductions in tax payments to the government. Recession brought a decline in taxable income and tax revenue; unemployment cut down payments for social security taxes. These "automatic stabilizers" seem to have had an important moderating influence on the 1949 recession.

The mildness of this decline had an important influence on monetary policy. Economists, bankers, business leaders, and legislators began to think that perhaps the built-in stabilizers had become strong enough to protect the economy from the onslaught of severe depression. Stagnation views receded into the background. Fears that the use of the monetary weapon might bring on a slump were dissipated. It was a change in the climate of opinion favorable to a bolder use of monetary policy.

Evidence of growing dissatisfaction with the subservience of the Federal Reserve System to the Treasury appeared in the hearings of a Senate committee which had begun an investigation in the summer of 1948. It was the Subcommittee on Monetary, Credit, and Fiscal Policies, appointed by the chairman of the Joint Committee on the Economic Report, and was headed by Senator Paul Douglas. Its report was published in January 1950.

Many interesting questions were considered by this committee. Officials of the Treasury and the Reserve System, as well as business leaders and commercial bankers, were called upon to make statements. On the question of past relations between the Treasury and the Board, the report stated that where the two agencies had differed, it was the Treasury that had prevailed. The report went on to say that if the Federal Reserve had been willing to assert its independence, the tighter monetary policy involved in the unfreezing of short-term rates, referred to above, would have been initiated earlier and carried further.

One of the recommendations of the Douglas Committee read as follows:

> As a long-run matter we favor interest rates as low as they can be without inducing inflation, for low interest rates stimulate capital investment. But we believe that the advantages of avoiding inflation are so great and a restrictive monetary policy can contribute so much to this end that freedom of the Federal Reserve to restrict credit and raise interest rates for general stabilization purposes should be restored even if the cost should prove to be a significant increase in service charges on the public debt and a greater inconvenience to the Treasury in its sale of securities for new financing and refunding purposes.[11]

After June 1950 the Korean War greatly increased inflationary pressures. Anticipatory buying by consumers, a scramble by business firms to keep covered against future requirements, and government stockpiling sent prices soaring. Wholesale prices rose 11 per cent during the second half of 1950 and consumer prices 5 per cent. This splurge of buying was basically due to the expectation of future shortages and price increases. Consumers and businessmen had not forgotten what had happened to commodity markets in World War II.

Various moves were made to check this revival of inflation. A new voluntary credit-control program got under way. Orders were issued limiting the civilian use of aluminum, copper, and other industrial materials. In December 1950 President Truman declared a state of emergency; and a general freeze on prices and wages was imposed. However, because of exemptions and loopholes, this freeze only slowed down the rise in prices.

The sharp spurt of inflation generated by the war greatly disturbed the monetary authorities. On August 18, 1950, in seeking to recapture an area for independent action, the Federal Reserve Board announced that it had approved raising the discount rate at the Federal Reserve Bank of New York from 1.5 to 1.75 per cent. In taking this action the Board came into conflict with the Treasury, which on the same day announced a $13.5 billion refunding program with no increase in interest rates.[12] The Board had already warned the Treasury that the rates on the new issues were too low.

Since there was grave danger that the exchange offer would fail, the System itself bought the new issue from the proceeds of sales of other securities from its portfolio. In this way strong support for the refunding operation was given without involving an increase in the government bond holdings of the Reserve banks. This episode, sometimes called "a declaration of independence" by the Reserve System, marked a milestone in the struggle of the System to free itself from Treasury domination.

These events were followed in early 1951 by increases in reserve requirements of two percentage points on demand deposits and one point on time deposits. Meanwhile, controls were imposed on consumer credit, and the Board was given authority to regulate loans secured by real-estate mortgages. Margin requirements on security loans were raised from 50 per cent to 75 per cent.

The failure of the Reserve System to cope with the inflationary forces generated by the Korean War is clearly evident in Table III. Though member bank reserve requirements rose by $2.8 billion during 1950 and the early part of 1951, these banks were able to meet the large requirements without strain. The Reserve System furnished the necessary reserve balances by adding to its holdings of government securities. These open-market operations, with the assistance of other factors, more than offset the contractive effect of $2.5 billion of gold exports. The report of the Reserve Board for March 7, 1951, showed excess reserves of $716 million, only about $100 million below the level of December 29, 1949. There was, however, a decline in free reserves of about $200 million.

The return of inflationary pressures comparable to those of 1946–1948 finally convinced the Administration that the Federal Reserve authorities should be given some freedom and independence in the management of the money-banking system. In January 1951 there began a series of conferences between the Federal Reserve and the Treasury. President Truman attended these meetings, and it was reported that to effect an agreement he had to bring some pressure on the Treasury. On March 4 an announcement was made that "a full accord has been reached to assure the successful financing of the Government's requirements and, at the same time, to minimize monetization of the public debt."[13]

TABLE III

CHANGES IN MEMBER BANK RESERVES—
DECEMBER 29, 1949, TO MARCH 7, 1951
(*in billions of dollars*)

Factors Causing Change*	Effect on Reserves
Federal Reserve credit	
Security holdings	+3.4
Discounts and advances	+0.1
Other factors affecting reserve bank credit	+0.4
Gold holdings	−2.5
Currency in circulation	+0.5
Other factors (net)	+0.8
Reserve balances of member banks	+2.7
Required reserves	+2.8
Excess reserves	−0.1
Free reserves (excess reserves less borrowings)	
December 29, 1949	.72
March 7, 1951	.51

* See footnotes to Table I, p. 61.

This announcement marked an important turning point in the history of monetary policy in the United States. Since March 4, 1951, the Reserve banks have been relieved of the necessity of maintaining a fixed pattern of rates. Though the system has continued to engage in open-market operations to maintain orderly conditions in the market and to facilitate Treasury financing, there has been no policy of keeping government bond prices above the parity level. As a matter of fact, by the end of March many Treasury issues were selling below par.

Revival of Monetary Policy

TRANSITION TO "FREE" MARKETS AND STABLE PRICES: 1951–1953

Soon after the accord was announced, the Treasury put out a new issue of bonds bearing 2.75 per cent, which were offered in exchange for outstanding long-term issues bearing 2.5 per cent. This move was designed to take some of the weight of potential liquidation off the market and at the same time to destroy the obsession that the Treasury must never pay more than 2.5 per cent for long-term money. Meanwhile, the system continued its support purchases but in decreasing amounts and at declining prices. The yield on long-term government bonds which had averaged 2.32 per cent in 1950 gradually rose during 1951 and 1952, reaching 2.87 per cent in early March 1953. The yield on three-month Treasury bills advanced from 1.2 per cent in 1950 to 2.01 per cent in March 1953.

Fears regarding the dire consequences of abandoning par support for long-term governments proved unfounded. Institutional and other investors did not rush to liquidate their holdings. The explanation is to be found partly in the skill with which transition from pegged to "free" markets was managed and partly in the decline that had taken place in the proportion of government securities among the assets of financial institutions. Though it cannot be said that the liquidity of these institutions had come near the danger point, nevertheless they were not as readily disposed as formerly to sell off large quantities of the most liquid of their assets.

The transition to relatively free markets was not accomplished overnight. There was at first some doubt as to how much freedom would actually be permitted. The probability of continued intervention by the system in support of Treasury refundings and its promise to maintain "an orderly market" suggested that some control would be retained. Under these conditions the brokers and dealers who made up the market were influenced not only by their estimates of the forces of demand and supply but also by what they thought the system planned to do.

Such limitations on the freedom of the market were gradually reduced as the reserve authorities modified their methods of operation. Mr. Martin, who had succeeded Mr. McCabe as chairman of the board of governors, speaking in Detroit in April 1953, referred to a change in the attitude of the system toward the market:

> Gradually our emphasis has been shifting toward a realization that we should not be the judges of what an orderly market is; that our efforts should be directed more toward correcting disorderly conditions . . .[14]

Another change of technique was the concentration of open-market operations on securities of short maturity. Since the prices of such securities are less affected by purchases and sales than the prices of those of longer maturity, the System kept its market interference to a minimum by confining its operations to issues of the former type. Still another move toward freedom was the withdrawal of support for Treasury refundings. This policy was first tried out in December 1952 and again in February 1953. On both occasions the refundings were successful.

The period from early 1951 to early 1953 was one of expanding business activity, stimulated at the beginning by increasing defense expenditures and later by an upsurge in consumer spending. Business outlays for new plant and equipment remained high throughout the period. To facilitate this expansion, member banks increased their loans and investments from $106 billion in March 1951 to $118 billion in the same month of 1953. Demand deposits went up from $88 billion to $94 billion and time deposits from $29 billion to $33 billion.

As indicated in Table IV, the Federal Reserve banks during this period kept member institutions supplied with enough reserves to permit them to meet the growing credit needs of business. Reserve requirements rose and so did reserve balances. At the same time, however, the Reserve System put some pressure on member banks. As shown at the bottom of Table IV, the borrowings of members as of March 11, 1953, exceeded excess reserves by $850 million—a

TABLE IV

CHANGES IN MEMBER BANK RESERVES—
MARCH 7, 1951, TO MARCH 11, 1953
(*in billions of dollars*)

Factors Causing Change*	Effect on Reserves
Federal reserve credit	
Security holdings	+1.7
Discounts and advances	+1.1
Other factors affecting federal reserve credit	−0.1
Gold holdings	+0.7
Currency in circulation	−2.6
Other factors (net)	+0.4
Reserve balances of member banks	+1.2
Required reserves	+1.6
Excess reserves	−0.4
Free reserves (excess reserves less borrowings)	
March 7, 1951	.51
March 11, 1953	− .85

* See footnotes to Table I, p. 61.

marked contrast with the situation on March 7, 1951, when excess reserves exceeded borrowings by over $500 million.

The increase of $1.1 billion in discounts and advances—an item made up almost entirely of loans to member banks—marks the restoration of the discount rate to an important role. The significance of this change is described by Mr. Martin in the speech referred to above:

> Primary reliance is once more placed upon the discount mechanism as a means for supplying the variable short-term needs of individual banks for reserves. Experience has demonstrated that when member banks are heavily in debt to the Federal Reserve Banks, the tone of the money market is tight. Marginal loans are more likely to be deferred and some credit risks may have to shop around for accommodation. Conversely, when member bank borrowing is low, the tone of the money market tends to be easy and credit accommodation is less discriminating. The Federal Reserve borrowing privilege and the discount rate, after years of disuse, have come to play once more

their intended role as flexible, impersonal instruments of monetary management.

This was a period of transition for prices as well as for monetary policy. The consumer price index, which had risen from a monthly average of 102.8 in 1950 to 111 in 1951, advanced to only 113.5 in 1952 and 114.4 in 1953. From then until early 1956 the index moved in a sidewise direction. Wholesale prices, which had increased sharply in 1950 over the level of the preceding year, actually declined in the two following years—chiefly because of a slump in farm prices. The index stood at 115 in January 1951 and at 109.6 in December 1952. It subsequently rose to around 111 and remained near that point till near the end of 1956.

Many factors contributed to this leveling-off in prices. One was the huge investment in plant and equipment that had been undertaken since the end of World War II. The industries of the country, with greatly enlarged capacity to produce, were turning out record-breaking amounts of material and finished goods. A second factor was the economic "hangover" from Korea and swollen inventories resulting from the scramble for commodities in the latter part of 1950. The increased rate of savings also had a part to play. Personal savings in relation to disposable income increased from 5.9 per cent in 1950 to 7.8 per cent in 1951 and 1952. There was also some tightening of mortgage credit by the Housing and Home Finance Agency of the federal government.

The moderate pressure on member banks revealed in Table IV should perhaps be given some credit for what happened to prices. The Patman Committee,[15] which was appointed in April 1950 and reported in June 1952, was almost unanimous in its opinion that monetary policy played an important part in checking the decline in the value of the dollar; and some members expressed the belief that an earlier unpegging of the market would have reduced the rise of prices following the Korean War.

THE RECESSION OF 1953–1954

In the early months of 1953 business was running in high gear. Industrial production, employment, and personal income had reached peacetime peaks. Retail sales, expenditures on new construction, and other economic indicators gave every evidence of boom conditions; and the monetary authorities became worried lest the boom be carried to excess and the growing pressure of demand on resources explode into another sharp inflation. They therefore increased somewhat their pressure on bank reserves, forcing member institutions to increase their borrowing from Reserve banks. As the credit demands of business expanded—together with the demands of the government (which was at that time running a budget deficit)—interest rates advanced. The market yield on three-month Treasury bills, which averaged 1.72 per cent in 1952, rose to 1.88 in the spring of 1953. The yield on long-term government bonds went up from 2.68 per cent in 1952 to over 3 per cent in May 1953. There was also some tightening in the residential-mortgage market, largely because of the relative unattractiveness of the official rates that had been set up for federally aided loans. The effects of credit restraint, however, were offset in some degree by an increase in the income velocity of money (the ratio of GNP to the stock of money).

In June 1953 business activity began a slow but steady decline which continued for about a year. This recession was in many respects similar to that of 1948–1949. There was a drop in the index of industrial production from 137 in July 1953 to a low of 123 in March 1954. Spending on producers' durable equipment turned down. Unemployment jumped to a high of 3,724,000 persons in March 1954. As in the preceding recession, there was a shift from inventory accumulation to liquidation.

In the second quarter of 1953 inventories expanded at an annual rate of $5.4 billion. By the first quarter of 1954 they were contracting at the rate of $4.2 billion. Meanwhile total federal government expenditures diminished from $62.2 to $55 billion, largely as the result of the cease fire in Korea. The curtailment of spending resulting from these two factors was at an annual rate of more than $17 billion. Their depressive influence was partly offset by an increase in net foreign investment.

As soon as signs of recession appeared, the system abandoned tight money and used all the weapons in its arsenal to promote easier credit. Reserve requirements were reduced in July 1953 and again in June and July 1954. The discount rate was cut down from 2 per cent to 1.75 per cent in February 1954, and then to 1.5 per cent in the following April. Open-market purchases of securities, which began in a small way in May 1953, increased in June and continued at irregular intervals throughout the year. By October the excess reserves of member banks exceeded their borrowing by about $400 million. By December Federal Reserve policy had become one of "active ease."

Despite the fairly prompt reversal of policy, the credit squeeze of April and May 1953 was by some observers given a great deal of the blame for the business setback beginning in June and July. Senator Douglas, for example, insisted that the monetary authorities went too far and too fast and that the shift from tight to easy credit did not come soon enough.[16] There may well have been some causal connection between the policy of tight money and the decline in business inventories and in spending for producers' durables. Both inventories and industrial equipment were being financed in part by borrowed money, and the expectation of further credit stringency may have acted as an incentive to contraction in these areas. However, inventories which played a leading role in the recession did not begin to decline until September.

The whole question of the effect of changes in credit conditions on business activity and prices is still being debated. It is generally agreed that pressure on bank reserves will have a twofold impact: (1) through higher interest rates, and (2) through credit rationing by lending banks. Rising rates of interest restrain total expenditures in the economy by making debt incurrence less attractive. When banks are short of reserves, they tend to raise their credit standards, scale down loan commitments, and shorten the maturity of loans. Since it takes some time for a change in the reserve position of the banks to work through to a change in their charges to borrowing customers, it is likely that the direct rationing of credit acts more quickly than the restraining influence of higher rates of interest. In the longer run, however, the more fundamental and powerful influence is probably exerted through changes in the cost of borrowing.

The question is complicated by lack of comprehensive data on the rates charged by banks for the various types of loans; and reliable information on the rationing activities of banks is even harder to obtain. Moreover, psychological factors, which are often of great importance, are difficult to appraise accurately. In April and May 1953, when credit stringency developed, there was considerable apprehension among banks and their customers that the stringency would increase in the autumn, when credit needs expand seasonally. Such fears made the banks put additional stress on liquidity at that time and caused them to tighten up business lending. There was a decline in the income velocity of money.

The story of monetary policy during the recession is suggested in Table V. Despite an increase in government security holdings by the system between March 1953 and October 1954 amounting to $500 million, total reserve balances declined. This drop was attributable mainly to gold outflow and a decrease in the indebtedness of member banks. The latter is indicated in the shrinkage in discounts and advances. Member bank debts to the system, which amounted to $1,202 million in March 1953, had been virtually all repaid by October 1954. There was a shift in the reserve position of the banks from net borrowings of $850 million to net free reserves of $600 million.

This easing of pressure on reserves produced a general decline in rates of interest. The yield on three-month Treasury bills, which averaged 2.19 per cent in April 1953, had dropped to less than 1 per cent by the spring of 1954. The long-term government bond yield declined from 3.26 in May 1953 to 2.6 per cent in August 1954. The average rates charged by commercial banks on business loans went down from 3.73 per cent in June 1953 to 3.6 per cent in July 1954. These banks expanded their loans and investments, and their deposits continued the steady climb which had been going on since the end of World War II.

The Treasury and the Federal Reserve System joined forces in an interesting financial maneuver in November 1953 designed to circumvent the statutory debt limit. The system sold direct to the Treasury $500 million of notes; and the latter made payment by issuing to the Reserve banks gold certificates against half of its holdings of free gold. These notes were immediately retired with the increased deposits set up in Reserve banks; and the Treasury was then able to borrow an equivalent amount in the market without exceeding the statutory debt limit. The reserves of the member banks were not affected.

The business setback of 1953–1954 was of moderate proportions. Despite the depressive influences of falling inventories and federal expenditures, GNP went down only about 4 per cent and personal consumption expenditures actually rose. An important supporting factor was the maintenance of foreign demand for United States products. American exports continued throughout 1953 at the high rate prevailing in the latter part of 1952. The fact that the recession did not turn into a cumulative spiraling depression—as many had feared—raised the confidence of businessmen and bankers in the inherent stability of the American economy. As in the 1948–1949 re-

TABLE V

CHANGES IN MEMBER BANK RESERVES—
MARCH 11, 1953, TO OCTOBER 27, 1954
(*in billions of dollars*)

Factors Causing Change*	Effect on Reserves
Federal reserve credit	
Security holdings	+0.5
Discounts and advances	−1.0
Other factors affecting reserve credit	−0.2
Gold holdings	−0.8
Currency in circulation	−0.2
Other factors (net)	+0.4
Reserve balances of member banks	−1.3
Required reserves	−1.6
Excess reserves	+0.3
Free reserves (excess reserves less borrowings)	
March 11, 1953	− .85
October 27, 1954	.60

* See footnotes to Table I, p. 61.

cession, the automatic stabilizers seemed to be working. Despite the difficulty of measuring the impact of Federal Reserve action, the apparently quick response of the economy to credit ease raised monetary policy another notch in the estimation of the financial community.

RECOVERY AND BOOM, 1954-1956

Early in 1954 the rate of inventory liquidation slackened and retail sales picked up. In the fall a general expansion got under way. GNP, which had fallen from an annual rate of $369.3 billion in the second quarter of 1953 to $357.6 billion a year later, rose to $367.1 billion in the fourth quarter of 1954. The year 1955 was one of exuberant expansion.

This expansion was aided and abetted by an increasing volume of credit. Member banks, whose lending power had been built up during the recession, raised their loans by over $20 billion between October 1954 and March 1956. Consumer debt went up by $600 million in 1954 and $6.1 billion in 1955. Expansion in home mortgage lending was stimulated by the easing of terms. Private housing starts, seasonally adjusted, rose from an annual rate of a little over 1 million in January 1954 to nearly 1.5 million in December.

In retrospect it appears that credit relaxation at this time was pursued too vigorously and that easy credit conditions were maintained too long. In fact, in December 1954 the money managers became concerned about the inflationary possibilities of their policy. They curtailed government security purchases and forced member banks to borrow to meet year-end demands for currency and credit. In January 1955, because of the continued rise in stock prices, the margin requirement for loans on stock-exchange collateral was raised from 50 per cent to 60 per cent. In February it was advanced to 70 per cent. During these two months the system sold $1.3 billion of bonds, forcing member banks to borrow additional reserves. In April the discount rate was raised from 1.5 per cent to 1.75 per cent. In the late summer and fall of 1955 the system again sold bonds. By the end of November the discount rate had been raised to 2.5 per cent.

As indicated in Table VI, the decrease in the security holdings of Reserve banks between October 27, 1954, and March 28, 1956, was $900 million, and member bank borrowing increased by about the

TABLE VI

CHANGES IN MEMBER BANK RESERVES—
OCTOBER 27, 1954, TO MARCH 28, 1956
(*in billions of dollars*)

Factors Causing Change*	Effect on Reserves
Federal reserve credit	
Security holdings	−0.9
Discounts and advances	+0.9
Float	+0.3
Gold holdings	−0.1
Currency in circulation	−0.2
Other factors (net)	+0.1
Reserve balances of member banks	+0.1
Required reserves	+0.2
Excess reserves	−0.1
Free reserves (excess reserves less borrowings)	
October 27, 1954	.60
March 8, 1956	− .62

* See footnotes to Table I, p. 61.

same amount. Between these dates the $600 million of free reserves disappeared, to be replaced by a net indebtedness of 620 million. Under the influence of tightening credit, bonds declined in price as their yields increased. There was a general rise in rates of interest. The rate on three-month Treasury bills went up from 0.98 per cent to 2.38 per cent and that on long-term issues from 2.65 per cent to 3.00 per cent. Bank charges on short-term business loans advanced from an average of 3.55 per cent in October 1954 to 3.93 per cent in March 1956.

Despite this credit tightening, the year 1955 was one of expanding business activity and increasing indebtedness. GNP went up from $361.2 billion in 1954 to $391.7 billion in 1955, crossing the $400 billion mark in the fourth quarter of the latter year. The FRB index of industrial production advanced from 125 to 139. Unemployment went down. Commercial banks expanded their business loans by about $7 billion. Consumer credit outstanding increased by over $6 billion. The terms on government-backed mortgages were tightened. VA appraisal requests and FHA applications decreased. But, despite a declining trend in housing starts, the total for the year was 1,328,900 —a near record—and mortgage indebtedness rose by $10 billion.

Credit stringency forced the commercial banks to satisfy the growing demand for loans by selling securities. When these securities were purchased by non-bank investors, desposits were liquidated and reserves were freed for loan expansion. As a result, active deposits were substituted for idle deposits, and the turnover of deposits increased. During the seventeen-month period beginning at the end of October 1954 the member banks reduced their security holdings (mostly government issues) by $11 billion. Insurance companies and mutual savings banks also sold Treasury obligations, while individuals, corporations, and government trust funds added to their holdings. The shift out of bonds into loans reduced the liquidity of the banks. The ratio of loans to deposits increased from 35 per cent to 47 per cent. Treasury issues averaged 44 per cent of the total loans and investments of commercial banks in October 1954, and a year later averaged 30 per cent.

The shift from securities to loans lowered the quality of commercial bank assets. Since government securities are without risk as far as the payment of principal is concerned, when these securities as a percentage of total assets decline, the proportion of so-called risk assets increases. In other words, the security sales of this period made inroads into the assets upon which banks rely for secondary reserves. As a result, banks became more and more selective in their lending policies.

As bank credit tightened, business firms began to look around for other ways of meeting their growing financial needs. They became increasingly willing to get along with lower cash balances in day-to-day business. They also availed themselves of idle bank balances held by others, inducing them to surrender these balances in exchange for securities. In this process industrial concerns were joined by non-bank financial institutions. The result of their activities was to raise further the velocity of circulation of money.

Since World War II, changes in velocity have played a more prominent role in business fluctuations than changes in money supply. Total demand deposits and currency moved roughly sideways from 1945 to 1948 at around the $100 billion level and then gradually increased to $134 billion at the end of 1957. Velocity, on the other hand, fluctuated closely with the economic cycle. The approximate monetary equivalent of the increase in velocity in 1948 was $18.9 billion; in 1953, $27.3 billion; in 1956, $7.6 billion. In the recession years 1949 and 1954 the turnover of money declined,[17] the monetary equivalent being −$3.2 billion and −$5.2 billion, respectively.

THE RECESSION OF 1957

During 1956 there was a slowdown in the rate of economic expansion. The FRB index of industrial production, which had risen fourteen points the year before, gained only four points. Housing starts declined further. This slackening in the pace of expansion continued in early 1957, and in August the boom ended. Though the percentage of the labor force unemployed did not begin to increase until November, by September another recession had gotten under way.

Prices, however, which had begun to rise again near the beginning of 1956, continued to move upward. The consumer price index advanced from 114.6 in February 1956 to 121.6 in December 1957; and the wholesale index during this period went up from 112.4 to 118.4. In 1958, while wholesale prices moved roughly sideways, the consumer price index edged upward until July.

The combination of rising prices and declining business activity put monetary policy to a severe test. The Reserve authorities, with their eyes fixed on the price trends, persisted in keeping money tight. The indebtedness of member banks to Reserve institutions continued to exceed their excess reserves; and the structure of interest rates advanced further. The rate on three-month Treasury bills rose from 2.3 per cent in March 1956 to 3.6 per cent in October 1957. The yield on long-term government bonds went up during this period from 2.9 per cent to 3.7 per cent and that on high-grade corporate bonds from 3.1 per cent to 4.1 per cent. Bond prices correspondingly went down. The average interest charge on short-term commercial bank loans rose from 3 per cent to around 5 per cent. The Federal Reserve discount rate, which was 2.5 per cent at the beginning of 1956, was raised in April and August of that year as well as in August of 1957, when it reached 3.5 per cent.

This policy was sharply criticized.[18] It was pointed out that the Federal Reserve System was missing both its main objectives, that there was neither full employment nor price stability. Critics contended that by raising the cost and availability of credit the System hastened the downtrend of business and yet failed to check the rise of prices.

Indeed it is hard to understand why the System waited until November 1957 before making a decisive move toward easier credit. In the early part of the year doubt as to whether the economy actually was in recession was understandable. There was a leveling off but not much in the way of decline. After Labor Day, however, when the usual seasonal upturn failed to appear, it became clear that a recession was in the making. There was disagreement among Reserve officials on the proper course to pursue. In August, when the discount rate was raised, some of the Reserve banks were reluctant to fall in line.

There was much complaining during 1956 and even more in 1957 about the unevenness of the impact of credit restraint. Home builders, school boards, and municipalities were said to be especially hard hit because of their dependence on the bond market for funds. Small business concerns were suffering because, unlike large corporations, they had to rely mainly on bank borrowings for financing. A demand arose in Congress for some means of sheltering these types of borrowers from the rigors of tight money.

It is interesting to observe that in 1957 the income velocity of money rose to a peak of about 3.3. This increase cushioned the impact of the restrictive monetary policy of that year. Some economists believe that this 3.3 rate is a near maximum and adduce in support of their contention the high interest rates prevailing in the first half of 1957.[19] If this is so, the cushioning effects of changes in velocity on credit tightening are likely to be weaker in the future. In short, the economy has just about grown up to the excessive supply of money and near money developed during World War II.

The economic downturn of August 1957 cannot be attributed solely to the failure of the Reserve authorities to shift promptly from restrictive to expansionary measures. Federal government purchases of goods and services declined by $1 billion (annual rate) between the first and the fourth quarter of 1957. The high level of output during the two preceding years had resulted in an accumulation of durable goods which led to a decline in demand. As the recession proceeded, there were further reductions in the output of consumer durables—especially automobiles—and a decrease in business capital outlays.

There were increasing doubts as to the effectiveness of monetary policy to control an inflation induced by rising costs. The inflationary movements of 1946–1948 and 1950–1952 had developed in an economy whose productive facilities were fully engaged. Prices had been forced upward mainly because the supply of goods and services could not be increased fast enough to meet the growing demand. The inflation of 1956–1958, however, seemed different. It was said to be a "new inflation."[20] Since surplus capacity in many industries had developed by 1957, the rise of prices could hardly be attributed to the pressure of demand against productive resources. It was a cost-push rather than a demand-pull inflation. Producers were raising their prices to recoup themselves for rising labor costs. These costs were controlled, not by the Reserve authorities, but by the unions.

Despite frequent urgings by the President, there was no disposition on the part of unions voluntarily to moderate their wage demands. Though the monetary authorities might have refused to provide the money necessary to enable higher wages and higher prices to be paid, such restrictive action would have generated unemployment and would have been vigorously opposed both in Washington and in the country at large.

Does this mean that price stability and full employment are basically incompatible? Some observers answer no to this question. They point to the 1952–1956 period, when wages were rising and prices were stable. They argue that the rate of increase in labor productivity slackened in 1956 and 1957 because of special circumstances such as the introduction of many unskilled workers into the labor force and the fact that the tremendous volume of industrial equipment introduced in prior years had not been digested.[21]

Others argue that the post-Korean stability of prices arose from special conditions in agriculture that caused declining prices for food and other farm products. When these prices firmed in 1956, the inflationary trend was resumed. It is asserted that our economy has a built-in bias toward inflation, a bias based on the dominant role of the unions in setting wages and on the commitment of the government to maintain full employment. Some would add a third factor— the system of administered prices, which makes large corporations virtually certain of being able to pass on higher wage costs in the form of higher prices.

The Reserve System shifted to an easy-money policy in November 1957. The discount rate was reduced in four steps from 3.5 per cent to 1.75 per cent at the end of April 1958. Beginning in late February, two reductions were made in the reserves that member banks were required to hold against demand deposits. Requirements for central reserve city banks were cut from 20 per cent to 18 per cent; and for reserve city banks from 18 per cent to 16.5 per cent. These changes, together with some open-market bond purchases, placed a large amount of additional lending power at the disposal of commercial banks.

Some of the new funds thus made available were used by member banks to increase their holdings of government securities, which rose by over $6 billion. These acquisitions strengthened the banks' liquidity, which had been weakened during preceding years of loan expansion. Some of the additional reserves served to offset the tightening effect of gold exports, which began to assume large proportions in the early months of 1958. The new lending power that was made available also enabled the member banks to pay off their debt to the System. On November 6, 1957, net borrowed reserves amounted to $360 million. By April 1958 the members as a whole had acquired free reserves of $550 million. These and other changes are indicated in Table VII.

As the result of this easing of credit, interest rates declined. The yield on ninety-day Treasury bills went down from 3.58 per cent in October 1957 to less than 1 per cent in the following May. Rates on commercial paper and bankers' acceptances followed a similar course. But long-term bond yields and the rates charged by commercial banks to their borrowing customers proved stickier. High-grade corporate bonds which were yielding 4.1 per cent in October were still yielding above 3.6 per cent six months later. The prime rate charged by commercial banks was about 4.5 per cent in November and around 3.5 per cent the following May.

The sluggishness of bond yields and commercial bank lending rates led to some criticism directed at the Federal Reserve authorities. It was said that a quicker and sharper reduction in such yields would have encouraged more long-term borrowing by corporations and checked the decline in capital spending. The System's practice of restricting open-market operations to short-term securities was also criticized. This practice was adopted, it will be recalled, shortly after the accord of 1951. The critics insist that, because it takes considerable time for shifts in short-term securities to work through to the long end of the market, the "bills only" doctrine has been partly responsible for the failure of bond yields to decline more quickly.

The loans of weekly reporting member banks fell by about $1 billion during the six months following November 1957. It is doubtful, however, that cheaper bank credit would have had any appreciable effect in checking this decline. Inventory liquidation, which played a

TABLE VII

CHANGES IN MEMBER BANK RESERVES—
NOVEMBER 6, 1957, TO APRIL 2, 1958
(*in billions of dollars*)

Factors Causing Change*	Effect on Reserves
Federal reserve credit	
Security holdings	+0.2
Discounts and advances	−0.7
Float	−0.1
Gold holdings	−0.3
Currency in circulation	+ .5
Other factors (net)	0.0
Reserve balances of member banks	− .4
Required reserves	− .7
Excess reserves	+ .2
Free reserves (excess reserves less borrowings)	
November 6, 1957	− .36
April 2, 1958	.55

* See footnotes to Table I, p. 61.

key role in the recession, was attributable more to a decline in sales and the prospect of further declines than to anything that happened to the cost of borrowing. Yet it is unfortunate that easy money was not given full opportunity to show what it could do.

THE ECONOMIC REVIVAL OF 1958–1959

April proved to be the low month of the 1957–1958 recession. The upturn was, as usual, the result of a variety of causes. State and local governments continued to increase their purchases of goods and services. Corporations, for the most part, maintained their dividends. There had been a slight increase in defense spending, and the market for government-supported mortgages had begun to improve. Support to consumer buying power resulted from the decline in revenues from personal and corporate income taxes; and additional stimulus came from the rise in payments for unemployment compensation. Monetary policy was also a factor in the upturn. It is doubtful whether the turning point would have come so soon if credit had not been eased.

Easy money, however, did not long continue. In fact, a shift toward credit tightening came in August 1958. This move was preceded by a dramatic rise in long-term interest rates attributable in part to the unloading of bonds by speculators. The latter was caused by unexpectedly large bond offerings during the first half of 1958 and the doubts that developed as to the ability of the Treasury to finance its deficit at existing rates of interest. Yields on Treasury bills rose from 0.635 per cent in May to 3 per cent in October; and yields on government bonds went up from 3.2 per cent during this period to over 3.7 per cent. High-grade corporate-bond yields advanced from 3.67 per cent to 4.1 per cent.

On August 1 the Board departed from its "bills only" doctrine and stepped in to support the bond market. This action was designed to aid the Treasury in its $16.2 billion refunding operation.[22] But the speed with which the Federal Reserve System offset this action and its refusal to check the subsequent decline in bond prices foreshadowed the restrictive credit move that came two weeks later. In the meantime, on August 4, the board raised the 50 per cent margin requirement for loans on stocks to 70 per cent. The market, therefore, was not taken completely by surprise when the discount rate was raised on August 15 from 1.75 per cent to 2 per cent.

This shift of policy followed a different pattern from the similar shift undertaken three and a half years before. At the end of 1954 the Board began to put pressure on member bank reserves but did not raise the discount rate till April 1955. In 1958, however, the increase in the discount rate preceded the reduction in member bank reserves! Free reserves, which had averaged $500 million during the first six months, did not begin to decline till August. By October they had dropped to around $100 million. From Table VIII it will be seen that there was a $1.7 billion outflow of gold and a $600 mil-

TABLE VIII

CHANGES IN MEMBER BANK RESERVES—
APRIL 2 TO OCTOBER 29, 1958
(*in billions of dollars*)

Factors Causing Change*	Effect on Reserves
Reserve bank credit	
Security holdings	+1.7
Discounts and advances	+0.3
Float	+0.2
Gold holdings	−1.7
Currency in circulation	−0.6
Other factors (net)	+0.1
Reserve balance of member banks	0
Required reserves	+0.2
Excess reserves	−0.2
Free reserves (excess reserves less borrowings)	
April 2, 1958	.55
October 29, 1958	.11

* See footnotes to Table I, p. 61.

lion increase of currency in circulation, and that the Federal Reserve System did not fully offset those contractive influences.

This credit restraint, even though not severe, met with considerable criticism. It was feared that the Reserve System would choke off —or at any rate hold back—the economic revival that was beginning to gain headway. Never before had credit been tightened so early in a recovery movement. Though the FRB index of industrial production had risen from 126 in April to 138 in October, and personal income had reached an all-time high, 7 per cent of the labor force was still unemployed in early 1959.

The consumer price index remained virtually unchanged from August 1958 till the spring of the following year. The fact that consumer prices stopped rising can hardly be attributed to the August increase in the discount rate. What happened was a decline in food prices sufficient to offset continuing increases in other items. In April 1959, as this is being written, few observers are expecting price stability to last. Many look for some further tightening of credit as the Reserve System keeps up its fight against inflation.

Conclusion

This survey of monetary policy suggests that the Federal Reserve System, despite mistakes, has on the whole exerted a stabilizing influence on the American economy. The three postwar recessions would probably have been more severe and the rise of prices sharper had there been no intervention from the central bank.

Though this conclusion seems rather tame and unexciting, anything more definite and meaningful would be hard to substantiate. Because many forces have been at work to make fluctuations in prices and employment more or less severe, it is impossible to identify and measure with precision the impact of Reserve policy. Moreover, since it is only during the latter half of the postwar period that the Federal Reserve System has had some freedom from Treasury domination, there has hardly been time enough for the Reserve bankers to show what they can do.

It should also be kept in mind that the problem which confronts them is one of great difficulty. We have seen that the effort to hold back inflation has at times interfered with the task of maintaining full employment and vice versa. The tightening of credit, which in early 1953 was undertaken as an anti-inflationary measure, had something to do with the business downturn in the summer of that year. The easing of credit in 1954, which helped to promote recovery, was a factor bringing about the resumption of inflation early in 1956. Delay in relaxing credit curbs in 1957, which was widely criticized, was attributable largely to a determination on the part of the System to avoid the excessive ease of 1954. Tightening of credit in the third quarter of 1958 may have slowed down the pace of the recovery at that time getting under way. It is apparent that the path between the objectives of full employment and price stability is narrow and difficult.

The pressure of organized labor for higher wages has not made the task any easier. It is not certain how much unemployment would be necessary in order to dissuade the unions from making wage demands in excess of gains in labor productivity. Recent union activity, however, seems to indicate that this required amount of unemployment is greater than would be tolerated by the public. Even if the Employment Act of 1946 were not on the statute books, Congress would surely be aroused by any action of the Reserve authorities designed to raise the level of unemployment.

The monetary authorities suffer under a number of other handicaps. The instruments of control are far from perfect. Many commercial banks are outside the System. The power of the Board over member banks is weakened by limitations on its authority to specify reserve requirements and by its lack of specific control over consumer and real-estate credit. The influence of a change in interest rates on the spending decisions of business firms is often quite small. The corporate income tax makes the government pay more than half of any increase in interest charges that result from credit tightening. Companies that finance themselves out of reinvested profits—and there are many—are not sensitive to changes in the availability of loan funds. Because of this blunting of the control instruments, the Reserve authorities must bear down heavily if they want to get results. But drastic action meets with public opposition, especially when the impact is uneven.

Monetary policy has at times come into conflict with fiscal policy. Some of these conflicts have been mentioned on preceding pages; and the whole subject is given a more extended treatment elsewhere in this volume. The Reserve authorities acting alone cannot hope to succeed in stabilizing prices and eliminating unemployment; much less can they be expected to accomplish these ends if the government acts in opposition.

There is ground for hope that some of the conditions hampering our central bankers will be removed and that conflict between monetary and fiscal policy will be reduced. For years various congressional committees, as well as the President, have been calling for a national monetary commission to study these problems. Since the prospect of getting an impartial survey of the whole financial system under government auspices seemed remote, the Committee for Economic Development recently decided to set up a Commission on Money and Credit to examine the financial structure of the nation and make recommendations for improvement. This undertaking may help to promote a more efficient banking system and a better coordination of monetary and fiscal policies.

Notes

[1] These figures and others cited in this chapter for GNP and its components—employment, wages, government finance, housing starts, and international transactions—are taken from Appendix E of the *Economic Report of the President,* January 1958.

[2] These figures and others cited in this chapter relating to money and banking are taken from those issues of the *Federal Reserve Bulletin* that deal with the month under discussion.

[3] See A. H. Hansen, *Full Recovery or Stagnation* (New York: W. W. Norton & Company, Inc., 1938), Chapter XIX.

[4] *Twenty-Eighth Annual Report of the Board of Governors,* May 28, 1942, p. 1.

[5] See Frank A. Garfield, "Transition Forecasts in Review," *Papers and Proceedings of the American Economic Association,* May 1947, pp. 71–80.

[6] R. J. Saulnier, H. G. Halcrow, and H. H. Jacoby, *Federal Lending and Loan Insurance* (Princeton, N. J.: Princeton University Press, 1958). This book contains a description and appraisal of federal aid to housing.

[7] See *Thirty-Fifth Annual Report of the Board of Governors,* June 30, 1949, pp. 12–15.

[8] *Thirty-Second Annual Report of the Board of Governors,* June 14, 1946, pp. 7–8. See also the *Thirty-Fourth Annual Report,* April 9, 1948, p. 8.

[9] Allen Sproul, "Monetary Management and Credit Control," *American Economic Review,* June 1947, pp. 337–350.

[10] This press release was reprinted in the *Federal Reserve Bulletin,* July 1941, p. 776.

[11] *Report of the Subcommittee on Monetary, Credit, and Fiscal Policies of the Joint Committee on the Economic Report,* 81st Congress, 2nd Session, 1949, p. 2.

[12] Operation described in the *Thirty-Seventh Annual Report of the Board of Governors,* March 31, 1951, pp. 9–10.

[13] *Thirty-Eighth Annual Report of the Board of Governors of the Federal Reserve System,* June 30, 1952, pp. 1–9.

[14] This speech was reprinted in the *Federal Reserve Bulletin,* April 1957, pp. 330–335.

[15] *Report of the Subcommittee on General Credit Control and Debt Management of the Joint Committee on the Economic Report*, 82nd Congress, 2nd Session, 1950, pp. 31–36.

[16] The critics were led by Senator Paul Douglas and Mr. Marriner S. Eccles. Chief defender was George M. Humphrey, Secretary of the Treasury. See *Barron's*, August 10, 1953, p. 49.

[17] Warren L. Smith, "On the Effectiveness of Monetary Policy," *American Economic Review*, September 1956, p. 600.

[18] See *Federal Reserve Policy and Economic Stability, 1951–1957*, Senate Committee on Banking and Currency, 85th Congress, 2nd Session, pp. 65–66.

[19] See L. S. Ritter, "Income Velocity and Anti-Inflationary Monetary Policy," *American Economic Review*, March 1959, p. 120.

[20] See E. H. Chamberlin, *An Economic Analysis of Labor Union Power*, (Washington, D. C.: American Enterprise Association, 1958). Also L. E. Gallaway, "The Wage-Push Inflation Thesis, 1950–1957," *American Economic Review*, December 1958, pp. 967–972.

[21] For a view that inflation can be avoided, see *Defense against Inflation* (New York: Committee for Economic Development, May 1958).

[22] See W. W. Riefler, "Open Market Operations in Long-Term Securities," *Federal Reserve Bulletin*, November 1958, pp. 1260-1274.

FOUR

☆

INCOME INEQUALITY
SINCE THE WAR

☆

ROBERT M. SOLOW

With the revival of classical problems come classical ideas and classical quotations. We are often reminded these days of what Ricardo wrote to Malthus in 1820: "Political economy you think is an enquiry into the nature and causes of wealth; I think it should rather be called an enquiry into the laws which determine the division of the produce of industry amongst the classes who concur in its formation." We are less often reminded that because Ricardo said it does not necessarily make it so. But, right or wrong, it is interesting to ask why Ricardo and his modern followers should have attached such importance to distributive shares.

Of course the classical theory of economic development hinged on the theory of distribution to some extent. For example, landlords were supposed to consume and merchants to save. But in turn this reflects something deeper. I think it is fair to say that the classical economists were interested in distributive shares because they viewed this breakdown as a picture of the structure of society itself. Rent, wages, interest, and profits corresponded to distinct social classes. This is especially clear in Adam Smith's statement:

> The whole annual produce of the land and labor of every country . . . constitutes a revenue to three different orders of people; to those who live by rent, to those who live by wages, and to those who live by profit. These are the three great, original and constituent orders of every civilized society, from whose revenue that of every other order is ultimately derived.

(Yet for all that, it is clear what Smith thought political economy was an enquiry into.)

There is still a lot of home truth in this picture, although the boundaries have grown fuzzier in the more successful capitalist economies. The fuzziness is of two kinds. In the first place, the identification of social class with source of income is probably not clear-cut. A substantial number of persons, or what is more to the point, families, receive both property income and wages or salaries. Moreover property income receivers hardly make up a homogenous "order." In this country property income bulks large both at the very top and at the very bottom of the income distribution; but to bracket the widowed rooming-house operator with the Texas oil millionaire would be a little artificial, although not without an occasional grain of truth. In much the same way the split between manual and white-collar workers has provided literature—and life—with important class distinctions in spite of the fact that both groups fall into the same slot in the national accounts. In the case of professionals, executives, and the like, this sociological difference has an economic counterpart. Much of what is inevitably recorded as salary income is really, from the economist's viewpoint, a return on capital previously invested in the acquisition of education, training or, for that matter, the social graces.

This is far from a complete catalogue of the ways in which the standard distributive breakdown fails to coincide with class structure; but it leads me directly to the second kind of fuzziness. The observed categories of income do not correspond exactly to the distinction we should like to draw in theory. One thinks first of the large rent component in the earnings of highly skilled people. The profits of unincorporated businesses are also compounded of a mixture of property income and the service earnings of the owners, and we have little but conjecture to help us to separate the two. (In the case of the family farm, the problem is somewhat easier and some success has been achieved.) Rather different in nature but no less inconvenient is the fact that our tax system has in recent years provided a powerful inducement to transform what is "really" one kind of income into what is nominally something else. Executive salaries are converted into capital gains and deferred pay. In closely held corporations it often pays to convert profits into salary and escape corporate income taxes. The reverse operation may also be profitable. And above all there is the inducement to convert large incomes of any kind into capital gains and thus escape both high marginal tax rates and, incidentally, the national accounts.

Yet even if the outlines are fuzzy, it is worth surveying the facts of income distribution with an eye to their more sociological implications. The subject is too interesting to pass up. This essay is meant as an informal survey, nothing more. I propose to assemble a few of the available facts, make a few comparisons with other times and other places, and point out what implications I can see for the evolution of social classes. Economic analysis I leave aside; that is too serious a subject for this light-fingered treatment.

There is a large sociological literature on social stratification, of course. I can claim to have scratched its surface, but I cannot claim to have drawn real blood. Much interesting material has been collected and analyzed, but it does not seem to have led any body of systematic, empirically tested theory.[1] More's the pity, for every invidious instinct in the human frame calls for just that.

The Functional Distribution of Income

There is still point in beginning with distributive shares, for this is where economic activity makes its direct contact with the distribution of rewards among persons. Table I gives the Department of Com-

TABLE I

NATIONAL INCOME BY DISTRIBUTIVE SHARES, 1929–1957*
(IN PERCENTAGES)

Year	Compensation of Employees	Proprietors' Income (Nonfarm)	Proprietors' Income (Farm)	Rent	Corporate Profits (before Tax)	Interest
1929	58.2	10.0	6.8	6.2	11.5	7.3
1930	61.8	9.8	5.4	6.3	8.7	7.9
1931	66.5	9.4	5.4	6.4	2.7	9.7
1932	73.2	8.0	4.5	6.4	−4.7	12.7
1933	73.4	8.0	6.0	5.0	−5.0	12.4
1934	70.0	9.4	4.9	3.5	2.2	10.0
1935	65.3	9.5	8.8	3.0	5.1	8.4
1936	66.1	10.0	6.2	2.8	7.7	7.2
1937	65.1	9.6	7.6	2.8	8.4	6.4
1938	66.6	10.1	6.4	3.8	6.4	6.8
1939	66.1	10.0	5.9	3.7	7.8	6.3
1940	63.8	10.3	5.6	3.6	11.2	5.5
1941	61.9	10.4	6.2	3.3	13.8	4.3
1942	61.9	10.1	7.3	3.3	14.3	3.1
1943	64.4	9.9	6.7	3.0	14.0	2.2
1944	66.4	9.9	6.3	3.0	12.6	1.8
1945	68.0	10.5	6.5	3.1	10.2	1.8
1946	65.5	11.9	7.7	3.5	9.6	1.7
1947	65.3	10.0	7.4	3.3	12.0	1.9
1948	63.6	9.7	7.5	3.2	13.8	2.0
1949	65.2	9.9	5.9	3.7	13.0	2.4
1950	64.3	9.5	5.5	3.5	14.6	2.5
1951	65.1	9.0	5.8	3.3	14.4	2.5
1952	67.2	8.9	5.2	3.4	12.7	2.5
1953	68.9	8.6	4.4	3.4	11.9	2.9
1954	69.4	8.7	4.2	3.5	11.0	3.3
1955	68.9	8.4	3.7	3.1	12.6	3.3
1956	69.8	8.1	3.4	3.0	11.9	3.5
1957	70.9	8.0	3.2	2.9	11.3	3.6

* Economic Report of the President, January 1958, p. 126.

merce breakdown of national income by relative shares annually since 1929. This series represents a purely nominal attribution. To come closer to a true market imputation we would have to know how proprietors' income is in fact divided between the return to property and the wages of management. This is at best conjectural, but to fix the orders of magnitude Gale Johnson has estimated that property earns about 35 per cent of nonfarm entrepreneurial income, while in agriculture the property share has fallen from about 43 per cent to about 35 per cent over the last fifty years.[2] If this is so, then the labor share of the national income stood at 69 per cent in 1929 and rose to 78 per cent in 1957,[a] with most of the increase occurring at the expense of interest and rents. Gross corporate profits held their own.

Before we look more closely at these figures, it is worth remarking that they show factor shares as the market pays them, not as individuals receive them. The distribution of economic welfare depends more directly on command over goods and services as measured by disposable income. Table II makes a step in this direction by measuring relative shares in disposable income, as roughly estimated by Frane and Klein.[b] Note that Table II returns to the nominal basis; no attempt is made to impute entrepreneurial income to its economic source. The difference between Table I and Table II reflects primarily the different size distributions of labor and property incomes and the differential incidence of the corporate income tax and the tax on corporate profits. In principle there is no reason to stop with Table II. It is arguable that for some purposes one ought to add the undistributed part of corporate profits to the property share. This amounted to 30 per cent of post-tax corporate profits in 1929; it was negative in 1930–1936, rose to 58 per cent in 1947–1951, and fell to 44 per cent in the succeeding five-year period. For some purposes variations of this magnitude ought not to be allowed to discolor our picture of how society distributes economic rewards. The inclusion of undistributed profits would yield a series intermediate between Tables I and II. Similar questions could be raised about the treatment of capital gains, particularly when the label that goes on an increment to net worth is at least partly open to decision by its owner.

One more qualification to Table I may play an important role in comparison over long periods of time and from country to country

[a] Kuznets has estimated this figure to be slightly higher.
[b] Even this makes no attempt to distribute the benefits of governmental and other nonmarket activity.

TABLE II

DISPOSABLE INCOME BY DISTRIBUTIVE SHARES*
(IN PERCENTAGES)

Year	Wages and Salaries	Farm	Nonwage Nonfarm
1929	61.9	6.7	31.4
1930	63.7	5.2	31.1
1931	65.2	5.2	30.4
1932	66.9	3.4	29.7
1933	67.5	4.9	27.6
1934	68.2	4.5	27.3
1935	66.2	8.4	25.4
1936	67.6	5.7	26.7
1937	66.5	7.9	25.6
1938	68.1	6.7	25.2
1939	67.9	6.4	25.7
1940	68.2	6.6	25.2
1941	68.8	7.5	23.7
1942	70.0	8.9	21.1
1943	73.2	8.5	18.3
1944	73.5	7.8	18.7
1945	73.3	7.8	18.9
1946	70.6	8.8	20.6
1947	71.5	8.7	19.8
1948	71.7	8.4	19.9
1949	72.4	6.4	21.2
1950	72.8	6.2	21.0
1951	73.5	6.8	19.7
1952	74.5	6.0	19.6
1953	75.9	4.9	19.3
1954	75.4	4.5	20.2
1955	76.3	4.0	19.9
1956	76.7	3.7	19.6

* *Productivity, Prices and Incomes,* Joint Committee Print (Joint Economic Committee, 85th Congress, 1st Session, 1957), Washington, D. C.: Government Printing Office, p. 123.

but is less significant in the short run. For well-known reasons our national accounts impute no income to government property but measure the national income originating in government solely by the compensation of employees. When the government's share of economic activity is subject to wide fluctuations, one may have to allow for the bias introduced by this accounting convention. For the last twenty-five or thirty years a calculation of distributive shares for the private sector alone has the effect of lowering the figures in the first column of Table I by some 4 or 5 percentage points, but it makes little difference to the over-all picture.

I have dwelt long enough on the difficulties of exact interpretation. What do the figures show about postwar American society? Clearly the market has dispensed a larger share of the goods of the world to labor. This stands out from Table II; the wage-salary share of disposable income has increased fairly steadily from 62 per cent in 1929 to 77 per cent in 1956. If entrepreneurial incomes were allocated, the change would be a little muted but could hardly be eliminated.

On the face of it, one might be tempted to attribute all of this increase to redistribution through taxes and transfers, since Table I appears to show no such systematic increase. But I think this would be a mistake. The increase is there too. What hides it is the commonplace fact that in the short run the wage share tends to rise in depressions and fall in booms. The high readings for the thirties need no further explanation. That this countercyclical movement still operates can be seen from the behavior of the wage-salary share in 1949 and again in 1953–1954. What is significant is that since the war the labor share has risen above the 1929 level and has continued to rise through a period of sustained prosperity.

Formally the increase has been at the expense of agriculture, interest, and rents. About the decline in the agricultural share nothing need be said except that it runs parallel to the decline of agricultural employment as a fraction of total employment. The whole sector has shrunk. It is impossible to say how much of the shrinkage in interest and rents reflects the return to specific forms of property and how much corresponds to a change in methods of financing. As forms of income, however, interest and rent have lost ground, and, to the extent that a class badge attaches to their receipt, the same can be said about *rentiers*.

Between 1929 and 1957 the relative share of income from unincorporated business fell by a third, from 17 per cent to 11 per cent. Almost two-thirds of this we have already attributed to labor, to be canceled off against the increase in employees' compensation. The small remainder represents a further decrease in the relative claims of property against the national product. But the sociological importance of this trend is better measured by the full labor-and-property decline, and it may exceed even that. The small independent proprietor who so caught the imagination of Alexis de Tocqueville and James

Bryce has dwindled still further in significance in the last thirty years, off the farm as well as on. Enterprise in this sense, it is plain to us all, is no longer an important highway of economic and social mobility.[c] The figures collected by Gale Johnson show this to have been happening since the turn of the century and, if Wilford King's data are to be believed, perhaps since the Civil War.

These comparisons over long periods are most interesting but necessarily delicate. The Department of Commerce series begins in 1929, which is especially tantalizing since the very beginning of their span is dominated by the Great Depression. As one goes back in time, the basic data become poorer and the definitions are not quite the same. Thus minor fluctuations must not be taken too seriously. But Johnson, in the article already cited, has made an effort to achieve comparability, and some further conclusions can be drawn. In the first place, since the wage-salary share averaged about 60 per cent in the decade of the twenties, the appearance of increase in Table I, with due allowance for the depression, is not voided when the base is extended back beyond 1929. Secondly, since it appears that about 55 per cent of the national income was paid out to employees in the decade 1900–1909, the tendency for this share to increase—to 60 per cent in the twenties and closer to 70 per cent in the last five years —has endured for a full half century.

As against this, the figures in Table I supplemented by those just given do tend to overstate the extent of the swing in favor of labor income. There are three reasons for this. First, the full fifty-year span encompasses a substantial increase in the government's share of economic activity and brings into play the purely statistical bias already noted. Second, account must be taken of the measurable decline in noncorporate entrepreneurial income, which was already substantial during the first quarter of the century. Since something over half of this income is imputable to labor, the effect is to raise the labor share all along the line, but noticeably to diminish the upward gradient. Third, the long-run decline of agricultural income introduces special problems of its own. Money returns in agriculture are and have been lower than those in industry. This is counter-

[c] This statement needs some qualification. In the trade and service area there is still a large turnover of new enterprises. R. Bendix and S. M. Lipset have collected some data which indicate that among manual workers the prospect of opening an independent business is an important, if not uniformly successful, opportunity for social mobility.

balanced (and partly explained) by the higher purchasing power of agricultural money incomes.

Comparisons across countries are also dubious, but they are too interesting to omit. Table III gives some figures for western Europe compiled by the ECE (Economic Commission for Europe). (Much more detail as well as a full explanation of methods is available in

TABLE III

COMPENSATION OF EMPLOYEES AS SHARE IN NATIONAL INCOME*
(IN PERCENTAGES)

	1938	1949	1955
Austria	—	57.1	58.1
Belgium	45.7	54.6	53.9
Denmark	—	52.9	55.9
Finland	50.4	61.8	61.2
France	52.0	56.0	59.1
Western Germany	55.4†	60.8‖	63.6
Ireland	51.6	49.0	51.6
Italy	40–42	—	48–50#
Netherlands	50.7	53.3	54.1
Norway	50.2	54.7	55.4
Sweden‡	52.0	59.8	62.7
Switzerland§	49.2	60.0	58.5
United Kingdom	62.7	71.5	71.1

* *Economic Survey of Europe, 1956* (Geneva: United Nations, 1957), Chap. VIII, p. 3.
† 1936.
‡ Share of GNP.
§ Share of net domestic product.
‖ 1950.
1954.

the source quoted.) The biggest danger in interpreting Table III is to forget that the share of unincorporated enterprise—especially farms—differs widely from country to country. In 1955, for instance, it was 31 per cent in France, of which well over a third was agricultural, and 10 per cent in the United Kingdom, of which under a quarter was agricultural. Obviously this may have a substantial effect on the true labor shares. However, inter-temporal comparisons within countries are probably not much affected by this. Every country on the list, with the revealing exception of Ireland, shows wages and salaries taking a larger share of the national income in 1955 than they did before the war.[3] This parallels the American development. There is a difference though. In over half the cases in Table III the change was substantially complete by 1949, and in most of the others it was well under way. In the United States, on the contrary, the share in 1937[d] was the same as in 1949, with the postwar increase coming later. It is possible that the depth of the depression of the thirties in this country muddies all such comparisons.

Fortunately, since unincorporated businesses are about equally unimportant in the United States and the United Kingdom, we may pursue this most interesting comparison. The wage share has moved in approximately the same way in the two countries. In 1938 the labor share was a bit higher in the United States; by 1949 it had increased sharply in the United Kingdom and, if anything, fallen slightly here; and by 1955 a solid increase in the United States had moved the two figures into approximate equality. I think it is the similarity rather than the residual differences that should be stressed. It would take a very detailed analysis to track down the minor differences to their source. For example, the wage share in agricultural income in the United Kingdom is roughly twice that in the United States; presumably this reflects primarily a difference in the proportions of hired and family labor rates rather than anything more fundamental. A sector-by-sector analysis would be of some purely economic interest, but for my present purpose it is more important simply to note that the postwar shift in favor of wages and salaries is common to the two great Western industrial countries (and western Germany as well) and may well be largely independent of direct political action. If this shift carries with it any significant social change, it should be visible on both sides of the Atlantic.

If the change is not a political fact, what is it? Many potential causes suggest themselves; but to sort them out would require a full-scale assault on the theory of distribution. It is hard to attribute the increase in the wage-salary share to any improvement in the bargaining strength of organized labor; it is not clear that this is a useful characterization of the years since 1951. Of course there is a tautological sense in which any increase in wages and salaries relative to other income can be described as an improvement in the bargaining power of labor (though not necessarily of organized labor) or of an increased investment in labor skills. It is tempting to ask whether the rise after 1951 may be a reflex of the postwar investment boom, a symptom of

[d] I chose 1937 rather than 1938 since the latter was a year of sharp recession.

the relative abundance of capital (and an elasticity of substitution less than unity). No doubt there are other clever ways in which one could account—after the fact—for a decline in margins over prime costs.

All such effects can work themselves out either more or less uniformly within major industry groups, or instead, largely through shifts in the importance of various sectors. E. F. Denison's finding is that the increase in the percentage of national income distributed as employee compensation between 1929 and 1950 was essentially all attributable to changes in the industrial composition of the nation's output.[4] It seems unlikely that all of the sharp change since then could be accounted for in this way; intra-industrial forces seem also to have been at work.

If society were as simple as Adam Smith believed it to be (or as it may have been in 1776), we could draw a neat, clear-cut conclusion: "The order of people who live by wages" has gained at the expense of the others. In fact, I believe something like this to be true, although some minor amendments are required which will take a bit of the edge off the assertion.

There is a small, but not negligible, number of persons and families who receive wages and salary income and other incomes as well. In 1949 something more than a fifth of all men with any income at all had income from more than one source. For women the fraction was closer to a tenth.[5] It seems likely that many of these multi-source incomes are dominated either by labor income or by property income.

A more important amendment to the spirit of the Smithian conclusion is that the distinction between property incomes and labor incomes is easily confounded with the distinction between rich and poor. There is good reason for this—there is a close connection. But it is far from perfect. Consider the following facts. About 80 per cent of all spending units had, in 1956, some income from wages and salaries. But among the lowest fifth of the families ranked by income fewer than half had any income of this kind. And among the top fifth about 85 per cent had received some income from wages and salaries.[6] Similarly, in 1948 employee compensation accounted for about a third of the income of the top 1 per cent of the income distribution and almost half of the income going to the top 5 per cent.[7] The reverse side of the coin is the fact that about a sixth of all interest and rental income goes to families at the lower end of the income scale. Some of those widows and orphans do exist. The point could be documented more systematically, but enough has been said to suggest that an increase in the labor share need not necessarily mean an equalization as between rich and poor.

Fortunately, some other evidence is available for the years 1948 and 1949. In the first place, the increase in the labor share does not seem to have been primarily a phenomenon of the upper reaches of income distribution. In 1939 the top 5 per cent earned 18 per cent of the wages and salaries paid out in the nation; ten years later this figure had dropped to 11 per cent. This went along with a fall in the share of all income claimed by the upper-income groups. Over the same decade the fraction of the income of the top 5 per cent accounted for by wages and salaries fell from 53 per cent to 44 per cent.[8] Thus at least up to 1948 there was no tendency for "labor" income to become more concentrated at the upper end of the income scale. There is no way of knowing whether the top 5 per cent continued to become less dependent on wages and salaries after 1948; but since the trend of prices has continued upward, it seems likely that they did.

We can go a bit farther. Within the class of wage and salary workers there seems to have been a visible equalization of earnings between 1939 and 1949.[9] Thus not only have wages and salaries gained at the expense of property incomes but also low-wage groups have gained relatively more than high-wage groups. At this point our discussion of the broad functional distribution of income meshes inevitably with two other bases of classification: the occupational pattern of earnings, and the distribution of income by size. We look at some details in turn.

Occupational Earnings Differentials

There are two kinds of information which can be brought to bear on the problem of changes in the economic status of occupations and broader occupational groups. One is the extensive literature on occupational wage rates and wage differentials. This is a literature for specialists.[10] Another source, which throws more direct light on our problem, is the census data on annual earnings by occupation. This is very neatly summarized in the book by Herman P. Miller already cited, and this section is in turn largely summarized from there.[11] Since the 1940 census collected income information only with respect to wage and salaries, our comparisons leave out of account any other sources of occupational income, self-employment in particular.

The basic fact is that between 1939 and 1951 wage and salary income became more equally distributed among recipients. The equalization is most noticeable among male workers, presumably because the increase in the proportion of part-time workers among women tends to distort the picture. Table IV shows the percentage of all wage or salary income received by each quintile of wage and salary earners for the years 1939, 1945, and 1951.

It is interesting to observe that most of the equalization process was complete by 1945. The direction of change thereafter was the

TABLE IV

PERCENTAGE OF ALL WAGE OR SALARY INCOME RECEIVED BY EACH
QUINTILE OF WAGE OF SALARY RECIPIENTS 1939, 1945, 1951*

Wage or Salary Recipients	1939	1945	1951
Both sexes			
Lowest fifth	3.4	2.9	3.0
Second fifth	8.4	10.1	10.6
Third fifth	15.0	17.4	18.9
Fourth fifth	23.9	25.7	25.9
Highest fifth	49.3	43.9	41.6
Male			
Lowest fifth	3.5	3.8	4.9
Second fifth	9.0	12.4	13.1
Third fifth	15.5	18.5	19.3
Fourth fifth	23.3	25.4	24.4
Highest fifth	48.7	39.9	38.3

* Herman P. Miller, *op. cit.*, p. 104.

same, but further movement toward equality was rather slower, which suggests that the main cause of the equalization was the approach to full employment from the relatively depressed conditions before the war. Full employment was achieved during the war; the subsequent prosperity prevented any relapse, but there was less push toward further equalization. Years ago Horst Mendershausen pointed out that, although the wage share of aggregate income tended to rise in depressed times, the distribution of income within the working class tended to become more unequal, largely as a result of the uneven incidence of unemployment. It seems reasonable to attribute some of the change between 1939 and 1945 to the reduction in unemployment from one-sixth to something like 2 per cent of the labor force.

But a relatively tight labor market has still other effects on the structure of occupational earnings. Occupational differentials tend to narrow. (Secular forces seem to be working in this direction too.) Between 1939 and 1951 median wage or salary income of course increased sharply in all occupations. But the increases were relatively greatest among laborers, semiskilled workers, and skilled workers, and relatively less sharp among professional, managerial, clerical, and sales workers. Thus those groups which in 1939 were clustered toward the bottom of the ladder had the largest relative increases to 1951. In 1939 the median salary in the class of "managers, officials, and proprietors, excluding farm" was about three times the median wage of "laborers, except farm and mine." By 1951 it was less than twice as large.

The annual *Surveys of Consumer Finances* contain some similar figures for more recent years, but they are not at all comparable with the census data. In particular, the *Survey* figures are on a spending unit rather than an individual basis and refer to total income rather than wage and salary income only. The picture they show is a somewhat different one. The income of self-employed businessmen had the sharpest relative gain between 1951 and 1956. Interestingly enough, the next most favored groups were professional workers on the one hand and unskilled and service workers on the other.

Returning now to the decade following 1939, we see that the tendency for the lower ranking occupations to gain relative to the better paid ones is observable even on a much finer occupational classification. For example, Miller gives figures for 118 occupations ranked by the median wage or salary income in 1949 (with only full-year workers included, to eliminate the direct effect of irregular employment). All the 17 occupations in which the median wage or salary income increased by 150 per cent or more were in the lowest paid half of the list; of the 33 occupations whose median income failed to double between 1939 and 1949, 29 were in the upper half of the list.

Two more changes contributing to the equalization need to be mentioned. Even within fairly narrow occupational classes income differentials decreased, at least among men. Whether intra-occupational irregularity is measured by the interquintile range or by the share of total income going to the highest fifth of recipients, there was a decrease in about nine-tenths of the occupations in the census classification.

Lastly, there was a slight shift in the occupational composition of the labor force, indicated in Table V. The socially and economically lowest ranked occupations declined most in relative numbers, and the middle occupations gained more than the very top ones. These changes might be expected to contribute to both the over-all increase in the level of annual earnings and to their diminished dispersion.

The pattern of changes since 1950 has been slightly different. As Table V indicates, 1956 showed a gain in relative numbers for the professional and clerical groups, largely at the expense of the skilled and unskilled manual laborers and occupations connected with sales and agriculture. This probably represents a net upgrading, and probably also a slight further decline in inequality. As between 1940 and 1956, the major changes are the decline in agricultural occupations, the increase in professional, managerial, and clerical employment, and the redistribution within the group of manual workers, with the skilled and semiskilled categories gaining at the expense of unskilled and domestic service workers.

The economic implications of all this are clearer than the sociological ones. In particular, the movement out of agriculture is pretty clearly a response to the growth of better paid job opportunities in

TABLE V

OCCUPATIONAL DISTRIBUTION OF EMPLOYED PERSONS,
1940, 1950, 1956

Major Occupation	1940	1950	1956*
Professional, technical, and kindred	8.0	8.9	9.5
Farmers and farm managers	11.5	7.8	5.7
Managers, officials, and proprietors, except farm	8.1	9.1	9.9
Clerical and kindred	9.8	12.4	13.7
Sales	6.9	7.1	6.2
Craftsmen, foremen, and kindred	11.6	14.0	13.3
Operatives and kindred	18.1	20.1	19.8
Private household	4.7	2.5	3.3
Service, except private household	7.2	7.7	8.5
Farm laborers and foremen	7.0	4.3	4.5
Laborers, except farm and mine	7.0	6.2	5.6
Wage and salary workers	75.1	81.0	82.6
Self-employed	21.8	17.1	14.9
Unpaid family workers	3.1	2.0	2.2

* Average of April and October. *Statistical Abstract of the United States,* 1957, p. 212.

the urban-industrial sector; but it is less clear that this is felt by the people involved as an unambiguous upward movement. A more careful analysis of the data would have to consider a more detailed breakdown, at least by sex and color. Otherwise some of the shifts may be misunderstood. For example, the increase in the percentage of clerical workers is for the most part a consequence of the heavier representation of women in the labor force. On the other hand the increase in the percentage of craftsmen and other skilled workers is largely masked by the influx of women. The apparent decrease in the skilled fraction between 1950 and 1956 hides an increase in the percentage of males in this category. The increase in service workers is also a phenomenon of the increasing employment of women.

The social significance of changes in the occupational structure as well as in the patterns of income by occupations has been the subject of much discussion among sociologists. Students of social stratification seem to be agreed that there is more to social class than income or occupation or even occupation *and* income. At the same time, however, *concrete* discussion of social stratification seems to be carried on almost entirely in terms of occupation, income, or indexes which are so closely correlated with those two as to yield essentially nothing additional. For example, Warner has been most explicit about the distinction between social and economic status, yet the six variables that went initially into his "Index of Status Characteristics" were occupation, amount of income, source of income (wealth, work, relief, etc.), home type, residential location, and amount of education. Subsequently, amount of income and education were dropped from the index; but, even so, it would seem that economic factors will still dominate the result.[12]

There is still further evidence in a recent study by Kahl and Davis.[13] They compared nineteen different indicators of status on the same group of people and naturally found high intercorrelations among the indexes. A factor analysis yielded the interpretation that the two most important underlying common factors were occupational position and quality of house and residential area. Amount of income had a rather anomalous position in the factor analysis, probably partly for sociological and partly for purely technical reasons. Certainly the correlation between income and any one of the standard rankings of occupations by social prestige would be very high.

There seems little doubt that occupation is the best single indicator of social-class position in American society. Moreover, an interesting paper by Inkeles and Rossi[14] concludes that industrial societies otherwise so diverse as the United States, the Soviet Union, Japan, Great Britain, New Zealand, and Germany all seem to attach prestige to various occupations in a roughly similar way.

Altogether, then, we have concluded that there has been in recent years a slight shift in favor of labor incomes and against incomes from property; at the same time, the distribution of people among occupations has changed in such a way as to promote equalization.[e] Similar movements have occurred in the earnings of various broad occupational groups and in the distribution of earnings within even narrow occupational groups. To anticipate another conclusion, the distribution of income by size has also become a bit, but only a bit, more equal in the last decade as compared with earlier periods. In view of the close connection between economic status and social status, all this suggests that postwar full employment has brought with it a consistent but slight narrowing of social-class differences.[f] There has been no revolutionary reversal of traditional differentials, but merely a small equalization, in the economic field at least. The long-run implications may be important. In the nature of the case, the comparisons made so far tend not to reveal what has happened to the two polar groups in economic status, the very rich and the very poor. At least a little light will be thrown on this matter in later sections.

The Size Distribution of Income

When all is said and done, one of the reasons we care about the distribution of income is that we care about the distinction between rich and poor. Particularly in a society whose ideology is heavily equalitarian, the existence of large inequalities in income is a source of intellectual puzzlement and emotional strain. The sources of inequality—how much is personal ability, whether genetic or environmental; how much is inherited wealth; how much is chance; how

[e] This trend is not a recent development. It goes back at least to 1910 and perhaps earlier. A recent study of the payrolls of a single factory over the period 1919-1954 confirms these conclusions. See L. Soltow, "Income Equality in a Factory Payroll," *Southern Economic Journal*, Vol. XXV (Jan. 1959), pp. 343-348.

[f] It seems plausible that the suburbanization of the last decade—not unconnected with full employment—may have resulted in some equalization with respect to the other important index of social status, quality of house and residential area. But this question had better be left to experts, if there are any.

much is the tendency of any initial advantage to increase itself; how much is inherent in the social or economic rules of the game—all this is too deep a question to be discussed here. But we can at least sketch the facts of the size distribution of income in the years since the war and compare them with the earlier period and with concurrent developments in Europe.

Table VI gives the relative distribution of personal income before personal income tax for 1935–1936 and at intervals during and since the war. Certainly, the most striking impression the figures make is to confirm the belief that this is a facet of economic life which changes slowly when it changes at all. Between the beginning and end

TABLE VI

DISTRIBUTION OF PRE-TAX PERSONAL INCOME BY QUINTILES AND TOP 5 PER CENT OF CONSUMER UNITS, SELECTED YEARS.*

Quintile	1935–1936	1941	1944	1947	1950	1954	1956	% Change 1935–1936 to 1954
Lowest	4.1	4.1	4.9	5.0	4.8	4.9	5.0	20
Second	9.2	9.5	10.9	11.0	11.0	11.4	11.3	24
Third	14.1	15.3	16.2	16.0	16.2	16.6	16.5	18
Fourth	20.9	22.3	22.2	22.0	22.3	22.4	22.3	7
Highest	51.7	48.8	45.8	46.0	45.7	44.7	44.9	–14
Top 5%	26.5	24.0	20.7	20.9	20.4	20.5	20.1	–19

* S. Goldsmith et al., "Size Distribution of Income since the Mid-Thirties," *Review of Economics and Statistics*, Vol. XXXVI (Feb. 1954), p. 9.
S. Goldsmith, "Income Distribution in the United States, 1952–1955," *Survey of Current Business*, June 1956, p. 12.
S. Goldsmith, "Size Distribution of Personal Income," *Survey of Current Business*, April 1958, p. 10.

of the period represented, real GNP increased 2.5 times, prices doubled, the unemployment rate fell from 20 per cent to 2.5 per cent; and against this background the relative distribution of income changed by inches. But change it did, and pretty consistently.

This leads to the second conclusion one can draw from Table VI —that over two decades there was a distinct movement toward equality. In 1935 the 20 per cent of families with the highest incomes earned more than half of all the income. By 1954 this fraction had fallen by a seventh, and the top 20 per cent of families had a bit less than 45 per cent of the total. For the top 5 per cent of families the decline was even sharper. Their share of the melon diminished by a fifth from 26 per cent to 20 per cent in 1956. Each of the four lower quintiles increased its share of personal income, with the second highest quintile making a relative gain substantially smaller than the others.

A third conclusion is of some importance because it fits in with some observations made earlier. Most of the movement toward equalization was complete by 1947, possibly even by 1944. Since 1947 there has been a slight further tendency for the three middle quintiles to gain at the expense of the top fifth. But this change is small as compared with that distinguishing the prewar period from the postwar period as a whole. Once again the suggestion is that the source of the equalization was the full employment brought about in the first instance by the war and maintained with only minor interruptions since.

The *Survey of Consumer Finances* has collected not quite comparable data annually since 1947.[15] They indicate essentially no further change between 1954 and 1956. It is remarkable that the income shares by deciles for 1956 and 1948 are identical. The steady increase in the labor share of national income since 1950 seems to have made no visible difference to the size distribution of personal income. Quite possibly the position of functional groups within the income distribution has changed, but the over-all degree of inequality has not budged.

It should be remembered that the quintiles of Table VI are not groups of constant membership. Family incomes rise and fall relative to each other regularly with the life cycle and irregularly with the varying fortunes of individuals, businesses, occupations, and industries. Moreover, the high end of the distribution in any year is likely to contain many families whose incomes are temporarily above their "normal" level, and conversely for the bottom group. Hence the over-all degree of income inequality (though not necessarily its trend over time) is exaggerated by distribution of annual income. A more useful measure of inequality would be provided by distributions of income over longer periods than a year, even up to lifetimes. Such distributions would of course show less inequality than the annual ones. How much less would depend on the degree of income mobility, on the rate and extent to which families circulate through the income pyramid. This is a fascinating and important question on which we have very little information. Some figures are available for a few postwar years from the *Survey of Consumer Finances*, but since I know of nothing comparable[16] for prewar years, they are of little help. Of equal interest would be some light on income mobility between generations. This is where inherited wealth and early environmental advantage would play their parts.

I shall return to this problem in the next section in connection with the upper-income groups. Here it is worth stating that there is some evidence that the rate of intergenerational *occupational* mobility remained roughly constant between 1910 and 1940.[17] This statement is at least partly independent of the long-run changes in the occupational structure itself. The latter effect adds to the total of mobility. That the rate of occupational mobility should not have declined may be found surprising, since it has sometimes been argued that much of the occupational mobility of fifty years ago was attributable to such demographic factors as the flow of immigrants, who provided a pool of unskilled labor, and to the failure of the educated and professional groups to reproduce themselves. The impact of these factors has certainly diminished over the years. Yet there is no strong evidence to support this view. If in fact there was little change in the rate of occupational mobility between 1910 and 1940, there would seem to be even less reason to expect any further rigidity to have appeared since 1940. One would expect the persistent prosperity, together with the continued spread of higher education, to have improved mobility chances, if anything.[18]

Some roughly comparable evidence for 1950 bears out this hypothesis.[19] The extent of self-recruitment in the professional and managerial occupations is no larger and perhaps somewhat smaller. Perhaps more important, the route from sales and clerical jobs for the father to professional and managerial employment for the son was more heavily traveled in 1950 than in 1942 and more heavily traveled in 1940 than in 1910. The extent to which the sons of semi-skilled and unskilled laborers remain semiskilled and unskilled laborers also declined slightly between 1940 and 1950, with more of the sons going into skilled, white-collar, and eventually higher occupational positions and a substantially larger percentage of the sons moving directly into professional and managerial jobs. Presumably this is one of the important fruits of the public school system. The fact that median earnings in white-collar occupations are no higher and perhaps lower than those in skilled manual or even in some semiskilled manual jobs is less important than the fact that sales and clerical employment is often a means of entry (either between generations or for the same individual) into the better paid and "higher class" professional and managerial jobs.

So far we have looked at the distribution of income as the market imputes it to individuals and families. The distribution of actual consuming power is of course further modified by taxation before it becomes available to families. It is worth taking a look at the distribution of disposable income by size, since it is perhaps a better measure of the extent to which the differential availability of goods and services has changed over the years. There are two conventional aspects to the distribution of Table VII which require mention. Once again, capital gains and/or the undistributed net profits of corporations are excluded from the definition of income, with a corresponding apparent worsening of the position of top groups. Secondly, although the effects of personal and corporate income taxes and certain transfer payments are allowed for in the figures, there are other real-income-redistributing activities of governments (such as the provision of recreational facilities and schools) which are excluded.

Table VII shows about what one would expect. The progressive nature of the federal income tax is reflected by the greater equality of the distribution of post-tax income as against that of pre-tax income. But the difference is slight. And the trend toward equalization, at least over the period 1941–1954, goes at about the same rate whether or not one takes account of income tax. The main difference is that, although on a before-tax basis the fourth quintile slightly increased its share between 1941 and 1954, on an after-tax basis it

TABLE VII

DISTRIBUTION OF FAMILY PERSONAL INCOME AFTER FEDERAL INDIVIDUAL INCOME TAX LIABILITY, BY QUINTILES FOR CONSUMER UNITS RANKED BY SIZE OF AFTER-TAX INCOME, 1941, 1950, 1954, 1956.*

Quintiles	1941	1950	1954	1956
Lowest	4.3	5.1	5.3	5.3
Second	9.9	11.4	12.0	11.9
Third	15.9	16.8	17.3	17.1
Fourth	23.0	22.7	22.7	22.7
Highest	46.8	44.0	42.7	43.0
Top 5%	21.7	19.2	18.4	18.0

* Same as Table VI, p. 109.

suffered a slight decline.[g] It is too bad that the 1935–1936 distribution has not been adjusted for taxes, but it is unlikely that these conclusions would be significantly altered.

Perhaps a more concrete view of the extent and change of inequality is given by such comparisons as the following. On a before-tax basis, in 1935–1936 the mean income in the top quintile was about thirteen times the mean income in the bottom quintile; in 1941, twelve times; in 1947, nine times; in 1950, ten times; and by 1954 down to nine times again. On an after-tax basis in 1941 the mean income in the top fifth was about eleven times that in the bottom fifth; in 1950, a bit over 8 times; and in 1954, exactly eight times.

Table VIII provides some comparisons between developments in this country and in a few of the industrial countries of western Europe. In all cases the movement over time has been toward equality; in all cases (except possibly Sweden) the movement has been slight. One important difference shows up between European and American experience. In the United Kingdom, the Netherlands, and Sweden, where figures are available both for an immediately postwar year and for a still later one, there is some evidence that the process of equalization has continued past the end of the war. In this country, it will be remembered, we found that after 1947 only very small changes took place in the pre-tax distribution of income. But in the United Kingdom the share of the top quintile fell by more between 1949 and 1955 than it had between 1938 and 1949. In the Netherlands the whole process seems to have begun after 1946. Sweden started in 1935 with the most unequal distribution of any we have recorded and wound up in 1954 with one of the least unequal. One is tempted to connect this with the fact that, of all the countries represented, real personal income per head increased fastest (between 1938 and 1954) in Sweden.

Contrasting this country with Europe, we started off in the thirties with a slightly less equal distribution of personal income than the United Kingdom, about the same as the Netherlands, and a rather more equal distribution than in Germany or Sweden. By 1954 we had more equal distribution than the Netherlands and western Germany, about the same as the United Kingdom, and a trifle less than Sweden. It appears that in recent years the lowest quintile has had a noticeably

[g] The after-tax distributions are perhaps sufficiently more conjectural than the before-tax that such minor differences ought to be discounted.

TABLE VIII

DISTRIBUTION OF TOTAL INCOME BEFORE TAX BY QUINTILES, SELECTED COUNTRIES, SELECTED YEARS

Quintile	United Kingdom 1938	United Kingdom 1949	United Kingdom 1955	Germany Pre-war 1936	Germany Western 1950	Netherlands 1938	Netherlands 1946	Netherlands 1950	Sweden 1935	Sweden 1945	Sweden 1948	Sweden 1954*
Lowest	33.2 }	7.2	10.7†	3	4	28.5 }	3.2	4.2	22.7 }	2.4	3.2	5.6
Second		9.8	22.0‡	8	8.5		8.4	9.6		8.6	9.6	11.2
Third	16.8	15.0		15.5	16.5	19.0	14.4	15.7	21.2	15.3	16.3	17.1
Fourth	50.0 }	20.5	23.6	20.5	23	52.5 }	21.0	21.5	56.1 }	23.1	24.3	23.3
Highest		47.5	43.7	53	48		53.0	49.0		50.6	46.6	42.8
Top 5%	29.5	23.7	20.2	27.9	23.6	28.9	27.3	24.6	28.1	23.6	20.1	17.0

Source: *Economic Survey of Europe, 1956* (Geneva: United Nations, 1957), chap. IX, p. 6.

* Unadjusted tax records; adjusted figures might give slightly lower shares of upper groups, slightly higher shares of lower groups.

† Lowest three deciles.

‡ Fourth through sixth deciles.

smaller share of total income in the United States than in the United Kingdom or in Sweden. Whether this is a consequence of the extent of social security programs, or of demographic facts, or of still other economic and sociological factors would require detailed investigation.

I think it is a fair summary of Tables VI and VIII to say that the similarities among the five countries surveyed are considerably more striking than the differences. And this is so whether one looks at the picture statistically or in terms of changes over time.

A few comparisons of the distribution of income after tax can be made from Table IX. About the only new evidence that is revealed is the indication of somewhat heavier progression at the top brackets of the United Kingdom income tax as compared with ours, and this hardly comes as a surprise.

No discussion of income inequality is complete without some mention of the demographic changes which play perhaps the most important role of all in the movement toward equalization. The trends revealed in Table X would presumably show up even more strongly if it were possible to carry the data backward in time. While the average number of persons per family declined over-all between 1935 and 1952, the decline was far larger in the lowest quintile of the income distribution than elsewhere, so that even a constant degree of inequality on a family basis would be converted into an equali-

TABLE IX

DISTRIBUTION OF TOTAL INCOME AFTER TAX BY QUINTILES, SELECTED COUNTRIES, SELECTED YEARS

Quintile	United Kingdom			Netherlands		Sweden		
	1938	1949	1955	1946	1950	1935	1945	1948
Lowest		8.3			4.8		2.7	3.5
	35.7		12.0	7.3		9.9		
Second					10.4		8.8	10.5
			23.8	20.8				
Third		51.0			17.0	13.5	16.1	17.7
Fourth			24.8	21.9	22.8	22.5	24.0	25.2
	64.3							
Highest		40.7	39.4	50.0	45.0	54.1	48.4	43.1
Top 5%	24.7	17.7	15.5	23.2	19.5	25.6	21.3	16.9

Source: *Economic Survey of Europe, 1956* (Geneva: United Nations, 1957) chap. IX, p. 22.

zation on the per capita basis that is most significant for economic welfare. The rich may be getting richer, but it is no longer so true that the poor have children. In 1935 the average number of minor children in the lowest fifth was a third again as large as in the top fifth; by 1952 it had fallen to approximate equality. Perhaps even more revealing is the extent to which families in the bottom quintile now tend to be headed by old people. In 1935 the median age of the family head was forty-three in the bottom fifth and forty-six in the top fifth. In 1952 that median age was still forty-six at the top, but it had risen to fifty-four at the bottom. In 1952, 52 per cent of the *families* (Table X does not include unattached individuals) in the bottom quintile were two-person families, against 24.6 per cent at the top; and 30 per cent of the families at the bottom were headed by persons over sixty-five, against only 8 per cent at the top. Finally, as the second panel of Table X shows, the higher families in the distribution have always been characterized by a higher average number of earners; but this tendency has grown much more pronounced over time.

THE RICH

As with heights, weights, and intelligence quotients, it is the extremes of income and wealth which attract attention. So it is worth saying something about the two tails of the distribution. With respect to the upper 1 per cent of incomes, we have Kuznets' exhaustive study,[20] from which the following details are extracted. Kuznets arrayed his data in a way slightly different from most. Income-size distributions, for obvious reasons, ordinarily rank income per family or other reporting unit; but Kuznets, dealing with tax returns, adjusted his size classes to make allowance for the number of children and other dependents represented on each return. Thus, to an approximation, he has ranked families by income per capita. From the consumption side this is undoubtedly the more useful arrangement.

There are some further technical problems connected with Kuznets' figures which it would be inappropriate to describe fully here. He works with three income concepts: a basic variant, an "economic-income" variant, and a disposable-income concept. I shall stick most closely to the first, though it is conceptually the least satisfactory, because only for the basic variant is full detail available with respect to the sources of income. The basic variant is the sum of employee

TABLE X

FAMILY COMPOSITION AMONG FAMILIES OF TWO OR MORE
PERSONS, BY QUINTILES OF FAMILY MONEY INCOME
BEFORE TAX, SELECTED YEARS

Quintile	1935–36	1941	1944	1947	1949	1952
			Average Number of Persons			
Lowest	3.73	3.55	3.10	3.25	3.26	3.19
Second	3.93	3.63	3.38	3.50	3.48	3.55
Third	3.92	3.67	3.64	3.63	3.61	3.63
Fourth	3.87	3.65	3.74	3.69	3.60	3.63
Highest	3.98	4.00	3.83	4.13	3.89	3.72
			Average Number of Earners			
Lowest	1.10		.98		1.07	1.02
Second	1.17		1.18		1.32	1.34
Third	1.24		1.32		1.39	1.44
Fourth	1.34		1.53		1.59	1.63
Highest	1.52		1.83		1.98	1.96
			Average Number of Children under 18			
Lowest	1.40	1.30		1.09	1.18	1.11
Second	1.51	1.35		1.28	1.25	1.35
Third	1.42	1.31		1.31	1.34	1.40
Fourth	1.29	1.10		1.19	1.22	1.31
Highest	1.07	1.00		1.09	1.01	1.07
			Median Age of Family Head			
Lowest	43					54
Second	39					43
Third	40					41
Fourth	41					42
Highest	46					46

Sources: S. Goldsmith *et al.*, *op. cit.*, p. 15.
"Income Distribution", supplement to *Survey of Current Business* (Washington,
D.C.: Government Printing Office, 1953), p. 69.
S. Goldsmith, *op. cit.*, p. 20.

compensation, entrepreneurial income, rent, interest, and dividends. Economic income makes an adjustment for imputed rent and certain other technical exclusions. Disposable income excludes federal income tax payments and includes net realized capital gains. Still further problems arise with the treatment of undistributed corporate profits; these will be mentioned below. Kuznets analyzes the share of the upper groups in the income of the total population and also in the income of the nonfarm population. I shall stick primarily to the latter, since otherwise interpretation is beclouded by the long-run changes in the status of agriculture, which need no documenting here.

It is important to realize how far down the income scale the top 1 per cent reaches. The bottom of this group extended to per capita income (before tax) of $2,100 in 1933, $4,200 in 1929, and $5,600 in 1946. These are not trivial incomes, but neither is the top 1 per cent restricted to the immoderately rich.

With these sketchy qualifications, what do the figures show? Between 1919 and 1938 the top 1 per cent of individuals took 13 per cent of all income of individuals in the basic variant, 15 per cent of economic income, and 14 per cent of disposable income. To two significant digits this is also true when we compare only the nonfarm population. Sticking now to the basic variant and the nonfarm population, the top 1 per cent averaged 6 per cent of all wages and salaries paid to individuals, 20 per cent of entrepreneurial income, 16 per cent of rent, 25 per cent of interest, and 62 per cent of dividends. About 38 per cent of all property income went to this group. Turned the other way round, 31 per cent of the income of the top 1 per cent was wages and salaries as against 70 per cent for the nonfarm population; 18 per cent was entrepreneurial income, as against 12 per cent; 4 per cent was rent as against 3 per cent; 14 per cent was interest as against 7 per cent; and 33 per cent was dividends as against 7 per cent. Thus we confirm what was noted earlier: the top groups get most of the dividends, but property income is far from all they get. If we attribute half the entrepreneurial income to services and half to property, then the latter accounted for about 60 per cent of the income of the top 1 per cent over the period 1919–1938.

Kuznets' most striking finding is that the share of total income received by the upper 1 per cent (and indeed the upper 5 per cent) has declined fairly steadily since 1929. Using the basic variant, the share of the top 1 per cent averaged 13.3 per cent of nonfarm income in 1919–1938, stood at 12.1 per cent in 1939, and fell to 8.8 per cent in 1948. After tax the corresponding figures are 12.3, 10.9, and 6.5 per cent. Very similar results appear when corporate savings are added to disposable income, although the decline is somewhat milder. If corporate savings are included but realized net capital gains are excluded as representing much duplication of corporate savings, the following figures emerge. Comparison can be made only with the total population and only up to 1946. The share of the top 1 per cent stood at 13.1 per cent in 1919–1938, 12.6 per cent in 1939, and 8.5 per cent in 1946. In all these cases the decline in the share of the top 5 per cent was just about as sharp as that of the more exclusive 1 per cent.

If we look more closely at the period before 1939, it appears that the share of the upper group began to fall off at least as far back as 1929. There was a partial recapture between 1933 and 1936, and then the decline continued as described.

There were also significant shifts in the composition of income at the top of the distribution. Most notably the top 1 per cent became less dependent on salaries, interest, and dividends, and more dependent on entrepreneurial income. Between 1939 and 1948 the fraction of this group's income which took the form of salaries fell from 36 per cent to about 31 per cent; the fraction which was interest fell from 10 per cent to 5 per cent; that which was dividends fell from 31 per cent to 25 per cent. In the same decade the fraction which was entrepreneurial income was barely holding its own as a share of the nation's personal income.

Before drawing conclusions from this fact we have to make some cautionary remarks. Most important, the "top 1 per cent" we speak of is a group of changing composition. Some individuals no doubt remain in it over long stretches of time, but others appear and disappear. In particular, at any point of time one may expect the top 1 per cent to contain many individuals who are experiencing temporarily high incomes which cannot be expected to endure. Now wholesale prices doubled between 1939 and 1948 and of course for many entrepreneurs this meant substantial profits. At the same time, the same price rise offers opportunities and reason for many upper-income people to convert other forms of property income and indeed also salary income into realized and unrealized capital gains (which do not appear in these basic variant source breakdowns). In this light the shift to entrepreneurial income does not necessarily become illusory or unimportant. Our conclusion probably ought not to be simply that the permanent economic basis of upper-class status has changed, but rather that war and inflation are likely to work in favor of entrepreneurial and independent professional groups at all levels of income and status but especially at the top. It would be interesting and important to know whether this tendency continued after 1948. The fairly steady, if small, decline in entrepreneurial income as a share of all income since 1948 suggests that it may not have.

There was a parallel movement in the share of the top groups of countrywide (but nonfarm) totals of various income types. In 1939 the upper 1 per cent took 6 per cent of all wage and salary income; by 1948 this had fallen to 3.5 per cent. Similarly, the share of the top 1 per cent in all interest fell from 22 per cent to 14 per cent and in all dividends from 56 per cent to 48 per cent. But the same group's share of entrepreneurial income increased from 19.5 per cent to 23 per cent. More sharply, the share of the top 5 per cent in entrepreneurial income rose from 36.5 per cent to 49 per cent.

Allan Cartter has recently[21] made some parallel calculations from British income-tax statistics. They indicate a rather similar movement in the fortunes of the top 1 per cent in Britain. By and large, the upper group started in 1938 with a slightly higher share in Great Britain than here, and, while there was a decline to 1948 in both places, the decline there seems to have been a bit milder than in this country. But once again one is struck more by the similarity of the two countries' experiences than by the differences.[h]

One would like to know more about the composition of the upper-income group in our own and other societies. Especially, it would be useful to know something about the rate of turnover, the extent to which the membership of the group changes from year to year or even from generation to generation. Unfortunately, the raw materials are not at hand for a systematic attack on this question of income mobility. Some facts about the recruitment of the business elite, by generations, will be summarized in a moment, but they bear on a slightly different problem. Kuznets reviews what pieces of evidence there are about income mobility; they all relate to the prewar period

[h] Cartter goes on to suggest that even the addition of pro rata corporate savings to personal income is not enough, and some (perhaps all) of corporate profits tax liability ought to be imputed to individuals if one is interested in the income distribution as the market shapes it. I would prefer to dodge the problem of tax incidence thrown up by this procedure and restrict attention to income as received.

and most of them to such out-of-the-ordinary intervals as 1916–1922 and 1929–1933. A Wisconsin sample showed that of the top 5 per cent of state income-tax returns in 1929, two-thirds were still in the top 5 per cent in 1930 and just under half were still in the top 5 per cent in 1935. By that time the percentage seemed to have stabilized (at least through 1937), with enough returns reappearing to make up for those which disappeared. A Delaware study in 1937–1938 showed somewhat greater stability, perhaps naturally, in view of the different economic climate. Of the top 5 per cent of returns in 1937, 83 per cent were still in the top 5 per cent in 1938 and 12 per cent more were in the second 5 per cent band.

For a brief period, 1948–1951, the *Survey of Consumer Finances* collected sample data which permit a rough inference about income mobility in the top 5 per cent during these postwar years. Consumer units sampled and asked about their current incomes were also asked to recollect their incomes in the previous year. Since the data suggest that the well-known tendency to under-report income, especially by forgetting casual sources of income, was even more markedly present in these recollections, any inference is necessarily unsafe. But it appears that in the group with money incomes of $7,500 and over, which in those years amounted to the top 5 or 6 per cent, only about two-thirds remained in the same income class in the following year. What happens over longer periods of time it is impossible to say. Kuznets offers the guess that in passing from a size distribution of annual income to one based on income over a longer accounting period, say five to ten years, the share of the top 1 per cent should be cut by about a fifth and that of the top 5 per cent by about a seventh.

For many purposes one would rather know about the families or other consumer units with the highest incomes than those with the highest incomes per capita. Apart from the possible existence of economies of scale of consumption for large families, there is the added fact that, so far as class position is concerned, the family may be taken as the indivisible unit, labeled with an aggregate income. This may be especially true at the upper-income levels. Actually there is not much difference in the over-all picture. Taking families and unattached individuals together, in 1935–1936 the top 1 per cent, with family incomes ranging down to a bit under $10,000, took about 13 per cent of all personal income. By 1947 the top 1 per cent extended to a money income of $20,000 and got only 8.4 per cent of the total. In 1950 the 1 per cent group ended at incomes around $22,000[1] and collected between 8 and 9 per cent of the total. There is not enough detail in the published statistics to carry this story forward to 1954. We can look at the top 3 per cent of all families and individuals: they took about 21 per cent in 1935–1936, 16 per cent in 1947, a bit over that in 1950, and 15.5 per cent in 1953 and 1954. This suggests that the upper strip of families had taken most of its before-tax licking by 1947 and any further movement must have been slight.

There is not much to be said about the composition of the upper-income groups (demographically, occupationally, etc.) that is not fairly obvious. There are some specialized studies (such as those on the business elite) but none which gives a complete survey of the way in which the income classification both cuts across and corresponds to other marks of social status.

No one will be surprised to learn that most of the large individual incomes (say of $10,000 and over, which corresponded in 1951 to about the top 1 per cent) were received by men rather than women, and whites rather than Negroes. Nor will it come as a shock that of the top 1 per cent of male incomes ($15,000 and up in 1951) about 70 per cent were earned by nonfarm managers, proprietors, and officials, and independent professionals, although these groups comprised only about 13 per cent of all employed males. It may be found a little more surprising that if one cuts down as far as the top 5 per cent of all income recipients or the top 8 to 10 per cent of male income recipients, the group of skilled manual occupations begins to be represented proportionally to its bulk in the population.

The age pattern of the top group is also about what one would expect. Ages between thirty-five and fifty-five are heavily over-represented in the top band of income recipients. Ages under thirty and over sixty-five are under-represented. This pattern is much reduced when income is put on a rough per capita basis, because of the tendency of the very young and very old income recipients to have few dependents. The life cycle of earnings is of course not independent of occupation. Different occupational groups have different

---

[1] It is to be noted that the consumer price index stood at 59 in 1935–1936, 96 in 1947, and 103 in 1950. Thus in real-income terms the bottom edge of the top 1 per cent did not rise quite as precipitously. The 1947 and 1950 equivalents of $10,000 in 1935–1936 would be something over $16,000 and $17,000, respectively. Of course the consumer price index may not accurately reflect living costs for this class of families.

earnings patterns. The earnings peak is reached rather later for the professional, managerial, and skilled manual occupations than for most others. To conclude this rather sketchy catalogue of characteristics, college-educated earners bulk much larger in the top 5 per cent than they do in the population. But this correlation no doubt duplicates the occupational differences already noted. Finally, there is a tendency for the high incomes to be earned in large cities. This effect approximately evens out (or did in 1947–1948) at communities of 50,000–100,000. Rural areas, farm and nonfarm, show a deficit in the top group. Interestingly, when these rural-urban and city-size differences are accounted for, there appears to be little systematic regional variation left as residual.

Most careful studies of elite groups have been conducted with a much narrower occupational base than is implicit in what has been said so far. Perhaps the most interesting and useful information available is that on the occupants of the very top positions in the business hierarchy. Here, since we have the good fortune to possess two roughly parallel studies[22] about one generation apart in time, comparative statements are possible. The Warner and Abegglen investigation distributed questionnaires to some 17,000 business executives in 1952; since the sample was selected from the major executives of large firms, one would guess that the people concerned would almost all come from the highest one-tenth of 1 per cent of the income distribution (in 1952 this would represent family incomes of more than $50,000). Unfortunately, in such questionnaire studies financial questions are left unasked, presumably so as not to prejudice the response rate. Nevertheless, much information is provided on the composition of an important segment of the very highest incomes and on the rate of intergenerational, not year-to-year, mobility into this group.

The occupational distribution of the fathers of the members of the business elite in 1928 and in 1952 is exhibited in Table XI. One notes immediately that the business elite in both periods was recruited very largely from the higher occupational reaches of the population. In 1928, 44 per cent came from the major executive, large business owner, and professional classes, and in 1952 the figure was 38 per cent.[j] Another 27 to 28 per cent of the fathers were minor executives

---

[j] It is less clear where we ought to place the sons of owners of small businesses. In 1928 the questionnaire defined a small business as one with annual sales under $50,000. The same definition was used in 1952, despite a 60 per cent increase in

TABLE XI

THE OCCUPATION OF THE FATHERS OF 1928
AND 1952 BUSINESS LEADERS

Occupation of Father	Percentage in 1928	Percentage in 1952
Unskilled or semiskilled laborer	2	5
Skilled laborer	9	10
Farmer	12	9
Clerk or salesman	5	8
Minor executive	7	11
Owner of small business	20	17
Major executive	17	15
Owner of large business	14	9
Professional	13	14
Other	1	2

Source: L. Warner and J. C. Abegglen, *op. cit.*, p. 45.

or owners of small businesses. And yet the picture is very far from being one of a closed business elite. In 1928 one-sixth of the sample had originated in families headed by manual or white-collar workers, and in 1952 this percentage had risen to about a quarter. Moreover in the 1952 data some 3 per cent of the fathers who were foremen and included in the minor executive group might better have been classed with the skilled laborers.

There is a significant sense in which the gross figures of Table XI overstate the degree of mobility into the business elite. It is true that 15 per cent of the 1952 sample had fathers who were laborers (more if one includes the foremen) and only 14 per cent had fathers who belonged in the professions. But it is equally true that in 1920 (about the time at which these people became self-supporting) 46 per cent of the adult male population were laborers and only 4 per cent were professionals. Thus the group of laborer fathers contributed only one-third as many sons to the business elite as they would have on

the general price level. In 1952 the large business owner class can be further broken down into 6.3 per cent of the fathers who owned businesses with annual sales between $50,000 and $100,000, and 2.4 per cent who owned businessess with annual sales over $100,000. The two generations might be more comparable if some of the 1928 small business owners were transferred into the large business owner class.

the basis of sheer numerical representation, while the group of professional fathers contributed three and a half times as many. When account is thus taken of the occupational structure of the population at large in the fathers' generation, it turns out that the sons of executives and large business owners are heavily over-represented (roughly eight times "chance"); next come the sons of small business owners and professionals, with a ratio of about 3.5. The only other occupational group to be over-represented is that of foremen, with a ratio of 1.33. Then come white-collar workers (.80), skilled laborers (.63), farmers (.45), and unskilled/semiskilled laborers (.16). The special significance of the white-collar jobs, especially sales occupation, is very clear.

Perhaps more significant than the absolute extent of mobility into the business elite are the changes that took place between the two generations. Here again it is necessary to take account of the evolution of the over-all occupational structure. When this is done, it turns out that the rate of mobility from the manual and white-collar groups into the business elite increased slightly between 1928 and 1952; the rate at which the professional and business classes contribute to the group of business leaders declined noticeably; and sons of farmers about held their own. Thus this evidence agrees with Rogoff's, quoted earlier, in denying that the class structure in this country (at least as represented by occupation) has become more rigid over the years. If anything, there appears to have been a slight loosening. Of course there are two interpretations that can be placed on this result. One is to say that the facts belie the common evaluation of the lack of fluidity of the American class structure. The other is to suggest that what the facts deny is the belief that in the Good Old Days the class structure was much more open than it is now. There is other historical evidence to suggest that the "poor boy makes good" story has been overdone by historians of the nineteenth century.[23]

It must be remembered that a survey of "arrived" business leaders in 1952, men who average around fifty-five years of age, no doubt reflects in large part the social conditions of a much earlier period (and perhaps in this case the intervening Second World War). One may wonder what a similar study in 1975 will show. The evidence accumulated in this paper suggests that the recent push toward openness and equality in the income and occupational structure occurred when the depression of the thirties gave way to the Second World

War and the subsequent prosperity, with little further change in the last few years. It may be that the boom of the forties and fifties still has some work to do in connection with the kind of socioeconomic mobility we have been discussing. In particular, the spread of higher education may have this effect. Both samples of business leaders were, by the standards of their times, highly educated groups. In the Taussig-Joslyn sample 32 per cent were college graduates and another 13 per cent had attended college. The corresponding figures for the later sample were 57 per cent and 19 per cent. (In 1950 only 13 per cent of males thirty years and over in this country had ever attended college.) More remarkable is the fact that in the Warner-Abegglen sample 35 per cent of the sons of laborers had been graduated from college and another 20 per cent had been to college. Among the sons of white-collar workers no fewer than half had been graduated from college and another 20 per cent had had some college education.

THE POOR

Every society—certainly every industrial society—has its relatively poor people. But one can hardly leave it at that in good Tory fashion. It makes a lot of difference, whether one is analyzing or evaluating a society's performance, who the poor people are and how poor they turn out to be, both in absolute terms and relative to the others. It makes a lot of difference to the economist, to the sociologist, and to anyone interested in public policy whether the poor turn out to be, say, an economically active urban proletariat, or an unemployed proletariat, or a semifeudal peasantry, or a group disadvantaged in other less specifically occupational ways. As it happens, poverty in this country is in large part, though by no means entirely, a problem of agriculture, of the South, of the Negro, of old age, of broken family status, and of physical and mental illness. And this description seems to be becoming more applicable over time. The problem of extreme poverty is none the less urgent on this account; but it appears to be primarily a classical "social" problem rather than a symptom of malfunctioning of the economic system in Marxian or other terms.

There is no point here in worrying about precisely what standard of living is to be used as a definition of poverty. The regular Bureau of Labor Statistics definition of an "adequate standard of living" is often mistakenly supposed to represent the border between destitution and subsistence. Even by American standards it is not quite that.[k] Instead, depending on the data at hand, I shall use the lowest third or the lowest fifth or a money income of $2,000 per year in 1948 as a rough definition.[1]

The first characteristic of the poor to be noted is that by and large they consist of small families and unattached individuals, which already suggests a heavy incidence of the aged, the divorced, and the widowed. This is of some importance in judging the extent of the trend toward equality. It was earlier noted that the share of the lowest fifth of consumer units increased only slightly in absolute terms between 1935–1936 and 1950. In 1935–1936 the lowest fifth had only 4.1 per cent of all personal income and by 1950 this had risen only to 4.8 per cent. But if we consider only families, excluding unattached individuals, the bottom fifth had 4.2 per cent, about the same in 1935–1936, and this had risen more than twice as rapidly, to 6.1 per cent in 1950. The extent of equalization brought about by full employment and inflation was even greater when we confine ourselves to the economically active. The inactive, including many with incomes fixed in money terms, have suffered relatively. In fact, even a relative improvement in the adequacy of old-age pensions is likely to show itself perversely in income-distribution statistics to the extent that it permits a number of the aged to live in independent households. There they are registered by the census taker as having very low incomes; in earlier years they might have been counted as part of a larger household with a larger total income.

Some more figures will clinch the point about unattached individuals. In 1948 about 15.5 million consumer units, that is, about one-third of all consumer units, had money incomes less than $2,000. Of these about 9.6 million were families, about one-fourth of all families, and 5.9 million were individuals, almost three-fourths of all individuals.

Restricting attention now to urban people, the demographic facts in Table XII make a clear pattern. In 1950, 6.3 per cent of all urban consumer units had net money incomes under $1,000, and another 12.3 per cent between $1,000 and $2,000. In the under $1,000 class,

---

[k] In 1947 it represented a family of four with five rooms to live in, hot and cold running water, stove, refrigerator, washing machine, meat for dinner several times a week, and a chicken or roast on Sunday.

[1] In 1946–47 an urban family of four would have required an income of about $3,000 to meet the "adequate" budget described above.

TABLE XII

PERCENTAGE DISTRIBUTION OF LOWER INCOME URBAN CONSUMER UNITS BY 1950 ANNUAL NET MONEY INCOME AND FAMILY CHARACTERISTICS

Characteristics	Total	Income Class Under $1,000	Income Class $1,000 to $2,000
Per cent of urban families	100.0	6.3	12.3
Family size			
Single consumers	13.5	62.8	35.2
2 persons	32.2	29.5	41.4
3 persons	23.2	4.7	12.6
4 persons	17.3	2.2	5.5
5 persons	8.1	.6	3.3
6 or more persons	5.7	.2	2.0
Occupation			
Self-employed	23.4	9.8	8.8
Salaried professionals, officials, etc.		1.2	3.2
Clerical and sales	13.1	2.4	8.9
Skilled	17.8	1.1	4.2
Semiskilled	17.1	1.9	13.7
Unskilled	14.9	19.4	28.2
Not gainfully employed	13.7	64.2	33.0
Age of head			
Under 25	3.9	.5	5.9
25–34	21.8	3.6	12.7
35–44		4.8	12.0
45–54	59.9	12.4	15.7
55–64		19.3	23.2
65–74	14.4	35.5	21.1
75 and over		23.9	9.4
Race			
White	90.2	83.7	78.3
Negro	9.4	15.8	21.1
Other	.4	.5	.6
Family type			
Husband & wife only	22.9	19.9	26.3
Husband & wife, oldest child under 6	14.0	1.6	6.3
6–15	17.3	1.7	4.3
16–17	3.2	.1	.9
18 & over	10.4	2.1	3.0
1 parent, oldest child under 18	1.9	1.9	7.0
Other adults, 18 and over	22.2	70.3	46.3
All other	8.1	2.4	5.9

Source: *Characteristics of the Low-Income Population and Related Federal Programs,* assembled by the staff of the Subcommittee on Low-Income Families, Joint Committee on the Economic Report. Joint Committee Print, 84th Congress, 1st session (Washington, D.C.: Government Printing Office, 1955), p. 32.

62.8 per cent of the units consisted of single persons, and 29.5 per cent of two persons. In the $1,000 to $2,000 class the corresponding figures were 35.2 per cent and 41.4 per cent. In the urban population at large the figures were 13.5 per cent and 32.2 per cent. As to age, about 60 per cent of the under $1,000 units were headed by persons over sixty-five, and similarly for about 30 per cent of the $1,000 to $2,000 group. Among all urban families 14 per cent fell into this category. Sixteen per cent of the lowest group of families were Negro, and 21 per cent of the next, as against 9 per cent in the urban population. In the lowest group less than 10 per cent of the units contained children; in the second group just under a quarter; in the urban population just under half.

The smaller size of the poor families means, of course, that the extent of the inequality involved is somewhat overstated. Another factor which inevitably has the same effect is the collection of family-income data on an annual basis. This means that some of the families appearing in the bottom class are there only temporarily and are able to draw on savings or other sources of assistance which do not appear in their income statements. Of course there is a reverse effect which compensates partially, but not completely. The bias in question is exemplified in a sample study of urban families made by the Bureau of Labor Statistics in 1950. The families with total money incomes under $1,000, $1,000–$2,000, $2,000–$3,000, and $3,000–$4,000, respectively, had average disposable incomes of $633, $1,539, $2,553, and $3,537, respectively, and expenditures for current consumptions of $1,217, $1,738, $2,701, and $3,570. In the case of the very lowest group the excess of outlay over income was financed by an average decrease in assets of almost $600, which suggests that many of these families were experiencing transitory low income because of illness, unemployment, or other bad luck. When one takes into account that the average family size in the four classes was 1.6, 2.0, 2.7, and 3.2, respectively, it turns out that total pre-tax incomes in the ratios 1:2.4:4.0:5.5 are translated into per capita consumption expenditures in the ratios 1:1.1:1.3:1.5, which is quite a difference in inequality. Even if one compares the lowest class with the group receiving incomes from $7,500 to $10,000, a before-tax income ratio of 14:1 is converted into a per capita consumption ratio of 2.5:1. Let me state immediately my belief that it would be fatuous to draw Polly-anna conclusions from these comparisons or from the other figures in this section. The last comparison leaves out of account the fact that the $7,500–$10,000 families added about $1,000 to their assets on average, while the lowest group often resorted to savings after other income was exhausted. Also, to indicate that inequalities are in fact somewhat less severe than the gross figures would suggest is by no means to suggest what the appropriate degree of inequality may be. Diagnosis is the first step. This is especially true when inequality tends through differences in health, education, etc., to perpetuate itself into succeeding generations.

We may now survey briefly some of the remaining characteristics of low-income families. Most important is the extent to which subsistence agriculture contributes to the problem of poverty. In 1948, for instance, farm families accounted for about one-sixth of all families in the United States. But they accounted for 40 per cent of the families with *money* incomes under $1,000 and 30 per cent of those with money incomes between $1,000 and $2,000. In 1954, farm families had dropped to about one-eighth of the total, but they now accounted for some 30 per cent of the families whose income was less than $2,000 in 1948 dollars.[m]

Within the population of rural and farm families there is a further regional bias. In 1954, 45 per cent of all such families lived in the South, but the South provided 65 per cent of all the farm families with money incomes under $1,000 and 52 per cent of those with money incomes between $1,000 and $2,000. Put differently, about half of all farm families had incomes under $2,000, but two-thirds of southern farm families had incomes under $2,000, as against one-third elsewhere. Within southern agriculture, the incidence of low incomes was a bit higher among Negro families than among whites.

The disproportionate contribution of the South to the group of poor families carries over even to city life, although considerably reduced. In 1950, 17 per cent of consumer units in large northern cities had incomes after tax of less than $2,000; 23 per cent of consumer units in large southern cities. In small cities the corresponding figures were 22 per cent and 33 per cent.

Statistics for the country at large confirm the earlier evidence about the relation of age to poverty in urban areas. Moreover, there is some evidence that families headed by aged persons form an increasing fraction of the low-income families. In 1948 one-quarter of all fami-

---

[m] At the risk of being tiresome it must be pointed out that the real-income differential against agriculture is less than this. Income in kind is omitted, and no account is taken of the higher purchasing power of the farm dollar.

lies earning less than $2,000 were headed by persons aged sixty-five and over; in 1954 it was one-third. A similar development has occurred among unattached individuals. In 1948 a third of all with incomes under $2,000 were sixty-five or over; in 1954 it was two-fifths. This development may have persisted over a longer span of time. In 1939 one-third of the lowest quintile of families and individuals were older couples, families headed by women, or women living alone. In 1951 no less than half of the lowest quintile consisted of families of this description.

Finally, it is illuminating to look at the labor-force status of the heads of the low-income families. Figures are given in Table XIII. It will be seen that in 1948 about a quarter of the low-income families (under $2,000) were headed by people not in the labor force; by 1954 this fraction had risen to about 40 per cent. (Part of this rise is an illusion due to the rising price level.) More interesting, because it is something we have not yet noted, in neither year were more than 5 per cent of the low-income families headed by unemployed workers. In some ways it is a good thing to find the lower end of the income distribution populated by the elderly and retired. It may suggest that

TABLE XIII

EMPLOYMENT STATUS OF FAMILY HEADS BY TOTAL MONEY INCOME OF FAMILY, UNITED STATES, 1948 AND 1954 (IN THOUSANDS)

Total Money Income (in current dollars)	Total	Head Employed	Head Unemployed	Head Not in Labor force
1948				
Total	38,530	31,870	1,140	5,520
Under $1,000	4,020	2,400	130	1,490
$1,000–2,000	5,580	3,880	290	1,410
$2,000–3,000	7,950	6,600	320	1,030
$3,000 and over	20,980	18,990	400	1,590
1954				
Total	41,934	34,129	1,225	6,580
Under $1,000	3,714	1,920	143	1,651
$1,000–2,000	4,616	2,646	245	1,725
$2,000–3,000	4,983	3,753	235	995
$3,000 and over	28,621	25,810	602	2,209

Source: *Characteristics of the Low-Income Population and Related Federal Programs,* assembled by the staff of the Subcommittee on Low-Income Families, Joint Committee on the Economic Report. Joint Committee Print, 84th Congress, 1st session (Washington, D. C.: Government Printing Office, 1955), p. 32.

the society has become rich enough to provide more adequate maintenance for the period of retirement, especially to the extent that many of the retired may be able to maintain consumption out of accumulated savings rather than current income.

Once again I remind the reader that, even if we were to ignore the aged, the handicapped, the broken families, the subsistence farmers, and limit ourselves to the able-bodied, economically active urban labor force, there would still be one-fifth of the population in the lowest quintile of the income distribution, and they would receive lower incomes than the rest. Some of them would be at or near what our society considers a decent standard of living. It appears that within this narrower group the degree of inequality would be substantially smaller than in the larger society to which the published data apply. But, precisely because it refers to the economically active members of society, many people would consider the remaining inequality all the more inequitable. And that would lead me to questions which properly belong to welfare economics.

Conclusion: De Tocqueville and All That

The sweep of centuries has a fascination denied to mere decades. It would be exciting to trace the distribution of income from the beginning of the country's history, to observe the rise and fall of regions, classes, and occupations. But the earliest facts are beyond recovery, and it is not until recently that any systematic and reasonably accurate sources of information have appeared. This essay has been limited to comparison of the decade before and the decade after the Second World War; and so I have made no use of earlier figures which go back, though with considerable inaccuracy, to the establishment of the federal income tax just before the First World War.[24]

Facts aside, there is certainly a widely held belief that American society has fallen from grace and is still falling. In the beginning was equality. At least so the picture emerges from De Tocqueville's pages of a century and a quarter ago. There are moments when he seems to be claiming a rough equality of income and wealth: "It is not only the fortunes of men that are equal in America; even their acquirements partake in some degree of the same uniformity." But on closer reading it appears that it is income mobility he means, and with it social mobility and social equality.

I do not mean that there is any lack of wealthy individuals in the United States; I know of no country, indeed, where the love of money has taken stronger hold on the affections of men and where a profounder contempt is expressed for the theory of the permanent equality of property. But wealth circulates with inconceivable rapidity, and experience shows that it is rare to find two succeeding generations in the full enjoyment of it.

So the state of grace was not equality of fortune but rather the instability of fortune.

Much of this characteristic American equality or mobility De Tocqueville attributes to the prevalence of agriculture and the tendency for inheritances to be divided. "When the legislator has once regulated the law of inheritance, he may rest from his labor." And he sees a danger to equality and even to democracy in the growth of manufactures. The division of labor may be the making of pins—but the ruin of society. "For if ever a permanent inequality of conditions and aristocracy again penetrates into the world, it may be predicted that this is the gate by which they will enter."

Was De Tocqueville as acute a prophet as he was an observer? Just halfway between his time and the present another great European traveler considered the question. "Does equality exist in the United States?" asked James Bryce, writing in 1894. And his answer:

Clearly not as regards material conditions. Sixty years ago there were no great fortunes in America, few large fortunes, no poverty. Now there is some poverty (though only in a few places can it be called pauperism), many large fortunes, and a greater number of gigantic fortunes than in any other country of the world.

And his forecast was also pessimistic:

One may surmise that the equality of material conditions, almost universal in the last century, still general sixty years ago, will more and more diminish by the growth of a very rich class at one end of the line, and of a very poor class at the other end.

Bryce also thought of the small farmer as the bastion of economic and social equality, and moreover:

At present nothing seems to threaten that system of small proprietors tilling the soil they live on which so greatly contributes to the happiness and stability of the commonwealth.

Thus there was supposed to be a fall from grace that had already begun by 1890, and some hold that it has continued ever since. But one anomaly in the picture of the nineteenth century should be mentioned. Present experience does not at all suggest that agriculture generates an equal distribution of income among its practitioners. Did it really do so under the technical and economic conditions of the nineteenth century, or did a deceptive appearance even then hide the inequality which tends to characterize any risky business? One must admit the possibility that early nineteenth-century agriculture was conducted under different, less capital-intensive, conditions than modern cultivation requires. If so, some support is lent to the traditional view.

How does the hypothesis of increasing inequality stack up against the facts reviewed earlier in this essay? We have found that there is indeed inequality, and from top to bottom substantial inequality—and, interestingly enough, that agriculture these days contributes heavily to the extent of inequality rather than the reverse. But we have also found a tendency, slight but persistent, for the degree of inequality to decrease over the last two and perhaps three decades. There is some evidence that the movement toward equalization was a consequence of the wartime recovery from depression and of the more or less sustained prosperity of the postwar period. And, equally significant, it is a sea change which roughly parallels the developments in the advanced industrial countries of western Europe during the same period. So if there ever was a state of grace and a fall from it, the fall has been at least temporarily arrested, with even a trace of a counter-gravitational rise.

Here we may permit ourselves the luxury of a look at the data for an earlier period. In 1918 in this country the highest 14 per cent of income receivers received about 40 per cent of the total income; the top 5 per cent received 26 per cent.

By comparison, in 1944 and 1946 (to take years at the end of another war), the top 5 per cent had 21 per cent of all personal income and the top 14 per cent some 36 per cent. It must not be concluded from this that there has been a slow but steady equalization over this whole generation: there were ups and downs in the interim. But the hypothesis of increasing rigidity in the income structure seems not to fit the facts.

Taussig quotes some British income-tax statistics from 1904 which cast another ray of light.[25] In that year the families in roughly the top 12 to 15 per cent tier of the income pyramid had about one-half the total income of the British people, as against the 40 per cent just reported for the United States at a date fifteen years later. Small differences are meaningless in figures so crude as these. What strikes one is once again the similarity of British and American experience in the twentieth century.

It seems, then, that forecasts of continuing polarization of classes, whether they come from De Tocqueville and Bryce or from Marxian doctrine, have not come true—at least not so far as sheer income distribution is concerned.[n] If there ever was a paradise of material equality in the United States, it must have existed well before 1890 and have been spoiled by the apple of manufactures by 1890. Since that time there has been some change, slow but fairly persistent; but it has been a change for the better. The paradise has not been regained—but one begins to wonder if it was ever really there to be lost. I would hazard the guess that income distribution in America a century ago was not nearly so equalitarian as the commentators of the period have suggested.

If the charge of increasing inequality is not proved (and the N. Rogoff and Warner-Abegglen evidence suggests the same verdict on the side of social mobility), our survey also suggests that the picture of America as an equalitarian mutation from the polarization of Europe will not stand up either, at least not on the income-distribution figures. What facts there are seem to indicate that there has not been any great difference on this score between Great Britain and the United States in the last quarter or half century, and much the same can be said of the rest of industrial western Europe. Instead, the gross outlines have been similar and the direction of change roughly the same. The evidence will not support a strong assertion, but if the evidence suggests anything it suggests this. Interestingly and amusingly, some sociologists are now beginning to suggest that the whole picture of social mobility falls into this pattern—that, in fact, the class structure (perhaps occupational structure would be more accurate) in the advanced countries of Europe is about as open as that in the United States—and that history shows more mobility in the Euro-

[n] Here is yet another forecast: "An enlargement of the leisure class and a diminution of the proportion of income going to the laborer are the natural concomitants of material progress under the system of private property."—F. W. Taussig, *op. cit.*, p. 222.

pean past and less in the American than ideology would have us believe.[26]

Of course the social equality observed by De Tocqueville and Bryce was more a matter of attitude and symbol than of dollars and cents. Casual observation suggests that in this sense American society is still more equalitarian than English and continental European.[°] If so, this kind of equality is no doubt supported by the failure of incomes to concentrate still further, but it must have other historical and social roots besides. Finally, in comparing Europe and America, one may ask whether it makes sense to talk about relative income inequality independently of the absolute level of income. An income four times another income has different content according as the lower income means malnutrition on the one hand or provides some surplus on the other. No doubt—and fortunately—the notion of subsistence is a sometime thing. But one suspects that the availability of enough surplus to postpone the entry of children into the labor force and to provide education and training is an important step in breaking down the barriers between noncompeting groups.

Notes

[1] For a useful survey see Bernard Barber, *Social Stratification* (New York: Harcourt, Brace and Company, Inc., 1957).

[2] D. Gale Johnson, "The Functional Distribution of Income in the United States, 1850–1952," *Review of Economics and Statistics*, May 1954, pp. 176–177.

[3] For an international comparison of wage structures see Part 2, and especially Chapter 13, of L. Reynolds and C. Taft, *The Evolution of Wage Structures* (New Haven, Conn.: Yale University Press, 1956).

[4] E. F. Denison, "Distribution of National Income," *Survey of Current Business*, June 1952, p. 18.

[5] See Herman P. Miller, *Income of the American People* (New York: John Wiley & Sons, Inc., 1955), p. 36, Table 13.

[6] *Federal Reserve Bulletin*, August 1957, p. 893. The main source of

[°] My colleague Paul Samuelson suggests that perhaps in America money counts socially for more, relative to caste symbols, than it does in Europe. And since there is more opportunity to lose and acquire wealth than to lose or acquire the more caste-like indication of status, inequality in the things that count in America may be less than inequality in what counts abroad.

income in the bottom quintile is, of course, pensions, annuities, and other transfers.

[7] Simon Kuznets, *Shares of Upper Income Groups in Income and Savings* (New York: National Bureau of Economic Research, Inc., 1953), p. 67.

[8] *Ibid.*, pp. 66–67.

[9] Reynolds and Taft, *op. cit.*

[10] Some references are given in a paper by J. J. Spengler, "Changes in Income Distribution and Social Stratification," *American Journal of Sociology*, Vol. LIX, No. 3, Nov. 1953, p. 251, n. 4.

[11] Chapters V, VIII, IX and Appendix C.

[12] See Barber, *op. cit.*, pp. 176–179 where further references are given; also R. R. Kornhauser, "The Warner Approach to Social Stratification," in *Class Status and Power*, edited by R. Bendix and S. M. Lipset (Glencoe, Ill.: Free Press, 1953), pp. 224–255.

[13] J. A. Kahl and J. A. Davis, "A Comparison of Indexes of Socio-Economic Status," *American Sociological Review*, Vol. 20, 1955, pp. 317–325.

[14] A. Inkeles and P. H. Rossi, "National Comparisons of Occupational Prestige," *American Journal of Sociology*, Vol. 61, 1956, pp. 329–339.

[15] See, for instance, *Federal Reserve Bulletin*, July, 1954, p. 12, and August 1957, p. 893.

[16] Some scattered evidence is summarized by Kuznets, *op. cit.*, pp. 131–134.

[17] N. Rogoff, *Occupational Mobility* (Glencoe, Ill.: Free Press, 1953). This study refers only to the environs of Indianapolis and hence may not be typical.

[18] For the role of education in promoting occupational and social mobility see S. M. Lipset and R. Bendix, "Ideological Equalitarianism and Social Mobility in the United States," *Transactions of Second World Congress of Sociology* (London: International Sociological Association, 1954); Vol. II, p. 34; and P. S. West, "Social Mobility among College Graduates," p. 465 in *Class, Status and Power* cited earlier. There is of course an extensive and meandering literature on social mobility.

[19] G. L. Palmer, *Labor Mobility in Six Cities* (New York: Social Science Research Council, 1954); also Herman P. Miller, *op. cit.*, p. 31.

[20] S. Kuznets, *Shares of Upper Income Groups in Income and Savings, op. cit.*

[21] Allan M. Cartter, "Income Shares of Upper Income Groups in Great Britain and the United States," *American Economic Review*, Vol. XLIV, Dec. 1954, pp. 875–883.

[22] See F. W. Taussig and C. S. Joslyn, *American Business Leaders* (New York: The Macmillan Company, 1932); and W. L. Warner and J. C.

Abegglen, *Occupational Mobility in American Business and Industry* (Minneapolis: University of Minnesota Press, 1955).

[23] See, for instance, William Miller, "American Historians and the Business Elite," *Journal of Economic History*, Vol. IX, Nov. 1949, pp. 184–208.

[24] *Income in the United States: Its Amount and Distribution, 1909-1919*, by the staff of the Nationl Bureau of Economic Research (New York, 1921).

[25] F. W. Taussig, *Principles of Economics*, third rev. ed. (New York: The Macmillan Company, 1921), Vol. II, p. 254. Chapters 47, 51, and 55 make interesting reading even today.

[26] An interesting paper by Morris Janowitz, "Social Stratification and Mobility in West Germany," *American Journal of Sociology*, Vol. XLIV, (July 1958), pp. 6–24, reaches somewhat different conclusions.

FIVE

☆

FEDERAL FISCAL POLICY
IN THE POSTWAR PERIOD

☆

E. CARY BROWN

In the period following the Second World War, stabilization policy has had to cope with both inflations and recessions. A review of this period can throw some light on its success or failure. Was the need for action seen promptly or was there a substantial lag? Was the prescription proper in terms of the seen need? How fast was policy adjusted to the new situation? What mixture of automatic and discretionary policy was used? Was the Administration hampered by the legislature, or was it the reverse? There are so many aspects of policy into which one can probe that some considerable narrowing down of the subject is necessary.

The first limitation is imposed by the title. This essay will deal only with fiscal policy and not with other aspects of stabilization policy, such as money and cost-price relationships. This leaves us with government spending, taxing, and borrowing problems. But, because debt problems are so intertwined with monetary management, and because monetary policy is being discussed in another chapter, this essay will be restricted to taxing and spending policies.

Even this narrowed conception of fiscal policy requires further restriction. In what follows we judge fiscal policy solely by reference to its consequences for economic stability, and not with reference to its effects on resource allocation, income distribution, or growth. Such a judgment cannot, therefore, be final. It would have to await an appraisal of all the results of the fiscal action.

Even so circumscribed, a number of problems remain. We must, for example, agree on what constitutes a fiscal action. The most helpful rule, it seems to me, is that fiscal inaction results from the maintenance at a constant level of real government purchases of goods and services and tax and transfer rates. Thus, if tax yields rise under an unchanged tax structure as income rises, no action is considered to have been taken. Such an interpretation creates some awkward problems. One cannot draw a sharp line between automatic and discretionary policy and expect it to hold up in all situations.[a]

[a] Samuelson early pointed out the arbitrary nature of the distinction between automatic and discretionary policy. See Paul A. Samuelson, "Principles and Rules in Modern Fiscal Policy: A Neo-Classical Reformulation," *Money, Trade, and Economic Growth: In Honor of John Henry Williams* (New York: The Macmillan Company, 1951).

TABLE 1*

GOVERNMENT BUDGET ACTIVITY IN 1947 PRICES, QUARTERLY TOTALS, SEASONALLY ADJUSTED, AT ANNUAL RATES

Year and Quarter	G_T	G_F	$G_{S\ and\ L}$	T_T	$G_T - T_T$	$G_T - .8T_T$	T_{Gross}	$T_{Personal}$	$T_{Corporate}$	$T_{Ind.\ Bus.}$	T_{SS}	Transfers	Net Interest Paid	Subsidies Less Current Surplus	P_{G_T}	P_{G_F}	$P_{G_{S\ and\ L}}$
(1)	(2)	(3)	(4)	(5)	(6)	(7)	(8)	(9)	(10)	(11)	(12)	(13)	(14)	(15)	(16)	(17)	(18)
1945-1	129.9	120.4	9.6	59.9	70.0	82.0	69.0	26.7	16.2	18.8	7.3	4.3	4.1	.7	75.9	75.4	81.0
45-2	127.5	118.1	9.6	59.2	68.3	80.1	69.1	26.4	16.2	18.9	7.6	5.2	4.5	.2	76.4	75.8	81.5
45-3	104.1	94.4	9.9	51.8	52.3	62.7	63.7	25.5	11.2	19.2	7.7	6.1	4.7	1.0	77.0	76.4	82.0
45-4	70.2	59.9	10.3	43.1	27.1	35.7	62.1	25.0	9.6	19.8	7.7	12.2	5.0	1.8	78.6	78.1	82.7
1946-1	43.3	31.3	10.7	34.7	8.6	15.5	56.9	21.8	7.3	20.2	7.5	14.7	5.4	2.1	82.0	84.4	83.8
46-2	34.4	23.0	11.1	38.7	-4.3	3.4	59.8	22.4	9.4	20.6	7.3	13.4	5.4	2.3	87.0	88.6	85.7
46-3	29.9	19.0	11.3	42.6	-12.7	-4.2	59.1	22.4	11.6	19.7	6.5	11.7	5.0	-.2	96.0	96.8	91.2
46-4	29.9	18.7	11.7	43.7	-13.8	-5.1	58.5	20.6	12.8	18.9	6.1	10.2	4.6	-1	99.0	99.0	94.5
1947-1	28.2	16.2	12.2	44.1	-15.9	-7.1	59.0	21.9	12.3	18.6	6.3	10.4	4.5	.0	99.4	99.5	97.3
47-2	27.8	15.3	12.6	42.3	-14.5	-6.0	57.1	21.6	10.8	18.5	6.2	10.1	4.5	.3	99.6	99.8	99.3
47-3	28.6	15.7	12.9	38.8	-10.2	-2.4	56.2	21.5	10.8	18.6	5.3	13.6	4.4	-.6	100.3	100.6	100.8
47-4	29.7	16.0	13.5	42.6	-12.9	-4.4	56.6	21.3	11.2	19.0	5.1	10.3	4.2	-.6	100.9	100.6	102.6
1948-1	30.5	16.8	13.5	43.0	-12.5	-3.9	57.3	22.0	11.7	18.6	4.8	10.4	4.1	-.6	102.4	100.6	106.2
48-2	34.3	20.4	13.7	40.6	-6.3	1.8	54.8	19.4	11.7	18.9	4.8	10.1	4.1	.0	103.9	100.7	110.4
48-3	36.9	23.0	14.2	40.8	-3.9	4.3	54.2	18.5	12.0	18.9	4.8	9.5	4.0	-.2	106.1	100.8	112.8
48-4	37.5	23.1	14.8	40.8	-3.3	4.9	54.1	18.8	11.1	19.3	4.9	9.1	4.1	-.0	107.2	101.1	113.8
1949-1	40.0	25.1	15.4	38.2	1.8	9.4	53.0	17.4	10.6	19.5	5.4	10.4	4.3	.0	107.8	102.1	113.8
49-2	41.1	25.6	15.6	37.0	4.1	11.5	52.2	17.5	9.3	20.1	5.3	10.9	4.3	.0	108.0	103.8	113.7
49-3	40.2	23.8	16.2	38.2	2.0	9.6	53.3	17.4	9.3	20.7	5.3	11.1	4.3	-.4	108.2	105.6	113.5
49-4	40.0	22.9	16.6	37.7	2.3	9.8	52.8	17.5	9.3	20.7	5.3	11.1	4.3	-.3	108.4	106.9	113.6
1950-1	38.0	20.4	17.0	33.9	4.1	10.9	58.0	18.4	12.3	21.1	6.2	19.5	4.4	.6	108.6	107.4	114.0
50-2	36.5	19.2	16.9	43.2	-6.7	1.9	61.6	18.8	14.6	21.9	6.3	13.3	4.4	.6	109.7	107.7	114.6
50-3	36.3	19.2	17.3	53.5	-17.2	-6.5	67.8	19.0	19.3	23.2	6.3	10.2	4.3	-.2	112.0	107.9	115.4
50-4	40.0	23.0	17.7	54.5	-14.5	-3.6	69.2	21.2	19.6	21.8	6.6	10.2	4.3	.2	114.9	109.0	117.2
1951-1	44.0	26.8	18.0	62.7	-18.7	-6.2	77.0	24.7	22.8	22.5	7.0	9.8	4.2	.3	118.5	114.1	119.8
51-2	49.8	32.0	17.8	58.1	-8.3	3.3	72.7	24.9	19.3	21.5	7.0	10.0	4.1	.5	121.4	121.2	122.7
51-3	54.6	36.9	17.1	56.7	-2.1	9.2	70.8	25.0	17.0	21.8	6.9	10.0	4.1	-.1	122.5	122.6	126.5
51-4	58.2	40.6	17.3	59.3	-1.1	10.8	73.2	25.9	18.1	22.2	7.0	9.9	4.0	-.1	123.0	121.7	128.2

	(1)	(2)	(3)	(4)	(5)	(6)	(7)	(8)	(9)	(10)	(11)	(12)	(13)	(14)	(15)
1952-1	58.7	41.0	17.3	62.4	-3.7	8.6	26.7	70.3	17.3	22.6	4.1	.0	123.0	120.7	129.7
52-2	63.0	45.3	17.7	60.9	2.1	14.3	28.7	75.1	15.6	23.6	4.1	.2	122.8	119.9	130.3
52-3	65.4	47.8	17.7	61.2	4.2	16.4	28.8	75.3	15.8	23.5	4.1	.2	122.0	118.7	130.8
52-4	66.3	48.3	18.2	64.1	2.2	15.0	29.2	78.3	17.4	24.3	4.1	-.3	121.4	117.0	131.6
1953-1	69.1	50.5	18.5	65.7	3.4	16.5	29.7	80.3	18.2	25.0	4.1	-.2	121.0	116.7	132.9
53-2	70.9	52.7	18.1	66.4	4.5	17.8	30.0	81.0	18.4	25.2	4.2	-.2	120.6	116.0	134.4
53-3	69.1	50.9	18.3	65.4	3.7	16.8	29.8	79.9	17.6	25.2	4.1	-.3	121.2	116.0	135.2
53-4	69.3	50.2	19.0	60.6	8.7	20.8	29.6	75.3	13.5	25.2	4.2	-.6	122.0	116.7	135.9
1954-1	65.5	45.9	19.5	58.2	7.3	18.9	27.1	73.8	13.9	24.8	4.3	-.4	123.0	117.5	136.2
54-2	60.8	40.7	19.9	57.7	3.1	14.6	27.1	74.5	14.4	24.9	4.3	-.2	124.4	118.5	136.9
54-3	60.2	39.8	20.5	57.3	2.9	14.4	27.2	74.1	14.1	24.7	4.3	-.2	126.1	119.8	137.7
54-4	58.4	37.8	20.7	59.5	-1.1	10.8	27.7	76.7	15.4	25.4	4.3	-.3	127.3	121.0	138.4
1955-1	59.6	38.3	21.2	63.2	-3.6	9.0	28.9	80.7	16.7	26.2	4.3	.1	128.3	122.3	139.0
55-2	59.4	37.7	21.5	64.8	-5.4	7.6	29.6	83.1	17.2	27.3	4.2	.6	129.0	123.2	139.8
55-3	59.4	37.7	21.7	67.7	-8.3	5.2	30.1	85.4	18.3	27.6	4.3	.0	130.0	123.9	140.8
55-4	59.5	37.7	22.0	69.5	-10.0	3.9	30.3	87.4	19.4	28.2	4.4	.1	131.5	125.0	141.6
1956-1	58.8	36.4	22.4	70.0	-11.2	2.8	32.3	89.0	18.4	28.3	4.6	.7	133.0	126.8	143.0
56-2	58.6	36.0	22.6	69.4	-10.8	3.1	32.6	89.0	17.8	28.6	4.7	1.0	135.4	129.0	145.6
56-3	58.5	36.1	22.5	68.3	-9.8	3.9	32.4	88.1	16.9	28.6	4.7	1.0	137.7	131.0	148.0
56-4	59.4	36.9	22.6	70.7	-11.3	2.8	32.7	91.1	18.8	29.2	4.8	1.3	139.4	132.7	150.0

Columns (2)–(4) are from U.S. Department of Commerce, *National Income, 1954 Edition*, Tables 45, 46 and 49, deflated by the appropriate price index for government goods and services in Table I—Column (16) for all government, Column (17) for the federal government, and Column (18) for state and local government. These indices have been developed by freehand quarterly interpolation of the Commerce Department's annual implicit deflators of government purchases, *National Income, 1954 Edition*, Table 41, Lines 13-15. This interpolation was based on the quarterly movement of the consumer price index.

Column (5) is from USDC, *ibid.*, Table 45, deflated by the consumer price index.

Column (6) is column (2) minus Column (5).

Column (7) is Column (2) minus 80 per cent of Column (5).

Columns (8)–(15) are from USDC, *ibid.*, Tables 46 and 49, divided by the consumer price index.

* G_T=Total government purchases; G_F=federal government purchases; $G_{S \text{ and } L}$=state and local government purchases; T_T=total taxes less transfers; T_{Gross}=total taxes; $T_{Personal}$=personal taxes; $T_{Corporate}$=corporate income taxes; $T_{Ind. Bus.}$=indirect business taxes; T_{ss}=social security taxes; P_{G_F}=price index of federal government purchases; P_{G_T}=price index of total government purchases; $P_{G_{S \text{ and } L}}$=price index of state and local government purchases.

What happens to tax yields will inevitably affect decisions regarding changes in the tax structure. It is, perhaps, best to think of all actions as discretionary, but in one case heavier reliance is placed on automatic yield changes, whereas in others more emphasis is given to revision of tax yields by structural changes.

Our rough measurement of budget changes will rely on the national-income concepts of the Department of Commerce. "Government expenditures" represent their series on purchases of goods and services. Both annual and quarterly data (seasonally adjusted) in 1947 prices[b] are shown in Table I.

The tax yields and transfer expenditures are also based on national-income concepts. This means that tax yields generally refer to collections, except in the case of the corporate tax, which is based on the accrued liability. Both quarterly and annual data are shown in 1947 prices (Table I),[c] with a breakdown between federal, state, and local shown in Table II.

The difference between government purchases and taxes less transfers is the national-income concept of the budget surplus or deficit. This figure is charted for each of the subperiods discussed as a rough approximation to the impact of fiscal policy on demand. But it is unsatisfactory for this purpose in two important respects.

First, expenditures are not a wholly satisfactory measure of the effect of government activity on demand. Quite aside from many subtle effects government spending may have on economic activity, expenditure may inadequately measure gross effects.[1] The actual impact of government activity may be more closely related, in some instances, to contract awards, for example, instead of expenditures, especially when they are changing rapidly. Even directly induced expenditures may not be counted, as, for example, when post offices are built privately and leased to the government. Expenditure then embraces only the annual lease payment.

[b] At the time this paper was prepared, only annual data in constant prices were available from the Department of Commerce. Now, they have taken an important step forward and developed a quarterly series. Our quarterly series represents the deflation of their quarterly series in current prices by a price index. Our price index represents a rough quarterly interpolation of the annual Commerce price index in the government sector, the interpolation based on the movement of the consumer-price index.

There are some differences between our results and the new Commerce series, but they are not serious. It did not seem feasible at this late stage to incorporate the new data.

[c] The consumer price index was used to deflate the tax-transfer series.

Second, this view ignores the fact that the direct effects on total demand of government purchases are probably larger than the direct effects of taxes and transfers, since the latter must work through private disposable incomes before affecting private purchases. A somewhat better idea of the demand effects can be secured, then, if government purchases are compared with, say, 80 per cent of taxes and transfers.[2] In some instances this concept will be followed.

With this advice as our guide to indicate crudely the impact of government fiscal action, we proceed to a chronological review of postwar fiscal action. We then attempt to judge whether the action was reasonable, judged solely from the point of view of its effects on stability. The focus is primarily on the executive branch of the government, the action it recommends, and the action taken. We take at face value recommendations for tax changes, regardless of their motivation. Obviously, in the political process recommendations are made that are not wanted for their own sake but because they will make a tidy political record, embarrass the opposition, or lead through political compromise to the desired end result. The fascinating game of fiscal politics is, however, not our subject matter here. Nor are we particularly interested in the quarrels between the executive and legislative branches, although they will appear from time to time. Nevertheless, certain broad judgments must be made of the character of congressional response to administrative recommendations, and they come out in this review.

Appraisal of political action, no matter how academic, cannot help being controversial. Many of the conclusions reached are inevitably matters of judgment. On such matters one cannot expect unanimity. Indeed, our institutional arrangements can be improved and strengthened only through discussion, analysis, and debate.

Immediate Postwar Inflation: 1945 (4)–1948 (2)

The first of the three postwar inflationary periods followed immediately after demobilization. It was characterized by very little unemployment and by excess demand. But what fiscal steps were actually taken?

EXPENDITURE POLICY

Governmental expenditure policy was that of reducing, sharply and rapidly, war outlays to peacetime proportions. These purchases

Table II

Net Taxes in 1947 Prices

FEDERAL

Period	Personal tax and Nontax Receipts	Corporate Tax Accruals	Indirect Business Taxes	Contributions for Social Insurance	Transfer Payments	Grants-in-Aid	Net Interest Paid	Subsidies less Current Surplus of Gov't. Enterprises	Net Taxes
1945	24,084.2	12,718.8	8,858.6	7,151.0	5,356.4	1,081.2	4,143.4	1,884.0	40,347.6
1946	19,683.0	9,919.5	9,055.9	6,299.9	10,567.5	1,270.7	4,775.6	1,856.8	26,487.7
1947	19,650.0	10,679.0	7,874.0	5,008.0	8,887.0	1,738.0	4,117.0	571.0	27,898.0
1948	17,629.2	10,987.5	7,507.5	4,186.2	7,101.0	1,843.0	3,878.1	598.5	26,889.8
1949	15,181.8	9,193.1	7,648.1	4,628.4	8,206.8	2,088.7	4,056.5	692.8	21,606.6
1950	16,866.4	15,827.3	8,379.8	5,480.0	10,098.1	2,170.1	4,111.0	1,072.5	29,101.8
1951	22,580.6	18,559.1	8,189.1	6,088.1	7,444.1	2,129.3	3,916.6	1,099.9	40,827.0
1952	26,191.0	15,939.8	8,845.2	6,200.4	7,484.0	2,214.4	3,856.5	849.6	42,771.9
1953	26,977.6	16,257.1	9,332.4	6,143.5	8,061.0	2,343.5	3,901.7	701.9	43,702.5
1954	24,221.9	13,844.4	8,353.6	6,739.4	9,643.0	2,394.3	3,982.0	968.7	36,171.3
1955	26,256.9	17,128.0	9,196.3	7,784.3	10,423.3	2,540.6	3,948.4	1,518.5	41,934.7
1956	28,818.2	17,233.5	9,481.0	8,647.1	11,073.4	2,689.7	4,266.5	1,968.2	44,182.0

Table II (cont.)

STATE AND LOCAL

Period	Personal tax and Nontax Receipts	Corporate Profit Tax Accruals	Indirect Business Taxes	Contributions for Social Insurance	Transfer Payments	Net Interest Paid	Current Surplus of Gov't. Enterprises	Net Taxes
1945	1,849.2	565.4	10,432.0	477.2	1,644.2	433.7	939.5	12,185.4
1946	1,887.7	529.8	10,841.6	559.6	1,880.9	336.0	899.1	12,500.9
1947	1,856.0	604.0	10,784.0	575.0	2,226.0	253.0	798.0	12,138.0
1948	1,990.5	621.7	11,414.4	657.9	2,681.9	244.0	757.2	12,515.8
1949	2,312.8	567.1	12,643.1	750.0	2,688.7	253.1	862.5	12,515.8
1950	2,543.6	714.4	13,647.0	893.4	3,173.0	264.4	883.2	14,193.7
1951	2,571.8	754.4	13,840.7	932.3	2,515.1	226.8	939.2	15,243.6
1952	2,719.5	689.9	14,775.0	1,038.7	2,634.6	241.1	965.6	16,296.5
1953	2,844.5	670.2	15,864.4	1,132.9	2,682.8	270.9	1,054.6	17,313.0
1954	3,156.2	635.5	16,680.8	1,315.1	2,786.5	333.1	1,161.4	18,612.9
1955	3,525.2	798.0	18,177.7	1,389.4	2,947.1	390.6	1,324.4	19,829.4
1956	3,753.5	790.4	19,246.9	1,491.3	3,003.3	444.0	1,432.0	21,877.0
								23,266.8

Source: USDC, Tables VIII and IX, divided by consumer price index.

fell by more than half in two quarters, measured in 1947 prices—from a rate of $104 billion in 1945 (3) to $43 billion in 1946 (1)—and remained around $30 billion for the bulk of the period, although they rose somewhat at the end (Chart I). All of the decrease and more was in federal government purchases—from $94 billion to $31 billion in the same period, to a low of $15 billion in 1947 (2). State and local government purchases were beginning their steady expansion of an

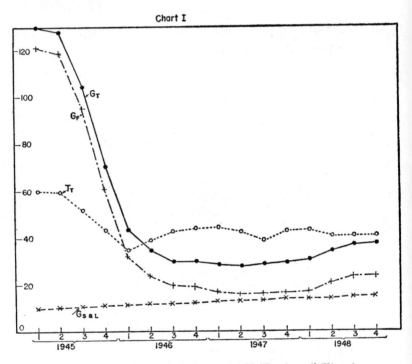

Chart I

Seasonally adjusted annual rates in 1947 prices (billions).

average of somewhat more than $1 billion per year (in 1947 prices) throughout the postwar period.

The general policy of the Administration at this time was to minimize purchases of goods and services in order to reduce inflationary pressures. Expanded programs, such as those that had to be undertaken in the first part of 1948 for Marshall Plan aid and defense, were recognized as expansionary, and led to the decision to retain existing taxes.

TAXATION AND TRANSFER POLICY

Federal government tax and transfer policy involved several specific legislative decisions in this period. First were the reconversion problems covered in the Revenue Act of 1945 and the GI Bill of Rights of 1945. Second, those connected with the expansive subsequent period in which were enacted two attempted tax reduction measures of 1947; finally, the Revenue Act of 1948 with which this period closes.

1. Reconversion

The Revenue Act of 1945 was the major reconversion tax bill.[a] Action was initiated on October 1, 1945, following V–J Day, and it was sped to enactment on November 8, 1945. It provided major tax reduction beginning in 1946 at an estimated rate of $6 million per year at prices and incomes ruling at about that time, in the following areas:

a) Corporation taxation—repeal of the excess-profits tax, but continuation of the carry-back of unused excess-profit credit for one year; and reduction of the corporate income-tax rate from 40 to 38 per cent.

b) Personal taxation—reduction by 3 percentage points in each bracket of personal income tax rates, with a further reduction of 5 per cent of the total tax, and the elimination of the vestige of the so-called victory tax by applying surtax exemptions to the normal tax.

c) Excise taxation—continuation of wartime rates.

d) Social security—postponement to January 1, 1946, of scheduled increase in tax rates from 1 to 2.5 per cent.

Looking back from our present vantage point, we can conclude that they were improper adjustments to the inflationary situation actually faced in 1946 and 1947. The policy error can be attributed primarily to an incorrect forecast of the kind of action needed, not an incorrect reaction to the situation actually expected. Both Congress and the Administration were under heavy pressure for substantial tax reduction in the face of an expected large increase in unemployment in 1946 and later years. To some extent the Administration resisted these pressures, but they unquestionably helped to shape the

[a] The Tax Adjustment Act of 1945, enacted earlier in the year, was a measure designed primarily to ease the financial position of business firms. It provided for the speeding of tax refunds already due business firms under existing law.

program formulated. Had the inflation been clearly foreseen, the Administration would surely have taken the line that it later took, namely, that tax reduction in the face of inflationary pressures was unwise.[e]

Perhaps the thorniest question that arose in discussion of the bill was repeal of the excess-profits tax. Its repeal was a close thing politically, with the weight of the Administration probably decisive. The consequences on inflationary pressures of its repeal are difficult to appraise. On the one hand, various direct controls rested on an uneasy compromise between many groups in the economy—business, labor, farmers, consumers—which was shattered by removal of the excess-profits tax. On the other, a high rate tax, especially with lower rates in prospect, reduced supply incentives, which increased inflationary pressures, subject to the qualification that private incomes after tax would be lowered by the taxes collected.

On balance, short-run direct effects of the tax were probably unimportant. The stimulus to wasteful spending does not seem to have been quantitatively significant.[f] The demand-reducing effects of the tax collections would also have been slight in the short run, given the substantial liquidity of the reconversion period. The indirect effects in stimulating higher wage demands and the abandonment

[e] Roy Blough, the chief tax adviser in the Treasury at this time, put a high gloss on the Treasury position. He argued that the Treasury position was not designed to increase effective demand in the face of an expected recession, but rather ". . . to remove from the tax laws three special wartime provisions that Congress had indicated it wished to remove as soon as possible after the close of the war. The Treasury proposed (1) to repeal the excess profits tax . . .; (2) to reduce the income tax by the 3 percentage points that had been added to each bracket when the 'victory tax' was transformed into the normal tax; and (3) to reduce the excise taxes to their 1942 levels. . . ."—*The Federal Taxing Process* (New York: Prentice-Hall, Inc., 1952), pp. 249–250.

To argue that this was the purpose of the Treasury program is not to excuse it for its consequent inflationary effects on total demand. Secretary of the Treasury Vinson in testimony before the Ways and Means Committee placed major emphasis on reconversion problems, but at the same time indicated the desirability of the legislation as a defense against deflation. See the summary in Randolph E. Paul, *Taxation in the United States* (Boston: Little, Brown & Co., 1954), p. 410.

[f] The same incentives were present in 1945 and in 1946: in 1945 because the excess-profits tax was repealed as of the end of the year; in 1946 for firms falling below their exemption because the carry-back of unused exemptions was continued in that year. Yet investigation of this period leads to no clear-cut picture of excessive costs being incurred for tax reasons. See the present author and Richard Eckaus, "Operation of the Carrybacks of World War II during the Reconversion Period," *National Tax Journal*, V (September 1952).

of various price and wage controls, then, may have been decisive. The early destruction of wartime controls may well have been the most fateful consequence of reconversion fiscal policy.

2. Expansion

In any event, the fiscal stimulation to total demand was sharply reduced through 1945. The over-all government budget deficit shrank from $70 billion at the beginning of 1945 to a surplus of $4 billion in 1946 (2). Throughout the rest of the period until the tax reduction in 1948, the budget surplus was in excess of $10 billion, peaking at $16 billion in 1947 (1). While government budgets might not have been as contractionary as they should have been, their direct impact on demand was still aimed in the proper direction even after allowing for the fact that perhaps 20 per cent of taxes come out of savings.[g]

The federal government's contribution toward stability was even larger than all other governments combined. As already noted, state and local expenditures expanded regularly from 1945 onward, while their tax yields expanded at a slower rate. Thus the federal government had to maintain large budgetary surpluses, larger than we had ever had in our previous history—a truly remarkable achievement. The achievement consisted primarily of holding up the existing tax structure, which in turn no more than held up real tax yields, although some gains were made by the elimination of certain wartime subsidies and the reduction of GI transfer payments.

It is perhaps worthwhile to emphasize the behavior of tax yields over this period. They rose over one-third in current prices—from $46 billion in 1946 (1) to $60 billion in 1948 (1). Yet in 1947 prices they remained almost constant—$57 billion in 1946 (1) and again in 1948 (1) just before the cut in personal taxes of 1948. It is commonly believed that progressive personal income-tax yields will automatically rise in real terms as prices rise. Yet such was not the case in this inflationary period. For the nine quarters ending with 1948 (1), the seasonally adjusted annual rate of personal tax yields (federal, state, and local) varied between $20.6 and $22.4 billion in 1947 prices. Federal personal tax collections alone were $19.7 in both 1946 and 1947 on an annual basis. In this period, therefore, these progressive taxes were essentially neutral as price stabilizers.

---

[g] On the assumption that a tax dollar reduces demand by only 80 cents, the government budget would still have been contractive from 1946 (3) through 1948 (1).

The story regarding corporate income taxes seems essentially the same, although they dipped more in the reconversion period. Indirect business taxes, as one would expect, fell off slightly both at the federal level and in total. Social security contributions dropped most sharply in real terms, partly from a reduction in the number of covered employees, but primarily from nearly constant money collections. Transfer and net interest payments also fell. One is driven to the conclusion from this brief survey that tax yields did not act as automatic fiscal stabilizers of the price level, effective as they may have been as stabilizers of income. In this period, then, expenditure cuts provided the initial budget surplus, while the *status quo* in the tax structure maintained this position.

For maintaining a deflationary fiscal policy, President Truman's administration can take a full measure of credit. Congress did not make the task easy. The first Republican Congress in over two decades was pressing to make good its campaign promise of tax reduction, and the large budget surpluses were an open invitation for such a policy. To achieve a deflationary policy required the indefinite continuance of excise taxes at their wartime rates under the Excise Tax Act of 1947 rather than their automatic reduction as provided by the wartime legislation.[h] It also required opposition to tax reduction for individuals as provided by Republican-sponsored tax-reduction bills.

The President hewed a consistent line. In his 1947 *Budget Message* he stated:

> As long as business, employment, and national income continue high, we should maintain tax revenues at levels that will not only meet current expenditures but also leave a surplus for retirement of the public debt. There is no justification now for tax reduction.[3]

Again in his first *Economic Report* in 1947:

> In the present economic situation, it is clear that it would be unsound fiscal policy to reduce taxes.[4]

In his *Economic Report* in July of that year:

[h] In 1945 the Administration recommended reduction of excise taxes to their 1942 rates (Paul, *op. cit.*, p. 410). But by 1947 the President in urging retention of the wartime rates stated: "When the time comes for excise tax revision, the Congress should review the entire group of excise taxes rather than concentrate attention on those that were imposed or increased during the war."—*Budget Message of the President for Fiscal Year 1948*, p. M11.

Under current economic conditions, the accumulation of a Federal surplus counteracts remaining inflationary influence, reduces the national debt, and leaves us in a better position to deal with changing developments, whether domestic or international.[5]

Despite this counsel Congress passed tax-reduction bills in 1947 and 1948 that provided $4 billion cuts in personal income taxes. The 1947 bills were undertaken, it was said, in order to meet a possible deficiency of demand when Congress was not in session or because of the lag in effective tax reduction after its need was recognized.[6] Both bills, however, encountered Presidential vetoes.

In late 1947 the Administration continued to view its major domestic economic problem as that of countering inflation. Indeed, President Truman called Congress into special session in late 1947 and suggested methods of dealing with it in the special message of November 17. Nevertheless, no legislation resulted.

Again, in his *Economic Report* of January 1948, he advised:

Taxes at present are providing revenues substantially larger than expenditures. It is important to maintain this favorable balance as long as the inflationary trend continues.[7]

But the growing pressure for tax reduction throughout the country was forcing some modification in his original position, and he continued:

However, certain adjustments need to be made immediately in order to protect those in the lower income groups hit hardest by inflation[8]. . . . Certain tax changes now will help those millions of families whose disposable incomes have lagged more and more behind the increased cost of living during the past year and a half.

I therefore propose that the Congress enact legislation extending a cost-of-living tax credit of $40 for each taxpayer and each dependent.

To offset this decrease in government revenues [of over $4 billion per year], corporate taxes should be increased sufficiently to yield an equivalent amount.[9]

This surely was a controversial program for dealing with inflation. At best it looked as if demand for output would remain unchanged; and, if corporate taxes were not as effective in cutting back demand as personal tax reduction was in expanding it, inflationary pressures would be higher. Since the Administration took the view that higher corporate taxes would not reduce investment spending, one can legitimately charge it with proposing an expansionary program, although it would have denied this. In any event, stated in the cloudy way that it was, the President's tax program must surely have weakened the Administration's policy position. Yet pressures were so powerful for tax reduction by then that nothing might have saved it. The Revenue Act of 1948, under which personal income and estate taxes were cut by $5 billion on a full-year basis, became law over the Presidential veto.

Economic activity showed some signs of slackening in the first quarter of 1948—the first such on a seasonally adjusted basis since 1945. Yet there was no clear evidence that the postwar boom was over at the time of the passage of the 1948 legislation. Indeed, the reports of the congressional committees accompanying the bill advocated tax reduction in order to combat inflation! It was argued in these reports that supply would increase through the greater incentives provided by lower taxes and that this would close the inflationary gap.[1] While one may cavil at the faulty argument,[j] Congress had come to the position that fiscal action, desirable as it might be on other grounds, should also be justified by reference to the effects on stabilization. Warped though their analysis was, it was, perhaps, an improvement over completely ignoring the issue.

Withholding rates were changed by the legislation on May 1, 1948, less than a month after the act's passage on April 2, 1948, and disposable income rose sharply in the third quarter of 1948. While consumption also rose somewhat, most of the change in disposable income was reflected in saving. If the consumption effect had been more marked, this tax reduction could be given some blame for reactivating the price rises of the third quarter of 1948. But it appears more reasonable to suppose that the tax reduction did little short-run damage and helped to shore up demand in the subsequent recession.

Thus we come to the end of a curious period. It started with in-

---

[1] "By lowering tax rates in both the lower and upper income brackets, your committee's bill will increase the incentives of labor and management to produce, and will increase investors' willingness to assume business risks. For these reasons H.R. 4790 will increase production. This in turn will decrease inflationary pressures."—U.S. House, Committee on Ways and Means, *Report to Accompany the Revenue Act of 1948*, Report No. 1274, January 27, 1948.

[j] It is, of course, technically possible for tax reduction to be deflationary provided that supply expands enough to more than offset the additional spending resulting from the tax reduction and from the additional income generated by the added output. This is, however, a fairly large order and requires quite extraordinarily elastic supply schedules or extraordinarily low marginal spending-income ratios.

correct action taken for the correct reasons: tax reduction to fill up a nonexistent deficiency in demand. Economic intelligence was poor, not the reaction to it. The period ended with correct action taken for incorrect reasons: tax reduction to cure an inflation. Since the inflation had almost ceased to exist, this action turned out relatively satisfactorily.

The Recession of 1949: 1948 (3)–1950 (2)

The signs of the 1948–1949 recession were hard to read. But, after making allowances for this obscurity, one can criticize the Administration for the extraordinarily long time it took to recognize them.

Both the *Midyear Economic Report* and a Presidential message to Congress on July 27, 1948, requested re-establishment of the excess-profits tax". . . . in order to provide a Treasury surplus and a brake on inflation."[10] This fiscal program was actually a repetition of the ones proposed by the Administration in late 1947 and early 1948, whereby tax burdens would have been rearranged. But, because the personal income tax had been reduced by the Revenue Act of 1948, that portion of the program was dropped and the increase in corporate taxes retained. Later still, in August, Chairman Keyserling of the Council of Economic Advisers testified to the Banking and Currency Committee that inflation was still the major danger.

Even on into 1949 the Administration's legislative program as outlined in the State of the Union Message and supported in the *Economic Report* of January was directed against inflation. The President stated under a heading of "Policies to Combat Inflation": "It is essential to sound fiscal policy to have a budget surplus now. . . ."[11] He then went on to propose an increase of $4 billion per year in added revenues principally from additional corporate taxation but also from estates and gifts, upper and middle brackets of the personal income tax, and perhaps added excises. In addition, he proposed an increase in social security contributions and careful limitation on federal expenditures. This program would, of course, have had a clear-cut deflationary impact. Yet, with almost every index sagging, it was defended vigorously in February 1949 by Chairman Keyserling before the Joint Committee on the Economic Report.

But by the time of the *Midyear Economic Report* of 1949 the weakening of demand had become clear to the Administration. For example, in this report the President noted the absence of inflationary strains. He therefore spoke out against reductions in his expenditure program at that time, but, curiously, he believed that

> Under present conditions, immediate tax increases should be limited to raising estate and gift tax rates and closing the loopholes in their administration. . . . At the same time, the tax on transportation of goods . . . should be eliminated. Furthermore, the loss carry-over provisions in the corporate income tax laws should be liberalized. . . . The net effect of these three changes in our tax structure, taken together, will be favorable to the expansion of business activity, without causing a significant net loss in total receipts. No changes in the tax laws which would result in a larger net loss in revenues would be justified at this time.[12]

By the beginning of 1950 the President in his *Economic Report* stated his belief that the economy had passed from inflation to stability and that the process would be completed by the rearrangement of taxes previously recommended. At the same time he decried the current budget deficit, ". . . principally because of the drop in incomes and employment in 1949, the untimely tax reductions in 1949, and the continuing heavy demands of national security programs."[13]

Despite this clumsy activity on the part of the Administration, the actual fiscal behavior of governments taken as a unit and of the federal government alone contributed to stability. Government purchases of goods and services in 1947 prices surged upward by $7 billion from 1948 (2) to their peak of $41 billion in 1949 (2) (Chart II). They continued at nearly this high rate through 1949, only falling back somewhat in the first half of 1950—a rather providential piece of timing. Although most of this change was carried out by the federal government, little credit can be given to its discretionary stabilization policies. The expansion by the federal government was due almost entirely to expenditures dictated by international tensions —an involuntary expansion from the stability viewpoint—and somewhat from increased purchases of appoximately $2 billion per year of agricultural products, an automatic spending response to changes in agricultural prices. State and local governments had a steady and continuous rise in expenditures throughout the period under review —about $3 billion for the whole period.

Net taxes and transfer payments declined sharply, a factor also contributing to stabilization. From 1948 (1) to the trough in 1949 (3), taxes less transfers in 1947 prices fell by $5 billion. This de-

Chart II—Government Expenditures and Taxes, 1948-1950
Seasonally adjusted annual rates in 1947 prices (billions)

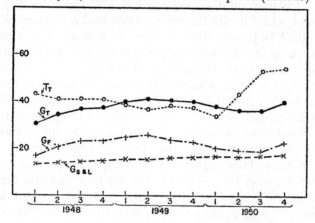

crease can be attributed to the algebraic result of four major factors:

1. The personal tax reductions provided by the Revenue Act of 1948 took effect for years beginning in 1949, with witholding changes effective on May 1, 1948. The change in annual rate of tax collection amounted to $4 billion.

2. Social security contributions increased over $1 billion.

3. Indirect business taxes increased $2 billion, primarily the result of state and local tax activities.

4. Total yields automatically decreased with changes in national income in 1949, particularly personal and corporate income taxes, but these did little more than offset increases at state and local levels. In total they were of the order of $4 billion.

How much credit can discretionary fiscal policy take for the observed reduction of net taxes, a not inconsiderable factor in cushioning the decline? Almost none, it would appear from the list. The 1948 tax reduction was taken, it was said, to remove inflation, not recession, and probably was undertaken for its own sake. The *increases* in social security contributions and in state and local indirect taxation were surely not designed as anti-recession devices. But the automatic decrease in tax yields was surely an important cushion in 1949, although by 1950 it was little more than offsetting state and local tax increases.

It is an understatement to say that little credit can be given the

Administration for the reasonably stabilizing fiscal behavior observed in the recession. Its policy position was a difficult one to understand. Consider the program it proposed in July 1949 and again in January 1950, and contrast it with the one recommended in January 1948 and January 1949. In January 1948 President Truman asked for a program in which personal tax credits of $40 per capita would be offset by corporate tax increases amounting to about $4 billion in the face of a situation generally regarded as inflationary. To his credit, President Truman firmly opposed over-all tax reduction at this time. But no one would characterize his 1948 program as sharply deflationary. Indeed, the increase in consumption spending from the proposed tax credit would probably have more than offset the decrease in corporate spending from higher corporate taxes. By January 1949 inflationary pressures had slackened. Yet the fiscal program President Truman urged was one of considerably greater inflationary impact than that proposed in the preceding year. He had dropped personal tax reduction but retained the corporate tax increases. Not until July 1949 and January 1950, when no one had any doubts that the economy was undergoing a recession, did the Presidential fiscal recommendations come back approximately to their position during the inflation—namely, to holding taxes constant. It is difficult to reconcile these two positions of the Administration, or to agree with Caplan that the reaction of the Administration was satisfactory once the economic situation was fully sized up, although such recognition was slow in coming.[k] The Administration grudgingly accepted a budget deficit. Fortunately, the recession proved to be primarily an inventory turn-around, and little more had to be done to pull the economy out of its slump. Fortunately, also, the Administration's fiscal requests in this period were largely ignored by Congress.

Yet these fiscal recommendations did set in motion a new tax bill in 1950. While recovery seemed under way, there was a sharp rise in unemployment in February, and this hastened action. The tax message of January 23, 1950, contained a detailed program for tax rearrangement that would have resulted in additional revenues of about $1 billion per year. Excise taxes, especially on freight transportation, were to be cut to the extent that tax loopholes were plugged. In addition, $1 billion were to be secured from revised

[k] "Unlike its poor record in diagnosing the turning point in the economy, the record of the government was very good during this phase of the recession."— Benjamin Caplan, "A Case Study: the 1948–1949 Recession," in *Policies to Combat Recession*, Universities—National Bureau Committee for Economic Research, (Princeton, N.J.: Princeton University Press, 1956), p. 50.

estate and gift taxes and a rise in the corporate income tax from 38 to 42 per cent on large corporations. Surely one would not argue that this program was an expansionary one.

In the House, where the bill was debated for nearly half a year— in and out of committee—it finally emerged as essentially a tax-rearrangement measure, additional revenues coming entirely from the speeding up of corporate tax collections. Excise taxes were cut $1 billion on a broad front, and the balance was sought by raising the corporate tax to 41 per cent and by comprehensive loophole-closing provisions. But the bill also provided for reductions in the holding period (from six months to three months) for long-term capital gains, and expanded, rather than contracted, the percentage-depletion provisions. Its passage came on June 29, shortly after the Korean invasion, which was to force complete reconsideration of fiscal policy.

The Korean War: 1950 (3)–1953 (2)

Hearings were begun in the Senate on July 5 on the House bill with the understanding that, should there be serious war developments, action on the bill would be suspended. Less than a week later Secretary Snyder recommended such suspension; and on July 19 President Truman reported to Congress on the economic problems of the Korean War. He recommended more taxation, an amount that would come as close as possible to matching additional expenditures. His detailed stopgap tax recommendations were contained in a letter of July 29 to the chairman of the Senate Finance Committee. They consisted of the conversion of the House bill to one sharply increasing revenue by $5 billion per year through (1) eliminating the excise-tax reductions and other revenue-losing provisions of the bill, but retaining its loophole-closing features; (2) raising corporate income-tax rates on 1950 incomes to 45 per cent; and (3) increasing individual income-tax rates through removal of the percentage reductions in rates provided under the revenue acts of 1945 and 1948, effective October 1, 1950.[1]

The House bill was thus revivified. The Senate Finance Committee promptly began work on it and reported out nearly a month later a bill raising $4.5 billion essentially along the lines recommended by the President. Although some important amendments were made to the bill on the Senate floor, notably the amendment instructing the

[1] Withholding-rate changes were also made effective as of that date, and only one-fourth of the elimination of percentage reductions in tax rates applied to 1950 incomes.

tax committees to prepare a retroactive excess-profits tax as soon as practicable, it became the Revenue Act of 1950. The new law became effective October 1—a remarkably rapid reversal of legislative policy. This speed was possible because a tax bill was already under way, and thus only half of the standard legislative journey had to be traversed. Even then, however, it was nearly three full months before the enactment of the new legislation despite the urgency of the occasion.[m]

Chart III—Government Expenditures and Taxes, 1950–1953

Seasonally adjusted annual rates in 1947 prices (billions)

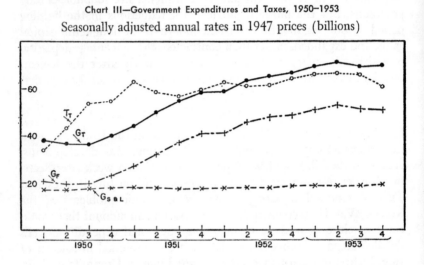

As a consequence, government fiscal action shifted from a budget surplus in 1950 (2) of $7 billion to a surplus of $17 billion in 1950 (3), and of $19 billion in 1951 (1) (Chart III). The surplus continued through 1952 but at a lower rate. Adjusting taxes for the approximate fraction coming out of savings, the direct effects of government fiscal action on demand seem to have been impressively contractive through 1951 (1). This remarkable performance accompanied an expansion of government purchases from a low in 1950 (3) of $36 billion to $50 billion by midyear 1951.

This prompt fiscal action was undoubtedly an important factor

[m] Professor Walter W. Heller points to this episode as one justifying, by its prompt response, greater reliance on discretionary policy. Certainly it can be considered as one of the better fiscal performances. But he reports the action as taken in a matter of weeks. Actually, a surprisingly long time was taken despite the prompt recognition of need and the rather noncontroversial nature of the action. See his article, "CED's Stabilizing Budget Policy after Ten Years," *American Economic Review*, Vol. XLVII (Sept. 1957), pp. 634–651.

in explaining the puzzling price stability of 1951.[n] After the sharp rise of nearly 20 per cent in wholesale prices from the middle of 1950 to the beginning of 1951, their general course was downward throughout the war period. With some lag, they fed into the consumer-price index. It, in turn, rose about 10 per cent and then remained essentially stable at the higher level throughout the war period, with transportation and rents showing the largest increases.

Two other pieces of fiscal legislation made their contribution to price stability in this period. First, the excess-profits tax called for in the Revenue Act of 1950 was provided in the Excess Profits Tax Act of 1951. Work was begun on it November 15, 1950, following receipt of the President's letter asking for a retroactive tax to July 1, 1950—the beginning of defense mobilization—that would raise $4 billion. Despite the fact that an excess-profits tax is a desperately complicated business, and the tax this time was considerably more complex than that of the Second World War on which it was modeled, it took less than two months to enact—on January 3, 1951. Here again is an impressive legislative achievement, considering the bitter opposition it faced from those who wanted no more taxes, or a higher corporate income tax instead of an excess-profits tax, or a tightening of renegotiation of war contracts.[o] The ultimate law was estimated to

[n] Bert G. Hickman in his monograph *The Korean War and United States Economic Activity, 1950–1952*, Occasional Paper 49, (New York: National Bureau of Economic Research, Inc., 1955), attributes the relative stability of the economy after its initial price rise to the inventory decumulation (both consumer and business) that could be undertaken in 1951 after the accumulations of the earlier period. He writes: "The outbreak of the Korean War in June 1950 was followed by eight months of strong inflationary pressure, due largely to abnormally heavy buying by consumers in anticipation of possible future shortages. However, the anticipated shortages did not develop, and early in 1951 consumer demand fell off. . . . In the period (1950–1952) . . . the key to an understanding of trends in economic activity is to be found in the behavior of consumers—that is, in the private, rather than the public, sector of the economy. The wide fluctuations in consumer spending that occurred during 1950–1951 were largely independent of variations in income and were strongly influenced by changing short-term expectations." (p. 203.)

It is our belief that fiscal policy in this period is deserving of a larger accolade than that given by Hickman, although relative balance is difficult to establish. The data for this period are consistent with the view that there was a gradual restoration of a more normal consumption-income relationship following the heavy consumer purchases in the immediate postwar period. While in any single quarter consumer spending did not relate closely to income, it did over annual periods in a way indicating the importance of fiscal policy in containing the rise in disposable income.

[o] The procedure for renegotiation of war contracts was amended by the National Military Establishment Appropriation Act of 1950 and the Renegotiation Act of 1951, passed on March 23, 1951.

yield $3.3 billion by raising the corporate income-tax rate to 47 per cent and providing an excess-profits tax. In computing this tax, taxpayers were permitted a credit based on average earnings in the period 1946–1949 or specified percentages of invested capital, with a minimum of $25,000. A tax of 30 per cent was imposed on taxable excess profits (in addition to the income tax), with a 62 per cent over-all limit on income and excess-profits taxes.

Later in the year the other major piece of fiscal legislation—the Revenue Act of 1951—was enacted. It was started on its way at a time when large deficits faced federal budget makers. Defense expenditures were just beginning to mount toward peak levels. From the low of $19 billion in 1950 (3) federal expenditures in 1947 prices were to rise to $40 billion by 1951 (4) and reach a peak of $53 billion in 1953 (2). In his messages to Congress and the *Economic Report* filed at the beginning of 1951, President Truman asked for substantially additional taxes to keep pace with rising expenditures. His tax recommendations were for immediate enactment of an additional $10 billion of revenue and for consideration later in the year of further taxes after determination of receipts and expenditures had become clearer. The $10 billion was to be fairly evenly split between the personal income tax ($4 billion), the corporate income tax ($3 billion), and excises, primarily of the demand-shifting variety ($3 billion). In addition, the standard recommendation was made for the closing of loopholes.

Secretary Snyder initiated legislative activity by his appearance before the Ways and Means Committee on February 5 to spell out in detail the administration program. The subsequent history of the legislation was long and stormy, passing the House on June 22 as a $7.2 billion measure, the Senate on September 28 as a $5.5 billion bill, and finally enacted on October 22 to yield $5.7 billion. Approximately $2.3 billion were from the personal income tax, primarily through rate increases that averaged 11 per cent to 12 per cent. Withholding changes became effective on November 1, and one-sixth of the added rates were to apply to 1951 incomes. Corporate income taxes were expected to yield $2.2 billion through an additional 5 percentage points on the income tax that raised it to 52 per cent on income over $25,000. Three-fourths of this rate were to apply to 1951 corporate income. The additional excise-tax yield of $1.2 billion was mainly to come from the old stand-bys—liquor and tobacco—although other commodities shared some of the increases, such as cars, trucks, and sporting goods, and the 3.33 per cent tax

on electrical energy was repealed, also effective November 1. In signing the bill the President indicated his dissatisfaction and stated that
he would shortly request additional revenues in order to maintain a
pay-as-you-go fiscal system.[p]

The retroactive character of this legislation resulted in a sharp
rise in tax revenues in 1951 (4) and 1952 (1), as individuals and
corporations adjusted their tax payments and accruals to the higher
tax provisions. But from then on the government was making heavy
expenditure drains on the economy that were by no means offset by
tax yields. The gap between the two was to rise to a peak of nearly
$9 billion in 1953 (4) for all governments. For the federal govern-
ment alone, a deficit of approximately $2 billion was recorded in
calendar years 1952 and 1953. President Truman reiterated his request for more revenues in the early part of 1952. In his *Economic
Report* he pointed out his initial request in 1951 for $10 billion in
revenue, only half of which was met by the Revenue Act of 1951.
He therefore requested ". . . at least enough additional revenues to
reach the revenue goal proposed last year, by eliminating loopholes
and special privileges, and by tax rate increases."[14] But by now
Congress evinced no interest in further tax legislation, and, indeed,
the degree of stability in the economy was high. Consumer prices
were essentially stable, wholesale prices were falling, and unemployment was less than 3 per cent of the labor force. And so it continued
through the rest of the year.

On the whole the fiscal performance during the Korean War
deserves high marks. Action came promptly after the need for it was
correctly ascertained. While more revenue was requested in the later
stages of the war than turned out to be necessary, the pressure in this
direction was a salutary one. Thus prompt action meant that direct
controls could be weak, since their role was merely that of buttress-
ing fiscal and monetary policy, not the other way round as in the
Second World War.

Post-Korea and Recession of 1954: 1953 (3)—1954 (4)

After assuming office at the beginning of 1953, the Eisenhower administration embarked on a program designed to end the Korean

[p] Secretary Snyder had informed the Ways and Means Committee in his appearance on April 2 that the second part of the President's program could be
postponed until January 1952, in view of the budgetary developments then
expected.

hostilities, slash spending and taxes, halt price inflation, and eliminate wartime economic controls. This latter action was first taken in February. There was a fear that it would result in an initial sharp upsurge of demand for goods and services, and a tighter money policy was followed. But the upsurge did not take place. Hence it seems doubtful whether these controls had been playing much of an active role in keeping down effective demand. Prices had been relatively stable right along. The wholesale price index had reached a peak in early 1951 and had fallen fairly steadily since that time. Consumer prices had grown very slowly. Yet monetary tightness continued through May of 1953.

Along with these actions went strenuous efforts to cut budget expenditures in order to bring the budget into balance. Yet actual expenditures on goods and services declined very slowly through 1953. In the tax field, the excess-profits tax was scheduled for automatic repeal on June 30, 1953. Chairman Reed of the Ways and Means Committee seized this opportunity to update by six months the automatic reductions in the personal income tax that would have reduced rates to their levels under the Revenue Act of 1950, and considerable political pressure was gathering behind his proposal.[q] To blunt this pressure, the President sent a message to Congress on May 20, 1953, decrying the budgetary situation and making commitments for tax reduction. Official and semiofficial commentaries have largely ignored his significant statement. It is with a sense almost of rediscovery that it is reproduced in some of its detail here:[15]

> Tax receipts will apparently fall considerably short of our necessary expenditures during the next fiscal year. In view of this fact I have come to the conclusion that no reduction in tax rates should become effective during this calendar year. . . . Under present conditions of high business activity, coupled with a budget deficit, a tax reduction would not be consistent with attaining the vital financial objective of a sound dollar.

He went on to recommend:

> 1. The excess profits tax should be extended as now drawn for 6 months beyond its present expiration date of June 30.

[q] Chairman Reed's bill, H.R. 1, to advance the automatic reduction in personal income taxes to July 1, 1953, had been passed by the Ways and Means Committee on February 16, 1953, but had remained bottled up in the Rules Committee.

2. The reduction in the regular corporate tax rate from 52 per cent to 47 per cent, now scheduled to go into effect on April 1, 1954, should be rescinded.

3. The increase in the old-age insurance tax from 1½ to 2 per cent on both employees and employers, now scheduled to go into effect next January 1, should be postponed until January 1, 1955.

4. The reductions in excise taxes, which would take place next April 1 under present law, should be rescinded pending the development of a better system of excise taxation.

5. I believe that a reduction in personal income taxes can and should be made effective next January 1. This reduction will amount to about 10 per cent on the lower and middle incomes, graduating down to between 1 and 2 per cent on the highest brackets. While this reduction is in accordance with existing law, it would have been impossible to accomplish on the basis of the previous administration's budget without additional deficit financing with its resultant inflationary pressures. A reduction will be justified next January only because of reductions in proposed expenditures which the present administration has already been able to make and because of additional economies we expect to achieve in the future.

6. As you know, the Ways and Means Committee of the House of Representatives is currently engaged in a comprehensive reexamination of the existing tax structure. To help achieve this objective, I have asked the Secretary of the Treasury to present by the end of the year recommendations to remove existing inequities of our tax structure, simplify the needless complications which have developed over the years in tax laws, and generally secure a better balance of tax revenues.

Note the heavy emphasis given to pure budgetary considerations rather than to the economic situation as it then appeared or would appear: no tax reduction in 1953 because there would be a budget deficit; tax cuts in 1954 only because of the reduction in expenditures that had been or would be made. There is some oblique reference to "high business activity" and "inflationary pressures," but the latter seem to be equated with the budget deficit. Surely the interpretation given in a subsequent *Economic Report* that ". . . it seemed reasonable to expect that in another six or twelve months the boom might recede and that at such a time some reduction in taxes would become appropriate. . . ."[16] seems to be a rationalization after the fact.

The diagnosis, then, was that the situation seemed inflationary. The fiscal program was conformed to this diagnosis and aimed in a deflationary direction for the moment. It was surely a gamble to recommend tax reduction for 1954 at this time, since the future course of the economy was by no means clear. Yet firm action was needed, or premature tax reduction would have been forced on the Administration. At the same time it was made clear by the Administration that it was not holding up taxes permanently. Both Secretary Humphrey and Undersecretary Folsom of the Treasury strongly emphasized the need for ultimate repeal of the excess-profits tax after its temporary six-months' extension, the former before the Ways and Means Committee on June 1, and the latter before the Small Business Committee on May 21. There was no question about the Administration's commitment at this time.

Shortly after these deflationary steps were taken, the economy began to hesitate. GNP slackened off in the third quarter and hit bottom in the fourth at a rate $10 billion lower than 1953 (2). Not until 1954 (4) was it to rebound from this trough to the earlier peak rate of 1953 (2).

The initial drop of $10 billion in GNP was, through 1953, essentially a switch of $8 billion (annual rate) from inventory accumulation to decumulation. This change is attributed primarily to the sharp cutbacks in federal government orders that changed the rate of spending by $13 billion, in 1947 prices, between 1953 (2) and 1954 (4) (Chart IV).[r] There were minor changes in other components. Consumer expenditure fell slightly despite the fact that personal and disposable income remained unchanged at seasonally adjusted annual rates. (Government transfer payments rose slightly and undistributed corporate profits absorbed the balance of the change in GNP.) Nonresidential construction remained virtually the same, but the other components of domestic investment fell off slightly. Foreign investment went up by $1.3 billion, and government purchases fell by about the same amount.

Following the deflationary fiscal action of sharp expenditure reduction and postponement of excess-profits tax repeal, expansionary

---

[r] Bert G. Hickman, "The Contraction of 1953-4," *Review of Economics and Statistics*, Vol. 40 (February 1958), attributes the inventory disinvestment to reduced defense expenditures and also to reduced consumer outlays. This latter view seems harder to sustain. The change in consumer spending was only $1 billion on a seasonally adjusted basis, and clearly should be treated with care. Even if there were in fact such a change, one would not expect inventory decumulation to be timed so closely with it. The linkage of stock of inventories to seasonally adjusted purchases requires considerably more examination.

federal action came through automatic changes in the budget—in price supports, transfers, and automatic tax reduction as income fell. These fiscal adjustments were powerful indeed. The developing recession was followed closely by the Administration,[17] but the large tax reductions—excess-profits tax repeal and personal income-tax reduction—previously agreed to in May were undertaken on January 1. Their timing was indeed fortunate. This luck is reminiscent of the 1948 tax reduction that bolstered the 1949 recession. The estimated full-year revenue reduction was $7.4 billion, but the lowered level

Chart IV—Government Expenditures and Taxes, 1953–1955

Seasonally adjusted annual rates in 1947 prices (billions)

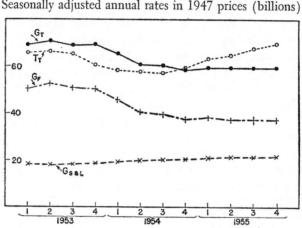

of economic activity at this time would place it at a slightly lower level. In any event, these reductions were well short of the deflationary impact resulting from the $15 billion cut in expenditures.

Another version of this period is contained in the various economic reports of the President and the statements of Chairman Burns of the Council of Economic Advisors. In January 1954 the President wrote:

> As the year wore on, tax policy was continually reviewed by the Treasury, not only from the viewpoint of moving toward a budgetary balance, but also in the light of the economic situation at large and the part that fiscal policy could play in contributing to economic growth and stability. By late September it was clear that the existing danger of inflation had passed, and that the prospective reduction of

Federal expenditure would justify some tax reduction. The Secretary of the Treasury therefore announced in the plainest possible language that the Administration, besides relinquishing the excess-profits tax, would not seek to postpone the reduction of the personal income tax, averaging approximately 10 per cent, scheduled for January 1, 1954.[18]

This "announcement" was apparently made in a speech to the American Bankers Association on September 22.[19] A reading of it does not indicate anything other than a repetition of the Administration's position established by the President's earlier statement as well as the testimony of the Secretary of the Treasury himself.

In January 1955 the *Economic Report* gave a still different version. Special credit is claimed for ". . . the announcement of sizeable tax reductions before it was generally known that an economic decline was actually under way. . . ."[20] The reference seems to be to the Secretary's speech, not the President's statement, since the latter gave no hint that a decline might be under way.[s] Another curious aspect of this view of the steps taken in policy formulation is that Secretary Humphrey's speech was delivered on September 22, yet the first serious mention of recession in Cabinet meetings is reported to have been on September 25.[21]

At any rate, the commitment entered into earlier regarding tax reduction was timed fortuitously to offset the deflationary effects of the Administration's policy of expenditure reduction. There were other steps, however, which further decreased taxes and others which offset this action of which brief mention should be made.

1. The President pocket vetoed, August 6, 1953, a bill repealing the 20 per cent tax on movie admissions on grounds of revenue loss and unfair discrimination. Its full-year effect would have been about $150 million.

2. The President and Congress failed to implement the freezing

---

[s] Chairman Burns gave the same version of the policy steps in his important talk to the Economic Club of Detroit, October 18, 1954. He stated: "Late in September, 1953, when it seemed plain that an economic decline had already begun but when unemployment figures still continued to move downward for seasonal reasons, the Government announced that it would make sizeable tax cuts for individuals and corporations effective in January, 1954, so that people would have more money to spend or invest."—(*U.S. News & World Report*, October 29, 1954, p. 44.) Burns's later discussion of this period, even when he was no longer a spokesman for the Administration, continues to ignore the role of the President and the commitments the Administration had made. His description differs little from the preceding. See Arthur F. Burns, *Prosperity without Inflation* (New York: Fordham University Press, 1957), pp. 30–31.

of social security taxes called for in the May presidential message. On January 1, 1954, the tax rate rose from 1.5 to 2 per cent, and the yield increased on an annual basis by $1.3 billion.

3. The Administration opposed the Excise Tax Reduction Act of 1954. In his January 1954 budget message the President spoke against lowering total excise-tax yields. Secretary Humphrey made a statement in opposition to the cut before the Ways and Means Committee on March 2, 1954.[22] Nevertheless, this bill became law on March 31, 1954. It reduced revenues by $1 billion through cuts in excise taxes (other than gasoline, liquor, and tobacco) to rates of 10 per cent, with the rate on household appliances reduced to 5 per cent.

4. The Administration opposed further tax cuts in connection with deliberation on the Internal Revenue Code of 1954.[t] Because of widespread unemployment at this time, considerable agitation, largely from the Democratic side, arose for further tax cuts to stimulate the economy.

On the expansionary side was the Internal Revenue Code of 1954, the cornerstone of the Administration's fiscal program, designed to reduce revenues at least $1.4 billion in the first fiscal year of its operation. While it was reasonably well timed as a tax-reduction measure, its major purpose was certainly not to expand purchasing power but to achieve structural tax reform. Secretary Humphrey assured both congressional tax committees that it would have been introduced when it was regardless of the position of the economy, whether receding or inflating. After an acrimonious journey through Congress, this bill became law on April 16, 1954. It made a host of detailed changes, but the largest and most discussed provided a dividend credit equal to 4 per cent of dividends received (after excluding $50 per dividend recipient),[u] permitted more rapid methods of depreciation to be used, increased deductible medical expenses to the excess over 3 per cent of gross income (rather than 5 per cent as previously), and granted limited deductions for child care and for retirement income.

By 1954 (4) GNP had recovered $10 billion to its pre-recession rate of 1953 (2). There was expansion from the low point in con-

[t] President Eisenhower in a speech to the nation on March 15, 1954, *Annual Report of the Secretary of the Treasury*, 1954, p. 221. Secretary Humphrey stated that ". . . . We cannot stand any further loss of revenue" to the Senate Finance Committee on April 7, 1954.—*Ibid.*, pp. 228–229.

[u] The Administration originally asked for a dividend credit which ultimately would have amounted to 15 per cent of dividends received after an exclusion of $100 per recipient.

sumption and investment, but sharp contraction in the government sector. Consumption spending had risen $11 billion from 1953 (2), almost entirely the result of increases in purchases of nondurable goods and services by an amount exceeding the $7 billion rise in disposable income. Domestic investment was up over $7 billion— residential construction was up substantially, inventory accumulation had recovered most of its recession losses, nonresidential construction remained about constant, but plant and equipment continued to fall. Foreign investment added $2 billion to demand for goods and services.

How much credit can fiscal policy take for the mildness of this recession? Examination of changes in the government's budget position shows it to have expanded in 1953 (4) and 1954 (1) and then contracted. The following seems to have happened. In 1953 (4) automatic tax reduction took place before the expenditure cuts could become effective. By 1954 (1) expenditure reduction began to take hold, but the scheduled tax cuts also went into operation in this quarter and they were substantially offsetting. Thus the combination of automatic and discretionary fiscal changes shored up demand initially, while monetary policy had a chance to stimulate residential construction. As recovery set in, fiscal policy acted increasingly as a drag. Had attention been focused on the shifting budget position of the government at full employment, its discretionary action would have been increasingly deflationary. Indeed, by 1955 the budget surplus was averaging $7 billion in 1947 prices—a sharp change from the $9 billion deficit of 1953 (4). More recovery credit, therefore, must be given to automatic fiscal action than to discretionary policy, with an important assist from foreign investment.[v]

Inflation Once More: 1955 (1)—1957 (3)

After the recovery had gathered force in 1955, wholesale prices began creeping upward, primarily because the fall in farm prices had been brought to a halt. By the middle of 1957 wholesale prices were 7 per cent above their 1955 level. In mid-1956 consumer prices began reflecting these increases, so that by mid-1957 they were 6 per cent

[v] I would agree with A. E. Holman's careful appraisal of fiscal policy in this period as ". . . remarkably similar in 1949–50 and 1953–5 . . . ," provided we take account only of the tax side. Inclusion of the expenditure side shows a marked difference. See "The Eisenhower Administration and the Recession, 1953–5," *Oxford Economic Papers*, Vol. 10, (Feb. 1958), p. 53.

above the 1954–1955 level. The pressure on prices seems to have been fed by every sector. GNP rose $67 billion in current prices between 1954 (4) and 1957 (2). Consumer money expenditures expanded $38 billion, but by less than disposable income, which in turn rose less than personal income, thanks to automatic stabilizers. Only 10 per cent of the expansion of consumption was in durable goods. The government sector and domestic investment rose equally in money terms—about $13 billion. While residential construction was actually down, business purchases of durable goods were going ahead briskly. State and local expenditure rose somewhat more than federal, but both components had risen by considerable amounts. Foreign investment, primarily because of the Suez oil shortage, had pushed up $3 billion. A picture of general expansion on all fronts is evident.

The budgetary position of all governments combined had shifted markedly. By 1956 budget surpluses averaged nearly $11 billion per year in 1947 prices. Government purchases had fallen off slightly in real terms—from $60 billion in 1955 (1) to $59 billion in 1956 (4). Hence the direct effect of government fiscal action on demand was deflationary as compared with the preceding recession.

The primary stabilizing effect exerted by the federal government was through reduction in purchases and in the large automatic increase in personal and corporate taxes yielded by the existing structure. No new enactments of any magnitude were made or recommended,[w] although the scheduled reductions in excise and corporate taxes (as of April) were postponed in each year, 1955–1957. Indeed, almost every budget message in this period contained hopes for tax reduction, with emphasis on the budget position rather than on the economy. In January 1954 the President stated:

> I am anxious to have taxes reduced as fast as that can be done without building up inflationary deficits. It is the determined purpose of this administration to make further reductions in taxes as rapidly as justified by prospective revenues and reductions in expenditures.[23]

In 1955 he held:

> Our economy is strong and prosperous, but we should not dissipate our economic strength through inflationary deficits. I have,

[w] Each year did see the unsuccessful recommendation that postal rates should be raised to eliminate the postal deficit. Not much credit can be given on stabilization grounds, however, since this recommendation was made every year, in prosperity or recession.

therefore, recommended to Congress extension for one year of present excise and corporate income tax rates which are scheduled for reduction on April 1, 1955, under present law. . . . Any other course of action would result in either (1) inadequate expenditures for national security, or (2) inflationary borrowing.[24]

And in the *Budget Message* in 1956 the President mused:

> So, in the present state of our financial affairs, I earnestly believe that a tax cut can be deemed justifiable only when it will not unbalance the budget, a budget which means provision for some reduction, even though modest, in our national debt.[25]

The fiscal program of the Administration for dealing with these slowly increasing prices was passive—a holding onto existing spending and taxing structures. Hope was placed on monetary policy and appeals to labor and management to follow non-inflationary price-wage policies.

While this period was a relatively quiet one on the fiscal front, the effects on excess demand and inflation of two major fiscal policies are worth further discussion. The first is the accelerated-depreciation provision of the Internal Revenue Code of 1954. The other is the major highway program initiated in 1956.

Some economists credit the inflationary pressures of 1956–1957 to the boom in purchases of producers' durable goods and credit or blame the accelerated-depreciation provisions enacted in 1954 for this result. That there was such a boom is clear. In real terms producers' durables rose nearly 16 per cent from 1954 to 1956.[26] Moreover, they rose as a percentage of the expanded GNP. Nevertheless, this shift is not entirely out of line with past recoveries. The 1938–1939 recovery resulted in an expansion of over 10 per cent in producers' durables. In 1950 it was considerably more—but this recovery is clouded by the Korean War. From 1949 to 1950 (2) the increase in real terms was slightly over 11 per cent. Whether we can attribute the 1956 bulge to the 1954 depreciation provisions is another question. The determinants of investment are a notably weak spot in economic analysis. Yet some provisional appraisal of this view must be made despite its necessarily tentative nature.

In sum, the data are not inconsistent with this interpretation, although any kind of conclusive testing would require more formal specification of the investment function. Consider first the timing of producers' durable goods. The pickup in demand for business durable goods came in about the second half of 1955. Since the depreciation provisions were enacted in April 1954, it would seem reasonable for business firms to begin to take advantage of them on a large scale only after study, debate, formulation, and placement of orders, a process that might well take six months to a year or more. But unfortunately this timing is also consistent with the view that the short-term movement of producers' durable goods lags behind the movement in GNP by about this length of time, and that we observe a reasonably normal reaction of these purchases to the 1955 recovery in other sectors of the economy. Note that the trough in producers' durables was not reached until 1955 (1), whereas the GNP trough came in 1953–1954. In 1949 the trough for producers' durables came in 1950 (1), compared with essentially the same quarterly GNP rates from 1949 (1) to 1949 (3).

A second kind of question we can ask is whether the expansion in producers' durables is found in industries that would use and benefit from accelerated depreciation. The regulated industries, rails and utilities, for example, viewed these provisions with many doubts. Here we find that, of the increase in annual rate of purchases from 1954 to 1956 of over $8 billion, half was in manufacturing, over $2 billion in utilities and rails, and nearly $2 billion in trade, service, and the like. This test is also, unfortunately, inconclusive. While these purchases by manufacturing firms represented a 36 per cent increase in 1956 over 1954, the purchases by rails represented 33 per cent, by the communications industry nearly 60 per cent, by trade over 30 per cent, with considerably lower figures (less than 20 per cent) for some of the other major groups. We can only conclude that the data are not inconsistent with this hypothesis, though they certainly do not confirm it.

The other major fiscal issue revolved around the federal highway program. Reference to it was first found in the President's 1955 *Budget Message* and *Economic Report*. At this time he requested that the federal government, at a cost of $27 billion, bear nearly all the costs of modernizing interstate highways over a ten-year period. He then intended that the program be financed by an independent authority from the excess of federal revenue from gasoline and lubricating oils over the then current amount of federal grants-in-aid for roads.[27] Over a thirty-year period these revenues would have equaled ten years' expenditure. This proposal was the one developed by the President's Advisory Committee on a National Highway Program headed by General Clay. It was severely criticized in Congress. While termed self-liquidating, it provided for added expenditures of nearly $3 billion per year without any added revenues—only an allocation of existing revenues was called for. The borrowing by the highway authority was to be exempt from the debt limit against which the Treasury was continually bumping. As a government corporation, however, it would have borrowed at higher interest rates than the Treasury. There were other more technical objections raised.[28]

The program as initially formulated was a transparent device, through which Congress quickly saw, for avoiding the debt limit. The Administration seemed to take the old position that borrowing by the Treasury was inflationary whereas borrowing by a government corporation was not. It appeared to be wholly unaware that it would have increased inflationary pressures at a time when they could be ill afforded. Attention was focused on the effect on the executive budget. The enormous potential of the program as a counter-cyclical measure was barely discussed.[x]

Indeed, so much criticism was aroused by this inept financial proposal that Congress developed what was essentially its own program.[y] While a separate authority was created for managing the highway program, new taxes were voted which would partially, although not wholly, offset the expansionary effects of the additional highway expenditures. The final program provided for average expenditure of slightly more than $2 billion per year, primarily from stretching out the construction period from ten to thirteen years. The added tax revenues were from higher taxes on gasoline and other motor fuels, on tires, and on trucks.[z] It was estimated that they would cover less than half of the federal cost,[aa] so that over the long run the program would be expansionary. However, since the new taxes were collected faster than the added expenditures could be undertaken, this legisla-

[x] A side glance was given it. "Although a steady pace of construction, financed through the sale of bonds to the public, would normally be the best procedure, expenditure and financing plans could be adjusted in the interests of general economic stability."—*Economic Report of the President*, January 1955, p. 62.

[y] The Administration backed off sharply from its initial proposals. See the testimony of the Secretary of the Treasury before the House and Senate Committees referred to in Footnote 28. See also *Economic Report of the President*, January 1956, p. 84.

[z] They added 1 cent per gallon on motor fuels, 3 cents per pound on tires and camelback, 2 per cent of the manufacturer's value of trucks, buses, etc., and $1.50 per 1,000 pounds on trucks and buses weighing over 13 tons.

[aa] The revenue estimate was $14.8 billion over a sixteen year period.

tion initially exerted some deflationary pressure.

On the whole, this period was not a particularly attractive one for a fiscal policy. While the expenditure-tax line was largely held, there was little constructive fiscal action to cope with inflation; and the road program as initially formulated was obviously the reverse.

The Recession of 1957 (4)—1958 (2)

Both the Administration and Republican and Democratic congressional members were driving for tax reduction in 1957 and again in 1958. There was obvious controversy in the Administration at the time of the preparation of the budget for the fiscal year 1958. Upon its release the usual press conference was dominated by Secretary Humphrey rather than the director of the Budget Bureau. Secretary Humphrey openly invited Congress to squeeze more water out of the budget or face ". . . a depression that will curl your hair."[29] Congress took up the challenge and cut down expenditures wherever it could. The Administration was criticized for giving ineffective and vacillating support to its own budget program and for failing to formulate a stronger program to halt the continuing rise of prices. The President did recommend, in the fiscal field:

> Government can strengthen the enterprise system at this time by preserving a balanced budget. Accordingly, the Congress should continue tax rates at their present levels, and Federal expenditures should be strictly limited.[30]

Secretary of Defense Wilson had imposed a $38 billion defense-spending ceiling. Since spending in the first half of 1957 was running ahead of that rate, there were sharp cutbacks on order placements in the middle of the year. Moreover, the debt was pressed against the legal ceiling, following a decision not to ask for a raise in it. There were slow-ups in expenditure that forced severe financial hardship on many firms. These cutbacks were an important factor contributing to the 1957 recession, but at that moment there was little concern over the consequent slow growth of unemployment from April 1957 onward.

The successful orbiting of the Russian Sputnik in early October was the first major shock requiring fiscal action. The initial reaction of the Administration was to belittle the Russian effort and talk up our own. But talk soon turned to expanding certain aspects of the defense effort. The Republican party had essentially abandoned its position in favor of tax reduction by November. The Democrats, with whom rested control of the Ways and Means Committee, had, however, scheduled tax hearings for January 7, 1958, presumably to discuss methods of reducing taxes. But their position, too, changed as they called for sharp step-ups in the defense program to match the Soviet effort.[31]

The mid-November position of the Administration regarding the forthcoming budget was stated by the President to be that of cutting back sharply many categories of nondefense spending to keep total expenditures in fiscal 1959 at the 1958 level. He also indicated, however, that he would not let budget-balancing considerations limit the defense program.

By the turn of the year the signs of gathering recession became clear. The Administration took an optimistic view of it, nevertheless. The budget it submitted in January was based on income forecasts that were immediately attacked as unrealistically high and were shortly to be proved so. A deficit of $400 million was expected by the Administration for the current fiscal year, and a small surplus of $500 million for fiscal 1959. Because of the Administration's belief that confidence was the major ingredient for an economic recovery, a recommendation for expansionary fiscal action was missing in the *Budget Message* and the *Economic Report*. The President did propose tax reduction to small business to the tune of approximately $140 million per year, a renewal of a recommendation he had made on July 15, 1957.[bb] In addition, government workers were to be given higher pay that would amount to $1.1 billion, and payments to states from the highway trust fund were expected to rise $0.6 billion. But the President also recommended an increase in postal rates of $0.7 billion and the further postponement of the scheduled July 1 decrease in tobacco, liquor, and auto excises, and the corporate income tax. Indeed, both the administrative budget and the cash-consolidated budget were expected to show a small deflationary shift between 1958 and 1959.

A vigorous policy discussion gathered force, picking up speed after

[bb] It consisted of accelerated depreciation on $50,000 of used property acquired in any year; a partnership option for stockholders of closely held corporations; an option to pay the estate tax over a ten-year period; and ordinary loss treatment, with some maximum, on losses from investment in stock of small corporations. It was, essentially, enacted as Title II of the Technical Amendments Act of 1958.

the sharp increase in unemployment between December and January.[cc] Shortly before the congressional Easter recess, April 4–14, it reached a peak. Pressure for tax reduction seemed irresistible. But apparently congressional soundings at home showed that the public was less concerned about the recession than Congress had thought. A noticeable slackening of pressure for expansionary fiscal policy followed on its return.

The debate covered most of the policy facets. In one group were those favoring tax reduction for its own sake. Some urged various types of income-tax reduction from increases in personal exemptions, of primary benefit to low-income groups, to devices aimed at stimulating effort, thrift, and investment by the wealthier. Others favored excise-tax reduction in order to revive demand for specific consumer durable goods, an area of demand notably weak, or to aid the railroad and transportation industry by repealing the tax on freight and passenger transportation. Still others advocated business-tax reduction by way of accelerated depreciation or rate cuts.

A time dimension was also added to the tax-reduction controversy. Since prices had moved slowly upward throughout the recession, there were fears that a recovery would add fuel to these fires. Therefore, some schemes for tax reduction carried terminal dates; for example, a tax-withholding holiday of a few weeks or months, with appropriate change in tax liabilities in the following April.

Other advocates of expansionary fiscal policy wished to see larger government programs in areas they thought were seriously lagging. Although most favored expansion of the military program, other programs, such as research, education, highways, foreign aid, rivers and harbors, and other public works, did not lack for support.

Throughout the recession, however, the Administration essentially stood pat, relying on automatic fiscal responses and monetary policy to achieve stability. A strategy meeting of the Republican congressional and Cabinet officers early in the year was reported to have reached the decision that both a tax cut and increased public works spending should be considered by summer if there were no midyear economic upturn. But it was expected by this group that business activity would turn upward without such aid. As the recession developed, the Administration seemed to favor a speed-up of existing public works and procurement programs and then, if that failed, a

[cc] It rose from 5.0 to 6.7 per cent of the labor force, a seasonably adjusted increase of from 5.0 per cent to 5.8 per cent.

tax cut.[32] Nevertheless, the Democrats characterized the policies as inactive and inadequate. Stung by their criticism, the President released an *Economic Statement* and a *Fact Paper* on February 12 outlining the steps he had taken to counter the recession. In the fiscal area, primary emphasis was placed on the $.6 billion rise in the highway program, the placing of a higher rate of defense contracts in 1958 than in 1957, the civil public works expansion of $.3 billion, and the announcement of a $2 billion post-office modernization program.[33] This was not, however, a particularly reassuring picture. The expansion in highway spending had been provided in the initial legislation in 1956. The added defense-contract awards represented merely a restoration of the cutbacks of the preceding year, with little or no expansion in defense output.[dd] The post-office modernization program of $2 billion was a five-year program, with at most $175 million to be spent in 1958 and that contingent on the passage of the higher postal rates on out-of-town first-class mail that would have collected at least as much in added revenue.[ee]

Congressional pressures for more activity mounted in March as action began on bills that would cut taxes, expand highways, housing, and other public works. The President on March 8 sent the minority leaders of the House and Senate a letter outlining steps that had been taken to cope with the recession, especially those since his February 12 statement. The major items involved a federal extension of exhausted state unemployment benefits through loans to states, acceleration of procurement programs, added capacity for lending under the housing program, and suspension of certain spending limitations under the National Highway Act.[ff] The extension of state unemployment benefits, estimated to cost $600 to $800 million, while obviously a helpful step in expanding demand, was subjected to

---

[dd] "What is more, high Administration officials are now willing to concede that they overrated somewhat the stimulative effect of the planned 50 per cent increase in defense orders in the current half year over the last half of 1957. They concede that this will mostly just make up for orders not placed last year." *New York Times*, March 9, 1958, p. 54.

"The sharp step-up, disclosed earlier by President Eisenhower as part of his anti-recession program, doesn't represent much additional buying. Instead, it reflects the efforts of the armed services to catch up with their original contract-letting schedules after a delay last summer and fall." *Wall Street Journal*, March 14, 1958, p. 4.

[ee] The Administration was not entirely clear at first on this contingency. *Wall Street Journal*, February 12, 1958, p. 3.

[ff] The so-called "Byrd Amendment" limited spending to the amount of money in the highway trust fund.

criticism. First, it was held that it discouraged states from strengthening their unemployment-compensation programs.[gg] Second, an extension of unemployment benefits was, technically speaking, a measure to soften recessions and not a device to raise full-employment demand and thus stimulate recovery. The highway program, it was estimated, would make possible $600 million in new contracts, but only in the last half of 1958.[34]

The whole program was yet something less than Congress thought desirable. By the middle of March expectations were high that a tax-reduction program would soon be announced. There was much jockeying between the Congress and the Administration to reap the political benefits from priority and a fear on both sides that such competition would produce a premature cut. An agreement between Speaker Rayburn and Secretary Anderson, neither of whom was a strong advocate of tax reduction, to inform each other in advance of any proposals, calmed the atmosphere,[35] as did unofficial estimates of budget deficits of $1 billion in 1958 and of $5 billion in 1959 without any tax reduction.[36] In addition, several steps were taken or proposed by the Administration to accelerate existing programs. Congress was also busy with further highway bills which involved a speed-up as well as additions to the highway program, a rivers and harbors bill, and a loan program for state and local public works.[hh]

But following the congressional recess in the first half of April a stiffening attitude was plainly evident. The President vetoed the rivers and harbors bill on April 15, belittling its contribution to economic recovery.[37] No attempt was made to pass it over his veto.[ii] The farm price-support freeze had been successfully vetoed at the end of March. The highway bill, however, was approved on April 16.[38] By mid-April a deficit of $3 billion in 1958 and $8 to $10 billion in 1959 was in prospect.[39] The crucial action that indicated the shift in congressional sentiment came on the measure to extend certain excise taxes for another year beyond July 1, 1958. It was reliably reported that the House leadership and the Treasury were attempting

[gg] A statement by 19 academic labor economists takes this view. *New York Times*, March 23, 1958, p. 42.

[hh] A careful appraisal of these programs is made by Edwin L. Dale, Jr., *New York Times*, April 6, 1958, IV:7. He speaks of one estimate within the government that the added spending for all these programs would equal $1 billion in annual rate by the end of 1958.

[ii] A modified version meeting his objections went to him for signature on June 25. *Congressional Quarterly, Weekly Report*, No. 26, June 27, 1958.

to develop a legislative procedure ". . . aimed at burying all broad tax cuts for the year."[40] It was successful. The inevitable tax-cutting amendments to this extension act were beaten back in the House. On the Senate floor amendments repealing the excise tax of 3 per cent on freight transportation and of 10 per cent on passenger transportation were successful. However, only the freight amendment survived in conference and the President signed the bill. Better news on the economic front sharply reduced interest in expansionary fiscal action.

Present signs give a clear picture that the bottom of the recession was reached by the middle of the year. Little assistance was given by the federal government. Perhaps the reported vigorous differences of opinion within the Administration stalemated any prompt and decisive action.[41] Perhaps the absence of Arthur Burns to carry weight in Cabinet meetings and counter some of the arguments used to support inaction was felt. The carrying out of this passive policy by the Administration resulted in much beclouding of the actual position of the economy through carelessness about seasonal adjustments, unjustified reliance on the "prediction" that things would soon be better, and gross overstatement of the efficacy of the Administration's reaction to the recession. Certainly the policy of holding the fiscal line until the situation clarified was a defensible one and did not need such shabby support. The major criticism to be made is not of the policy itself but of the reasons given in support of it and the ways in which it was implemented. There was complete failure to make a clear-cut presentation of the issues to the public for decision and advice.

Secretary Anderson took his post at the beginning of the recession. He apparently played a key role in the Administration's policy formulation. Yet his economic views were sometimes obscure and not always consistent. On April 24, for example, at approximately the depth of the recession, he published an article on the virtue of increased consumer saving as a device for strengthening the nation.[42] Congressional leaders were also somewhat reluctant to move. Speaker Rayburn obviously had doubts about the efficacy of tax reduction as a recovery device, and Majority Leader Johnson was putting no pressure on him.

Nevertheless, the debate over policy developed interesting objections to fiscal activity. By the time the recession was deep enough for fairly strenuous action to be called for, it had become widely accepted that new public-works programs would be ineffective recovery devices. However, this was partly a question of semantics, since the acceleration of *existing* public-expenditure programs was given first priority. Opposition to tax reduction also took many forms. Some held it to be ineffective in inducing added consumer expenditure, especially if of a temporary character. Others argued that a permanent tax reduction would amount to so little per week as to have no effect in inducing purchases of durable goods. In some cases these arguments were coupled with the view that, since added budget deficits would be inflationary, although no added spending would result, the consequence would be inflation without recovery. And, finally, some thought that tax relief to the employed would not feed the unemployed.

That there is little proved theory regarding the speed of response of consumer spending to changes in disposable income is an unfortunate fact. But what we do know regarding consumer response to income changes would lead to the expectation of some significant additional spending. The argument that it is too small to do any good is an argument for more, not less, tax reduction.[jj] To argue that it would be inflationary without having any effect on spending is to become ensnared in the mythology that deficits per se are inflationary. Unfortunately, this latter view has cropped up often in public statements over this period both in Congress and the Administration, from the President on down. This view should not, of course, be confused with the quite reasonable one that the added consumer spending from tax reduction may feed in slowly and cause *later* inflationary pressure when other demand recovers. But if this is the fear, there is surely no practical reason why such pressures could not be dealt with later when and if they arose. And, finally, the belief that tax reduction for the employed does not help the unemployed is primarily an argument about the distribution of income. Even on these grounds, however, the distributional difference is not as large as it might seem. Income-tax reduction, provided it induced added consumer spending, would result in the employment of those now out of work. They in turn would receive tax reduction on the wages that they would earn upon re-employment.

But perhaps the most powerful argument as the recession grew was the budget deficit itself. The forecast 1959 budget deficit auto-

[jj] The significant speech of April 10, 1958, by Howard C. Petersen, president of the Fidelity-Philadelphia Trust Company, and chairman of CED's fiscal subcommittee, gives emphasis to this view. *CED Release*, April 11, 1958, p. 5.

matically swelled from near balance to around $10 billion in a very few months in early 1958. The news was received with alarm by many. They took the position that further tax reduction could not be afforded. Others thought that fiscal policy was a failure, since recovery was not promoted by such a large deficit. Here again we see a failure to distinguish between deficits that arise passively from existing programs and those that arise from new legislation or from administrative action which increases government spending or decreases tax rates and yields at existing levels of income. One cushions; the other expands.

Although the economy had turned the corner, the recovery was weak. While there was some indication of need for further expansive fiscal action, none was discussed. On the contrary, following the 1958 elections, the Administration bent every effort to cut expenditures further.

Concluding Observations

What can we conclude from this excursion through approximately a decade of attempted economic stability? What lessons can be learned regarding the use of fiscal policy?

1. Economic intelligence has improved over this period. The slowness with which the 1949 recession was sensed contrasts sharply with the speed with which both the 1953 and 1957 recessions were detected. But with the improvement in knowledge has come increasing ability to distort. Public officials have not yet firmly accepted the view that political decision making will be improved by making available to the public as accurate a description of the existing state of affairs as it is possible to give. Instead, current statistics may be released incompletely; seasonal adjustments may or may not be made, depending on which result is most congenial to current policy positions; and meaningless or misleading comparisons may be emphasized. Oftentimes these data may be given especial emphasis by release through the White House or in press conferences.

This attitude on the part of public officials leads also to the official rewriting of economic history. The economic reports of the President, for example, are, unfortunately, quite worthless as descriptions of the course of fiscal policy. Instead of accepting the backing and hauling, inconsistencies, false starts, action on inadequate information, that characterize actual policy formation, they are written with omniscience and self-justification.

There seems little that can be done to suggest remedies for this situation. Obviously it is desirable to have public servants who assist rather than mislead public discussion. Perhaps an independent statistical body could release these data along with their interpretation of them, so that interested users would have some place to turn.

This administrative attitude toward knowledge has even extended to the creation of the data themselves. The most obvious and recent example is the budget estimate of January 1958. It was administration policy not to recognize a decline in incomes below the preceding year since such a decline would imply inadequacy of policy. As a result, the budget was obsolete by the time of its preparation.

It might lead to greater clarity in fiscal policy if the budget estimating procedure urged by the CED and other groups were adopted. Under such a procedure the "full employment" amounts of revenues and expenditures would be forecast. Such a budget could be supplemented in considerably less detail by one or two alternative budgets that indicated alternative forecasts of economic activity. In this way the politics of budget making could be further channeled toward giving the public more information on which to act.

The importance of such a procedure is heightened by the common failure to distinguish between movements along the aggregate demand schedule (automatic responses) from shifts in the schedule (autonomous changes). In a rapidly changing economic environment it becomes difficult for legislators and the public to know whether changes in the budget position result from modifications in the tax structure or spending rates, or from automatic budget reactions to variations in output.

2. Understanding of economic analysis has advanced considerably over the decade. As long as output was slumping in the last recession, public discussion of fiscal policy was concerned primarily with questions of timing and choice of fiscal instruments. This is as it should be. Some clouding of this impression is found toward the end of the recession, when the size of the budget deficit which was primarily a passive reaction to the recession frightened some, and when public statements were made that incorrectly equated budget deficits with inflation. But the business community has clearly advanced a great deal from its attitudes in the thirties.

3. Discretionary fiscal policies cannot claim much credit for

stabilization operations over this period. The 1945 tax remissions were premature; the 1948 tax cuts were carried out for precisely the wrong reasons; nothing much was undertaken in the 1949 recession except to carry out policies undertaken for other reasons; policy in the early portion of the Korean War was correct and effective; net deflationary fiscal policies were followed in the recession of 1953–1954; little or nothing was undertaken fiscally to reduce the inflation of 1955–1957; and in the 1957–1958 recession fiscal action was relatively slim.

Yet this is too harsh a judgment. There was less moving in the wrong direction as more understanding was acquired. Expenditures, the major shifts in which are marked primarily by changes in defense policy, have tended to be stabilizing factors in recessions and inflations. State and local governments have steadily increased expenditures and taxation throughout the postwar period, but the changes here have been predictable, helping in recessions, hindering in booms. Indeed, the degree of stability, both of price and employment, in the postwar period was extraordinarily high for this country.

4. Automatic fiscal stabilizers have played an enormous role in postwar recessions. They have sharply reduced the secondary repercussions on income from shifts in inventory accumulation or decumulation, thus aiding materially in stabilizing consumer expenditure, and, in turn, business investment in plant and equipment. Taxes and transfer expenditures show great sensitivity in real terms to changes in output. They do not show this same sensitivity to price changes, notably in the 1946–1948 period. This means that the economy is much less protected automatically against price change than it is against changes in output. Put in another way, automatic fiscal stabilizers are much stronger in reducing output fluctuations than price fluctuations. Their efficacy depends primarily on tax rates.[kk] As between the 1946 tax structure and that at the end of the period, there may have been some slight improvement, mainly from broadening social security coverage. As compared with the thirties and twenties, vast progress has been made. But as compared with, say, the middle of the postwar period, automatic fiscal stabilizers have been reduced.

5. One sees in this period a repetition of the following policy

[kk] Much too much credit in this area is given to trivial modifications in the tax structure that improve the timing of tax collections, such as extension of the loss carry-back from one year to two years.

pattern. First, there is a growing awareness of a recession or inflation, but more information must be gathered to be sure of the pattern. By the time of reasonable certainty, the economy is well into the inflation or deflation. In the case of recessions, where the problem arises most vividly, many fiscal instruments are then rejected as being too dangerous in their timing. New public works, for example, have often been placed in this category. Permanent tax reductions have also been viewed with alarm. And temporary reductions carrying a restoration date were rejected in 1958 because, it was argued, the additional purchasing power would be saved rather than spent because of their temporary character. Thus most fiscal instruments are discarded except the speed-up or slowdown of existing expenditure programs, and this procedure may offer inadequate flexibility. Thus discretionary fiscal policy is enormously weakened.

It points up a number of problems. Is there a factual basis for these arguments? Have we extended our knowledge of the timing of public-works outlays beyond the thirties? What kinds of expenditure patterns can arise under public-works programs? Have adequate plans been formulated? How much do we know about the speed with which permanent or temporary tax reductions feed into disposable incomes and consumer spending? Are there genuine differences between income and excise-tax reductions? Would tax credits for business investment work promptly? Are there other, more flexible, fiscal devices? In a word, much more research on the timing of fiscal policies must be undertaken before we can resolve some of these questions.

Unfortunately, the chance to try a promising fiscal device was rejected in the last recession. The interesting proposal of temporary tax reductions, including withholding tax forgiveness appears to be the most flexible fiscal change yet proposed. While not new,[11] it has never received as much support as it did in the 1958 recession. In essence, it permits a sharp, temporary change in the rate of disposable income without a commitment to a permanent change. Any amount of withholding forgiveness can be achieved when coupled with appropriate adjustment of final liabilities in the subsequent April. For example, if the starting income-tax rate were 20 per cent, three months' withholding forgiveness (and one declaration) would

---

[11] Albert G. Hart has had this idea for a long time. He spelled it out in a book written jointly with the present writer, *Financing Defense* (New York: Twentieth Century Fund, 1951), pp. 139–141.

result in a computation of final liabilities for the whole year at three-fourths of this rate, or 15 per cent. Half a year's forgiveness would result in the use of 10 per cent as the starting rate. In neither event would the permanent starting rate change.

In principle, it would permit a prompt flexible adjustment to the developing economic situation. It could be carried out on any scale believed desirable—one month or more up to twelve. And it should have powerful leverage, provided consumers will spend the proceeds. On this, further study is needed.

6. The inflexibility of government expenditure is impressive. Major policy changes—Marshall Plan, Korean War, post-Korean War, and post-Sputnik—took a long time appearing as changes in government expenditures. This behavior raises the question whether or not expenditures are a satisfactory measure of the impact of the government on economic activity or whether better series could be developed, such as appropriations, orders, output, or some combination of them.

7. It seems somewhat startling, but, with two exceptions, broad tax reductions or additions were undertaken only when there were (roughly) corresponding expenditure changes. In other words, discretionary tax changes have not been made for stability purposes. The tax reduction of 1948 was undertaken alone, but not to shore up a recession. On the contrary, it represented the giving away of a large budget surplus in an inflationary period. The other possible exception, on a small scale to be sure, was the 1954 excise-tax reduction of $1 billion over administration protests. But since expenditures were being cut by $15 billion at this time, even this reduction is not a genuine exception.

The generalization that all of us have made from time to time—that expansionary fiscal action will be taken promptly in a recession—and that, therefore, there is an inflationary bias in fiscal action is simply not borne out by the facts. Fiscal bias there may be. But the bias toward larger budget deficits in the time of recessions has not been present in the postwar period. In this country, therefore, we cannot take it as obviously true that a properly stabilizing fiscal policy will be undertaken.

Notes

[1] For a recent discussion of these issues, see Murray L. Weidenbaum, "The Federal Government Spending Process," in *Federal Expenditure Policy for Economic Growth and Stability*, Joint Economic Committee, papers submitted by panelists appearing before the Senate Subcommittee on Fiscal Policy, 1957.

[2] This percentage seems not unreasonable in the light of recent studies of private spending decisions. For further discussion see my paper, "Fiscal Policy in the Thirties: A Reconsideration," *American Economic Review*, Vol. XLVI, Dec. 1956.

[3] *Ibid.*, p. M5.

[4] *Economic Report of the President, January* 1947, p. 22.

[5] *Midyear Economic Report of the President*, July 1947, p. 27.

[6] See *Individual Income Tax Reduction Act of 1947*, U.S. House of Representatives, Committee on Ways and Means, Report No. 180, March 24, 1947; and *Individual Income Tax Reduction Act of 1947*, U.S. Senate, Committee on Finance, Report No. 173, May 14, 1947.

[7] *Economic Report of the President*, January 1948, p. 6.

[8] *Loc. cit.*

[9] *Ibid.*, p. 48.

[10] *Midyear Economic Report of the President*, July 1948, p. 7.

[11] *Economic Report of the President*, January 1949, p. 10.

[12] *Midyear Economic Report of the President*, July 1949, p. 8.

[13] *Economic Report of the President*, January 1950, p. 11.

[14] *Economic Report of the President*, January 1952, p. 25.

[15] *Annual Report of the Secretary of the Treasury, 1953*, pp. 204–207.

[16] *Economic Report of the President*, January 1954, p. 52.

[17] Robert J. Donovan, *Eisenhower: The Inside Story* (New York: Harper & Brothers, 1956) gives a vivid picture in Chapter 15 of the Cabinet concern and discussion.

[18] *Economic Report of the President*, January 1954, p. 54.

[19] Donovan, *op. cit.*, p. 210.

[20] *Economic Report of the President*, January 1955, p. 20.

[21] Donovan, *op. cit.*, p. 165.

[22] *Annual Report of the Secretary of the Treasury, 1954*, p. 242.

[23] *Budget Message of the President for Fiscal Year 1955*, p. M12.

[24] *Budget Message of the President for Fiscal Year 1956*, p. M5.

[26] *Budget Message of the President for Fiscal Year 1957*, p. M17.

[26] *Survey of Current Business*, July 1957, U.S. Department of Commerce, Table 40, p. 25.

[27] *Economic Report of the President*, January 1955, pp. 61–62. The amount of grants-in-aid at that time was $875 million per year.

[28] For detailed discussions see *Hearings on National Highway Program*, U.S. House of Representatives, Committee on Public Works, (1955); and *Hearings on National Highway Program*, U.S. Senate, Subcommittee of Committee on Public Works, (1955).

[29] *Congressional Quarterly Almanac*, Vol. XIII (1956), p. 691.

[30] *Economic Report of the President*, January 1957, p. vi.

[31] *Wall Street Journal* (New York), December 3, 1957, p. 3.

[32] For example, in the President's press conference of February 26, 1958, *Wall Street Journal*, February 27, 1958, p. 12.

[33] *Ibid.*, February 13, 1958, pp. 1, 54.

[34] *New York Times*, March 9, 1958, pp. 1, 54.

[35] *Wall Street Journal*, March 14, 1958, p. 2.

[36] *Ibid.*, p. 1.

[37] *Wall Street Journal*, April 16, 1958, p. 3.

[38] With misgivings, however. *Wall Street Journal*, April 17, 1958, p. 2.

[39] *Wall Street Journal*, April 23, 1958, p. 3.

[40] *Wall Street Journal*, May 12, 1958, p. 8.

[41] *Wall Street Journal*, April 25, 1958, p. 8.

[42] *Christian Science Monitor* (Boston), April 24, 1958, p. 14. At the same time the President was urging the public to save less and buy anything.

SIX

☆

CONTINUITY AND CHANGE IN AMERICAN LABOR PROBLEMS

☆

ABRAHAM J. SIEGEL
and
CHARLES A. MYERS

What are some of the more significant changes in the sources and character of American labor problems which have occurred in the recent past? What changes or continuities in the nature of these problems can we anticipate for the near future? These are the central questions with which we deal in this essay.

Any such survey is necessarily personal and selective. Impersonal digests of the data are hard to come by, and the record has yet to "speak for itself." There is no pretension here to the "whole truth" or to exclusively valid evaluation. It may be useful, therefore, to enumerate briefly some of the considerations which have shaped our own perspective for review of the past and speculation about future American labor problems:

1. *Work* and not alone the worker's eye view of and reaction to the world of work seems to us a more general context for discerning labor problems. Labor problems are thus seen as including but not confined to labor's problems.

2. The focus on "our" labor problems should not bar from view the fact that these are rooted as deeply in the *industrial* character of our society as in its American-ness. Specific or unique attributes of national character and environment have undoubtedly had a vital cumulative impact in shaping our problems, and we have tried to note these. The more general aspects of "our" problems, however, are comparable to the labor problems of any industrial society, and we have attempted to describe them in terms which would allow such comparability.

3. In keeping with these broader dimensions for perception, we have seen the general source of our labor problems as lying in the series of challenges put to us by the functional requirements of organizing work in modern industrial society—in the need for devising and maintaining a web of rule relating worker to work process, to employer, and to the state—and in the society's responses to these challenges. Modern industrialism creates a productive mechanism made up of an intricate web of interdependent parts and requires an equally complex body of rules and institutional arrangements to insure that the components mesh smoothly. Every industrial society will be confronted with the problem of setting and enforcing rules

concerned with the recruitment, training, commitment, and allocation of a labor force. Every industrial society faces the problems of
setting rules on time to work and not to work, on pace and quality
of work, on method and amount of pay, on movement into and out
of work and from one position to another. Every industrial society
grapples with the problem of devising rules pertaining to continuity
in the work process.

Finally, if rules are to be set, there must be established at each
relevant level of decision-making power some rule-making and rule-
enforcing procedure to define the distribution of power to make rules
governing the conduct of the work force. These are universal challenges—whatever the form of industrial society—and "our" labor
problems (and anyone else's) emerge from these challenges and from
the conflicts over procedure for the fixing of rules and from conflicts
over the substance of the rules themselves.

American Labor Problems: Antecedents to the Recent Past

By the 1930's American industrial development was far from in-
cipiency. It had been initiated "from below" by a middle class sparked
by the Protestant ethic, had proceeded at a relatively moderate rate,
and had developed in the mold of a relatively self-regulating market
mechanism organized in keeping with the strongly individualist,
laissez-faire principles of economic liberalism. A lavish endowment of
economic space had facilitated its progress and, together with an
early heritage of political and civil rights and an absence of feudal
restraints, had fostered a mobile and fluid society whose industrial
work force was replenished by wave after wave of immigration. There
was no "big push" or "forced draft" industrialization (such as we
have witnessed in the Soviet Union) involving swift, sharp transitions
from one way of life to another. There was no concerted emphasis
on investment which could come only at the expense of consumption.
There was no serious population growth pressure to impede increases
in per capita income. Advances in the technical organization of work
and in productivity permitted a secular rise in real wages over the
years. The direct role of government in the inception of industry and
in the establishment of procedural or substantive rules which controlled it was minimal.

The American labor story reflects the influence of these factors.
We obviously cannot here review or document in detail every major

and minor theme in this story. One of the principal themes, however
—the evolving contest over the process of "industrial government"
—is worth rehearsing as a prologue to the climactic events of the
1930's with which we begin our review of the recent evolution of
American labor problems. It is to this theme and to some additional
comments on the nature of work in American industry prevailing on
the eve of the upheaval of the thirties that we now turn.

THE LIMITED ASSAULTS UPON INDUSTRIAL AUTOCRACY

Workers (although not all workers) from early colonial times,
and with increasing vigor as industrialism matured, sought an effective voice in the industrial rule-making process. For more than
half a century before the Civil War sporadic, localized, and discontinuous incursions into collective bargaining were interwoven with a
variety of similarly small-scale, amorphous, and short-lived reform
panaceas aimed at guaranteeing a worker-voice in shaping the work
process and in distributing its proceeds. The tempo of development
was stepped up after the Civil War, and the decades to follow were
to see a chink in the armor of industrial autocracy introduced by the
effective organization of many of the skilled elite of the work force
in a number of trades, along with some islands of organization among
the less skilled. Leaders and would-be leaders quarreled with one
another over appropriate organizational structure and alternative
strategies; but by the turn of the century the pragmatic, limited-
function union had won the day. Samuel Gompers' "business union"
and the American Federation of Labor harbored the philosophical,
if not the precise structural, kernel of future labor organization in
America.

The employer's basic concern was to retain intact his unilateral
rule-making authority which the workers wished to breach and share.
From the beginning there were a few benevolent autocrats; but for
the most part the "labor problem" for the employer consisted in:
(1) attracting a labor force; (2) setting wages, hours, and other terms
and conditions of employment with more regard to the market than
to "what was on the worker's mind"; (3) weeding out "incompetents"
and "ne'er-do-wells"; and (4) steadfastly resisting any concerted
worker efforts to encroach upon this managerial monism in industrial rule making. If hours were long, how better protect the laboring
poor from the evils inherent in idleness? If wages were low, who could
challenge the "iron law" of competition? If conditions in the mill or

the mine were ugly and hazardous, we all knew that work, the onerous burden which we have borne since the fall from grace, was not the place for self-indulgence. If children labored alongside their elders, was this not at the behest of the latter and, further, what better training ground for industry, discipline, prudence, and the myriad other virtues we sought to inculcate in our young? And finally, if the manager ruled the roost in unequivocal and unhesitating fashion, this was simply because the rights and the interests of the laboring man were to be looked after "not by the labor agitators, but by the Christian men to whom God, in His infinite wisdom, has given control of the property interests of the country."[1]

The environment in which American industrial growth proceeded tended to retard the worker's efforts to change the *status quo* in industrial government and to support the employer's efforts to retain it. The pre-1842 application of the conspiracy doctrine to combat trade unions, the post-1842 judicial interpretations which carried the individualist heritage to great lengths in stripping labor of many of its tactics, the divisions made possible by a stream of immigrants drawn from diverse backgrounds, the recurrence of business depressions, the elitist emphasis of labor leaders reluctant to adapt trade-union structure and policy to the dynamics of a changing industrial technology, the generally adverse popular sentiment—all were factors (in addition to the employer's hostility) in minimizing the opportunity of workers to act in concert as an effective agency in industrial rule making. It is also important, however, to stress the factors which for a long time minimized the propensity of workers to join or organize unions. The relative abundance of economic resources and opportunity, the fluidity and mobility among social and economic classes, pools of reasonably adequate individual bargaining power, the continuing rise in real earnings, the confusing impact of the many internecine clashes of ideology within the house of organized labor—all reaffirmed the already individualistic worker, who was oriented to the chance to advance, in his disinclination to trifle with unionism.

Where clashes occurred, they were often violent and bloody with little quarter given or expected. If feelings ran high, there was good reason for the fervor: the stakes were big—a radical shift in the procedure for enacting and enforcing rules of the industrial game. The culmination of these pressures for extensive redistribution of power in the autocratically governed domains of industry did not

come until a quarter century ago, and it was to have many repercussions for the subsequent pattern of labor problems in America.

THE NATURE OF WORK

If national environment helps to explain the belated appearance
of social legislation and the more than a century of slow-gaited union
growth, the maturation of "industrial" culture had at the same time
sown and nurtured the seeds of future change. None could have
foreseen the drastic discontinuity in the going state of affairs which
this change was to occasion when it did come; but an astute observer
standing at the threshold of the thirties—granted that retrospective
prediction makes astuteness easier to come by—could at least have
pointed to changes in the technical organization of industry which
were bound to be reflected in the changing character of labor problems. Even in the national environment, a number of the earlier
deterrents to worker opportunity or proneness to organize for bargaining collectively with an employer had worn thin: restriction of
immigration and reduced social fluidity are examples. But perhaps
the more important change was the pervasive shift in the nature of
work which had occurred by the thirties. Increased concentration of
industry was accompanied by an inevitable loss of individual bargaining power; and the advanced technology which characterizes the
American industrial system—and especially the job specialization
and repetitiveness which characterize the mass-production assembly
line—had created an anonymity and an impersonalness in the work
place.[2] This point has been stressed *ad nauseam* but nonetheless bears
re-emphasis. Industrial work often became a "job," performed for the
economic security which wages would bring and not as a satisfying
experience in itself. The job, even if it always had been so regarded
to some extent, came more and more to be looked upon as a means
to other ends, and the continuity and size of the pay envelope became the most important consideration.

There were implications in this character of the work process as it
had evolved thus far in mature industrialism for the future concerns
and behavior of workers, employers, and government:

1. With little psychic income from his job and no significant
opportunity to control the decisions affecting it and, more important,
his earnings, the American factory worker in the thirties was ready
for a process or institution which would give him and his fellows
some measure of decision-making power over his wages, his job

security, and the conditions under which he worked. If there was resigned acceptance of the depersonalized nature of work, if the outlets for self-expression were few and becoming increasingly centered outside the plant gates, the worker could at least seek to secure and increase the payoff from the job and minimize the disutilities of work. He had witnessed the continued ability of employers in most industries to safeguard their traditional unilateral authority in rule making. But in some industries (like the railroads, big-city construction, printing, and a few others) he could take notice, as well, of the effectiveness of the trade union as a vehicle to bear him from industrial autocracy to industrial democracy. Provided other conditions were right, a substantial future growth in union membership was by no means out of the question.

2. Employers had been largely successful in preserving their "managerial rights." But beneath the surface bravado of the new welfare capitalism and despite the precipitous decline from 5 to 3 million members in American unions during the twenties, there lingered doubts about how best to employ this vouchsafed authority. The now-famous "Hawthorne experiments" by Harvard Business School researchers in the Chicago plant of the Western Electric Company had set out to test the impact on worker productivity of such patent work environment variables as hours of work, illumination, and so on, only to end by unearthing the major relevance for work of that submerged nine-tenths of the iceberg, "the factory social system." These studies had an important impact on the thinking of management about the nature of work and employee morale, as did many lesser studies and writings—before and after the Hawthorne experience—of social psychologists, industrial sociologists, and practitioners in the field. If for the moment the threat of outside (union) control had been parried, there was always the possibility of resurgent challenges. This increasing concern with the effects of the depersonalization of work on the worker set more and more employers on the trail of methods and techniques which could improve "employee morale." Personnel departments were established or expanded, industrial psychologists rode the waves of a surging expanse in the market demand for their services, "human relations" took on a specialized meaning as a new professional "discipline" crystallized in the wake of Hawthorne.

Our observer at the threshold of the thirties could have suggested that the changes which had occurred in the nature of work portended, insofar as employer behavior was concerned, an extension and proliferation of his increased concern with effective "human relations" techniques for utilizing (without sharing) his rule-making authority to get the best results from worker and machine. In fact, this line of employer concern *has* continued and developed side by side with (and in many instances closely related to) the more recent major strand of employer concern—the accommodation to extensive unionism and the sharing of rule-making authority. Personnel administration has grown in importance as a management function; directors and even vice-presidents of industrial relations have sprung up where only employment managers had grown before in less favorable soil; and the grim relentlessness of earlier references to subordinated application and unquestioning obedience have given way to the cheerier patois of participation and job enlargement—sometimes as an offset to union organization or growth, but sometimes, too, as a means of improving productivity and union-management relations in a unionized society.

3. The changing nature of work also had implications for the future role of government in the handling of American labor problems. The immense complexity of the work process and the interdependence of different sectors of the mature industrial economy suggest that the community could not tolerate, except at its own peril, any drastic disruption of the productive sector. This is, of course, a continuing problem in all mature industrial societies, the American included. But it need not involve extensive direct state intervention in the industrial rule-making procedure *provided* that alternative procedures exists and are reasonably effective in creating and administering a viable web of rule in industry. The Railway Labor Act in 1926 and the Norris La Guardia Act of 1932 harbingered a hitherto novel and direct intrusion of government into the industrial rule-making process; but the precise role which government was to play in the decades ahead had to wait on history.

As affairs turned out, in fact, this concern with maintaining continuity in production and with the minimization of the potential impact of worker protest was to be the rationale for the emergence of new public policy on the encouragement and protection of union growth and on the settlement of labor disputes. The preamble to the National Labor Relations (Wagner) Act of 1935 stressed the conviction that unorganized workers lacked the power to achieve a distribution of income which would support a healthy economy and emphasized the "burden" which labor disputes, caused by denial of the right to organize and bargain collectively, put on interstate commerce by disrupting it periodically. A similar philosophy was explicit or implicit in other subsequent measures of government intervention: social security, minimum wages, and wartime wage regulation and labor dispute settlement. Despite this expanded role of government in the past few decades, we have succeeded in developing effective alternatives; and we have managed, in contrast to other industrial societies, to get *relatively* less governmental intervention on this account. But all this anticipates the recent unfolding of our labor story.

The Last Quarter Century of American Labor Problems

A little over twenty-five years ago—in 1933—the stage was set for the social revolution which was to be sparked by the Great Depression and ushered in by the New Deal. The depression shattered the surface calm and the postwar complacency of the prosperous twenties. With nearly a third of the industrial labor force unemployed, economic chaos merged into seething political and social discontent with the existing order. Change was inevitable, and change there was to be. The initial problem of substituting pluralism for monism in industrial government, the array of subsidiary concomitant issues relating to this effort to effect a shift in rule-making procedure, and the problems induced by the subsequent broad success of the effort, triggered by the New Deal, constitute the single most significant set of labor problems in the recent past. But changes affecting American labor were not confined to those growing out of the New Deal reforms in the early thirties. This past quarter century has witnessed a great World War, a postwar boom mixed with "cold war," and some business recessions—all of which have placed their mark on American labor problems. Less obtrusively, and perhaps more significant for future than for past developments, the gradually changing composition of the work force and of technology has played a role in shaping our recent labor problems. This section centers on these developments.

THE TRANSITION FROM INDUSTRIAL AUTOCRACY TO
INDUSTRIAL DEMOCRACY

The Great Depression brought government into labor problems on a scale unknown in the twenties. The year 1935 saw the passage of the Wagner Act, protecting the right of workers to join unions and bargain collectively by forbidding certain "unfair labor practices" which employers had used to discourage union membership and to avoid collective bargaining. The act also marked a major modification in a cherished American trade-union principle of "exclusive jurisdiction" for particular unions, regardless of employee wishes, by providing for governmental (National Labor Relations Board) determination of "appropriate" bargaining units and for secret ballot elections conducted by the NLRB to determine whether the employee in that unit wished to be represented by a union and, if so, which one. In the same year the Social Security Act was passed to provide certain protections against individual insecurity; and in 1938 the Fair Labor Standards (wage-hour) Act completed the major tripod on which rested the growing power of the government in the labor-management relationship.

The reaction of organized employers was instantaneous and often drastic. Through their lawyers they challenged the constitutionality of this new legislation; and the major battle on the right of government to make rules protecting workers and restricting employers was fought over the Wagner Act. In a series of decisions notable for judicial recognition of the power of the federal government to intervene in areas hitherto protected by the twin sanctities of right of contract and state's rights, the Supreme Court of the United States— before it seated any Roosevelt appointees—upheld the constitutionality of the Wagner Act in 1937.

The die was cast, but the consequences of the toss were not yet accepted. Between 1935 and 1937 the NLRB was largely powerless to enforce its orders; after 1937 it had more power, but many employers still opposed efforts to unionize their employees. This resistance, not always initially violent, often erupted into violence as tempers were aroused, epithets exchanged, bricks thrown, tear gas used by company guards, beatings administered, and blood let. All of this is chronicled in the LaFollette Senate Committee hearings, perhaps one-sidedly, but with detail for all the world to see how in the mid-thirties American employers and the new militant unions fought over the crucial decision as to how the rule-making power in an industrial society was to be shared.

What is more remarkable about this context of violence, however, is the relative peacefulness into which labor-management relations have emerged less than twenty-five years later. The heritage of conflict which has plagued other industrial societies is surprisingly absent, despite the words of conflict sometimes used by each party as a prelude to serious collective bargaining.

The tripling of union membership between 1933 and 1940 was perhaps the most rapid growth of a union movement in any industrial society; the struggle over the rule-making process in industry was one of the most dramatic. The *élan* induced by the formation of the Committee for Industrial Organization in 1935, out of disgust with old-line AFL craft union failure to organize the mass-production industries successfully, captured the energies and imagination of many militant unionists, including socialists and Communists. Great organizing drives were planned; forces were marshaled to capture the citadels of nonunion strength in steel, automobiles, electrical manufacturing, rubber, etc.; campaigns were prepared preceding NLRB elections; strikes were called, and contracts negotiated and signed. The unions remaining in the AFL were galvanized into action by this competition; the whole union movement was revitalized as the locus of rule-making power in American industry shifted from employers alone to the combination of employers, unions, and a dash of government.

This transition from industrial autocracy to the kind of industrial democracy represented by "constitutionalism" in industry has grown steadily during the past twenty-five years. Management's unilateral right to manage is no longer unchallenged; for, as one writer has put it, "a union is an employer-regulating device. It seeks to regulate the discretion of employers . . . at every point where their action affects the welfare of the men."[3] Thus the process of rule making has had to be shared with unions, through them with workers, and to a lesser extent with government (through the legislation mentioned earlier) as part of a modern welfare state.

Within the framework (set by the government) of this new constitutional industrial democracy, unions in a large sector of industry have come to represent the "opposition" to management as the industrial initiator.

> All in all, we might say that a relationship is developing which projects management as "the government of the day" and unions as "the permanent opposition"—increasingly becoming a "loyal opposition" in the political sense. That is to say, it is an opposition that puts constant pressure on "the government" to improve the substance of the union contract every time it expires, and between negotiations serves as a policing agency in the enforcement of the

contract. Beyond the corporation, the "opposition" raises questions about unemployment, recessions, purchasing power, and, in general, government action to advance the welfare of the people.

We may in fact be witnessing the development of a private or voluntary constitutional framework for our economic life which is complementary to the formal constitutional framework of our political life. . . . This development of constitutionalism stands out as a major achievement in American industrial society. It has no counterpart in Europe. What looked like irreconcilable conflict in the 1930's has given way to an orderly, civilized way of adjusting differences. Legitimate power of self-made law has been substituted for illegitimate power of violence, or for law imposed by government.[4]

IMPACT OF THE WAR, POSTWAR PROSPERITY, AND THE COLD WAR

The wartime emergency wiped out the unemployment which had persisted as late as 1940, changed the composition and distribution of the labor force, and gave new stature and strength to trade unions as maintenance of high, uninterrupted production became the primary national industrial goal. Unions were still pressing for more members and for extended power in industry; and they found aid and encouragement from a government with other things on its mind (through the War Labor Board, especially its "maintenance of membership" compromise and its elastic wage controls). The resistance from employers was also less, because of the emergency and its cost-plus contracts.

While some strikes occurred despite "no-strike pledges," as either employers or unions defied War Labor Board orders (which represented direct government intervention), the dominant pattern was one of increasing union growth and of increasing labor-management accommodation. By the end of the war there were more than 14,000,-000 union members, an increase of almost a million a year during the war. Efforts at curbing inflation and imposing a lid on wages through the War Labor Board and the economic stabilization agencies gave an impetus to wage structure manipulations, an increasing interest in such techniques as job evaluation, and the spread of "fringe" benefits like paid vacations and holidays, reporting-in time, overtime rates, and shift differentials.

Postwar prosperity, interrupted only slightly by the business recessions of 1948-1949 and 1953-1954, brought continued union growth, but at a slower rate. By 1950 there were about 16,000,000 members, and eight years later only about 18,000,000. The reasons for this deserve fuller examination later, as they help forecast the future. To go back, the end of the wartime emergency and its controls sparked a series of union wage demands and strikes which made "industrial relations" a national problem of front-page concern. Late in 1945 President Truman called a labor-management conference to help stem what appeared to be a return to the open conflict of the thirties. While several agreements were reached on such important but less dramatic problems as the settlement of disputes arising under collective agreements through the growing practice of private voluntary arbitration, there was sharp disagreement between the top management and labor representatives over the precise substantive content of "management's right to manage." While constitutionalism had grown before and during the war, it had not reached the point (if it ever will) where management and labor spokesmen would determine on a nationwide basis precisely where the line was to be drawn to delimit the zone for joint decision making. Instead, decisions over what is or is not "bargainable" continue to be hammered out from day to day and year to year in the thousands of separate collective bargaining contracts which are continually being negotiated and renegotiated in the factories, mines, and transportation systems of America.

Postwar union wage demands were, however, successful in the inflationary period which followed the war and again the Korean War. In the first wage rounds of 1946 and 1947 Presidential fact-finding boards, and even Presidential intervention, helped unions to get a favorable settlement, although the pent-up demand for goods and services was more likely the coal that stoked the fires of postwar inflation. The Korean emergency brought some wage controls, although these did little to curtail the wage settlements made by the more powerful unions, riding the wave of government defense expenditures.[5] The problem of union wage demands and inflation is still with us, but the answers are no more satisfactory than before. Economists disagree on the impact of unions on wages, both in the short run and in the long run, although there is a growing balance of informed opinion that within recent years unions have exercised an independent influence on wage levels forcing employers to grant more in wages, as well as on other terms and conditions of employment which are more directly involved in the rule-making process, than they would grant in the absence of union pressures. The dilemma thus presented for unions and for those who recognize the other values which unions bring to an industrial society is well put by Neil Chamberlain:

> An anomalous situation has thus been developing in the United States whereby if those friendly to labor unions would aid them in escaping from regulations, they must plead the economic impotence of the organizations they would protect. If one admits that the unions fulfill the economic role which they claim and do in fact bring wage advantages to their members, he is faced with the difficult question of whether existing political and economic restraints are adequate to control the organized power which he champions.[6]

This dilemma is still with us, and unresolved. But the growing power of unions led Congress to pass the Labor-Management Relations (Taft-Hartley) Act in 1947, ostensibly to balance the employer unfair labor practices of the Wagner Act with some for unions, to add new restrictions on union practices such as the secondary boycott, and to inject the government directly into disputes which threatened or created a "national emergency." The year 1947, then, was a watershed between the 1933–1937 period of growing union power supported by government intervention largely on the side of labor, and the period since 1947 when union growth has slowed down and union power continues to worry not only employers and Congressmen but large segments of the public.

At the same time, the pressures of the cold war and the growing disillusionment of the CIO under Philip Murray with the tactics of the Communists in CIO unions after the war, led to the expulsion by the CIO of eleven Communist-dominated unions in 1950. The non-Communist majority in American unions had supported the Marshall Plan and other facets of America's postwar foreign policy; the Communists opposed them, and the lines were drawn away from the collective bargaining arena as well as in it.

By the fifties the American Labor Movement was, in the words of *Fortune's* labor editor, "coming of middle age." Writing in 1951, Daniel Bell said:

> The traditional Gompers attitude, with its focus on collective bargaining and the market situation, is replacing the social planners' unionism of the last decade and a half. If it is a unionism without a defined ideology, it is by no means a softened unionism. In its typically American quest for "more," it is still a relentless challenge to American business management.[7]

With the exclusion of the Communist left and the exhaustion of the non-Communist left, with the death or aging of many of the earlier militant leader-organizers like Murray, Hillman, Lewis, Dubinsky, and others, with increasing management acceptance of unionism, stabilization of bargaining, and entrenchment of national union leadership, the "organization men" (in American labor as in American industry) seemed to be replacing the "independent spirits." The trade-union leader was becoming more and more an "industrial traffic cop" (to use William Gomberg's phrase) and less and less the firebrand prophet of a new faith. Only a Walter Reuther remained to keep alive the earlier dream of social planning along with business unionism, and he had many critics within and outside the labor movement. The essential conservatism of the American labor movement was summed up by Bell in these words: "In the deepest sense, the present-day trade-union movement has accepted capitalist society."[8]

The verbal attacks on business continued; but such public theatrics were more a part of the strategy of winning support and adherents in collective bargaining than the symptoms of a class struggle-to-the-death between implacable adversaries. Organized labor and management in America always expected to settle their differences within the rules of a private-enterprise competitive economy. Labor has challenged management's right to make the rules within the plant; it has not challenged the "rules" of the economic system itself. There has been no taste in American organized labor for nationalization of the means of production; and the spreading disillusionment with this road to Utopia in western European labor movements has helped to reinforce the American conviction.

LABOR PROBLEMS INDUCED BY THE BASIC CHANGES IN RULE MAKING AND THE GROWTH OF LABOR ORGANIZATION

A number of significant problems were associated with or induced by the major transition in rule making during the past twenty-five years. Among these were problems concerning (1) structural change in labor organizations: (2) bureaucratization and internal union democracy, (3) the scope of rule making or collective bargaining, (4) the extension of union organization, (5) union tactics and objectives, (6) employer responses and policies, and (7) governmental intervention. Our earlier "broad-brush" review has touched on all of these; here we elaborate on some of these problems and emphasize those trends and developments which suggest the directions of future change.

1. The Formal Structure of Labor Organization

Union leaders in the thirties all saw eye-to-eye on the general objective of "industrial democracy." Agreement on the appropriate means and slogans for implementing the objective was another matter. If the new government policy of encouraging trade-union growth involved a crisis for employers, it had posed a major problem for labor leaders as well. Was the craft union or the industrial union the more appropriate organizational vehicle for "liberating" the worker? Or, put another way, who was organizable and how? The consequence of the vigorous debates over the primacy of horizontal exclusiveness versus vertical solidarity was schism in the ranks of organized labor. The split, in turn, undoubtedly had its major impact on the ensuing rate of organization. Without the revamped structure of unionism, it is doubtful whether organization could have proceeded at the rate and on the scale it did in many industries. In addition, however, the split affected the tone of twenty years of industrial relations by creating some serious rivalry and jurisdictional problems for union leaders which were bound to (and did) carry over to employers and the public.

After twenty years of disunity in the "house of labor," created originally when a number of unions led by John L. Lewis and Sidney Hillman formed the Committee for Industrial Organization and were expelled from the AFL for the crime of "dual unionism," the two federations finally merged in December 1955. During those twenty years the early and dramatic CIO, by organizing drives and victories in unionizing the major centers of American mass production, had sparked equally vigorous AFL efforts which soon overtook the CIO on the membership scoreboard but which had been rendered effective only by the gradual diminution of the craft-industrial distinctions between many unions in the two federations. While John L. Lewis and his mineworkers, the original driving force in the CIO, played musical chairs between AFL, CIO, and independent affiliation (their current status), the CIO, as we have seen, struggled with the problem of its Communist-dominated unions and expelled eleven in 1950. The earlier gaps in the respective assessments by the federations of appropriate economic and political policy narrowed over time; and a roadbed to *rapprochment* was heralded as well by the signing in 1953 and 1954 of no-raiding pacts which affected a substantial number of unions in both federations. These changes, along with the death of some of the original protagonists, helped to smooth the path for the negotiations which led to a united AFL-CIO, which today represents about fifteen million of the approximately eighteen million unionized workers in the United States.

The major battle over structural change which characterized the incipient stages of the boom for unions during the thirties—the craft versus industrial unionism issue—has given way to two new structural problems in the fifties: the appropriate degree of centralization at the federation level, and the backsliding within industrial unions created by dissatisfaction among skilled workers.

The constitution of the new federation gave greater powers to the federation than the old AFL could exercise over its "international" unions, which guarded their autonomy like the original states under the Articles of Confederation or like manorial barons in medieval Europe. How effectively could the federation use these new powers? A major test came with the Ethical Practices Codes which the AFL-CIO Executive Council adopted and applied to its member unions during 1957 when it expelled the teamsters and two other international unions (and suspended two others) for failing to adhere to these codes of moral standards in the conduct of their union affairs. This was a major shift in the center of power, foreshadowed by the earlier expulsion of Communist-dominated unions by the CIO and of the corruption-ridden Longshoremen's Union by the AFL.

At the same time, the second structural problem of the fifties began to plague some of the industrial unions. Flat cents-per-hour wage increases had narrowed the differential between skilled and less skilled; some skilled groups sought to break away from industrial unions under the liberalized craft-unit provisions of the Taft-Hartley Act, and industrial unions like the auto workers' were forced to set up "skilled-trades departments" and to seek special wage adjustments for these groups. The strike of the motormen on New York subways in 1957, in protest against their treatment under an industrial union, dramatized the same issue. Yet in this and other cases both employer and industrial union opposed the breakaway for obvious reasons, and a thoughtful public saw the dilemma here emphasized between freedom for the minority and stability in labor-management relations.

2. The Impact of Bureaucratization in Internal Union Government

The tendencies toward centralized power within unions—often condemned by the same people who demand "more responsibility" from union leaders—are reflected in the bureaucratization of internal union government. As unions have matured in this country (as well as in Sweden and Great Britain, for example), the administrative demands on union leaders supplant the combative and organizing ones. Growing centralization and bureaucratization are not confined to the "natural history" of unions; they are well known tendencies in every large organization.[9] But specifically for unions, which are organized for the benefit of members and which claim to be "voluntary" private organizations, they do pose the problem of internal union democracy. Is the union a "going concern" whose survival and growth take precedence over the rights of individual members? Can an institution representing the majority tolerate dissent and opposition from the minority? The Ethical Practices Codes promulgated by the AFL-CIO Executive Council gives answers to these questions which emphasize *voluntary* action by the union movement to protect these rights—as well as to root out corruption in the unions. But the disclosures of the Senate Select (McClellan) Committee (on Improper Activities in the Labor or Management Field) investigations during 1957–1958 led to an increasing demand for legal protection: some limited, some more drastic with motives which go beyond mere protection of individual rights and threaten the survival of present-day American unions. This mixture of motives is well illustrated by the movement for state and federal "right to work" laws.

The Labor-Management Reporting and Disclosure Act enacted in 1959 seeks to prevent and eliminate some of the breaches of trust, corruption, and disregard of the rights of individual employees which the McClellan investigations revealed. It thus represents an expansion of the government's role in the confrontation of what is likely to continue as a significant labor problem for the near future—the search for appropriate limits and constraints within which group responsibility and individual freedom in the conduct of labor–management relations may co-exist and flourish.

3. The Extension of Dualism in Rule Making

As unions have grown in strength during the past twenty-five years, and as employers and management representatives have learned to accommodate to this new institution, the scope of collective bargaining has widened; and the end is not yet in sight. The dualism in rule-making which characterizes free collective bargaining has spread from questions limited to wages, hours, and working rules to an increasing variety of bargainable issues. While management was and still is concerned with containing this dualism (the management prerogative issue), the futility of "drawing the line" was demonstrated, as we have seen, as far back as the President's Labor-Management Conference in 1945, when the management representatives spelled out bargainable and non-bargainable areas, and the union representatives countered with the statement that in specific situations and industries some managements and unions had in fact reached collective agreements on many of those "non-bargainable" issues. One of the most perceptive students of collective bargaining, Neil W. Chamberlain, has concluded:

> The wide range of subjects concerning which labor unions have insisted on having something to say has led management people to raise the question, where will it end? To this question there is no answer. It seems evident that the unions will ask for provisions on any matter which they conceive to affect their members significantly, and depending on their bargaining strength they may be successful in their demands.[10]

Even so, the American union movement has not sought to share managerial responsibility. It has not been attracted by the German union's drive for "co-determination," the Swedish labor movement's interest in "enterprise councils," or the British union's earlier (now less enchanted) drive for nationalization and labor representation on the boards which are managing nationalized industries. American unions, by and large, remain in the role of critics and controllers of private enterprise managerial actions which affect employees.

4. Organizing the Unorganized

Extending union organization has always been a major concern of American unions, summed up in the battle cry "Organize the unorganized!" The initial trade-union targets of manufacturing, mining, transportation, and public utilities, and big-city construction have largely been met; yet even here pockets of employer resistance such as the southern textile industry, the chemical industry, and a few others remain to plague particular unions. Approximately 75 per cent of the total labor force in manufacturing industries is represented by unions; but this contrasts with about 5 per cent in banks and insurance, roughly the same percentage in wholesale and retail trade and in government services, and less than 20 per cent in private service industries. The comparative difficulty of organizing these industries and occupations, many of which are "white-collar," led the labor editor of *Fortune* to conclude that there would be "No Boom for Unions" in the years ahead.[11] This view was disputed by Irving Bernstein, who analyzed union growth from 1897 to 1952 and concluded that the rate of growth has continued since 1946 in line with past trends.[12] But Bell's essential point about the future organizable areas, and the environment within which further gains are possible, was not refuted in our judgment. This point is developed further in our concluding section. In any case, with less than a third of the civilian nonagricultural labor force organized today, the organizer's problems are far from over.

5. The Transition in Union Tactics and Objectives

Union tactics have shifted as the American labor movement has matured and come of "middle age." The fighting, militant unions of the great organizing days of the thirties have largely changed into the administrative collective bargaining organizations which only occasionally (and less frequently) flex their muscles in periodic struggles with employers. Strikes, when they occur, are organized and conducted more like a "war game" than war itself. Economic pressures still play a part in reaching agreement, but under rules—written and implicit—which govern the conduct of the parties. Even the charges and countercharges which are released to the press and other communication channels are usually regarded by the principals, but not as often as they should be by the less sophisticated public, as tactics in the process of reaching a mutually acceptable compromise or agreement.

While union tactics have moderated and follow a more predictable pattern, objectives of unions have not basically changed. Perhaps there has been some increased emphasis on political action through lobbying and other pressures designed to secure the passage of legislation regarded as more favorable to labor, or to defeat hostile legislation. But Gompers' dictum of "support your friends and defeat your enemies" has not changed much; and, although CIO unions did form a Political Action Committee, no real effort to organize an

American labor party has ever been made. The pluralism of the American society both in its federal-state system and in the variety of institutional loyalties which Americans have, makes such an effort as highly unlikely in the future as it has been in the past.

But increased efforts by the labor movement to enter the legislative arena have developed with the passage of laws affecting workers nationally, such as the Social Security Act, the Fair Labor Standards Act, the Wagner and Taft-Hartley Acts. Support for amendments regarded as favorable to labor, often presented as also favorable to the American people as a whole, has grown, especially with the passage of the Taft-Hartley Act. Organized labor has also supported the Full Employment Act of 1946, and it has pressed continually for governmental policies which would assure full employment and provide increased services such as better schools and highways. The public good is emphasized; but these efforts also aid the unions in their direct collective bargaining objectives by creating an economic and political environment more favorable to gains at the bargaining table. The concern of the Auto Workers Union for federal action to halt the business recession of 1957–1958 was not unrelated to the fact that unemployment in the automobile industry made its bargaining position in 1958 the weakest it has been since the union was first organized in 1937. The dilemma is not only one confronting the union: if workers cannot achieve gains through collective bargaining and if they face continued unemployment, the nation may find them turning increasingly to the political road to achieve what they consider their due. If this happens on any large scale, the American labor movement will be quite different from what it has been historically and is now.

6. *The Employers' View of the Union*

The change in employer responses and policies toward unionism—from initially violent resistance to growing accommodation and sophistication—has already been mentioned. Employers have given greater attention, both in approach and in organizational developments like industrial relations and personnel departments, to problems of employer-employee relations; and this development seems irreversible.[13] Similarly, the number of managements which have learned to deal constructively with and to accept the continued existence of trade unions has grown, although there may seem at times to be a reversal of this trend in particular cases.

In recent years what appears to the unions as an attempt to undermine them may simply be a tactic by an aggressive employer to negotiate what he conceives to be a better collective bargaining settlement. Clothing the tactic in terminology on what is "right" may only be the equivalent of the union's supporting its demands with an appeal to what is "just." With these developments—sometimes called "Boulwareism" after the General Electric vice-president of industrial relations who took the initiative in propounding and practicing more aggressive employer tactics in collective bargaining —there has been a move toward stiffened resistance by employers in some firms and industries. While this has anti-union elements, the greater probability is that American employers basically accept (though often reluctantly) the prospect of continued union strength and simply want to counter it more effectively with sophisticated bargaining tactics. At a time when the wage-cost push is at least one factor in a rising price level, this may not be the unmitigated evil that unions would have us believe.[14]

7. The State's View of the Union

Finally, as we have seen in the earlier sections, the role of government in the American labor scene has been shifting. At the opening of this twenty-five year period, government actively intervened to bring social reforms which would help to redress an imbalance that existed in the twenties between labor and management and between employees and other income groups. The passage of the Taft-Hartley Act was a reversal of this trend, as government sought to "balance" the Wagner Act and to control some of the growing economic power of unions. Moreover, some provisions of the act, and the way the NLRB has interpreted them, involved more direct government intervention in the process of collective bargaining and in the terms which agreements may include. And the act's "national emergency" provisions reflected the growing concern of the public over major disputes which threatened the public health and safety, even though it may be questioned whether many such disputes do, in fact, result in "national emergencies."[15]

Government in the United States has become increasingly a rule maker in labor-management relations. We have moved from a situation in which government first set the broad rules within which collective bargaining and industrial risks could take place to one in which government is narrowing these limits and determining *what* the parties can do by private agreement between themselves. Thus governmental regulation of the administration of health and welfare funds is inevitable, as is some form of protection of the civil rights of union members within the union. Yet the threat of these regulations has served to increase the degree of self-restraint by unions, just as it did earlier by employers who were anxious to avoid NLRB cases. The AFL-CIO Ethical Practices Codes reflect the growing concern of unions with the threat of punitive legislation, and union-originated procedures such as the Public Review Board established by the United Auto Workers "to preserve the integrity of the union" are another example. Governmental intervention has also resulted in joint efforts to keep disputes out of government hands, as is illustrated in the growth of private voluntary arbitration, the establishment of the National Joint Board for the settlement of jurisdictional disputes in the building trades, and the no-raiding agreements between unions within AFL-CIO. Both employers and unions in the United States oppose the kind of governmental intervention represented by compulsory arbitration of labor disputes; and, even though some states have passed laws affecting public utilities, there has been no peacetime effort to introduce the kind of national system which is found in Australia, New Zealand, India, and some other countries. In sum, although collective bargaining is probably less "free" than it was at the outset of the twenty-five year period, it is still more "free" from governmental intervention than collective bargaining is in any other major industrial country. This, too, is a reflection of the values which most people share in the American democratic society.

The relative nonintervention has had its severest test recently during the controversy over the impact of unions on wages and prices. Demands are made by employer organizations that union "monopolies" be subjected to the antitrust laws (from which they were largely freed by a series of Supreme Court decisions during the thirties and early forties) and that their economic power be "curbed." Whether these groups also consider that wage controls might mean price and profit controls is not clear; nor is the connection between free collective bargaining, full employment, and price stability well understood. These issues are too complex to examine here, but it can be said that up to 1960, at least, the American people through their government had not yet taken a step down the road which would bring the full power of government into the collective-bargaining, private price making, free-enterprise process and possibly spell the end of them all. At the same time, neither organized labor nor big management had yet demonstrated the kind of self-restraint, as they have in other areas of their relationship, which would help to avoid and postpone increased governmental intervention.

GROWING IMPACT OF SCIENCE AND TECHNOLOGY

We conclude this review of a quarter century of American labor problems with a few comments on the impact of science and technology, which is likely to be even greater in the years ahead than it has been during the past twenty-five years. Private and public expenditures for research and development, according to one estimate, have risen ninefold since 1940, and "the total expended on basic research probably has trebled or quadrupled in the past ten years."[16] While private capital spending fell off during the 1957–1958 recession, a recent survey indicates that business research and development expenditures will increase by 1961 to 35 per cent above their 1957 level.[17] Assuming a Gross National Product of $560 billion by 1965, in line with long-term economic growth since 1940, the number of employed people in the labor force will rise from 63.2 million in 1955 to 74 million, even with an estimated 6 per cent reduction in working hours and minimum unemployment of around 2.4 million.[18] The impact of science and technology is such that the greatest occupational increases in employment are estimated to occur in the professional and technical, clerical and sales, and skilled craftsmen groups, while employment among laborers and farm workers will decline still further.

These projections reflect trends during the past quarter century or more. For example, employment in the goods-producing sector of the economy (mining, contract construction, and manufacturing) has been declining relative to employment in the services sector: particularly in wholesale and retail trade, finance, insurance and real estate, service industries, and government.[19] This shift from a goods to a services society, which occurs in all advanced industrial systems, has changed the composition of the labor force by increasing the "white-collar" occupations at the expense of the "blue collar." The labor force is better educated and tends to have different expectations as a consequence. We have seen how this has slowed down union growth in the last decade; and it will be a continuing problem for union organizing efforts.

Accelerated technological and economic change has accompanied the increased emphasis on industrial research and development; but in the expanding full-employment economy since the war, the labor

problems resulting from this have been minimal. The auto workers'
drive for the "guaranteed annual wage" (which became "supple-
mentary unemployment benefits" when the first agreement was
negotiated with Ford and spread to the rest of the industry) was,
in part, the result of actual or anticipated loss of employment as a
consequence of technical and economic changes. "Automation" is
only the most dramatic of technical changes; and fears of it increase
among workers in proportion to the extent that alternative employment opportunities, with provision for retraining and temporary lay-
off compensation, are not available.

The economy's concern for rising productivity has not yet clashed
head-on with labor's concern for security. American unions and unorganized workers have not basically opposed technological and
economic change; they have sought to control and moderate its
impact on them. The "annual improvement factor" which General
Motors and the UAW first negotiated in 1948 (and renewed in
subsequent contracts at higher levels) was presented by both parties
as a way of recognizing the need for higher productivity and technical
change while sharing the benefits of these with the labor force of
the company. Other labor-management agreements have worked out
different accommodations, without in most cases seriously limiting
management's ability to function efficiently. If anything, the pressures
of unions for higher wages and other gains which directly increase
labor costs have put additional pressures on management to increase
efficiency more often than union policies have directly hamstrung
managerial efficiency.

All of these postwar developments reflect, of course, the underlying
favorable level of employment, together with the primary concern
of American organized labor, for collective-bargaining progress at the
plant level. What the future brings will depend on one's assumptions
(among others) about the future level of economic activity in relation to the probable changing distribution of the labor force in line
with past trends, and the impact of these on the strength and policies
of the American labor movement. We turn now to some concluding
comments on the probable trends and drifts which lie ahead.

A Look Ahead

What continuities and what changes in our labor story (and in
the factors which shape it) do we anticipate for the near future and

what do these portend for the kinds of labor problems we are likely to encounter in the next decade or two? Many of our premises for projection have already been underscored in our earlier comments. To this extent, our look ahead affords an opportunity to recapitulate past trends as well as the occasion to speculate on further developments. We have made no effort at completeness in these speculations, nor should they be regarded as *predictions*. The best we can offer are *projections* premised on judgments about the imperatives and impulses transmitted by yesterday's trends and drifts rather than tomorrow's surprises. John T. Dunlop has aptly put this *caveat* for us:

> It should be possible to identify and to project underlying or secular tendencies in our institutions. But dramatic and substantial changes appear to take place in brief climactic periods of depression, crises, or war. In some respects these sudden changes only make evident forces that have been at work for long periods, as when a cliff crashes into the sea as a consequence of many years of erosion. The climacteric only reveals what was going on for a long time. In other respects, however, the specific conditions of depression, crises, and war themselves fashion the course of events and provide distinctive and new tendencies for many years. The distinctive influence of these climactic periods is a major indeterminateness and error term in all projections of trends into the future. All projections must be hedged against the possibility of such periods.[20]

SOME PREMISES FOR PROJECTION

1. We assume, first that there will be no sharp discontinuities in the prevailing cold war climate in international relations. If a look ahead is worth the venture at all, the obliterating impact of a hot war's transcontinental exchange of H-bombs and atomic missiles is the first thing to impound behind a *ceteris paribus* wall. Total peace in the near future is an equally remote alternative.

2. There will be no second Great Depression. George H. Hildebrand's (and our) optimism reflects the generally prevailing mood among economists on this score:

> In looking ahead ten years, the question naturally arises: will we have another great depression? I do not think so. We have learned a great deal about combating depressions. Tax policy, public spending and monetary policy are now recognized to be weapons of great power for stabilizing economic growth. Within the economy many forces are at work to sustain growth: longer range business planning, much

emphasis upon industrial research and development, broad investment opportunities for a growing urbanized population, and wage
rates that are reasonably well geared to rising productivity while
increasingly resistant to cuts during slack periods.

This does not mean that no fluctuations can ever again occur
in our economy. However, there is reason to believe we can prevent
another great depression; that long-term growth is a practical objective for policy.[21]

3. There will be continued general acceptance of the welfare
state and the concomitant role of social insurance as an instrument
of general economic welfare in addition to its traditional role of
securing individual welfare.

Today social insurance is deeply built into the general business
economy as well as into the family economy. It is an essential and
recognized aspect of industrial relations. Industries with private
welfare and pension plans build upon and integrate with social
insurance. Personal savings and investments are widely tied in with
social insurance expectations. Without OASDI many private retirement and life insurance plans would collapse. . . .

Income insurance plays a crucial and acknowledged role in maintaining buyer and seller confidence in continuous capacity to pay
which is a foundation of our instalment-purchasing consumption
patterns.

In short, the institution of social insurance is now being recognized as an instrument of business welfare as well as of individual
welfare. . . . Arthur Larson recently warned that it was vital that the
"American public in general, and the business community in particular" be apprised "that a complete income insurance system is
an indispensable adjunct both to a modern private-enterprise economy
and to a modern individualistic free society." We believe this view
is in fact beginning to break through the business community.[22]

4. We have already pointed to the changing composition of the
labor force and to the long-term drift to an increasingly automated
technology. We are confident of the general direction (if not the
precise year-by-year estimates) of the projection of these trends into
the next decade or two. Our labor force is an "aging" one. There
will be a continued increase in the number and proportion of women
workers and in the number of persons seeking part-time work. And
the turning point in the occupational structure of our work force
which came in 1956, when for the first time in United States history
the number of white-collar workers exceeded the blue-collar workers,

will not be reversed. Automation—even if we assume that it is extremely unlikely to "race through our economy like a forest fire" during the next decade or so—will nonetheless continue as a "lusty and fast-stepping development likely to pick up speed as time goes on."[23]

5. The continuing primacy of "security" as a major concern of workers is projected on the basis of past experience and buttressed by the implications of the forementioned premises for the future. The assumption of "no great depression" hinges in large part on the premise that the techniques we have for combating large-scale sustained unemployment will be utilized by either political party under the pressures of a security-conscious populace. The continuing and growing role of social insurance turns on the same security theme. The aging population in general and the projected increasing proportion of the labor force in the ages above forty-five suggest that increasing attention will be focused on stability and security rather than on mobility incentives. The displacement threat of automation will surely bring with it increasing concern for cushioning transitional shocks both to the worker and the community. The initial booing a few years ago and the more recent applauding of the UAW's supplemental unemployment benefits scheme by the union's members[24] is symbolic of the underlying emphasis on security which surfaces at the first threatening signs of gathering clouds.

6. The major breakthrough in the extensive transition from monism to dualism and, more recently, pluralism in the industrial rule-making process is behind us, and, where collective bargaining (with a minor assist from government in a still limited number of substantive areas) currently prevails, it will remain as the established mode of making and enforcing the variety of rules which affect an industrial work force. Employers who currently share decision-making power with unions have come increasingly to accept the continuance of this procedure for formulating a code of industrial jurisprudence. In his own recent look ahead at industrial relations in 1975 John S. Bugas, Vice-President, Industrial Relations of the Ford Motor Company, typifies this view when he anticipates that the UAW will continue to represent in the future, as now, the great bulk of hourly employees.

> I would also predict that we will continue to place basic reliance on the collective bargaining process for dealing with . . . differences and problems. . . . With all its imperfections—and there are many

of them—collective bargaining is the only process we in this country have been able to hit upon to resolve disputes between management and its organized employees in a manner consistent with our American ideals of individual freedom and free competitive enterprise.[25]

Implicit in our premise about the continuance of an already institutionalized collective-bargaining process is the additional assumption that the legal and social climate over the next decade or two will involve no drastic and abrupt changes to threaten the viability of this mode of rule making in industry.

Further, unions will continue to function chiefly (although not exclusively) as agencies for collective bargaining, and the structural trends to which we have pointed will continue. The bulk of organized labor will fall within the jurisdictions of a small (and perhaps increasingly smaller) number of national unions. These unions will be multi-industrial and multi-occupational in scope. The major bargain or bargains in many manufacturing industries will continue to provide "patterns" or "keys" for smaller and independently negotiated contracts. And the trend toward multi-plant, regional, and, to some lesser extent, even industry-wide bargaining is strong and steady. Increasing intercraft mobility, mechanization of craft operations, and the extension of jurisdiction to cover new jobs created by technological development, employer demands for "one bargain" with related crafts, the growing importance of the multi-plant corporation operating in a variety of industries (as defined by product categories), the general anti-competitive trend within organized labor effected by the merger, and the many advantages of size *per se* are but a few of the factors which have accounted for this increased centralization in collective bargaining.[26]

SOME LABOR PROBLEMS FOR THE FUTURE

What are some of the implications of our review of the past and of these premises for the character of tomorrow's labor problems? We outline first a number of considerations concerning the *procedural* aspects of fashioning work relationships in the near future and conclude with a few conjectures on the changing *substance* of the "rules" themselves.

1. *The rule-making relationships*

The anguished hue and cry against the disintegrating impact of Taft-Hartley notwithstanding, trade-union leaders had, as far back as a decade ago, ceased being seriously concerned with survival. By the late forties primary concern had gone beyond survival per se to expansion and extension of sovereignty. The next decade or two will pose a variety of issues for trade-union officialdom; by no means the least of these will continue to turn on the rate of union growth. How successful will be the efforts to extend union organization? Conjecture on this point is a first step toward speculation on the character of the industrial rule-making process which we may expect in the future.

There are many elements in our projected picture of tomorrow which, in combination, suggest that trade-union leaders may have to run hard merely to maintain an aggregate membership which will constitute a proportion of the growing nonagricultural work force roughly equivalent to the present one-third. Here are some of the formidable barriers to a successful major organizational breakthrough in the years ahead. A currently "bad press" will (whether deservedly or not is irrelevant) spill over for at least a few years into the future to tar the whole movement and impede recruiting. A continuing higher rate of growth in the services and white-collar sectors relative to the blue-collar areas and the concomitantly increasing proportions of women, professional, managerial, and technical workers will mean tougher organizational sledding on many of the counts which have traditionally obstructed organization in these sectors. The relatively small size of plant in the unorganized sectors of work no longer affords the economies of scale in organization which prevailed in the past. Industrialization in the traditionally hostile-to-unionism South and west south central areas continues with no indication that the cultural barriers to organization will break down in the near future. The growing suburbanization of the work force makes access to workers more difficult and helps to further the diffusion of nonwork-centered interests. Continuing generally high income levels (conceding that economic motives are not the sole spur to organization) will make the "underdog" appeal generally less effective. The increasing sophistication of management in adopting and adapting personnel policies and affording tandem benefits for unorganized workers will make extension of unionization all the more difficult.[a]

[a] The growing and continuing concern given by management to the development of effective employer-employee relations policy which stops just short of a formal sharing of rule-making power was discussed earlier. For an illustration of the broad concern with the issue, see the recently promulgated code of ethics drawn up by the National Association of Manufacturers; and for an interesting

Finally, there is the changed role of the labor organizer himself. The organizer who once considered his work a "calling" and thought in terms of selfless devotion to a "cause" has also come more recently to look upon his work as a mere "job" and has devoted much of his recent energies to organizing his own ranks to bargain collectively with his employer, the AFL-CIO itself, over terms and conditions of employment. This bureaucratized *esprit* somehow fails to conjure up images of a spirit of dedication which can be relied upon to advance on and conquer the citadels of the opposition, whatever the odds or the costs.

There are, to be sure, other factors which may mitigate the effects of those just listed: joining a union carries less of a stigma now than it did thirty years ago; there will undoubtedly be some second-and third-generation carry-over of union membership inheritance; continuing inflationary pressures over the next decade or two may coincide with wage lags in some unorganized sectors without built-in escalator clauses on top of improvement-factor clauses and thereby spur interest in unionization; and the merger and the no-raiding pacts will release more time from the musical chairs game of exchanging memberships—time which may be devoted to organizing new members. In addition, there may well be some major shake-up in the leadership approaches toward organization. The emphasis of the traditional bravado of the organizer's proclamation that "white collar workers are just like any other workers, but . . ." may be reversed to stress the overriding verities of what follows the "but" and result in a "new look" in organizational techniques aimed at professional and white-collar occupations. A la Madison Avenue, we may see a switch from "hard" to "soft sell", and we may witness an increasingly community relations oriented appeal. These qualifications, however, are likely to be of minor import in affecting the general projection of relative saturation of union growth for the near future.

How important or genuine a problem all this may present to the trade-union leadership is a matter of conjecture. The public image of the trade-union leader (and particularly the federation leader) *requires*, in a sense, that "organizing the unorganized" be considered and bruited as a "serious problem." The missionary is morally and

discussion of the detailed implementation of such policy in one specific instance, see Paul L. Davis, "Are Personnel Policies Different in a Non-Union Plant?" reprinted from Management Report No. 1, American Management Association, 1957.

publicly committed to extend the gospel of hope and liberation to all
potential converts to and benefactors from the faith. In his role as
proselytizer the labor leader will undoubtedly continue to talk about
and periodically act upon the need to organize the unorganized. In
those areas where organization is already substantial, the union
security clause can insure extension of the faith at a pace in step
with accretions to the labor force in these sectors; and we may see, in
addition, mopping-up campaigns which will be pressed with vigor
where the odds on success are about even.

Converting the aborigines in the trackless wastes of the services
sectors and the white-collar occupations is another matter entirely.
There will be rounds of proffering the lifeline to salvation, but the
odds here are heavy on repeated rebuffs. And the missionary, after
a few such disappointing rounds, may recall that he is simultaneously
bureaucrat and businessman with commitments to a going constitu-
ency of sizable (if minority) proportions. He may well end by hanker-
ing publicly after the bird in the bush and may even flourish the
organizational net occasionally. But at the same time, and in more
private moments, he may conclude that the gap between the ideal of
an all-encompassing unionism and the actuality of a going, if at times
uneasy, rule-making partnership in only a portion of work is not too
bad a showing after all. There will also be the continuing and perhaps
increasing efforts to attend to and protect the more immediate pressures and interests of those within the fold to occupy the bulk of his
attention; and the alternative path of more vigorous political activity
to improve and extend social welfare and insurance programs could
conceivably appease any residual yearnings which may be geared to
the definition of his role as "social movement" leader.

The projection of stability in the *relative* size of trade unionism is
not inconsistent with the further projection of an increasing role
for government as regulator of the procedural aspects of industrial
rule making. The *absolute* size of unionism is already substantial,
and it directly affects the working lives of many millions of workers.
The fact that unions are private and voluntary (although less so than
a quarter century ago) associations does not alter the fact that some
of the consequences of their internal operations and of their external
behavior may be legitimate matters for public concern and will not
deter continuing and perhaps increasing scrutiny and intervention by
government in a number of procedural problem areas. The problems
of corruption, violence, and industrial conflict will persist and receive

periodic attention, but, in the larger perspective, they will be relatively sporadic and minimal issues. Racketeers and despoilers of union treasuries have always been confined to relatively few unions; violence as a tactic in industrial relations has waned considerably, and there is little prospect for the resurrection of brute force as a major strategy in the future; and the impact of industrial disputes may exert even less strain on the volume and continuity of production in the future than in the past. The currently headlined problem of worker freedoms within the union is both more complex and more pervasive and promises to draw increasing attention not alone from government in its attempts to guarantee (without regulating in detail) secret elections, effective due process procedures, etc., in the internal affairs of unions but also from trade-union leaders as well. Provoked by the public limelight and emergent public policy to more careful self-scrutiny and self-corrective revisions in demonstrably defective attitudes and procedures, trade-union leaders are likely to give (as they have already begun) increasing attention to the relationship between themselves and rank and file members.

The projected failure of unionism to advance significantly beyond its current relative size should not be interpreted as a reversal of the trend toward affording the worker effective sanctions to protect his own interests in industrial rule making and enforcing. In the organized sectors of work the continued exercise of self-expression will be encouraged by the increasing efforts of both public and union leaders to insure an effective worker voice in an institutionalized union structure. In the nonunion sectors, workers' sanctions may be less direct but effective nonetheless. The potential ultimate sanction of available unionization, coupled with the pressures of market forces (in a context of relative labor scarcity, skill shortages, full employment goals, and progressive industrial growth), will push many managers in these sectors toward a "voluntary" democratization of personnel policy and procedure which may fall short of going procedure in the unionized sectors by no more than the union label. The substance of the emergent web of rule in these sectors will, at worst, lag and, at best, outstrip (to evade) union achievements. The democratizing impact of effective unionism in a minority but sizable portion of the work force, operative in a full-employment welfare state setting, may not spill over into the remotest nook and cranny of the nonunion sector of work but may well be pervasive enough to dispatch the traditional symbolic slogan, "Organize the unorganized!" to a gradual obsolescence through disuse following on the heels of repeated and continuing unsuccessful use.

2. *The web of rule*

What are some of the substantive issues which are likely to compel attention in the years ahead?

a) The problems of manpower utilization and allocation will increasingly concern unions, managers, and the public. The training and retaining of new skills for automation, the technological race spurred by the Sputniks, the relative scarcity of "prime" age groups in the work force, the increasing demands for professionals, managerial and supervisory personnel of a progressing industrialism—all will make more dramatic the urgency of utilizing fully and allocating appropriately available skills as well as the need to create by formal and on-the-job education the additional supply demanded.

The consequences of this emphasis on better utilization of manpower will be reflected in a number of ways. The increased number of younger people in the labor force by 1965, as well as the larger proportion of women over thirty-five, will require some re-structuring of jobs, possibly to arrange partial shifts to utilize part-time workers who either cannot or do not want to work a full day or shift. The shortages in the prime age groups by 1965 will put a greater premium on better selection, placement, and training of workers, especially if a firm wants to avoid a labor turnover. It will be easier for people in these age groups to move if they are dissatisfied, and management will consequently need to pay greater attention to how they are placed and handled. These shortages may also call for changes in job structure to make work more interesting and satisfying. There is increasing recognition that routine, specialized, repetitive tasks bring frustration to many people. Fortunately, automation may change a good deal of this by eliminating much of the routine, repetitive work performed by human beings and by requiring instead more maintenance and service workers. And what has been called "job enlargement"—adding varied and related duties to a man's job rather than overspecializing it—may become an increasing concern of management, particularly in dealing with professional and technical manpower. Finally, the relative shortages in the prime age groups will put a premium not only on the more effective utilization of younger workers and older married women but also on the so-called "minority" groups in the labor force—Negroes, other minority racial groups, and, not least, older workers over sixty or sixty-five who may be willing and able to continue working beyond the retirement limit.[27]

b) Automation will give a new dimension to some old and familiar labor and industrial relations problems. Perhaps the major problems will turn on the displacement of labor and the provisions of social shock absorbers to ease the transitions which major technical change will occasion. It is true that the introduction of automation involves considerable time between initiation and operation—"time for company, union and employees to plan and adjust, if they are adequately informed and provided with resources enough to get through the inevitable transition period."[28] And it should be re-emphasized that the impact of automation, which is, in particular cases, to eliminate jobs, will come at a time when there will be relative manpower shortages in the prime age groups, and we cannot even be certain that the larger number of young people entering the labor force between now and 1965 will become permanent employees.[b] These deterrents to consequences of catastrophic or alarming proportions notwithstanding, it would be foolish to pretend that automation will not abolish many jobs; and "there is bound to be a new influence at work which will strengthen the arguments of those who feel that wage earners ought not to bear the main brunt of technological change."[c]

In this connection, then, we are likely to see a number of problem areas rethought or given added emphasis in collective-bargaining negotiations. Typical among these basic questions are (1) the content and classification of new jobs, (2) the wage rates for such new or

[b] As we know, many young girls take jobs until they are married. Thus some of the Boston insurance companies find that introduction of "automation" in the office is necessary to avoid chronic labor shortages in the years ahead, just as the telephone company found that it could not have expanded its services to meet growing demand if it had not been able to introduce the automatic dial system.

[c] Shultz and Baldwin, op. cit., p. 17. A recent AFL-CIO publication stresses this point: "Unions in the United States are not opposed to and do not stand in the way of technological improvement . . . They typically cooperate with and indeed frequently encourage and stimulate management efforts to improve technology. . . . At the same time . . . unions are also greatly concerned about the manner in which technological change is introduced. They want an orderly procedure for joint management-union consideration of possible adverse effects on workers. . . . Unions believe that management has a positive responsibility to soften any blow of new technology on its workers. The workers should not be forced to carry all of the sacrifice or burden of adjustment. . . . To put it another way, management should devote some of the savings to be gained from introduction of new equipment to the easing of adverse effects on workers." AFL-CIO Collective Bargaining Report, April-May, 1958, p. 25.

changed jobs, (3) the selection of workers to fill the jobs, (4) provision for training or retraining required workers for the new jobs, (5) provisions for workers affected by demotion, transfer or severance. Thus the issues of hours of work, severance pay, guaranteed annual wages or supplemental unemployment benefits, wage structure and methods of wage payment, job classification and seniority units are all potential candidates for increasing attention and reconsideration. Further, the nature of technical change and the character of the labor force will most probably push in the direction of loosening or discarding many of the traditional rigidities built into current standards and procedures in these problem areas. Narrow and rigid job classifications fostered by discontinuous and highly specialized methods of production may well be broadened as automated processes integrate several operations and require more generalized knowledge of an operation.

The new emphasis on integration of heretofore separate and specialized operations and the prospects of increased job changes and personnel transfers to meet the demands for a more flexible work force will push in the direction of broader seniority units and expanded seniority standards. Continuous flow, round-the-clock operations may make second-and third-shift operations a more normal phenomenon; and technical advance will continue to support the long-run trend toward shorter hours. Individual piecework incentive systems and methods of wage payment are bound to be radically affected by automated technology and by the shift from goods to services occupations.

There are a few additional consequences of automation worth noting: (1) automation will permit greatly improved working conditions; and John Diebold has made the point that we can anticipate a substantially increased amount of leisure on the job.[29] The significance of this point is well put by Robert Dubin:

> It is one of the paradoxes of automated operations that the human work force associated with it will be more productive, yet require less attention to on-going operations. . . . In servicing on-going operations, a good deal of time will be spent in watching and waiting . . . the "tightness" of industrial discipline that has grown up to control behavior of machine operators will tend to be relaxed in favor of accommodating automation specialists in their self-image as professionals capable of policing their own personal behavior. These specialists will have greater freedom to associate freely with each

other, doing their work as necessary, rather than having to give the appearance of being continually busy.[30]

(2) Managers—over and above the concern of society at large—will find themselves increasingly concerned with appropriate training and education techniques in their efforts to obtain an adequate supply of scarce skills and as a consequence of worker demands for retraining provisions. These demands in the work force, and through the unions representing it, for company emphasis on retraining displaced workers for further employment *in the company* will be particularly strong if benefits provided by the various "fringe" security provisions of the employment contract remain contingent on continuity of employment with one company. Management will, in addition, be confronted with the problem of reviewing and revising the functional and organizational layout of its managerial operations.

(3) In addition to the problems of recruiting presented by the changing nature of work and the occupational distribution of the work force, trade unions will be faced with the disturbing issue of revamping and renegotiating traditional jurisdictional boundaries.

c) On the wage front, we expect that the issue of inflation will continue to focus increasing (if not exclusive) public attention upon the impact of trade-union wage policy. The general level of money wages has since World War II advanced by about 60 per cent and productivity by a little less than 30 per cent. Although unit labor costs had generally lagged behind price increases up to 1955, by then it was clear that labor costs were pushing prices and real wages were running ahead of productivity. There has been a good deal of dispute among economists over what has been the net effect of collective bargaining on the general level of money wages. What is less in dispute is the projection of a long-term, continued inflationary trend.[d] The reasonableness of this prediction is supported by the expectation of continued strong unions in those sectors in which

---

[d] Depending upon the assumptions made about the average annual rate of increase in money wages, the concomitant rates of increase in non-labor costs, and the offsetting average annual rate of increase in aggregate productivity, estimates of the rise in the general price level between now and 1975 have varied from about 20 to 70 per cent. See, for example, Lloyd G. Reynolds, "The General Level of Wages," in *New Concepts in Wage Determination*, edited by George W. Taylor and Frank C. Pierson, 1957; John T. Dunlop, "The Secular Outlook: Wages and Prices," paper presented to Conference on Changing Concepts of Compensation, 1957; and Clark Kerr, "The Prospects for Wages and Hours of Work in 1975," paper delivered at Michigan State University, 1957 and published in the volume edited by Jack Stieber, *op. cit.*

they are already established, the increasing relative scarcity of labor and specific skill shortages, the continued pressures for high levels of full employment and concomitant permissive monetary policy, the continuing high premium placed on labor peace, and the irreversibility of the shift from goods to services where productivity increases may be more difficult to come by. In any case, until the specific role of the trade union in this process is clarified and for just so long as concern continues over rising price levels,[e] there will persist this particularly contentious labor problem. Some will suggest extreme policy proposals such as broad reinterpretation or revision of the antitrust laws to make "big" collective bargaining impossible; others will minimize the scope of the problem. Daniel Bell has, for example, recently suggested that

> unions have reached the limits of collective bargaining. . . . By the "limits of collective bargaining" [he proceeds] I mean simply the growing awareness by unions that they can obtain wage and welfare increases equal only to the increases in the productivity of the country . . . the importance of the productivity wage-increase is that, despite the lingering rhetoric of militancy, unions have accepted the idea of limits to what can be obtained through collective bargaining. I do not mean to suggest that there will be no more bargaining. But we have here the *bureaucratization* of bargaining in the establishment of limits.[31]

This characterization is still far from the mark in describing the general approach toward collective bargaining today; but it may turn out to be a tolerably accurate description of tomorrow's mode in

[e]Sumner H. Slichter, for example, has recently questioned whether this issue warrants the attention it attracts or the worry it evokes. In a question put to Mr. Leland Hazard, who had stressed the primary importance of this issue, he states: "Mr. Hazard, aren't you greatly exaggerating this problem? . . . What has happened is that, instead of going up in . . . violent ways, having speculative booms followed by severe collapses, we haven't had speculative booms, and we haven't had severe collapses. Today something has become clear which we had in the old days but didn't see as part of the business cycle—the floorwalker's creep. I think our present problem is of secondary or tertiary importance compared to the problems we got rid of. We are much better off today than we've ever been. I don't think that creeping inflation is anything to be alarmed about. When you asked where shall we stop, I don't see necessarily why we should stop anywhere, though perhaps in the next ten or twenty years, as the white-collar population becomes dominant and the old-fashioned trade union becomes a smaller and smaller part of the community, we shall solve this problem not by policy but by social change." See *The Next Twenty Years in Industrial Relations, op. cit.*, p. 82.

bargaining. Unions have responded initially to the attack on inflation by disavowing all contributory responsibility. With continuing public interest, exculpation may be buttressed by repeated justifications of bargaining demands as non-inflationary (witness the UAW approach in early 1958); and with time the broad limits Bell talks of may actually come to be considered more in the nature of rough criteria than window-dressing rationalization for public consumption. Easing of inter-union rivalries and periodic hold-the-line efforts of employers reacting to restraining competitive forces (inter-industry product substitution, capital substitution, nonunion firm competition, etc.) will act here to complement the restraining effects of continued public scrutiny. Bell's limits, however, even under the most auspicious of conjunctures, would tend to be very rough indeed.

We have already briefly touched on a few of the wage structure issues which we may anticipate. In the long run the further compression of inter-occupational and inter-industry differentials may be expected to continue as disutility comes to assume an increasing primacy over skill in advancing industrialism accompanied by widespread educational (skill-producing) facilities. The trend may, however, be slowed down substantially in the next decade or so as skilled trades strive to reassert pressures for retaining differentials and as automation and spurred-on national security programs proceed at a rate faster than the rate at which new required skills are produced by the educational plant. Such decelerators, however, are not likely to reverse the process of compression which has now been proceeding for a long time. It is quite probable that by 1975 or 1980 the average margin for skill will be below the current figure of nearly 50 per cent. Clark Kerr has summed up the consequences of this new equality as follows:

> While there is turmoil and discontent in the process, when this period of change is over there will be more equality of net advantage among people, and this will have more favorable social and political consequences. Who then will be low-status and who high-status; who liberal and who conservative?
>
> This new wage system, with its greater equality, will not be the result of socialism but rather of industrialization. Wage structures around the world have behaved very much the same way, whether in Russia or the United States. The process of industrialization makes demands which go beyond the ideology of the nation. But this process of achieving greater equality of net advantage may come about rather

better and more readily under democratic capitalism, with its emphasis upon popular education and mobility and many centers of decision-making power, than in a more authoritarian system based upon an ideology, even an ideology emphasizing equality. As this process moves along, there will in the end, almost inevitably, be less tension in society as the wage structure conforms more nearly to "justice," as the poor become richer and the rich become poorer, as people have more nearly the same economic and social position, as political outlooks become more consistent one with another; and all this not as the result of an ideology but of industrialization and the pressure it exerts on the labor market.

d) Hours of work in the coming decades will not constitute a single issue, but a concatenation of issues pulling and hauling in different directions. When hours of work were very long, the bond which united the various efforts to shorten the work day and the work week was essentially a humanitarian one. But within the past century we have seen the work week about halved; and the hours issues of the future will not hang on excessive daily or weekly fatigue occasioned by overlong hours of work. As productivity increases, we shall undoubtedly see some share of this increase accruing to leisure as well as to income. But the proportions and the nature of the solutions will vary widely from work group to work group, union to union, location to location. It is likely, on the basis of the recent "moonlighting" binge, that the share going to income will be higher than that taken in increased leisure. Debates over the appropriate hours "standards," however, have already begun: a four-day week versus a six-hour day versus extended vacations and more holidays, etc. Kerr, in the paper referred to above, has in fact suggested that the upshot may well be that

> the concept of the "standard" work week may largely disappear in a welter of arrangements as men have more real choice in the distribution of their leisure hours. The new "standard," to the extent that there will be any "standard" at all, may be in terms of hours scheduled per year which now run a little less than 2,000 and by 1975 may be a little over 1,700. By that time we may be talking about a "1,700 a year" contract instead of a "40 a week" one. Putting it this way gives men a better chance to get an optimum distribution of their leisure time around the year and limits them less in their range of choices than does the emphasis on the scheduled work week alone (p. 12).[32]

e) A new "joint paternalism," introduced under the innocuous label of "fringe" benefits, has within the past decade and a half, in effect, wrought something of a minor revolution in the concept of the wage bargain. A network of private social security systems negotiated jointly by unions and employers has sprung up where once stood a few unilaterally and paternally conferred gratuities. Nor are the costs of these security systems any longer marginal additions to payrolls. Fisher and Chapman[33] have described the big costs of little fringes which on the basis of various estimates are said to run in the neighborhood of one-fifth of total payroll. The powerful security drives of the worker, the incentive (to improve morale and productivity, reduce turnover, etc.) motives of the employer, the failure of the public systems of social insurance to adjust benefits upward with inflation, and the widening range of security guarantees sought by workers have all propelled this movement. There is little to suggest that the first two interests will dampen in the near future. Yet, in the light of some of our comments concerning the impacts of automated technology and the needs for increased flexibility and mobility in the work force of the future, it is conceivable that some minor modifications in this new manorialism and its binding ties may be forthcoming. Individual employers, in the face of increasing displacement and work force reshuffling problems, may be unwilling or unable to shoulder the costs which worker demands for security will seek to impose upon them if continuity of employment with a single employer is the price of securing the various protections against health, sickness, and old-age hazards. The consequence may well be some sacrifice of the incentive value of security guarantees and an increased effort to spread the "fringe" cost burden via the introduction or spread of area-wide or industry-wide vesting of benefits. In addition, we may see an increasing concerted attempt to get society at large to shoulder more and more of these costs.

The major issue and some of the main battles of a quarter century ago turned on the transfer and redistribution of power to make and enforce rules governing work relationships. By the end of the next quarter century this issue will have receded into the background. The heritage of pluralism in American polity has been irreversibly extended to American industry. In the unionized sectors of industry collective bargaining has greatly enhanced the freedom and dignity of the individual worker, and a more intensive public scrutiny in the future will recall and periodically revitalize the responsibility of union leaders to the individual worker—a responsibility which is inherent in representation but which bureaucratization and cozy comforts occasionally tend to dull. The pressures for enhancing an effective worker voice in the nonunionized sectors of work have already been discussed. The dramatic problems centering upon the rule-making procedure in work are a part of the past.

Instead, the observer a quarter century hence may, in looking back, suggest that the major labor issues of the then recent past had turned on an extension of this theme of liberating the worker which went beyond the procedural aspects of rule making to the substantive impact of the rules themselves on the life of the worker.

In discussing the general sources and character of an industrial society's labor problems, we noted that any industrial society requires a web of rule relating worker to work process, employer, the state, and other groups in the society. The burden of this web of rule, however, as it affects the individual choice and mobility, can vary substantially. To the degree that rules impose rigid limitations, the burden on worker freedoms is comparatively heavy; to the degree that the breadth of the limits expands, it is comparatively light. The imperatives of industrialization may be such as to permit broader limits and increasing freedoms as advance occurs.

It is more than coincidence that many of the issues projected for the future involve either increasing efforts or trends in the direction of making this web of rule more flexible, gearing it to greater potential for individual tastes and preferences. Looser discipline requirements on the job, broader seniority units and easier standards, a greater individual option in the allocation of energies to work or leisure as uniformity in national standards for hours of work begins to wither—these were but a few of the possible consequences projected as emerging from the issues posed by the future; and each enhances the potential for increasing worker freedoms. Frederick Harbison has described the past as follows:

> Much of our effort in the past has been directed toward treating the common man fairly and equally. Seniority systems have been created to eliminate favoritism and discrimination; job evaluation has been used to provide equal pay for equal work. In working on things such as general wage increases, call-in pay, overtime, compensation for work on Saturdays and Sundays, vacations, pensions, supplementary unemployment benefits, sickness benefits and re-

lated matters, the concern has always been to establish rules for equal and non-discriminatory treatment of the various categories of manual and clerical labor. Above all, we have been interested in achieving *conformity* and *consistency*. We have become skilled in the arts of classification and categorization. In fact, industrial relations practices may be plagued today with an ailment called "a hardening of the categories!"[84]

To the extent that the future labor issues evolving in a highly advanced and opulent industrial society tend toward a loosening of the categories, as in many instances they could easily move, we approach the resolution of the heretofore frequently opposite pulls of the twin desires for security and freedom.

Notes

[1] Selig Perlman and Philip Taft, *History of Labor in the United States, 1896–1932*, Vol. IV, *Labor Movements* (New York: The Macmillan Company, 1935), p. 43. Letter by Mr. George F. Baer, president of the Philadelphia and Reading Railroad Company controlling anthracite mines, written in 1902 at the time of a strike, to a stockholder in reply to the stockholder's letter pleading that, as a Christian, the railroad president should grant a concession to the strikers, end the strike, and thereby earn the blessing of God and the thanks of the nation.

[2] Charles R. Walker and Robert Guest, *The Man on the Assembly Line*, (Cambridge, Mass.: Harvard University Press, 1955); and Daniel Bell, *Work and Its Discontents* (Boston: Beacon Press, 1956).

[3] E. Wight Bakke, *Mutual Survival: The Goal of Unions and Management* (New York: Harper & Brothers, 1946), p. 7.

[4] Benjamin M. Selekman, "Trade Unions:—Romance and Reality," *Harvard Business Review*, May-June, 1958, Vol. 36, No. 3, pp. 76-90. For a similar view, see Max Lerner, *America as a Civilization* (New York: Simon and Schuster, Inc., 1957). Lerner observes: "The greatest achievement of the trade-unions in the economy as a whole has been that they have made possible the government of industry by constitutional means. If the massive corporate empires had been the sole survivors and had bargaining with only the individual worker, and if collective bargaining had continued to be viewed as a conspiracy against the anti-trust laws, there could have been anarchy or tyranny in American industry" (p. 322).

[5] Clark Kerr, "Governmental Wage Restraints: Their Limits and Uses in a Mobilized Economy," *Papers and Proceedings of the American Economic Association*, Vol. 42, May, 1952, pp. 369–384.

[6] Neil W. Chamberlain, "Collective Bargaining in the United States,"

Contemporary Collective Bargaining in Seven Countries, Adolf Sturmthal, editor (Ithaca, N.Y.: Cornell University Institute of International Industrial and Labor Relations, 1957), p. 289.

[7] Daniel Bell, "Labor's Coming of Middle Age," *Fortune*, October 1951, p. 114.

[8] *Ibid.*, p. 150

[9] See, for example, Robert Michels, *Political Parties* (Glencoe, Ill.: Free Press, 1949); Will Herberg, "Bureaucracy and Democracy in Unions," *Antioch Review*, Vol. 3, No. 3, Fall 1943, pp. 405-417; and Richard A. Lester, *As Unions Mature* (Princeton, N.J.: Princeton University Press, 1958).

[10] Neil W. Chamberlain, *op. cit.*, p. 302.

[11] Daniel Bell, "No Boom for Unions," *Fortune*, June 1955, pp. 136 ff.

[12] Irving Bernstein, "The Growth of American Unions," *American Economic Review*, June 1954, pp. 301 ff.

[13] Douglass V. Brown and Charles A. Myers, "The Changing Industrial Relations Philosophy of American Management," *Proceedings of the Ninth Annual Meeting of the Industrial Relations Research Association*, December 1956, pp. 1–15.

[14] See Leland Hazard, "Trends and Future Problems in Collective Bargaining," *The Next Twenty Years in Industrial Relations* (Cambridge, Mass.: Massachusetts Institute of Technology, Industrial Relations Section, 1958), pp. 69 ff.

[15] Edgar L. Warren, "Thirty-six Years of National Emergency Strikes," *Industrial and Labor Relations Review*, October 1951, pp. 3–15.

[16] J. A. Stratton, "Science and Economic Progress," *Private Investment: The Key to International Industrial Development*, James Daniel, editor, (New York: McGraw–Hill Book Company, Inc., 1958), p. 177.

[17] Reported in McGraw–Hill's eleventh annual survey of capital spending, *Business Week*, April 19, 1958, p. 31.

[18] *Our Manpower Future, 1955–56: Population Trends—Their Manpower Implications* (Washington, D.C.: U.S. Department of Labor, Bureau of Labor Statistics, 1957). See also Sophia Cooper, "Labor Force Projections to 1975," *Monthly Labor Review*, December 1957, pp. 1443–1450.

[19] Rudolph C. Mendelssohn, "America's Changing Job Sources," *Employment and Earnings*, November 1957 (Washington, D.C.: U.S. Department of Labor, Bureau of Labor Statistics), reprint, p. 8.

[20] John T. Dunlop, "The American Industrial Relations System in 1975," *United States Industrial Relations: The Next Twenty Years*, Jack Stieber, editor (East Lansing, Mich.: Michigan State College Press, 1958), pp. 27–54.

[21] George H. Hildebrand, "The Worker and Collective Bargaining in the American Economy in the Next Ten Years," in *Proceedings of a*

Pension Plan Conference, presented by the California State Federation of Labor and the Institute of Industrial Relations and University Extension (Berkeley and Los Angeles: University of California, 1956), mimeo, p. 1.

[22] Herman M. Somers and Anne R. Somers, "Trends and Current Issues in Social Insurance," Reprint No. 97 (Berkeley: University of California, Institute of Industrial Relations, 1957), pp. 23–24.

[23] George P. Shultz and George B. Baldwin, "Automation: A New Dimension to Old Problems" (Washington, D.C.: Public Affairs Press, 1955), p. 7.

[24] See *The Christian Science Monitor,* June 5, 1958.

[25] John S. Bugas, *Industrial Relations—1975,* an address sponsored by the Labor and Industrial Relations Center of Michigan State University, April 24, 1957, p. 12.

[26] See Mark L. Kahn, "Contemporary Structural Changes in Organized Labor," *Proceedings of the Tenth Annual Meeting of the Industrial Relations Research Association,* September 1957, pp. 171–179; Sumner Slichter, "The Position of Trade Unions in the American Economy," unpublished paper prepared for the Arden House Conference of the Fund for the Republic, May 1, 1958, pp. 5–6; and George W. Brooks, "What Will Collective Bargaining Look Like in Twenty Years?" in *The Next Twenty Years in Industrial Relations, op. cit.,* pp. 3–21.

[27] Some of the points made here are summarized from Charles A. Myers, "Management's Challenge in the 1960's: Manpower," paper delivered at the Fiftieth Anniversary Conference of the School of Business, Northeastern University, Boston, Mass., April 26, 1958. An extended discussion of the problems concerning high-level manpower is to be found in Frederick H. Harbison, "The Utilization and Development of High-Talent Manpower in American Industry," in *The Next Twenty Years in Industrial Relations, op. cit.,* pp. 23–36.

[28] George P. Shultz and George B. Baldwin, *op. cit.,* p. 20. Many of the points made here on the consequences of automation are taken from this insightful study.

[29] Testimony of John Diebold in *Automation and Technological Change.* Hearings before the subcommittee of the Joint Committee on the Economic Report, 84th Congress of the United States, 1st session, October 1955, (Washington, D.C.: Government Printing Office, 1955), pp. 28–29.

[30] Robert Dubin, *The World of Work* (New York: Prentice-Hall, Inc., 1958), p. 198.

[31] Daniel Bell, "The Capitalism of the Proletariat?" *Encounter,* February 1958, p. 22.

[32] Clark Kerr, *op. cit.,* pp. 36–37.

[33] Austin M. Fisher and John F. Chapman, "Big Costs of Little Fringes," *Harvard Business Review,* Sept.-Oct., 1954.

[34] Frederick H. Harbison, *op. cit.,* pp. 34–35.

SEVEN

☆

DEVELOPMENT, DIVERSIFICATION AND DECENTRALIZATION*

☆

ALFRED D. CHANDLER, JR.

Decentralization, diversification, and research and development—these have become familiar words in the businessman's vocabulary. Yet their use is comparatively new. A generation ago only a few American industrial firms devoted extensive resources to research and development, made and sold a variety of products, and had decentralized managements. Even today these new forms of business strategy and structure have been adopted in only a relatively small number of industries. Moreover, where a company has taken on one of these new ways, it has usually adopted the other two.

The systematic application of science to industry through organized research and development has never been really widespread. As early as the 1920's three industries—the electrical, chemical, and rubber—accounted for by far the largest amount of money and personnel used in systematic research and development.[1] During the 1920's and 1930's petroleum and power machinery (including automobile and agricultural implements) companies began to build large development organizations. By 1938 three-fourths of the personnel working in organized industrial research were in these five industries. Other basic American businesses, such as steel, non-ferrous metals, paper, textiles, food, and those processing agricultural products, provided well below 25 per cent of the trained men in the nation's industrial laboratories.

The pattern has continued since World War II.[2] The only industries besides the prewar five to devote extensive resources to research and development have been aircraft and scientific instruments. As the aircraft industry has been largely government sponsored, it hardly has the same business problems as other industries. The government has also been the market for and has provided over 60 per cent of the funds used in the development of scientific instruments. This same government support has also been true of many of the newer products of the older electrical companies. On the other hand, in the automobile and power machinery industries the government provides less of a market and covers less of the cost of research and develop-

* *Editor's Note.* This study was supported by the Sloan Research Fund of the School of Industrial Management, Massachusetts Institute of Technology, and the Carnegie Fund.

ment, while in chemicals, petroleum, and rubber, government funds play an even smaller role.

Systematic research has led to the development of new products, new markets, and new processes. It also appears to have stimulated changes in external business strategies and internal management structures. Except in aircraft, the industries which have concentrated on research and development today handle the widest variety of different product lines. Firms in these same industries have tended to be the ones which have replaced the older, functionally departmentalized, centralized management structure with the newer, decentralized form made up of autonomous operating units and a general headquarters with policy-making and coordinating duties.[a] The purpose of this study is, then, to investigate more closely the nature of the connection between decentralization, diversification, and research and development. Or, to put it in the terms of a broad question, what has been the relationship between internal structure, external strategy, and economic and technological change?

In looking for answers to this question, the experience of fifty of the largest American industrial concerns has been examined. These fifty fall into nine major industrial categories. The companies include the forty-four largest by assets in 1948 as listed in the Brookings Institution's study, *Big Enterprise in a Competitive System.*[3] Five other companies from the next fifteen largest have been added to round out the major industrial categories. (See Table I.) Finally, Sylvania was added in order to include a third electrical company. This sample seems neutral and manageable and at the same time fairly significant. The companies, by any criterion, are among the most influential in American industry.

The nine industrial categories into which these fifty companies fall have, in turn, been classified for the purposes of this paper into three groups: the metals industries and those manufacturing agricultural products, the assembling industries, and the processing industries. Although this study will focus on the last group, since the greatest changes are currently occurring here, the experience of the first will have to be briefly summarized and the second told in more detail if the developments of the more recent period are to be fully understood.

---

[a] The difference between the centralized and decentralized structure is indicated in Charts I and II.

TABLE I

THE FIFTY COMPANIES

(Numbers indicate relative size according to 1948 assets)

I. Metals and Agricultural Processing

Steel	Non-Ferrous	Agricultural Processing
3. U.S. Steel	18. Anaconda Copper	16. American Tobacco
12. Bethlehem	21. Kennecott Copper	23. R. J. Reynolds
26. Republic	25. Aluminum Co. of	24. Swift
32. Jones & Laughlin	America	27. Armour
38. National Steel	39. International Nickel	28. Liggett & Meyer
44. Armco Steel	40. International Paper	34. Distillers—Seagram
	49. American Smelting &	Corporation
	Refining	36. Schenley Industries
	53. Phelps Dodge	Corporation
		41. United Fruit
		42. National Dairy
		Products
		43. Procter & Gamble

II. Assembling

Electrical	Power Machinery	Automotive
9. General Electric	17. International Harvester	2. General Motors
15. Westinghouse	57. Deere & Co.	10. Ford
[Sylvania]	59. Allis-Chalmers	22. Chrysler

III. Process

Rubber	Oil	Chemical
29. Goodyear	1. Standard (N.J.)	8. Du Pont
33. U.S. Rubber	4. Standard (Indiana)	13. Union Carbide
35. Firestone	5. Socony Vacuum	30. Eastman Kodak
56. Goodrich	6. Texas	37. Allied Chemical &
	7. Gulf	Dye
	11. Standard, California	
	14. Sinclair Oil	
	19. Shell Oil	
	20. Phillips Petroleum	
	31. Atlantic Refining	

Metals Industries and Those Processing Agricultural Products

The great corporation had its beginnings in the United States in the years after the Civil War.[4] In the 1870's the individual firms in the long-established metals and those in processing agricultural products were small, like those in nearly all American industries, and were concerned almost wholly with manufacturing. Except for what they could buy and sell in the immediate locality, they purchased their raw materials and marketed their finished goods through commission agents and other middlemen. By 1903, the year in which a slight business recession ended the great merger movement at the turn of the century, these and other American industries had become dominated by a few large firms. The great new enterprises now did their own marketing and distribution and purchased their own supplies. Where their supplies came out of the ground rather than from the farmer or another manufacturer, they often obtained control of their raw materials. By 1900 many major American industries had become, to use the words of the economist and sociologist, oligopolistic in their inter-firm relations and bureaucratic in their intra-firm organization.

The strategy that led to the rise of the great corporation was primarily that of vertical integration. The resulting structure usually became a highly centralized one. Both structure and strategy appear to be essentially a response to the coming of the nationwide and increasingly urban market created by the rounding out of the national railroad system in the 1870's and 1880's. The consumer-goods industries were the first to take advantage of the new national market. During the 1880's and 1890's the meat packers (Swift and Armour), the tobacco manufacturers (American Tobacco Company), the soap makers (Procter & Gamble), the distillers (Distillers' Security), the banana merchants (United Fruit), and the refiners of kerosene (Standard Oil) all built nationwide—and often world-wide—distributing and sales organizations and then created large buying departments.

The makers of producers' goods completed their integrated organizations a little later. This was probably because it took longer before the city became such a major market for producers' goods. Until the 1880's the railroad remained their primary market. Then, with the falling off of railroad construction and the rapid growth of the city, the nation's urban and industrial concentrations began to take the great share of the products of the metal industries and also those of the growing machinery industries.

In the new, large, vertically integrated corporations each major function was departmentalized. There was a sales department, a manufacturing department, a purchasing department or one that produced the raw materials. Finally, all these corporations had their financial departments. The vice-presidents who headed these functional units also worked frequently as an executive committee or council with the president in coordinating the work of the different departments and in charting the business course of the corporation as a whole. As the consumer-goods companies required a steady flow of goods from the ground or farm to the market, the control of the central office was tighter and more centralized than in the higher priced, lower volume producers' goods businesses.

In most cases, however, the coordination required to make integration work effectively led to a centralized operating structure. As a result, corporations that began as combinations of firms under the common ownership of a stock-holding company soon consolidated into centralized, functionally departmentalized organizations.[b] International Harvester, for example, tried for three years to maintain its five constituent companies as separate divisions, but then combined into a single centralized operating structure. (See Chart I.) E. I. du Pont de Nemours & Company did the same thing in 1902 when it consolidated the many powder-making firms it controlled through stock ownership and a trade association into a very similar centralized organization. Of the fifty largest companies in 1909, all but the United States Steel Corporation and two or three copper companies had some type of functionally departmentalized management structure whose headquarters office was primarily concerned with the flow of materials from mine to market.

By 1903 the typical American industrial corporation handled a single line of products for the national market and had an operating department to carry out each major industrial function. (See Chart I.) Often the manufacturing, marketing, or purchasing of the single line led to the development of by-products. The meat packers manufactured glue and fertilizer and used their marketing organization to distribute poultry and eggs. The steel makers had their cement, the oil refineries their vaseline and medicinal products. Yet these goods remained by-products and received little attention from any of the organization's main operating departments. For these companies, product diversification was not a conscious business strategy.

[b] In the steel and copper industry, control of raw material was often obtained primarily for defensive reasons—that is, to have an assured supply of the necessary raw materials. In the early years there was little attempt to include mining within the same managerial organization as processing and marketing. Also, in the metals industry, selling, distributing, and warehousing were relatively simple operations that could be handled by a comparatively small marketing department.

Chart I

Simplified Chart
Centralized, Functionally Departmentalized Structure

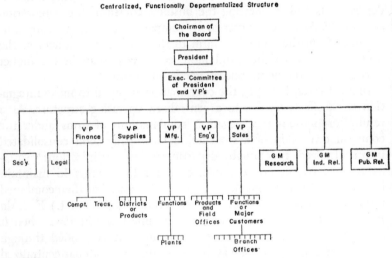

For the metals, the food, and other agricultural processing industries, the operating pattern set by 1900 has remained little changed over the past half century. Much the same firms make much the same line of goods; they compete with one another and are internally managed in much the same way. In the metals industry the only firms in Table I to be established after 1903 are National Steel (a merger of three older firms) and Kennecott Copper (which was earlier the supplier of raw materials for American Smelting and Refining, both financed largely by the Guggenheims). Actually, in the metals industry the trend has been, if anything, toward increasing centralization to coordinate more efficiently the flow from ground to consumer.

In the agricultural processing industries, political action encouraged a little more change. Two new tobacco companies were formed in 1911, after the dissolution of American Tobacco. The distilling industries were drastically hit by the coming of prohibition in 1920. The only other new firm on the list is National Dairy. In the mid-1950's nearly all the companies in these industries still handled a relatively few lines of closely related goods; and by 1955 all but National Dairy and possibly Kennecott and Schenley Industries were still managed through what was essentially a centralized operating structure.

The firms in these industries have been under little real pressure to change. Their basic markets, the sources of their raw materials, and the technology of their manufacturing stayed much the same in the years from 1900 to World War II. Even postwar developments have not caused drastic changes. Just as important, the manufacturing and marketing of primary metals and products based on the output of the American farm were comparatively little affected by the technological innovations resulting from the coming of the new sources of power and the application of physical and natural sciences to industry.

The Assembling Industries

Basic technological innovations had a great impact on the assembling and process industries. The years after 1900 saw the enormous expansion of the electrical industry, the coming of the automobile industry, and the great changes in the existing power machinery and implement industries. From 1900 until the coming of the Great Depression these new and expanding businesses and the goods that they produced seemed to have been a dominant stimulant for industrial change—change in the sense of the development of new products and processes and of new forms of business structure and strategy.

The manufacturing of engines and vehicles or frames in which the engines were used called for new methods of purchasing, manufacturing, and marketing. Their manufacturing, particularly, required the assembling of a great many parts and components; demanded the working out of a complex production flow, the development of new machine tools, and the devising of new manufacturing methods. Because the loss of one part could delay and actually stop production, the assembling companies felt a need to control parts and accessory firms. On the other hand, as they used relatively few basic materials in relation to their final product, they felt little pressure to go into the production of the primary metals. The marketing of complex power machinery to utilities, manufacturers, and other producers required a technically trained sales and service force, while the selling of durable machinery to the mass consumer market called for the development of new types of consumer financing and servicing facilities. Finally, the new ways of manufacturing and marketing caused the makers of engines and machinery to give more careful attention to systematic research and development. This was particularly true of the two great electrical manufacturers—General Electric and Westinghouse.

THE ELECTRICAL FIRMS

General Electric and Westinghouse, beginning as makers of lamps, generating, and other equipment for lighting, quickly moved into the manufacturing of machinery to generate and use electric power in industry and transportation. The scientific nature of their business led both companies to concentrate on technological development. "Competition," as Harold Passer points out, was "in reality between the engineering staffs of the two companies."[5] Each constantly worked to put out more efficient and newer types of engines, transformers, or generators than the other. By 1900 General Electric had gone so far as to set up a research laboratory for basic investigations into electricity which was placed under the direction of Dr. Willis R. Whitney, recruited from the faculty of the Massachusetts Institute of Technology.

Vertical integration, like competition and product improvement, encouraged the taking on of new products. A desire for an assured supply led both companies to purchase or form subsidiaries or departments to make parts and components. As the manufacturing departments did not expect to take all the output of these subsidiaries, the sales departments of both companies were soon marketing many types of switches, fuses, and other electrical engine parts. Similar needs brought General Electric into the plastic business.[6] Unable to purchase satisfactory insulating materials, in 1912 it turned its laboratories to studying the properties of resins. Two years later the company began to make and sell plastic materials.

Development and integration, however, were concentrated in one field—that of developing, manufacturing, and marketing electrical power and lighting machinery. Because both companies remained in this single producers' goods industry, they had comparatively little difficulty in managing their activities through centralized, functionally departmentalized, organizational structures similar to those then coming into use in the metals and agricultural processing industries.[7] The electric companies had smaller purchasing but much larger engineering departments than did the meat packing or steel firms. At headquarters their engineering and sales departments were divided along product lines—indicating the close relation between product development and competition. General Electric's sales department included, by the early 1900's, lighting, railway, power, and supply (parts and accessories) departments as well as its advertising division and its regional sales organization. The engineering department, with comparable product subdivisions, also included the research and the engineering laboratories. All in all, the organizational structure at General Electric and Westinghouse at the time of World War I looked quite similar to that outlined in Chart I.

The one major exception was the lamp business, where both manufacturing and marketing were quite different from the apparatus lines. At General Electric some lamps were made at the Harrison, New Jersey, plant; but the major production was carried on by the National Electric Lamp Association acquired in 1911. NELA operated separately from the rest of the company. Then, in the late 1920's, its activities and those of Harrison were combined.[8] The resulting Lamp Division continued in almost complete independence. Westinghouse, too, had its separate lamp-operating organization by World War I.

When the two companies began, in the years after World War I, to move beyond power machinery, the older structure was unable to meet the new needs, and more autonomous units similar to the lamp organizations began to evolve.[9] At both companies diversification resulted from two basic decisions. The first decision—that to develop consumer appliances—came as part of an effort to increase the demand for power machinery by expanding the nation's needs for electricity and also from a desire to keep the existing plant working more steadily—to avoid the feast-or-famine cycle of the apparatus business.[10] The second decision resulted directly from an agreement to exploit commercially the new and varied products developed in the research laboratories, such as electronic devices, alloys, and chemicals. Soon both of these new types of business were expanded for their own sakes. Continuing diversification, based largely on systematic research and development, became more of an explicit business policy.

The basic problems created by product diversification at the two electrical companies were greater in marketing than in manufacturing. This was true particularly of the new consumer appliances, for these durable goods, unlike power machinery, were sold in volume directly to the ultimate consumer. Their marketing required the creation of a chain of dealers and of retail outlets and the formation of organizations to help finance both customer and dealer. To sell these new products, General Electric formed in the late 1920's, its merchandising department with headquarters at Bridgeport, Connecticut. It long remained almost wholly a marketing department. Refrigerator parts were made at Schenectady and Erie, and the finished product was assembled at Erie; flat irons were manufactured in California, stoves and water heaters in Chicago, and so on. Their design, manufacture, and assembling were supervised by the older functional departments, but all were sold through Bridgeport. So, too, were radios after 1931. This arrangement had its defects, since both the manufacturing and selling units usually had different estimates as to markets and outputs. Moreover, the transferring of parts between plants was costly, and effective over-all control of product flow proved difficult.

Unlike appliances, products that came from the research laboratories tended to be organized in more autonomous units, since their engineering and maufacuring as well as marketing differed from procedures with consumer appliances and power machinery. So General Electric formed a separate subsidiary to handle the making and selling of X-ray equipment and another—Carboloy, Inc.—to handle its alloy business. Its chemical activities were consolidated in 1930 into a separate autonomous unit with headquarters at Lynn, Massachusetts. At General Electric, too, air-conditioning equipment, developed in the early 1930's, was soon placed within a semi-independent department handling its own sales and manufacturing.

By the early 1930's Westinghouse had similar autonomous units for manufacturing and sales of X-ray equipment and elevators. At Westinghouse the merchandise department came to have more control over other functions than did the one in General Electric. Formed in 1933

> as a separate operation distinct from the other Divisions of the Company. This Division includes not only the sales activities of such products as refrigerators, electric ranges, household appliances, etc., but also related engineering and manufacturing activities, whenever the main outlet for the product is through merchandising channels.[11]

Then came the appointment of "a separate manager" responsible for supervising engineering, manufacturing, and sales in other "main divisions of the Company's products."[12] Vice-presidents in charge of the functional departments now became essentially advisory officers responsible for coordinating engineering, manufacturing, marketing, and other policies of the different product units.

Until after World War II General Electric retained its complex structure which was partly functional and partly along product lines, partly centralized and partly decentralized. The first attempt at simplification came after the retirement of Gerard Swope, its brilliant president who for many years ran the company almost singlehandedly. While his successor, Charles E. Wilson, made some tentative beginnings at reorganization, the war delayed his plans. Then, in 1946, he turned over the problem to Ralph Cordiner.

Cordiner quickly redefined the company's activities along product lines by setting up six new major departments—apparatus, lamp, appliances, air conditioning, electronics, and chemical.[13] Each was headed by a senior executive who had all the necessary functions under his control and was responsible for the fianancial performance of all the products in his department. The older functional departments now became advisory staff units with planning and coordinating duties.[14] Committees of staff and operating men which usually included the three general officers (Wilson, Cordiner, and the chairman of the board) set over-all policies and plans.

When Cordiner became president in 1950, he carried the reorganization still further. He subdivided the product departments into over seventy units and eliminated the coordinating and policy-making committees. The managers of the smaller departments now had the same responsibilities and authority as had the former heads of the six product departments. Supervision and planning for several units were placed under a general divisional manager who, to keep him from interfering with the department heads, was given no staff of his own. At headquarters four new group vice-presidents were appointed. Individually they appraised the performance of the various departments and divisions placed under their guidance. Collectively they were—with the president, the chairman, and the head of the service departments—responsible for over-all policies. (See Chart II.)

Westinghouse, under the direction of Mark W. Cresap, Jr., under-

Chart II

Simplified Chart of a Typical Decentralized Structure

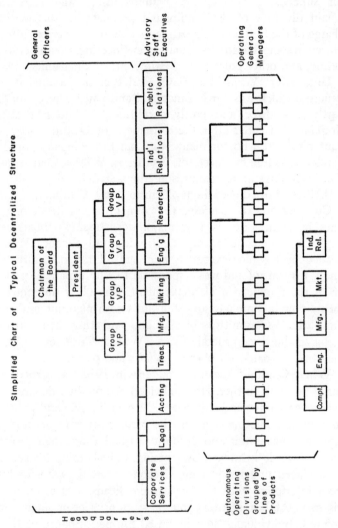

went a similar massive reorganization after 1950. The changes there resulted in a structure quite similar to the one Cordiner first set up at General Electric.[15] Operating activities were placed in four groups —apparatus, general industries, consumer products, and defense. The group vice-presidents, assisted by large staffs of their own, were given full responsibility for profit and functions. The older functional departments became explicitly advisory service units. Recently the company has increased the number of general offices at headquarters to five.[16]

In this way, then, the present decentralized structure, consisting of autonomous operating units and a policy-making coordinating headquarters with general officers and staff specialists, evolved at both the great electrical companies out of the older functionally departmentalized centralized organization. Fundamentally the new structure has been the organizational response to the strategy of product diversification developed in the 1920's. The manufacturing, marketing, and engineering of very different lines of products proved extremely difficult to handle within the old organization. The final resolution of the operating problems created by diversification came, however, only when two executives with strong interest in organizational matters—Cordiner and Cresap—devoted their full attention to reorganizing the existing structures. And both men became, once the new structure was completed, the presidents of their respective companies.

THE IMPLEMENT AND POWER MACHINERY FIRMS

The experience of the implement and power machinery firms and the automobile manufacturers had many parallels to that of the electrical companies. The essential difference is that they did not move much beyond the making of implements and power-driven machinery. Also, except for General Motors, they rarely attempted to handle both producers' and consumers' goods. Because they did not diversify much beyond power machinery, their product lines were pretty well completed by the 1930's; and, since they were less diversified than the electrical companies, their later reorganizations were less of a traumatic experience.

Allis-Chalmers and International Harvester, as well as somewhat smaller firms like Worthington (formerly International Steam Pump) and Borg-Warner and, to a much lesser extent, Deere & Company, were changed by the coming of the new sources of power in the early years of the twentieth century. Of these, only Allis-Chalmers exploited the new electrical machinery business. Created in 1901, as a merger of several steam power machinery companies, Allis-Chalmers quickly consolidated the operation of its constituent firms into a single centralized, functionally departmentalized organization. In 1904 the company, aware of the competitive challenge of the new sources of power, planned to make both electrical and gasoline-driven machinery. This decision called for a great expansion of both its engineering and sales departments which, like those of the electrical companies, quickly became divided along product lines. At first the company concentrated on electrical apparatus; and by 1910 it could report that "of the sales invoiced for the year, about 55 per cent were for the new lines of business which the company has recently developed and, of these new lines, about 75 per cent are electrical."[17] From that time on, Allis-Chalmers remained the third largest manufacturer of electrical machinery and apparatus in the United States.[18]

In the next decade the company shifted its attention to the internal-combustion engine; and by the end of World War I it had developed a line of tractors, earth-moving, and other construction machinery. After the war the company decided to build and sell tractors for farmers as well as for construction companies.

The decision to go into the agricultural tractor business quickly raised marketing difficulties. Allis-Chalmers sold its construction machinery equipment through independent distributors, while it sold directly to the flour, lumber, mining, cement, and utility companies through technically trained salesmen working out of the sales departments' district offices here and abroad. To reach the farmer, however, required warehouses, branch offices, and franchised retail dealers. Also, in order to compete successfully with International Harvester, Deere & Company, and other farm machinery firms, Allis-Chalmers' distributing organization needed a full line of farm implements. The company's engineers were soon hard at work designing harvesters, combines, and other agricultural implements. By 1940 Allis-Chalmers had become the third largest producer of agricultural machinery in the United States.[19]

As the tractor and implement business grew, these activities became more separate from the company's main operating organization. By World War II there was a separate factory and distributing organization, and the company had come to consider its business as being divided into two groups—the Tractor Division and the General Machinery Division. However, although there was a separate sales and manufacturing vice-president for tractors, the company continued to operate through a centralized, functionally departmentalized management structure.

Continued expansion in both tractor and general machinery lines led to a major reorganization in 1954.[20] It started, as did the first changes at General Electric, by making a growing *de facto* situation *de jure*. The operating activities became specifically divided into two groups. The tractor group now included three divisions—construction machinery, farm equipment, and buda (diesel) engine. The industries group included the power equipment, industrial equipment, and general products divisions. As at Westinghouse, each group vice-president had his own staff, including directors of manufacturing, engineering, and sales. With the disbanding of the old major functional departments (manufacturing, engineering, and sales), the other functional activities (research, public relations, industrial relations, and the controller's office) now became "service" departments, with advisory and auditing duties. No general officers were appointed besides the president and the chairman of the board. These two, in consultation with the busy group vice-presidents and senior staff officers, made policy and appraised the activities of the operating divisions.

International Harvester, unlike Allis-Chalmers, never diversified into electrical power machinery. At first it concentrated on adapting the gasoline motor to improve and expand its existing line of farm implements and machinery.[21] In the 1920's, however, as the prolonged postwar depression in agriculture cut down the buying power of the farmer, the company turned increasingly to the making of trucks and power machinery for industry. While this move beyond farm implements raised some new problems of production and of purchasing and control of materials, the major difficulties arose in marketing. Here Harvester's problems were just the reverse of those of Allis-Chalmers. The former had to create marketing and distributing outlets to sell in the cities to industry, just as the latter firm had to develop a rural sales organization. Until World War I the Harvester sales department continued to supervise the marketing of new products. To do this it set up a number of "specialty" departments. As the truck and industrial machinery business grew, the sales organizations became increasingly separated from the department's main organization.[22]

International Harvester did not wait until increasing growth and diversification caused an administrative crisis before it reshaped its organizational structure. Fowler McCormick, who became president in 1941, had developed a strong interest in the problems of organization and had been particularly impressed by the decentralized structure which General Motors used so effectively.[23] In 1943 he set up six new operating divisions—industrial power, motor truck, farm tractor, farm implement, fiber and twine, and Wisconsin steel.[24] The first two—industrial power and motor truck—were completely autonomous. Their managers had full responsibility for profits and sales and soon had under them executives in charge of engineering, manufacturing, sales, supply and inventory, labor relations, and a divisional comptroller. Managers of the next two divisions were responsible for all activities except sales. Since their goods went to the same market, they were sold and distributed through the general line sales department, which was basically the same marketing organization that had been set up shortly after the company's formation in 1902. The sixth division included the steel-making and mining companies that had come into the company with the 1902 merger.

McCormick next carefully redefined the duties of the remaining functional departments. Several were combined into two units—a vice-presidency of supply and inventory and a vice-presidency of merchandising services. The first, divided into three departments (estimate and order review, materials control, order and distribution), was to coordinate the flow of materials or, to use the wording of the 1943 annual report,

> to review orders, to place manufacturing orders, and to control all inventories of raw materials, purchased parts and work in progress, and after manufacture had been completed, to control inventories of finished machines and parts until they reached the hands of the dealers and users.

The vice-presidency of the merchandising services, also divided into three units (customer relations, sales operations research, and credits and collections), was an advisory and service organization. So also were the older engineering and manufacturing departments and the much newer industrial relations and public relations offices.

After the war the general office was more carefully defined. In 1946 three executive vice-presidents were appointed. They were given no specific administrative duties but were to specialize in a major functional area, such as sales, engineering, or finance. The senior staff officers were to assist the general officers to plan, to decide policy, and to appraise and audit divisional and company performance. For the latter task the meetings of the Operations Review Committee, consisting of the executive and staff vice-presidents, came increasingly to be used.

Smaller power machinery and implement firms, such as Worthington, Borg-Warner, Cherry-Burrell, and Thompson Products, have developed the same strategy and, much more recently, the same structure as the two leading companies in this field. Deere & Company has, until almost the present day, remained the exception.[25] Only since the retirement of a president in 1955 ended more than a century of direct family management has attention been turned to development and diversification.

Except for Deere, the coming of the new generators of power had a forceful impact on existing machinery and implement firms as well as creating great new ones. The older policies of vertical integration and of having a "full line" led to the production of many new products and to the development of others. Growing product diversification in turn led to *de facto* decentralization by World War II. But not until the late 1940's and early 1950's did such *de facto* structure become *de jure*. When the final reorganizations were made, the managers of the power machinery firms usually took as their model the management structure of the leading automobile company.

THE AUTOMOBILE COMPANIES

The automobile companies differed from the other power machinery firms in their concentration on the mass consumer market. High-volume production called for greater attention to factory layout, production engineering, and the development of highly complex, specialized machine tools. Mass marketing meant that more thought had to be given to style, comfort, product differentiation, and advertising. Both marketing and production encouraged vertical integration and management centralization.

Before the gasoline-driven car was over a decade old, Ford and General Motors had become the two leading automobile makers. Their founders, Henry Ford and William C. Durant, more than any other manufacturers, appreciated the potential of the great national market for a moderately priced car. To reach this market, Ford in 1908 put the Model T into production; and Durant, in the same year, formed General Motors. Ford increasingly met the requirements of rapidly growing production by internal expansion. Durant, on the other hand, relied more on external purchases to fill the needs of his car-making units. These differences in growth led to completely different operating structures and, in turn, greatly affected the response of the two companies to the leveling off of demand for new cars in the 1920's.

Ford's decision to concentrate on a single model brought more immediate success in a market where there was an insatiable demand for the inexpensive car.[26] To meet the enormous demand, Ford focused his efforts on improving and expanding production facilities. At his Highland Park works he developed the classic moving assembly line. Then at the River Rouge plant he carried out his dream of building a great factory into which flowed Ford-owned ore, coal, rubber, and glass and from which poured a vast stream of Model T's. With the realization of these plans Ford's manufacturing became, like his marketing and management organization, completely committed to the making of one single model for an ever-expanding market. When the market leveled off, the Ford Company was unable to meet the new situation. It quickly gave way to its more diversified and decentralized rival.

After Durant had formed General Motors as a combination of leading producers of the day—Buick, Cadillac, Oldsmobile, and Oakland—he concentrated, like Ford, on increasing production rather than purchasing new companies.[27] After 1915, when he came into full control of General Motors and enjoyed du Pont financial support, he increased his production facilities at existing and new plants. He also purchased many parts and accessory companies, bought large interests in leather, tire, gear, and body companies, and made long-term contracts with aluminum and steel firms. In these purchases and negotiations his motives were essentially defensive. He wanted to assure his car-making companies of an adequate and certain supply of materials at reasonable prices. Durant made no attempt to coordinate more efficiently the activities of the supplying and manufacturing units. Nor did he try to line up his cars to make the most of different types of demands for automobiles. Like Ford, Durant merely wanted to produce as many units as possible; but, unlike Ford, he preferred to do this through the purchase of facilities rather than through careful rationalization of production.

Durant left General Motors in the fall of 1920 at the time when the sharp postwar recession stopped automobile production and caught General Motors without the necessary operating capital. The du Ponts and J. P. Morgan, who provided the needed funds, installed a new management headed by Pierre du Pont and Alfred P. Sloan, Jr. The new executives immediately reshaped General Motors' market strategy and management structure. The basic strategic objective became "a car for every purse and purpose," while the new organization was one which Sloan had already suggested to Durant.[28]

Under Durant each operation had been left completely to its own. General Motors was, in fact, almost totally decentralized. To bring some sort of order and unity into the corporation, Sloan had proposed the creation of a central office to coordinate, appraise, and plan policy for the different units and the corporation as a whole. The operating divisions were to remain responsible for market and financial performance. The central office, Sloan suggested, should consist of staff specialists and general officers. The staff would provide the expert services and advice to the operating units and the general officers. These general executives included the president, the chairman of the board, the vice-presidents in charge of the financial and advisory staffs, and the group executives. The latter were made explicitly responsible for appraising the performance and for supervising a group of similar divisions. Sloan recommended separating the divisions into four groups—motor car, parts, accessories, and miscellaneous. This structure, which was changed only in detail after its adoption in January 1921, became a model for structural changes at International Harvester, General Electric, and elsewhere in later years.

Once the strategy of the full line and the decentralized structure had been shaken down, General Motors quickly outdistanced Ford both as to profits and share of the market. In 1925 General Motors had less than 20 per cent of the market and Ford more than 50. By 1940 their positions were almost reversed. Decentralization gave General Motors real advantages in effectively exploiting the variations in the no longer expanding passenger-car market. It also made relatively easy the development of the commercial vehicle, particularly the bus, and the creation of new and the expansion of older nonautomotive lines, such as Frigidaire and Delco. Durant had earlier taken the last two for special reasons. He had purchased Frigidaire in World War I as a means to keep his dealer and some of his manufacturing organization employed if car production was cut down.[e] Delco-Light, manufacturers of electrical equipment, was purchased partly to get the services of Charles F. Kettering.[29]

Kettering, as the head of the first research and development organization in an automobile company, at first concentrated on product improvement. Toward the end of the 1920's, however, his department not only worked on developing household and electrical appliances but also began developing the diesel engine. Soon, through its diesel manufacturing, General Motors was by far the largest maker of railway locomotives in this country. In this way the decentralized organization helped to encourage both development and diversification at General Motors.

Ford had also tried to diversify, but nearly all his ventures failed; and they failed primarily because the Ford organization was set up to handle only a single automobile model. For example, Ford in 1917 enthusiastically developed plans to make a cheap tractor that would revolutionize farming just as the Model T had changed passenger transportation. His tractor was adequately engineered, inexpensive, and popular; but it proved unsuccessful largely because he tried to handle it within his larger organization. As one of his major rivals, Cyrus McCormick III, pointed out:

> He overran his object when he gave his tractor to his dealers to sell. . . . Ford dealers in the country were well acquainted with their customers, but not their farm needs; and Ford dealers in the city had no sales outlet for farm goods.[30]

For a time Ford tried to develop a line of implements which were manufactured on contract to go with his tractor. Even this move was not enough to meet the competition from the established, widespread, fully stocked dealer organizations of International Harvester, Allis-Chalmers, John Deere, and others. Once the Rouge was in operation, the production, like the distribution, of the tractor could not be fitted into the existing organization. So in 1928 Ford stopped making tractors in this country.

Ford also built an excellent airplane; but, again, he was unable to produce and sell it effectively. Although his light truck business,

---

[e] As a wartime measure Durant had also moved into the tractor business, with the purchase of the Samson Sieve Grip Tractor Company. The venture was liquidated with large inventory loss in 1922, at the time when General Motors was meeting the major crisis created by the postwar recession. *Annual Report of the General Motors Corporation for 1922, December 31, 1922*, pp. 10-11.

which could be handled through his car-making and selling organization, was profitable, he made almost no attempt to develop other types of commercial vehicles. Nor did he develop a profitable parts and accessory business. Nor was he able to follow General Motors' example and move into diesel and other types of internal-combustion engines. Finally, Ford did not even develop a full line of cars. Until after World War II the Mercury and the Lincoln, accounted for a very small percentage of Ford's sales.

After World War II and the retirement and death of the elder Henry Ford, the company finally began to change its strategy and structure. The younger Henry hired Ernest R. Breech and other General Motors executives to rejuvenate the company. Breech began his new job, in *Fortune*'s words,

> by clapping the GM organizational garment onto the Ford manufacturing frame, trimming the garment here and pulling out the frame there. Nobody around Ford makes any bones about this, and indeed one of Breech's first acts was to send around copies of a semi-official GM text on decentralization.[31]

The new organization had its autonomous operating divisions and its group vice-presidents and its advisory and service staff. Since the 1947 change, Ford has rounded out its line, devoted more attention to Mercury and Lincoln, and revived its tractor, parts, and accessory businesses. Except for the Edsel fiasco, this imitative strategy and structure appear to have worked quite well.

Chrysler's story is closer to Ford's than General Motors', although Walter Chrysler began the present-day company by imitating the latter.[32] In 1928, with the purchase of Dodge and the creation of the DeSoto and Plymouth, Chrysler fashioned a full line of cars. Until World War II, however, his company concentrated on the Plymouth. Because he began in a time of declining demand, he had little trouble in obtaining his parts, accessories, and materials at a low price. So until World War II the company remained essentially an engine-making and car-assembling organization, operating through a centralized, functionally departmentalized structure. The great increase in demand after the war forced Chrysler to obtain control of some of its supplies. The war also turned the company, like Ford, to the making of products other than automobiles; and since the war the company has continued to produce a larger variety of products. After the retirement of K. T. Keller, Chrysler's successor as chief executive, it began to decentralize along the lines of the General Motors model. By 1955 it had its autonomous divisions, advisory staff, and policy-making general officers.

The experience of the automobile companies stresses how the existence of the volume market encourages product concentration and management centralization. Because of historical circumstances and because of the leading executives' concern with organizational principles and problems, General Motors was able to avoid both concentration and centralization. The decentralized structure permitted it to make the most of the automobile market and, in fact, of the potentials of power machinery used in transportation. Because of it, Kettering's research and development section was encouraged to develop nonautomotive products as well as to improve the automobile. Only after Ford and Chrysler had decentralized too did the first begin to move successfully into nonautomotive products like tractors and implements, and the second into air-conditioning and marine engines.

The limits of diversification for the automobile and power machinery firms seem to have been nearly reached. General Motors, Allis-Chalmers, and International Harvester have added few major products to their lines since World War II. Nor have Westinghouse and General Electric developed much new power machinery or apparatus outside of those needed primarily to meet military demands such as jet aircraft, missiles, and nuclear power. Research and development in the power machinery field have been concentrated on improving existing products and processes and on refining marketing and organizational techniques. As the government has provided the major markets as well as most of the funds for research and development in jet, missiles, and nuclear power, the needs of national defense have been the primary stimulus for technological innovation in the power machinery firms since the 1930's.

In the electrical industry many new nonmilitary products have been developed, and here the systematic application of science in research and development departments appears to have been the major innovating force. The new lines developed at General Electric and Westinghouse in the past twenty-five years have come largely out of the research laboratories. Applied physics has enlarged these companies' offerings in electronics, radio, television, control systems, and a number of scientific instruments. Applied chemistry has increased the offerings, particularly at General Electric, in plastics, silicons, and similar products.

The story of Sylvania Electric Products Inc., a newer company, stresses how applied chemistry and physics, rather than the demands of electric power, have led to growth and change in the electrical industry in recent years. Sylvania, formed in 1931 as a radio and lamp tube company, never made power machinery. During and after World War II it expanded rapidly into a variety of electronic, electric, and chemical products.[33] Rapid diversification soon led to decentralization.

Sylvania continued with a centralized structure until 1950, when the managers of the different product units were given control over sales and development, as well as manufacturing, and the functional offices at headquarters became advisory and service departments. Then, in 1954, the central headquarters were enlarged by the appointment of three "vice-presidents—operations," one for lighting, one for the other consumer goods businesses (radio and television, radio tubes, picture tubes, and parts), and a third for producers' goods (tungsten and chemical, atomic energy, and electronics). They, with staff vice-presidents, the president, and the chairman, concentrated on over-all supervision and policy making. The story at Sylvania has many parallels in other companies exploiting physics and allied sciences, such as the Radio Corporation of America, the Philco Corporation, and the American Optical Company.

Since the 1930's, then, applied science seems to have encouraged more product diversification than has the exploitation of electrical or petroleum-generated power. Systematic research and development have in fact encouraged many assembling firms, particularly in the electronics business, to make diversification a basic business policy. The laboratories are expected to develop a fairly steady flow of new products which may or may not be integrated into existing manufacturing and marketing organizations. For such a business strategy the decentralized structure has become almost imperative.

The Process Industries

In the process industries applied science has been in recent years even more of an innovating force than in the assembling industries. Just as the coming of the new sources of power revolutionized the petroleum and rubber businesses in the first quarter of this century, so has applied chemistry begun to transform them again in the years since World War II. Until the war many oil and rubber companies failed to utilize fully the broad potentials of chemical engineering because they concentrated on building a single line of high-volume, low-priced products necessary for the mass-produced automobile. Only radical changes in demand created by the war brought the gasoline and tire companies into chemicals on a large scale. The result has been a shift from product concentration to diversification and from management centralization to decentralization. Most large chemical companies, on the other hand, have been systematically applying science to the development of new products since World War I and have become as diversified and decentralized as any American industrial firms.

THE RUBBER COMPANIES

The experience of the rubber industry's "big four" emphasizes the connections between product diversification and management decentralization and between product concentration and management centralization. It also indicates the relation between a corporation's structure and strategy and the uses made of its research and development laboratories. The story is particularly clear since two of these companies—Goodyear and Firestone—focused their attention on a single line, the tire; while the other two—Goodrich and United States Rubber—although tending to concentrate on the tire, maintained a policy of diversification.

One reason for this division was that Goodyear and Firestone began as tire companies; but the other two, being older, already had established businesses before the automobile made the tire an important rubber product. Goodrich, beginning as a partnership in 1870, made belting, hose, cushioning, and other goods for industry. United States Rubber began in 1892 as a merger of a number of rubber boot and shoe companies.

Like so many early mergers, United States Rubber Company first centralized its activities by setting up a nationwide sales organization, a unified purchasing unit and, though more slowly, a consolidated manufacturing department.[34] After the turn of the century it began to diversify, because the demand for rubber boots and shoes had leveled off with the growing migration to the city and the increased paving of streets and roads. In 1905 the company entered the field of industrial rubber by obtaining closer financial and managerial control of the Rubber Goods Manufacturing Company.[35] By this time rubber to insulate electric wire and fixtures was a major product; and tires were quickly becoming another.

Increased production encouraged integration. In 1911 the company established plantations in Sumatra to avoid the extreme fluctuations of price and to have an assured supply available at a fair price. Earlier it had begun to reclaim rubber, setting up the Naugatuck Chemical Company to provide the essential sulfuric acid. In 1911 it purchased Raymond B. Price's rubber regenerating company. Price, who had developed a caustic soda process for rubber reclamation, then took over the company's reclaiming activities. At the same time he enlarged its small development department and set up its general laboratories for broad research in rubber chemistry.

Both diversification, with its various types of rubber processing, and the desire to find better ways to process raw and reclaimed rubber led to systematic research and development. The company's general laboratories, concentrating first on improving product and processes, developed before and after World War I a number of new accelerators and pioneered in finding rubber anti-oxides, such as VGB and BLE, and improved acids and heavy chemicals. Since these products had many uses outside the rubber industry, the company's chemical sales tripled in the 1920's. Soon, too, the laboratories began working on new products and processes, such as using latex (essentially the milk exuded from the cut bark of the rubber tree) directly as a raw material in a variety of products, including tire cord, dip, paper, and extruded rubber thread.

As it began to diversify its product line as a result of integration and development, as well as taking on the manufacture and sale of existing industrial rubber products, the United States Rubber Company gave more attention than most companies to its organizational structure. By 1917 President Samuel B. Colt, on the recommendation of Raymond Price's development department, separated the company's operating activities into four divisions (tire, general, industrial, footwear and clothing), a chemical subsidiary, and an overseas department to handle plantations and foreign sales. Except for the last, each unit handled its own manufacturing and sales; for coordination of manufacturing and sales of products for such different markets had been the company's biggest management problem. At headquarters the development, legal, and financial departments continued much as before. Besides forming an operating council of the president and the vice-president in charge of the product and functional departments, little was done specifically to define the functions of the central office and its relation to the operating units, or to expand the role of the central office through increasing the size and number of staff specialists and creating general executive officers.

Under Colt's successor, Charles B. Seger, the structure became again more centralized. Only after a financial crisis did the company's organization receive attention. In 1928 the du Pont family assured the company's solvency by purchasing 30 per cent of its stock. The du Ponts then put in a new management, headed by Francis B. Davis, who quickly set up a structure similar to the one which the du Ponts had had in their own company since 1921 and which they had seen Sloan use successfully at General Motors.

The company's operating activities were again segregated into a number of product divisions, including tire, footwear, mechanical goods, sundries, Naugatuck chemical, and divisions to handle the sale of crude rubber, liquid latex, overseas sales, and the company's rubber plantations.[36] Each department head was specifically given full authority and responsibility for the operations of his unit. Statistical and financial controls similar to those developed at General Motors and du Pont were set up as a means to check on divisional performance and to keep the general managers accountable. Functional officers were, for the first time, explicitly placed on an advisory staff basis with service and auditing duties. These included finance and accounts, planning and engineering, development, industrial and public relations, commercial research, advertising, purchasing, traffic, legal and patents. General supervision and policy formulation were now given to the Executive Committee, consisting of Davis and executives with long experience in the company. All were relieved of day-to-day administrative duties and each specialized in the activities of one function or type of product. Since 1929 this structure has remained relatively unchanged. Probably as a result of its decentralized organization, United States Rubber has remained one of the most diversified of the leading rubber manufacturers, and, with Goodrich, has one of the best records of development of new goods and improvement of existing processes and products.[37]

Goodrich's story has many similarities to that of United States Rubber. Beginning as a manufacturer of industrial rubber products, it too rounded out its line of rubber goods after 1900. It soon became even more of a pioneer in rubber chemistry than its largest competitor.[38] Development, by continuing to encourage diversification, helped to bring on decentralization. In 1930 Goodrich's centralized, functionally departmentalized structure was reorganized into four product divisions—tire, mechanical, footwear, and sundries. The onslaught of the depression and the resulting retrenchment, however, caused a return to centralization.

Then, under the impetus of continuing product development, *de facto* decentralization began to evolve. In 1936 the management set up a separate unit to manufacture and sell latex products. In 1940 Goodrich formed, with Phillips Petroleum, a jointly owned subsidiary to make synthetic rubber. Three years later the president created the Goodrich Chemical Division with its own development, manufacturing, and sales organizations. Expanding rapidly, it took over the synthetic rubber subsidiary immediately after the war. Finally, in 1953, the company became fully decentralized. Its structure included six autonomous operating divisions—tire and equipment, industrial products, footwear and flooring, chemical, Canadian, and foreign (a seventh, sponge rubber, was added the next year)—and a central office of advisory staff specialists and senior policy-making and appraising general officers.

Where Goodrich and United States Rubber considered all areas of rubber and rubber chemistry as their domain, Goodyear and Firestone until the 1930's focused the attention of their whole organizations on a single line of products for the volume market. They integrated vertically more than either of their major competitors. Besides extensive rubber fields, both had their own cotton plantations as well as textile mills for their tire cord and fabricating mills for their rims. Both gave much more attention to creating their own retail outlets. This concentration made development of new and diversified lines much more difficult. The two had had their chemical laboratories and development departments almost from their beginning, but their efforts were devoted almost entirely to designing better tires and finding more efficient ways to make them.[39]

Before the depression Goodyear's only major venture, outside of tires, was the building of dirigibles. However, the Goodyear Zeppelin Corporation, formed in 1923, proved only a little more of a business success than Ford's tri-motor airplane business. The depression and the rapid decline in the demand for tires turned Goodyear to industrial rubber goods. Even here its policy was to concentrate on a few large-volume items, often making only one grade or model. In 1938 the sales and accounting operations of the Industrial Goods Division were moved out of Akron and located at the division's manufacturing plant. However, the heads of the sales, manufacturing, and accounting units still reported to the heads of the functional departments in Akron.

The war had a greater impact; for the production of synthetic rubber turned Goodyear's development department for the first time to serious consideration of the opportunities in rubber chemistry. In 1943 a large central research laboratory was opened and soon began to work up products that might find profitable postwar markets.[40] In 1945 Goodyear created the General Products Division, with its own manufacturing and sales departments, to handle nearly all of the non-tire business, which now included air-foam, flooring, plastics, and some chemicals. In the next year a separate Chemical Products Division was organized. By the mid-1950's Goodyear had developed a *de facto* decentralized structure comparable to that of General Electric in 1945. It has three major product divisions—tire, general products, and chemical—but its central office does not yet include advisory staff specialists or a group of general officers to appraise performance and make policy. The control of day-to-day activities still seems centralized in Akron, as the relations between the older functional and the newer product divisions are not entirely clear and the senior executives spend much of their time in routine administrative work.[41]

Firestone's story is quite similar, except that here there is even less of a trend toward decentralization.[42] The Firestone Company concentrated on the tire until the depression, then moved into industrial goods. In its expansion the major policy was, apparently, to take on automobile parts and rubber and plastic goods which might be effectively sold through its tire retailing organization.[43] With the war, Firestone first began to take an interest in chemicals; and in 1945 it completed a large research laboratory. At the same time it set up a Products Development Division. However, the managers of its several manufacturing divisions continue to report to the vice-president in charge of production. In 1951 all sales activities were still centralized in Akron, as was research and development. Still focusing its energies much more on marketing than on rubber technology, Firestone has continued to maintain excellent profits and so has been under little pressure to alter its management structure.

In the rubber industry, then, the coming of the automobile inhibited two of the major companies and several smaller ones from exploiting fully the potentials of rubber chemistry. Concentration on low-priced, mass-volume product led to a highly integrated, centralized management organization; and this organization was, in turn, ill-equipped to manufacture and sell a variety of products based on rubber chemistry. Only a series of drastic events brought change. The depression indicated the dangers of concentration on a single line. The war exposed and trained the tire companies' personnel to advances in rubber chemistry and technology, particularly in synthetic rubber. Finally, the postwar boom created new demands for synthetic fibers, plastics, and rubber chemicals. These changes turned the tire firms slowly to product development and diversification which in turn are slowly bringing decentralization.

THE OIL COMPANIES

Many of the foregoing generalizations might be made for the oil companies. They too built great vertically integrated, centralized organizations based on a single line of products created by the coming of the internal-combustion engine. Because the production, transportation, refining, and consumption of gasoline, fuel, and lubricating oil called for even more of a continuous flow of materials than the making and selling of tires, central office coordination became more essential. However, because the process and products were based even more on chemical reactions than those in the rubber industry, the petroleum industry offered a greater opportunity for the application of the chemical sciences. The focus on gasoline, fuel, and lubricating oil prevented the petroleum firms from fully realizing the possibilities of petro-chemicals outside of their major line until World War II. The move into this new field has only just begun to bring a readjustment of older organizational structures.

The experience of the industry's oldest and largest company effectively illustrates the pattern. After the dissolution of the old Standard Oil Company (New Jersey) in 1911, what remained of it was a large refining and smaller marketing organization.[44] In the following years the Jersey company concentrated on building up its supply of crude, both here and abroad, developing a tanker fleet, expanding and adjusting its marketing organization to meet the demands created by the internal-combustion engine. Finally, in 1927, it reorganized its production, transportation, refining, and marketing subsidiaries and, at the same time, reshaped its central office functions. Besides the allocation of funds for capital expenditures and the setting of over-all policy, the central offices' primary task became the coordination of the flow of petroleum from oil well to customer.

Jersey Standard was the first oil company to establish a research and development department in this country. From the beginning that department concentrated on improving product and production. Walter C. Teagle had a broader objective when he first suggested setting up such a department. Writing in June 1919 to A. C. Bedford, chairman of the board, Teagle pointed out:

> Since you have been away, I have felt more than ever before the need for a thoroughly organized and competent research department, under an able executive, such a department not only to be confined to chemical research, but to general research in connection not only with production and refining of our products, but with the sales end of our business as well. There are, I am convinced, a number of products that could be manufactured in addition to the lines we are at present manufacturing, and the manufacture of those products would undoubtedly result in enhanced profits to the Company. General Electric and other concerns of a like character lay a great stress on their research department.
>
> They consider this department on a parity in importance with the manufacture and sales end of their business. Our research department up to date is a joke, pure and simple; we have no such thing, and on your return here I am anxious to discuss with you this entire question.[45]

To set up the new development department Teagle selected Frank A. Howard, a Chicago engineer and patent lawyer. Howard looked more to the tire companies than to General Electric for a suitable model for his department. The important task, he reasoned, was to apply the already existing backlog of scientific knowledge to the oil industry before attempting to strike out into new areas. And the place where the need for such application was the greatest and where the financial return would be the highest was in the bettering of existing processes and products.[46]

During the twenties and thirties the development department concentrated on making higher quality gasoline and lubricating oil in a more efficient manner. First it improved the tube and tank thermal cracking process; then it worked on an improved continuous vacuum distillation process. Next came the development of fluid catalytic cracking and superfractionating. The research organization also worked on improving the manufacturing of tetraethyl lead as an antiknock agent. Similar improvements were made in the quality and efficiency of lubricating oils by the use of additives such as Paraflow, developed in 1932. Also significant was the development of high-octane gasoline base stock, particularly for airplanes. Some of these advances were based on an agreement made in 1929 with the great German chemical organization, I. G. Farben, for the use of its hydrogenation process.

Howard's Development Company—it became a subsidiary in the 1927 reorganization—and the company as a whole paid little attention to the potentiality of chemical by-products or waste gases. Jersey Standard had in 1919 purchased Carleton Ellis's patents for making synthetic (isopropyl) alcohol, a solvent used in the rubber and textile industries and as an effective antifreeze; but it wanted these patents primarily because they related to a new tube and tank refining process. Jersey did put them to use by manufacturing alcohol and similar solvents at Bayway, albeit on a small scale. At first sold through the company's unit for marketing specialty products, alcohol sales were placed in 1932 under the Standard Alcohol Company. Other minor by-products—such as Flit, an insecticide; Nujol, a medicinal oil; and crayons—were sold after 1927 through Stanco. Yet the handling of all these items was considered essentially a peripheral activity. In 1928, when negotiations were under way with I. G. Farben, Jersey executives did actually study the possibility of a large-scale move into petro-chemicals. Apparently the marketing and management difficulties involved and the coming of the depression kept the company from such a venture.[d]

As in the case of the tire companies, it was World War II that finally brought Standard into the petro-chemical business on a large scale.[47] And again the prime stimulant was the huge demand for synthetic rubber. Jersey invented butyl rubber in 1937, and by February 1942 it had in operation a plant making butyl for waterproofing clothing, hose, and mining and conveyor belts. Already in 1941 Standard had completed plants to make buna N and buna S types of synthetic rubber, based on the I. G. Farben patents. In the same

[d] The division of fields agreement made between I. G. Farben and Standard Oil (N. J.) in November, 1929, when Standard obtained the rights to I. G.'s hydrogenation process, should not have inhibited Standard's development in the broad area of petro-chemicals. Solvents were the major field for petro-chemical development at that time, and these were explicitly exempted from the agreement. See Frank A. Howard, *Buna Rubber—the Birth of an Industry* (New York, 1947) pp. 249–251 and Chaps. III and IV.

years Standard began systematically to recover napthenic acids and to segregate and purify sulphonates. After 1945 the chemical business continued to grow by the development of plastics, detergents, agricultural chemicals, and other lines. The development company now began to study hydrocarbon synthesis as a source for chemicals as well as just for liquid fuels. The marketing of new chemicals as well as alcohol and some older products was given in 1947 to the Enjay Company. The development and manufacturing of chemicals continued to be handled by the operating departments of Esso Standard, one of the Jersey company's operating subsidiaries. For, in spite of all its growth, Standard's chemical business remains small in relation to the total volume of the gasoline, lubricants, and fuel oil trade.

With few exceptions, the story of integration, development, and diversification in the oil companies paralleled that at Jersey Standard up to World War II. The former Standard Oil firms (those studied here include Jersey Standard, Indiana Standard and California Standard, Socony-Vacuum, and Atlantic Refining) were largely refining and marketing firms and so, in the years after 1911, concentrated, as did Jersey Standard, on obtaining an assured supply of crude oil. The younger companies (Gulf, Sinclair, Texas, Phillips Petroleum, and Shell) were just as anxious to have assured outlets for their crudes and so concentrated more on building or buying, refining, and marketing activities.[48] During the depression of the 1930's, when the demand for gasoline declined, nearly every major company underwent a simplification of its management as well as its corporate structure. The resulting operating organizations tended to be centralized ones, broken down into functional departments or subsidiaries.

During the 1920's nearly all the major oil companies quickly followed Jersey's lead in starting systematic research and development activities. These new development departments concentrated on lowering costs of producing and refining and on improving the quality of gasoline and oil. Then the war, with its demand for high-octane gas, explosives, synthetic rubber, and many types of chemicals, involved Gulf, Texaco, Standard (Indiana), and Atlantic in the petro-chemical business.

Only Shell had built up a large chemical business before 1941.[49] At Shell (the only foreign-owned company in Table I), the impetus came explicitly from abroad. In 1929 the directors of its European parent company decided to set up the Shell Chemical Company to make use of gases produced at Shell's California refinery. By 1940 the chemical company was a self-contained unit handling sales as well as manufacturing and was producing synthetic ammonia, a wide range of alcohols and ketenes, and other solvents and chemicals. By 1940 Phillips and Standard of California had also made a good start in petro-chemicals, but until after World War II these companies remained very much the exception.[50]

The delay in diversification was not because the oil companies failed to appreciate the potentiality of exploiting gases and liquids made in their refining processes and not used for gasoline and oil. Besides Shell, they had the example of Union Carbide and other chemical companies which had built plants alongside the major refineries for the manufacturing of chemicals. Undoubtedly the reason for the oil companies' hesitancy to move into petro-chemicals was that their whole huge organization was concentrated on the development, production, transportation, manufacturing, and marketing of a single line of products to one major market. As Williams Haynes has pointed out in his *American Chemical Industy: A History:*

> Production of chemicals by the petroleum industry appeared to be economically and technically sound, but most petroleum executives could not see what appeared to them to be a tiny market for a multitude of chemicals produced by a complexity of operations and sold to a long and diversified list of customers, tasks for which they had neither the technical nor the sales staff.[51]

However, product improvement and the development of catalytic refining and superfractionating processes in the 1930's and early 1940's provided new raw materials as well as technical knowledge and experience in chemical operations. Then the war and postwar industrial boom, with the growing demand for chemicals, provided markets outside of gasoline and oil for large-scale, low-cost processing operations. So, after World War II, nearly all the major oil firms began to diversify their product lines.

Postwar diversification has led to a variety of organizational responses. The ultimate result seems to be the creation of an autonomous unit like the Shell Chemical Company, which has control over its own manufacturing, market development, and sales and is fully responsible to the oil company's top management for its financial performance. Such is the Oronite Chemical Company, formed in 1943 by Standard of California to handle developing and marketing of industrial chemicals, and the smaller California Spray Chemical

Corporation, founded even earlier to handle agricultural chemicals. Immediately after the war, California Standard also gave both units control over manufacturing.

Of the companies studied here, only Atlantic continues (1959) to develop, manufacture, and sell its chemical products through the company's regular functional departments. Jersey Standard's Enjay Company is still only a marketing organization. So too is Socony Mobil's recently formed petroleum chemicals department. But Sinclair, in 1951, and Standard of Indiana, in 1952, formed subsidiaries to handle the development as well as the sale of petro-chemicals. In both cases the parent's refining department retained supervision of chemical manufacturing. Phillips, in 1952, went one step further and, following the example of Shell and Standard of California, gave its chemical subsidiary, formed in 1948, control over manufacturing as well as development and sales. In that same year Phillips thought it necessary to create a coordination department to help coordinate the flow of petroleum from well to refinery and then to the new chemical plants as well as to the marketing organization.

Since 1950 Gulf and the Texas Corporation have set up autonomous petro-chemical units.[52] Gulf, a latecomer, made the decision to move into chemicals on a large scale in 1950, and by 1954 it had a separate division for their development, manufacture, and sale. Until 1954 the Texas Corporation preferred to have its petro-chemical business handled by subsidiaries jointly owned with firms outside of the industry and with which it had no managerial connection. In 1944 it formed the Jefferson Chemical Company with American Cyanamid; a little later, the Coltex Corporation with Columbia Carbon; and in 1953, the Texas-United States Chemical Company with United States Rubber Company. In 1954, however, it set up its own research and technical department and the next year a separate petro-chemical department. Apparently Texaco had come to feel that it could not go on indefinitely setting up partly owned subsidiaries to handle new business which was becoming such an important part of the industry.

Both Texas and Gulf, when forming their petro-chemical departments, made, as Phillips had earlier, an extensive reorganization of their over-all management structures.[53] Gulf, in fact, in 1955 formed an organizational planning department to handle growing organizational needs and problems. The supervision and coordination of a number of operating units involved in the same integrated process present different management activities and problems from supervising and coordinating units making different products for very different markets but using the same source of supply and somewant similar processing techniques. If diversification in petro-chemicals continues at the current rate, the oil companies may have to decentralize their organizational structure still further. If so, both the make-up and duties of the policy-making generalists and of the staff specialists will require more study.

In the mid-1950's, then, the oil and tire companies were feeling the impact of diversification in somewhat the same way that the automobile and power-machinery companies did in the 1940's. Diversification here seems to have encouraged the formation of management structures similar to those fashioned in the machinery and in the two other rubber companies.

THE CHEMICAL FIRMS

The leaders in the chemical industry have not been inhibited to the extent that those in the tire and petroleum businesses were by concentrating on a single line of products. The chemical companies have always sold a variety of goods for the producers' market rather than a few lines of goods for the mass consumer market. Because their manufacturing has been a largely chemical process, and their products have been chemically created, their research and development departments have had probably as extensive a scope for innovation as any in American industry. It is hardly surprising that among American firms these companies have become the most diversified and have placed the most men and money on research and development. The slowness to diversify and decentralize in the chemical industry has come largely from the failure of a company's executives to appreciate the potentials of the chemical sciences or the need for an articulated management structure. The history of each of four of the largest chemical firms illustrates different aspects of these generalizations.

The experience of the biggest—E. I. du Pont de Nemours and Company—illustrates quite dramatically how diversification brought on decentralization. At the end of World War I the du Pont company was a highly centralized, functionally departmentalized organization handling a single line of products.[54] Although tentative steps had been taken toward diversification in 1914, 96 per cent of the company's business was still in the making and selling of high explosives. Paradoxically, it was the First World War that really turned the company to a carefully thought-out program of diversification—because the war drastically expanded the company's plant equipment, personnel, and profits.

By the middle of 1915 the company's president, Pierre S. du Pont, began to plan for the postwar use of what would otherwise be excess plant, trained men, and capital. He asked the development department to study intensively all possible fields for diversification chemically related to the making of explosives. On the recommendation of the department, the company continued to expand in the production of artificial leather and cellulose, which it had started to develop before 1914. It also moved into the paint and varnish field; began to work on dye, dyestuff intermediates, and allied organic chemicals; started to think of uses for heavy acids and water-soluble chemicals; and, finally, initiated experimental work on artificial silk.

This well-defined program made the transition from war to peace relatively easy. However, the company was soon having increasing difficulty in managing its new multi-product activities with the old centralized structure made up of four major departments—manufacturing, sales, development, and finance. The most serious problems now arose in its new paint business. The coordination between the manufacturing and the sales departments was particularly difficult, since paints, unlike most of the du Pont products, were sold to the small consumer rather than to the large producer. Coordinating committees were set up to help bring together development, manufacturing, and sales activities of the different products; but neither these committees nor the Executive Committee, consisting of the heads of the functional departments, had time to coordinate effectively or to formulate over-all policies and procedures. Finally, the pressures of the 1921 depression precipitated a fundamental reorganization of the company's operating structure.

Du Pont's first step in this pioneering change was, in the words of its annual report, "to segregate its five principal industries—Explosives, Cellulose Products, Pyralin [plastics], Paint, and Dyestuffs, placing each in charge of a general manager."[55] Artificial silk, still in an experimental stage, was left under a separate subsidiary. Each departmental manager had his own staff and full responsibility and authority for the development, manufacturing, and sale of his products and for the financial performance of his unit. Next, the functional departments—research, engineering, purchasing and accounting

—became advisory or service departments whose staff officers audited, advised, and helped to coordinate the work of the operating departments; and they also assisted the new general office. The creation of this office, the final step in the reorganization, was brought about by relieving the president and the Executive Committee of all day-to-day operating duties and so permitting them to concentrate on making over-all company policy. The committee's members, like the general officers at International Harvester twenty years later, came to specialize in certain functional areas.

Under this decentralized organization, which has in recent years often been copied, the du Pont company continued to diversify production. From its division and central research laboratories flowed a variety of new products. Product development, in turn, led to the formation of new and the reorientation of old operating departments. Vertical integration, by the purchase or development of units to make the more basic chemicals, resulted, as did the same policy at General Electric, in the creation of other operating organizations. Also, more staff or service offices were added at headquarters. The underlying structure, however, has changed little since 1921. This decentralized structure helped du Pont to make diversification a fundamental business strategy. The company has increasingly relied for income and volume on a flow of new products which often make many of the existing wares obsolete.

Union Carbide, the second largest chemical company, has for many years relied on a similar policy. Since its formation in 1917 it has steadily expanded through diversification. It too has had a decentralized organization; but, unlike du Pont, it was never centralized. Its basic management problem has been more that of General Motors, the creation of an effective coordinating and policy-making central office with staff and general officers.

The basic motive for the merger of four companies which became Union Carbide and Carbon Corporation was integration.[56] Each of the four concerns (Union Carbide and its subsidiaries, Prest-O-Lite, Linde Air Products, and National Carbon) supplied the others with raw materials or with a market for their products. Here, even more than in the power machinery companies, integration encouraged product diversification; for, although these companies supplemented one another, they sold many products to outsiders. Also, after 1917 the research laboratories in the various subsidiaries continued to develop new products. National Carbon, for example, pioneered in developing and marketing dry-cell batteries which found a booming market in the telephone and automobile industries. Prest-O-Lite, in working on sources other than calcium carbide for acetylene, opened up the whole new field of synthetic organic chemistry based on petroleum and natural gases. The petro-chemical field was further expanded by the Linde Company's work in developing techniques for separating gases.

To exploit more effectively the possibilities created by this chemical research, in 1920 the parent company set up another subsidiary, Carbide and Carbon Chemicals Corporation. This company, one of the very first to manufacture petro-chemicals in the United States, developed a wide variety of products for almost a generation before most oil companies entered the field. It moved into lacquer and nitro-cellulose products, while its work in accelerators, rubber vulcanizers, and, in the 1930's, butadiene and other rubber intermediates brought it into the rubber business. Its pioneering work in plastics led it to purchase the Bakelite Company in 1939. Other subsidiaries, particularly Electro-Metallurgical and National Carbon, had been from the first in the metals and electrical industries.

Because its products were so diverse and covered so many different business fields, Union Carbide and Carbon never considered uniting its operations into a single unified structure. However, its managers had to pay increasing attention to creating an effective central office. At first the central office did little more than approve capital expenditures and set dividend policies. It did make some efforts to see that technical advances and procedures developed in one division reached the others.

Slowly, during the late 1920's and early 1930's, both the functions and the duties of the central office and the activities of the different operating subsidiaries became more carefully defined.[e] By 1934 the different operating subsidiaries had been segregated into four operational groups: gas, electric furnace, chemical products, and carbon products.

At the same time, the coordinating and policy-making functions of the central office were further strengthened by building up a central advisory staff. By 1934 the advisory central staff departments in-

---

[e] In 1930, for example, Linde, Prest-O-Lite, Oxweld, and Union Carbide Sales Company were consolidated into one operating unit—the Linde Air Products, Incorporated. This unit handled the development, manufacture, and sales of oxygen, acetylene, calcium carbide, and welding and metal cutting equipment, *Annual Report of Union Carbon and Carbide Company for 1930*, p. 13.

cluded at least research and development, patents, engineering, traffic, and employee relations.[f] When in 1945 a corporate vice-president was named for each of the product groups, the central office at Union Carbon and Carbide achieved much the same type of structure that General Motors created in the 1920's. Since the war there has been an increase in the number of general officers at headquarters who, relieved of operating responsibilities, concentrate on policy planning.

The experience of the third largest chemical firm—Allied Chemical Corporation—underlines the need for effective management structure if even a chemical company is to grow through product development and diversification. Particularly, it emphasizes the need for a strong center as well as autonomous parts. Allied Chemical began as a combination, and its organizers gave diversification, integration, and the pooling of research as the reasons for the merging of five companies. Its committee on consolidation wrote late in 1920:

> Among the advantages which the Committee believes are to be derived from such a consolidation are: Greater diversification of output and correspondingly greater stability of business; closer adjustment of the production of basic and intermediate materials to the requirements for manufacture and their derivatives; and greater financial strength—not to mention the various economies in operation ordinarily available to an organization of the scope here contemplated . . . Intensive progressive research is—and will continue— an especially important feature of the chemical manufacturing business. In the opinion of the Committee, promotion of such research, through combination of material and personal resources of the consolidating companies, is alone a compelling reason for the proposed consolidation.[57]

The five combined companies did, indeed, support one another; but at the same time, like Union Carbide, each bought and sold many products from and to outside companies. Because the parent company failed to develop an effective central office, the five subsidiaries were unable to benefit as fully as they might have from the integration and the pooling of research and development activities.

[f] In the late 1920's the company tried to centralize its staff work still more through the creation of a central research laboratory. This apparently proved unsuccessful, and the laboratory was disbanded well before 1940. The role of the research department remained, like that of the other staff offices, largely one of providing interchange of information, coordinating policy, and supplying expert advice. There is a reference to the central research laboratory in the Company's *Annual Report for 1929*, p. 12.

Until World War II the company's headquarters included little more than the president, the chairman of the board, the treasurer, the controller, and a couple of vice-presidents. Headquarters failed to coordinate the activities of the subsidiary units, to systematize the exchange of information, or even to encourage the development of new products and processes. The primary function of the central office, which for fifteen years was wholly dominated by one man, Orlando F. Weber, was to allocate funds for capital expenditure and to set dividend and other financial policies. Weber, a man of many neuroses, believed in doing everything as secretly as possible; he disliked giving information even within his own company. Financially, Allied was successful enough, but as it developed few new products and did little to exploit available knowledge, it fell behind du Pont and Union Carbide in the size of its plant and personnel, in the volume and variety of its products, and in the amount of time and energy spent on research and development. By World War II the company had become known as "the bank with a pretty good chemical business on the side."[58]

Only after the death of Weber in 1945 and that of his protégé, H. F. Atherton, in 1949 did significant changes occur. Under the guidance of F. J. Emmerich, Allied's president after 1946, all subsidiaries became operating divisions, each headed by its own president. The activities were now more carefully and logically defined.[g] To improve interdivisional coordination, as well as to secure more expert advice and assistance, Emmerich began gradually to build up a central staff. By the mid-fifties Allied had engineering, traffic, employee, and public relations departments at headquarters. Most important of all, the company put much more thought and money into building research and development organizations, both in the divisions and at headquarters. Finally, in 1957, the responsibilities and duties of the central office were more clearly and explicitly defined. To strengthen the staff, strong executives were recruited from the divisions to become vice-presidents of the new advisory, marketing, and manufacturing departments. At the same time, two executive

[g] The reorganization was pretty well completed in 1952, with the creation of the Nitrogen Division, which took over the ammonia, nitrate, and fertilizer business. Manufacturing of these lines had previously been done by Solvay Process, and their sales were handled by the Barrett and the Solvay Divisions *Moody's Manual of Investment, American and Foreign, Industrial Securities, 1952* (New York, 1952), p. 2903. In 1958, as Allied's annual report pointed out, a new Plastics and Coal Chemicals Division was formed.

vice-presidents were appointed. These general officers were to help coordinate divisional and staff activities and, with the president and the chairman of the board, formulate over-all policy.

The creation of a strong central office, with its policy-making generalists and staff specialists, appears to have revived the company. Sales, plant construction, output, and profits have steadily increased. Since 1950 Allied has placed more new products on the market than it had in its thirty preceding years. Allied's experience thus indicates that the effective exploitation of scientific knowledge requires a rational management structure which, besides autonomous operating divisions, includes a strong central office to combine the different units into an integrated whole.

Eastman might be considered an exception to a more general pattern. Still, it has been more of an assembling than a processing firm. Eastman first entered the chemical business to carry out a policy of vertical integration.[59] In order to assure itself of supplies of acids and other materials necessary to making and processing photographic film, the company organized Tennessee Eastman soon after World War I. Chemical output at the Tennessee works quickly outran the needs of the main Rochester, New York, plant. Sales to outsiders began to be an important part of the company's business. Research and development at Eastman, however, concentrated on photographic equipment which its world-wide marketing organization was equipped to handle. Almost in spite of itself Eastman has become increasingly involved in the chemical business. This continuing product diversification has in the last year or so turned the company to examining its organizational structure. It is currently (1959) creating new autonomous operating units and redefining the role of its central office.

Other, more wholly chemical, companies have closely followed the structural pattern set by du Pont and Union Carbide. Carborundum, Glidden, Koppers, Pittsburgh Coke and Chemical, Hayden Newport Chemical, Stauffer Chemical, American Cyanamid, Spencer Chemical, Hercules Powder, Atlas Powder, Diamond Alkali, and Food Machinery and Chemical companies all have autonomous operating units and policy-making, appraising, and coordinating headquarters.[60] These firms have been able to develop, as have some electrical companies, a strategy of planned product "turnover"— that is, a policy of the constant development of new products to replace older ones. In so doing such chemical companies have not only created a great variety of new products in their own field but have also pioneered in other industries. They have innovated more in alloys and new metals than most steel and copper companies; in the development of petro-chemicals before most oil firms; in synthetic rubber as much as most rubber companies; in detergents more than most soap firms; and in fertilizers more than all of the older fertilizer companies.[61]

Summary and Conclusions

Diversification has altered the older ways of inter-firm competition. Competition has grown between firms in different industries making the same product, and it has come to be based more on technological development than on price and product differentiation. Competition has become as much a match between the research and development as between the marketing departments. Consider the differences between the rapidly growing plastics and the older copper industry. Copper mining, smelting, refining, and marketing have been carried out for over half a century by a few large firms which handle little besides copper and closely allied metals; and the primary competitive weapon, when used, has been price. On the other hand, nearly all the chemical, rubber, petroleum, and electrical companies studied here have large and active plastics divisions. Competition in plastics is less concerned with pricing and more with further investigations into the science of polymer chemicals and its commercial applications. It is a competition to develop new types of plastic materials, to locate new uses, new raw materials, and new ways of producing existing products. Moreover, the plastics business is only one of many in which these firms are engaged. In the companies and industries where applied science can be exploited, business strategy has become more concerned with the entering and leaving of different fields, lines of products, and markets. In the older industries like steel, copper, meat packing and, until recently, oil and rubber, such matters rarely concerned the policy makers.

Diversification in multi-industry activities, which is altering the older patterns of oligopolistic competition, has also changed the internal structure of the large corporation. It has helped to break down the huge centralized structures created to manage the vertically integrated corporations handling a single line of goods. The large functional departments have been divided into smaller units based on products. This has permitted more managers to become generalists, rather than specialists, and to become responsible, at an earlier age, for over-all market and financial performance. The shortening of the lines of authority, responsibility, and communication, the reduction in the number of management levels, and the more explicit delegation of decision making have helped to make many a large corporation less of a bureaucracy and more of an enterprise.

Management decentralization appears to have been largely a response to product diversification, and product diversification has been adopted most widely in the industries where the natural and physical sciences can be most effectively applied. Applied science has had its greatest impact in the process industries not only because the products of these industries are usually the result of applied chemistry but also, and even more important, because putting the new products into commercial production is less costly and difficult than in other industries. To say this another way, development, like research, is less risky. Pilot operations are less expensive, as the manufacturing of a new product often requires relatively little more than a change in raw materials or in the ingredient mix rather than, as in the mechanical industries, a heavy outlay for machines and tools. Yet in the assembling and mechanical industries, particularly the power machinery and electrical, there has been still more potential for the application of science to both the development of new products and the requirements of getting these products into production than has been true in the metal and metal-shaping industries. Steel, copper, zinc, and lead and the basic goods fashioned from them can be improved by applied physics and chemistry but not greatly changed. Only in the newer metals, like aluminum and magnesium, has there been the opportunity for much development. Of the metals firms studied here, only the Aluminum Company of America has made a concentrated effort to create new products.[62]

In the industries where the potential of research and development can be applied, concentration on a single line of goods for the mass consumer market has been a major factor inhibiting diversification. This has been true in the oil, tire, camera, and automobile companies and also in the older firms processing agricultural products. Partly because of an increasing use of applied chemistry, Armour, Schenley Industries, and Procter and Gamble in recent years have moved into new business fields such as pharmaceuticals, detergents, chemicals, and cellulose products.[63] All three have begun to reshape their long-established, centralized, functionally departmentalized organizations. Procter and Gamble, for example, set up in 1957 a typical decentralized structure with a central office and seven product divisions. Armour in 1958 and 1959 went through a comparable reorganization. Two somewhat similar food firms—General Mills and Borden—evolved similar structures before 1957, while a third—Quaker Oats—has, like the petroleum companies, a separate autonomous chemical division.[64]

While the decentralized structure has been the normal organizational means to manage a diversified product line, its creation has rarely come automatically. In most cases its introduction required a change in top management. The older executives usually had neither the awareness of the organizational needs caused by diversification nor a specific interest in defining organizational relationships. In nearly every company studied here, the organizational changes were made and carried out by a new set of senior executives.

Decentralization, diversification, and systematic research and development all reflect an increasingly complex technology and economy. Before the railroads had created a national and increasingly urban market, the industrial firm handled only a single line of goods and carried out one commercial function—that of manufacturing. The demands of the new market, with its ever-growing volume, encouraged the industrial concerns to do their own purchasing and even their own mining and their own marketing. The centralized, functionally departmentalized organizations fashioned to handle the new expanding business were still built around a single line of goods. The coming of the new sources of power after 1900 and the application of science to industry in the past twenty-five years not only made procurement, manufacturing, and marketing more complicated but also permitted many firms to increase the number of their offerings. The older centralized structure was unable to carry out the demands of diversification. The decentralized structure evolved, then, largely to meet the growing complexity in all aspects of development, purchasing, manufacturing, and marketing and to help assure the essential coordination between these functions for the individual products within the over-all diversified line.

Notes

[1] The most useful survey of the employment of funds for personnel in research and development is a detailed study based on the National Research Council's surveys by George Perazich and Philip M. Field, *Industrial Research and Changing Technology* (Philadelphia, photoprinted, 1940), especially Chaps. 2 and 3 and tables A-8, A-13, A-15, A-17 and D-1. Also useful were "A Development of Industrial Research in the United States," by Howard R. Bartlett, and "Location and Extent of Industrial Research Activity in the United States," by Franklin S. Cooper, both in National Resources Planning Board, *Research—A National Resource* (Washington, D.C.: Government Printing Office, 1941), Vol. II. The National Research Council surveys asked for information on laboratories "which definitely devote some time to research looking toward improvement and development of products" and which are not involved primarily in routine testing of materials and products, Perazich and Field, *Industrial Research*, p. 6.

[2] The report of the Bureau of Labor Statistics, Department of Labor, and Research and Development Board, Department of Defense, *Industrial Research and Development—A Preliminary Report* (Washington, D.C.: Government Printing Office, 1953), pp. 4–20, shows that 85 per cent of the aircraft research and development work and 60 per cent of the instrument development activities were financed by government funds. The government also financed a major increase in research work in the electrical industry. In the chemical industry, the government pays for less than 10 per cent of the research and development work, and in petroleum, under 5 per cent. Also useful are the National Science Foundation's *Science and Engineering in American Industry—A Final Report on a 1953–54 Survey* (Washington, unbound pamphlet, 1954), especially Charts 5, 8 and 11, and the National Science Foundation's "Research and Development Costs in American Industry, 1956," *Reviews of Data on Research and Development* (May 1958). Raymond H. Ewell, "Role of Research in Economic Growth," *Chemical and Engineering News*, 33: 2980-2985 (July 18, 1955), has some provocative ideas.

[3] A. D. H. Kaplan, *Big Enterprise in a Competitive System* (Washington: Brookings Institution, 1954), pp. 153-154. I have not included Western Electric because it is, for all intents and purposes, a part of the American Telephone and Telegraph Company, which takes nearly all its nonmilitary production, nor have I included the marketing firms on the Brookings list. Table I has been renumbered to take these omissions into account.

[4] The following is a very brief summary of a broader study, some of

the findings of which appear in Alfred D. Chandler, Jr., "The Beginnings of Big Business in American Industry," *Business History Review* (Spring 1959). Some of the information comes from Alfred D. Chandler, Jr., "Management Decentralization: An Historical Analysis," *Business History Review* (June 1956).

[5] Harold C. Passer, *The Electrical Manufacturers, 1875–1900* (Cambridge, Mass.: Harvard University Press, 1953), p. 263. The annual reports of the two companies provide additional useful information. Also helpful for the earlier period were *Thirty Year Review of General Electric Company, 1892–1922* (Schenectady, N. Y., published by the company, 1923); John W. Hammond, *Men and Volts: the Story of General Electric* (Philadelphia: J. P. Lippincott Co., 1941); John T. Broderick, *Forty Years with General Electric* (Albany, N. Y.: Fort Orange Press, 1929); Paul W. Keating, *Lamps for a Brighter America: a History of the General Electric Lamp Business* (New York: McGraw-Hill Book Co., 1954); John Clark, "The General Electric Company," a case study mimeographed in 1950 for use at the Harvard Business School; Arthur A. Bright, *The Electric Lamp Industry* (New York: The Macmillan Co., 1948); and Benjamin G. Lamme, *Benjamin Garver Lamme, Electrical Engineer: an Autobiography* (New York: G. P. Putnam's Sons, 1926).

[6] For General Electric see Williams Haynes, *American Chemical Industry: A History* (New York: D. Van Nostrand Co., Inc., 1949), VI, 187-189.

[7] The organizational structure is suggested fairly clearly in the annual reports of General Electric and Westinghouse and in the books on the two companies listed above. Passer's *The Electrical Manufacturers*, pp. 322-325, is particularly good on General Electric's initial structure.

[8] Keating, *Lamps for a Brighter America*, Chap. 15, Westinghouse Lamp Company is listed in the Westinghouse *Annual Report* as early as 1911.

[9] The story of General Electric between World War I and World War II is suggested in David Loth, *Swope of G.E.—The Story of Gerard Swope and General Electric in American Business* (New York: Simon and Schuster, Inc., 1958); Kent Sangendorph, *Charles Edward Wilson, American Industrialist* (a company publication, 1949); and *Fortune*, 3: 30 ff, 3: 39 ff (Jan. Feb. 1931), 21: 68 ff (Jan. 1940); 25: 65 ff (Mar. 1942) and the company's annual reports.

[10] *Fortune*, 21:102 (Jan. 1940) and Sangendorph, *Wilson*, p. 22.

[11] *Annual Report of Westinghouse Electric and Manufacturing Company for 1933*, March 12, 1934, p. 9. The information for the following comments on Westinghouse is based on the company's annual reports and *Fortune*, 17: 42 ff (Feb. 1931); 46:119 ff (Dec. 1952).

[12] *Facts and Figures for Stockholders—Westinghouse Electric and Manufacturing Company, July, 1938* (Pittsburgh, 1938), p. 3.

[13] *Fortune*, 35: 121 ff (May 1947); 48: 142 (July 1953); 52: 110 ff (Dec. 1955); *Sixtieth Annual Report of the General Electric Company for 1951*, March 10, 1952, pp. 11, 14-19; Lawrence M. Hughes, "G. E. Seeks Conquest of Business through Fanned-Out Management," *Sales Management*, 69: 26 ff (Oct. 1, 1952). Also useful were Ralph Cordiner, *The Implications of Decentralization*, General Management Series, No. 113 (New York: American Management Association, 1945), pp. 24-32, and *Problems of Management in a Large Decentralized Organization*, same series, No. 159 (1952), pp. 3-17.

[14] The advisory and service role of the vice-president in charge of marketing is well defined in Hughes, *op. cit.*, p. 122.

[15] *Annual Report of Westinghouse Electric Corporation for 1954*, p. 12, and *Fortune*, 48: 142 (July 1953); also Westinghouse organization chart for October 1952, printed in *Company Organization Charts*, National Industrial Conference Board, Inc., Studies in Personnel, No. 139 (n.p., 1953), pp. 137-138.

[16] *Annual Report of Westinghouse Electric Corporation for 1957*, p. 3.

[17] *Annual Report of Allis-Chalmers Company*, October 1, 1910.

[18] *Fortune*, 17: 42 (Feb. 1938).

[19] *Economic Concentration and World War II*, Report of the Small War Plants Corporation to the Special Committee to Study Problems of American Small Business, United States Senate (Washington: Government Printing Office, 1946), p. 137.

[20] *Annual Report of Allis-Chalmers Company for 1955*, p. 4.

[21] The information on the early years and early organization of International Harvester comes from Cyrus McCormick III, *The Century of the Reaper* (Boston: Houghton Mifflin Co., 1931), Chaps. 7-15; Bureau of Corporations, Department of Commerce and Labor, *The International Harvester Company* (Washington: Government Printing Office, 1913), especially Chap. 4; and the company's annual reports.

[22] McCormick, *op. cit.*, pp. 229-230.

[23] The information on Fowler McCormick comes from *Fortune*, 34: 111 ff (Sept. 1946) and a discussion with John Vance and E. Lieberman of International Harvester.

[24] *Annual Report of International Harvester Company for 1943*, pp. 14-15. The quotation in the following paragraph is from the same report and pages. The information on postwar changes at International Harvester comes from the company's annual reports and Christian E. Jarchow, "Harvester's Division Organization—A Decade of Experience," an address before the New Orleans chapter, Society for the Advancement of Management, Dec. 8, 1953.

[25] The comments on Deere & Company are based on a study of its annual reports. Those on Borg-Warner and the Worthington Corporation are based on a more cursory survey of their reports; for Cherry-Burrell

284 DEVELOPMENT, DIVERSIFICATION AND DECENTRALIZATION

and Thompson Products see National Industrial Conference Board, *Organization Charts*, pp. 36-37, 126-127. Also Remington Rand, makers of typewriters, tabulating machines, and other equipment, adopted a structure very similar to that of General Motors, *Organization Charts*, pp. 118-119.

[26] These generalizations about Ford and his company are based largely on Allan Nevins and Frank E. Hill, *Ford: The Times, the Man, the Company* (New York: Charles Scribner's Sons, 1954) and *Ford: Expansion and Challenge, 1915–1933* (New York: Charles Scribner's Sons, 1957); Edward D. Kennedy, *The Automobile Industry* (New York: Reynal and Hitchcock, 1941); Lawrence H. Seltzer, *A Financial History of the American Automobile Industry* (Boston: Houghton Mifflin Co., 1928), especially Chap. 3; Federal Trade Commission, *Report on the Motor Vehicle Industry* (Washington: Government Printing Office, 1939); *Fortune*, 35: 82 ff (May 1947), 45: 87 ff (March 1952) and 50: 123 ff (Sept. 1954).

[27] The story of the early years of General Motors comes from Arthur Pound, *The Turning Wheel* (New York: Doubleday, Doran & Company, 1934); Seltzer, *Financial History of the Automobile Industry, op. cit.*, especially Chap. 4; *United States of America v. E. I. du Pont de Nemours & Company, General Motors Corporation et al.*, U. S. District Court for Northern District of Illinois, Eastern Division, Civil Action No. 49C1071 (1953); and the corporation's annual reports.

[28] Sloan's role in the creation of the General Motors management structures is suggested by Ernest Dale, "Contributions to Administration by Alfred P. Sloan, Jr., and G. M.," *Administrative Science Quarterly*, 1: 30-46 (June 1956); A. P. Sloan, Jr., "The Most Important Thing I Learned about Management," *System*, 46: 137 ff (Aug. 1924); Donaldson Brown, "Decentralized Operation and Responsibilities with Coordinated Control," American Management Association, *Annual Convention Series*, No. 47 (New York, 1927) and "Pricing Policy in Relation to Financial Control," *Management and Administration*, 7: 195 ff, 283 ff, 417 ff (Feb., March, April 1924), and C. S. Mott, "Organizing a Great Industrial," *Management and Administration*, 7: 532 ff (May 1924). The later story of the corporation comes from the Federal Trade Commission, *Report on the Motor Vehicle Industry*; Kennedy, *Automobile Industry*; and the corporation's annual reports.

[29] T. A. Boyd, *Professional Amateur, the Biography of Charles Franklin Kettering* (New York: E. P. Dutton & Company, 1957), pp. 93–94, 117-118.

[30] McCormick, *Century of the Reaper*, p. 198.

[31] *Fortune*, 35: 88 (May 1947) and National Industrial Conference Board, *Organization Charts*, pp. 62-63.

[32] Information on Chrysler comes from the Federal Trade Commis-

sion's *Report on the Motor Vehicle Industry*; Kennedy, *Automobile Industry*; Walter P. Chrysler with Boyden Sparkes, *Life of an American Workman* (Philadelphia: Curtis Publishing Company, 1938); and the company's annual reports.

[33] The information on Sylvania comes from its annual reports; Don G. Mitchell, "Big Business in Small Plants," *Advanced Management*, 15: 2-5 (Dec. 1950); *Fortune*, 35: 113 ff (May 1937); and a mimeographed case study on Sylvania prepared by John Clark at the Harvard Business School.

[34] The annual reports of the United States Rubber Company have much detailed information; especially useful are those dated 1894, 1895, 1896, 1904, 1906, 1910 to 1914, 1917, 1918, 1921, 1929, 1938 and 1939. Constance McL. Green, *History of Naugatuck*, Connecticut (New Haven: Yale University Press, 1948), pp. 193-198, 201-204, 215-220, 232-237; Haynes, *American Chemical Industry*, Vol. VI, pp. 452-455; and *United States of America v. E. I du Pont de Nemours & Company, General Motors Corporation, et al.*, provide additional information.

[35] Victor S. Clark, *History of Manufactures in the United States*, Vol. III, *1893–1928* (New York: McGraw-Hill Book Co., 1929), p. 237, states that the United States Rubber Company was "allied" with the Rubber Goods Manufacturing Company from the first, but the nature of the alliance is not indicated.

[36] Major changes under Francis B. Davis in 1929 are mentioned in *Commercial and Financial Chronicle*, May 11, 1929, and in *Thirty-Eighth Annual Report of the United States Rubber Company for 1929*, p. 3.

[37] Compare, for example, the references to United States Rubber Company and Goodrich to those on Goodyear and Firestone in Haynes, *American Chemical Industry*, Vols. IV and V.

[38] Besides the company's annual reports, two booklets printed by its Sales Training Department and published by the company, *The Growth of an Ideal* (Akron, 1918) and *A Wonder Book of Rubber* (Akron, 1917), have useful information. Valuable too is a sketch of the company's research and development work in Haynes, *American Chemical Industries*, Vol. VI, pp. 190–195.

[39] Goodyear's Development Department was formed in 1908. Harvey Firestone hired a chemist (John W. Thomas, who in time became the company's president) in that same year. Information on Goodyear comes from Paul W. Litchfield, *Industrial Voyage* (Garden City, N. Y.: Doubleday & Company, 1954); Hugh Allen, *The House of Goodyear* (Cleveland, Corday & Grass, 1949), especially Chaps. 7, 9; Haynes, *American Chemical Industry*, Vol. VI, pp. 195–197; and the company's annual reports.

[40] The change in Goodyear's attitude toward the uses of research and

development and the potentials of rubber chemistry at this time is made very clear in David Dietz, *Goodyear's Research Laboratory* (Akron, published by the company, 1943) and *Harvest Research, the Story of the Goodyear Chemical Division* (Akron, published by the company, 1955).

[41] National Industrial Conference Board, Inc., *Decentralization in Industry* (New York, 1948), pp. 32–34, indicates the continuing strong central control. When Edwin J. Thomas succeeded Paul Litchfield, who was over eighty, as chief executive officer in 1956, he began to make some management changes. It is not quite clear what these have been, *Fortune*, 53: 61 (May 1956).

[42] The annual reports of Firestone Tire & Rubber Company say little. Alfred Lief, *The Firestone Story* (New York: McGraw-Hill Book Co.—Whittlesey House, 1951) has a little more information, as has Haynes, *American Chemical Industry*, Vol. VI, pp. 163–165.

[43] In 1936, for example, the Firestone Rubber Footwear Company, with a plant at Hudson, Massachusetts, was sold to United States Rubber Company, Green, *History of Naugatuck*, p. 220.

[44] The information on Standard Oil Company (N. J.) came from George S. Gibb and Evelyn H. Knowlton, *The Resurgent Years* (New York: Harper & Brothers, 1956) and *Fortune*, 21: 49 ff, 21: 61 ff (April, June 1940), 44: 98 ff, 44: 112 ff (Oct., Nov. 1951) and Haynes, *American Chemical Industry*, Vol. VI, pp. 389–403.

[45] Gibb and Knowlton, *The Resurgent Years*, p. 524.

[46] Frank A. Howard, *Organizing for Technical Progress*, a lecture delivered December 5, 1956, at George Washington University (New York, 1957), p. 2.

[47] Frank A. Howard, *Buna Rubber* (New York: D. Van Nostrand Co., Inc., 1947) tells the story in detail. Charles S. Popple, *Standard Oil Company (N. J.) in World War II* (New York, published by the company, 1952) has some additional data.

[48] The major source of data for all these companies was their annual reports. Additional information on Standard Oil of Indiana came from Paul H. Giddens, *Standard Oil Company (Indiana): Oil Pioneer of the Middle West* (New York: Appleton-Century-Crofts, Inc., 1955); on Shell Oil Company, from Kendall Beaton, *Enterprise in Oil: A History of Shell in the United States* (New York: Appleton-Century-Crofts, Inc., 1957); on the Texas Corporation, from Marquis James, *The Texaco Story: the First Fifty Years, 1902–1952* (published by the company, 1952); on Sinclair Oil Corporation, from *Fortune*, 6: 56 ff (Nov. 1932), 53: 117 ff (April 1956); on Socony Vacuum Oil Company from *Fortune*, 26: 111 ff (Nov. 1942), 27: 117 ff (Feb. 1953); on Phillips Petroleum Company, from *Fortune*, 50: 73 ff (Aug. 1954); on Atlantic Refining Company, from *Fortune*, 48: 128 ff (Aug. 1953); and on the Gulf Oil Corporation, from *Fortune*, 16: 79 ff (Oct. 1937), 49: 32 ff (Feb. 1954);

Sidney Swensrud, *Gulf Oil Company: the First Fifty Years, 1901–1951* (New York: Newcomen Society of North America, 1951); Craig Thompson, *Since Spindletop* (published by the company). The beginnings of formal research and development activities in Gulf, Atlantic, Standard of Indiana and Standard of California are described in Bartlett, "Development of Industrial Research," pp. 45–47.

[49] Shell's venture into chemicals is well told in Beaton, *Enterprise in Oil*, Chap. 9.

[50] Haynes, *American Chemical Industry*, Vol. VI, pp. 315–318; *Fortune*, 50: 73 ff (Aug. 1954).

[51] Haynes, *op. cit.*, Vols. V–XI.

[52] The following are from the recent annual reports of Gulf and Texaco and from Haynes, *op. cit.*, Vol. VI, pp. 234–235. Other oil companies with autonomous chemical units are Continental Oil and Standard of Ohio. Kenneth R. Kern, ed., *Corporate Diagrams and Administrative Personnel of the Chemical Industry* (Princeton: Chemical Economic Services, 1958), pp. 9, 34.

[53] In 1954 Standard Oil of California also underwent a major reorganization. *Annual Report of the Standard Oil Company of California for 1954*, p. 4; also the company's *Annual Report for 1952*, p. 3.

[54] The du Pont story comes from William S. Dutton, *Du Pont, One Hundred and Forty Years* (New York: Charles Scribner's Sons, 1942); Marquis James, *A. I. du Pont, Family Rebel* (New York: The Bobbs-Merrill Company, Inc., 1940); *A History of the du Pont Company's Relations with the United States Government, 1802–1927* (Wilmington, Del., published by the company, 1928); Haynes, *American Chemical Industry*, Vol. IV, Chap. 3, Vol. VI, pp. 125–137, and scattered references in the other Haynes volumes; *U. S. v. E. I. du Pont de Nemours & Co., et al.*, in the Circuit Court of the United States for the District Court of Delaware #280 in Equity (1909), *U. S. v. E. I. du Pont de Nemours & Co., General Motors Corporation, et al.*; Ernest Dale, "Du Pont: Pioneer in Systematic Management," *Administrative Science Quarterly*, 2: 25–29 (June 1957); William H. Mylander, "Management by Executive Committee," *Harvard Business Review*, 33: 51–58 (May–June, 1955; *Fortune*, 10: 65 ff (Nov. 1934), 42: 87 ff (Oct. 1950); and the company's annual reports.

[55] *Annual Report for E. I. du Pont de Nemours & Company for 1921*, p. 6.

[56] The information on Union Carbon & Carbide came from Haynes, *American Chemical Industry*, Vol. IV, Chap. 3, Vol. VI, pp. 429–438, and scattered references in the other Haynes volumes; *Fortune*, 16: 83 ff (Dec. 1947), 23: 61 ff (June 1941), 24: 49 ff, 24: 57 ff (July, Sept. 1941), 57: 123 ff (Feb. 1957); and the company's annual reports.

[57] *Prospectus for Allied Chemical & Dye Corporation for 1920* (New

York, published by the company, 1920). Data on this company came from Haynes, *American Chemical Industry*, Vol. IV, Chap. 3, Vol. VI, pp. 9–11, 45–49, 179–183, 292–296, 367–370, 391–395, and scattered references in the other volumes; *Fortune*, 1: 81 ff (June 1930), 16: 83 ff (Dec. 1937), 20: 44 ff (Oct. 1939), 50: 119 ff (Oct. 1954); and the company's annual reports. The most recent organizational changes are well described in *Chemical Week*, 84: 51–62 (April 11, 1959).

[58] *Fortune*, 50: 122 (Oct., 1954).

[59] The data on Eastman Kodak came from Haynes, *American Chemical Industry*, Vol. VI, pp. 138–141, and scattered references in the other Haynes volumes; Carl W. Ackerman, *George Eastman* (Boston: Houghton Mifflin Co., 1930); *Fortune*, 50: 76 ff (July 1954); and the company's annual reports.

[60] Organization charts and personnel listings for these companies are given in Kern, *Corporate Diagrams*. Other firms exploiting applied chemistry have developed similar structures, such as Corning Glass and Johns Manville. National Industrial Conference Board, *Organization Charts*, pp. 79–82, 97–98.

[61] The chemical companies' pioneering role in the metals industries is emphasized in Lawrence P. Lessing, "The New Metals Age," in *The Mighty Force of Research* (New York, edited and published by *Fortune*, 1953); and in petro-chemicals, synthetic rubber and fertilizers in Haynes, *American Chemical Industry*, Vol. V, pp. 108–110, Chap. 15, pp. 301–303, 389–390.

[62] There is a brief summary of Alcoa's experience in A. D. Chandler, "Management Decentralization," *Business History Review*, June 1956, pp. 155–156.

[63] *Ibid.*, pp. 164–165, 168–169 and the annual reports of the Procter & Gamble, Armour, and Schenley Companies.

[64] Kern, *Corporate Diagrams*, pp. 5, 16, 60.

EIGHT

☆

SOME ASPECTS OF CORPORATE ENTERPRISE

☆

M. A. ADELMAN

The American economy is an archetype or extreme example of what is loosely known as the Western world. Most of its work is done by corporations rather than by individuals or family groups; in many lines of industry, and for the economy as a whole, there is an impressive degree of concentration, so that a large part of the activity is accounted for by a few very large corporations. This kind of structure is chiefly the development of the past hundred years.

The economic significance of a big-business economy lies in its effect on prices and production: the amount, distribution, and growth of the national income. This essay, however, is concerned mainly with the noneconomic, or social and political, effects.* These noneconomic aspects often insinuate themselves into economic discourse in a disguised, inarticulate, and therefore unhelpful way; to identify them, at least, may be progress. Keynes remarked in his introduction to the first series of Cambridge Economic Handbooks that "the Theory of Economics is a method rather than a doctrine, an apparatus of the mind, a technique of thinking, which helps its possessor to draw correct conclusions." Economists have had some experience in breaking down large and fuzzy ideas like "production," "consumption," "savings," etc., into smaller and more specific concepts which can be tested against facts. Similarly, we may be able to take some steps toward breaking down no less large and fuzzy concepts such as "power," "big business," etc.

The Corporation in General

It is said that life imitates art. In the beginning was the concept of *homo oeconomicus*, the economic man, a bloodless creature with no functions or interests other than income and outlay. In time, there appeared the modern corporation. It is, of course, an imperfect device, as any human contrivance is imperfect, but in most areas it

* Such merit as this essay has is due to my deceased teachers, Morris R. Cohen and Joseph A. Schumpeter. There never lived two men more unlike in character and viewpoint; but each was a mind guided by a zeal to understand; and both would appreciate how their teaching has led me to a result with which, perhaps, neither of them would readily agree.

does far better at the specialized task of searching out the greater profit and shunning the lesser than do the individual or family firms which it has supplanted. Individual entrepreneurs and partners are human. The human condition has two great weaknesses: mortality and, in the interim, all the weakness and distraction that flesh is heir to. In an interesting paper, Scitovsky has pointed out that profit maximization by an entrepreneur is only the special case of constant marginal utility of income.[1] To put the same idea in less rigorous language: at some point, a businessman would rather go fishing than go hunt for yet another dollar; he would be viewed as rather queer if he didn't. To the corporation, however, this becomes merely another detail of cost and of economy of scale. Two vice-presidents would suffice if they could each work sixty hours weekly, but if their efficiency would suffer with a work load of more than forty hours, three will be hired rather than two because it is more profitable. Scitovsky's special case becomes the general case as soon as the business unit is liberated from the constraint of individual tastes, preferences, and work limits. This is the function of the corporation. It is a device to bring together people in an institution with profit as its only distinctive reason for existence.

The concept of the corporation as economic man is contrary to much writing in this field which considers the family firm, uniting ownership and management, as being much closer to the profit-maximizing unit of economic theory. The continued popularity of this view arises in part from the very success of corporate enterprise in making explicit—in order to diminish or overcome—the many barriers to profit-maximizing (chiefly gaps in information) in the real world. To a lesser extent, this view is a mistaken deduction from the demonstrable fact that in any given situation much business profit is actually a residual which may be distributed to nominal owners, or alternatively to managers, with no effect on economic behavior. The insiders may estimate their deserts rather liberally, or even misuse their position to increase their rewards at the expense of the stockholders. But this has little or nothing to do with the decisions the insiders will make, or will be forced by the market to make, as to the best scale and level of output, purchase of factors, investment, and so on. What is best for the company is best for the insiders; its profits are the source of their own private income.

Likewise, profits are the chief source of that survival or "security" which is so often, and so wrongly, set up as an alternative goal to profits. At any given moment, of course, there is usually a choice between greater profit with greater risk and lesser profit with lesser risk. A choice in either direction is an implicit prediction of where greater profits lie over the long run. The better choice is the one based on better information, strict rationality in interpretation, and available means to carry out the decision. On each ground, the modern corporation is usually (though not in all areas, or to an equal degree) a superior economic instrument; hence its survival power. The usefulness or meaning of wider theories of business conduct than "mere" profit making has yet to be shown.[2] The corporation is an imperfect instrument for the pursuit of strictly economic ends because it is operated by men on very scanty information. Railroads, automobiles, and aircraft are also imperfect instruments. They are, however, superior to horses, and they would not continue to exist if they were not a much better way of getting from one place to another.

If the existence of the corporation can be sufficiently explained on purely economic grounds, it follows that we cannot assume, but must look for, the links of causation between it and the social-political phenomena which are the object of our study. The most obvious place where corporate enterprise touches on noneconomic life is in its role as employer. True, large-scale organization of individuals into coherent groups, answerable to a very few decision makers, is older than recorded history. What is now called "the organization man," and the relation of superior to subordinate, was summed up perhaps as well as anywhere by the army officer in the New Testament: "I say to this man, Go, and he goeth; and to another, Come, and he cometh; and to my servant, Do this, and he doeth it."

What is distinctive about corporate enterprise is its mobilization of large numbers of men for avowedly economic goals—not in the name of any divinity or military leadership principle, but simply through a labor contract. If I had to choose a single statistical table which told the most about the history of the United States, it would undoubtedly be the one[3] which shows that in 1820 roughly three-fourths of the labor force were in agriculture and another eighth in "manufacturing and independent hand trades." Something like 75-80 per cent of the labor force were independent entrepreneurs, mostly farmers. Today, the proportions have been reversed. Of the total labor force of 64 million in 1956, 86 per cent were employees. Excluding government employment, 54 million were engaged in private industries, and 83 per cent of them were employees. Of 49 million persons in nonagricultural private pursuits, 87 per cent were employees.[4] And the reduction of the agricultural population continued apace; it fell by 17 per cent from 1950–1956, and by a third in the twenty to twenty-four year age group.[5] In short, as compared with the American economy of 130 years ago, there has been a tremendous narrowing of employment alternatives. From a nation of independent enterprisers, we have become a nation of employees.

This transformation within the business sphere (*i.e.*, outside of agriculture and government) seems to have been largely accomplished by the beginning of this century. So far as can be ascertained, the number of employment centers, *i.e.*, business firms, has remained at about one-twelfth to one-eleventh of the working population.[a] Concentration of employment among firms is of course quite impressive; in 1951 the largest three-fourths of 1 per cent of all business firms—those employing 100 or more persons—accounted for about 60 per cent of the employees. The largest 240-odd firms, those with 10,000 or more employees, had 19 per cent of private business firms' employment, and indeed about 11 per cent of the nation's entire labor force;[6] though it is no less true that 89 per cent of the labor force, and 81 per cent of the nongovernment, nonfarm labor force, is still outside the employment of the 240 giants.

This extensive separation of labor from direct ownership-management of capital has not been greatly offset by indirect ownership. In recent years, to judge by the results of the Survey Research Center, about 10 per cent of all households own some listed corporate stock and only 3 per cent own $5,000 worth or more.[7] Assuming a yield of 5 per cent of market value—quite high by current standards—this would correspond to an annual income from ownership of only $250. Smaller amounts can scarcely be called significant. About 7 per cent own a share, however small, in a business.[8] These two categories overlap and are not additive. If we had a corrected and nonduplicated total, it would not be correct to add it to the total of independent businessmen and professionals, since many of them obviously own stock or other forms of business property. Under the circumstances, it appears to be a generous estimate that, aside from these "independents," less than 10 per cent of the population own a significant

---

[a] This is a rough estimate made by extrapolating the estimates of the Department of Commerce backward according to the number of firms reported by Dun and Bradstreet, Inc., and their predecessors.

amount of any income-yielding property; while something upwards of 3 per cent (perhaps as high as 5 per cent) own a significant amount of corporate stock.

The divorce of the great bulk of the population from ownership of capital has not gone as far as it can go; but it has obviously gone far. If continued, it would of course in time approach the One Big Employer of the socialist state. It has probably become clearer in the last ten years that the chief objection to socialism is not strictly economic, but lies rather in its startling resemblance to the old-fashioned mining town where the one employer was also the landlord, the government, the school, etc., with the vital difference that there was a world outside the town which afforded means of escape for a few and, in time, of release for all.

It does not follow, however, that, because we have gone any given per cent of the distance between one employment center per unit of the gainfully employed and one employment center in the whole economy, we have gone any corresponding distance on a scale marked "liberty," "democracy," "progress," or anything else. It would be a strange (and strangely easy to understand) world if this were true. To be sure, economic and political divisions and classes are interrelated. The Founding Fathers of our Constitution, as able and hard-boiled a lot of political philosophers as ever convened, needed no instruction from Karl Marx on that score. James Madison's famous Number Ten of the Federalist papers is still a classic formulation of how the unequal distribution of property, and the various forms of property, are the everlasting source of "factions." But what neither Madison nor his fellows (except perhaps Thomas Jefferson, who was not a member of the convention, reflecting on his experiences in Europe) envisaged was a society where many or most of the population were without property and worked for someone else.

By the first half of the nineteenth century such a process was visibly under way, and it is instructive to read the reactions of some of the more sensitive and powerful minds to whom it was still a new phenomenon. A hopeful revolutionist like Karl Marx and a despairing conservative like John C. Calhoun agreed in their analysis of what was happening and was likely to happen. Marx, as is well known, thought that capitalist enterprise would be concentrated into fewer and fewer hands until the propertyless masses would revolt, and "the expropriators are expropriated."[9] It is doubtful that he expected this to be a neatly determinate process like the catastrophic rise of steam pressure in a boiler. But one may surmise that he considered as high a degree of proletarianization as exists in the United States today to be a sufficient condition for "the revolution."

Calhoun's defense of the slave system was that by uniting capital and labor in the person of the slave the otherwise irreconcilable conflict between capital and labor would be prevented. Hofstadter has pointed out that in Calhoun's thought there is to be found

> a labor theory of value and of a surplus appropriated by the capitalists; the concentration of capital under capitalistic production; the fall of working-class conditions to the level of subsistence; the growing revolt of the laboring class against the capitalists; the prediction of social revolution. The difference was that Calhoun proposed that no revolution should be allowed to take place.

He vainly urged that the stable slaveholding South offered a valuable conservative influence for the whole class-struggle-ridden North.[10]

The durability of the tradition is striking. Shortly after the First World War the British Prime Minister, Lloyd George, contrasted the stability of France, a nation of widely diffused property in small enterprises and peasant holdings, with the instability of Great Britain, the great bulk of whose population was composed of propertyless employees. This drew from Lenin the remark that not only was Mr. Lloyd George a clever man, but he had also learned much from the Marxists.[11] Yet Lenin's attempt to copyright the tradition was probably unjustified. Before then and since, the belief is almost unanimous —left, right, and center—that the diffusion of ownership of the means of production (as distinguished from goods used for personal satisfactions) helps stabilize our society. In the language of Judge Learned Hand:

> It is possible, because of its indirect social or moral effect, to prefer a system of small producers, each dependent for his success upon his own skill and character, to one in which the great mass of those engaged must accept the direction of a few . . .[12]
>
> Throughout the history of these [antitrust] statutes it has been constantly assumed that one of their purposes was to perpetuate and preserve, for its own sake *and in spite of possible cost*, an organization of industry in small units. . . .[13]

With this dominant tradition may be compared the opinions of De Tocqueville, who visited the United States about the time that Calhoun's thought was maturing, and who was also impressed by the rise of manufacturing and industry and the importance of economies of scale:

> Private persons can effect nothing in manufactures without combination; but the government naturally seeks to place these combinations under its own control.
>
> It must be admitted that these collective beings, which are called companies, are stronger and more formidable than a private individual can ever be, and that they have less of the responsibility for their own actions; whence it seems reasonable that they should not be allowed to retain so great an independence of the supreme government as might be conceded to a private individual.[14]

This language is strikingly contemporary, but the "reasonable" conclusion is not self-evident. Would not the newly powerful "companies" control the government rather than let it control them? De Tocqueville's answer was negative but cautious:

> I am of the opinion, upon the whole, that the manufacturing aristocracy which is growing up under our eyes is . . . one of the most confined and least dangerous. Nevertheless, the friends of democracy should keep their eyes anxiously fixed in this direction; for if ever a permanent inequality of conditions and aristocracy again penetrate into the world, it may be predicted that this is the channel by which they will enter.[15]

Unfortunately, De Tocqueville's reasons are not clearly stated. So far as we can guess at his thought, it is that the employer had no connection with the employees except the labor contract, and had no means of controlling their lives as the rural magnate did those of his serfs or tenants. The sharp separation of classes and the definition of personal roles by economic function rather than by time-honored relations with one's "natural superiors" were precisely what Marx was to emphasize so strongly as sufficient conditions for revolution. In De Tocqueville's system the result appeared to be rather a brake on the power of the capitalists which made their existence tolerable to the rest of society. To formulate the issue a little differently: The Marxist system predicted that the propertyless masses would be systematically exploited until they realized the power that lay in their numbers. Since pent-up forces tend to work with some violence, this would lead to revolution. In De Tocqueville's system the resistance of other social groups to the "manufacturing aristocracy" was in operation from the start. Marx had a model of delayed adaptation, leading to a cataclysmic break; De Tocqueville had a model of continuous adaptation to a new equilibrium.

The Social Impact of Big Business

Our object is not to decide which of these various prophets with honor had the best insight. But we are interested in how to reduce the issue to a set of smaller propositions for or against which some actual evidence can be found. The central concept is that of power. How is power registered so that we can tell whether it waxes or wanes in time and how it varies with the size of business? Some possible consequences of a society polarized between a few owners and a vast number of employees might be put down summarily: first, the small number of business units would acquire for their owners, by controlling the market system, a growing share of the national income. Second, a concentrated business system, particularly the larger units among it, would wield increasing power over government and insure that policies were increasingly favorable to them. Third, since the good jobs within the corporate system would be reserved increasingly to the heirs of the existing management, vertical mobility upward would become ever more difficult. Fourth, big business would give rise to big unions and big government.

INCOME DISTRIBUTION

The distribution of the national income seems, if we may trust general impressions, to be less unequal in the United States than anywhere else outside the British Commonwealth and the Scandinavian countries. Foreign observers are struck by the size of the American middle class. The greatest extremes of wealth and abysmal poverty are most characteristic of countries of small-scale enterprise. If this impression is correct, it is not wholly unexpected. The degree of industrial concentration, industry by industry and market by market, is generally less in the United States than elsewhere, and the degree of effective monopoly is considerably less, chiefly because markets are generally larger. The current attempts at freer trade in western Europe are basically an attempt to provide a larger arena for a more effectively competitive system, in imitation of the United States. It is likely, though it is not strictly necessary, that an economy with less monopoly would have a more equal distribution of income. We are on a somewhat firmer basis in exploring trends in the distribution of the national income. So far as concerns the United States, there is some reason to believe that the distribution has become somewhat more equal over the past forty-odd years. The share (before taxes) of the top 1 per cent and the top 5 per cent of all income-receiving units was roughly stable during 1913–1927, decreased in 1929–1939, and decreased rather more substantially during 1939–1948.[16] The decline was particularly marked in corporate interest and dividends, even after inclusion of undistributed corporate profits.[17] Kuznets' findings have given rise to much discussion and controversy,[18] which is as it should be; income is not a simple concept. But nobody has suggested that the data can be interpreted to support an increase in the share of the upper-income groups.

POLITICAL POWER

The hypothesis of increasing power over government may by verified by the method of *inputs* or that of *outputs*. On the side of inputs, one can cite the money available to any large business for public relations, to buy itself a reputation, project a corporate "image" according to the latest fashions, maintain lobbies at the seat of government, employ ex-officials, and so on. The method of inputs can be interwoven and reinforced with familiar names. Thus one can mention ex-generals who were hired by large business enterprises, proceed to blanket all ex-generals as a class into big business, then suggest quite an impressive togetherness of government and business by pointing out, for example, that over the past decade the Secretaries of State and both parties' candidates for President have all been either retired generals (Eisenhower, Marshall), or corporation lawyers (Acheson, Dulles, Stevenson).

The method of inputs has, obviously, great literary and labor-saving advantages. But a resident of Boston finds it difficult to forget that the Red Sox were at one time known as the Fenway Millionaires, able and willing to buy the best pitching, fielding, and hitting; but in the end they somehow lacked enough *games won* for either the spiritual afflatus of a pennant or the cash rewards of World Series play. It may be that organized baseball is right in using a measure of output rather than input. By this standard, the record of business in general, and big business in particular, does not seem impressive. This country has engaged in three major wars over the past century. A war is a period of great burdens and also opportunities for profit, when the operations and results of the various power mechanisms are most clearly evident. If we look at the major economic items of taxation, price control, and profits on war contracts, the pattern stands out quite clearly—increasing regulation and decreasing opportunities for gain. Or, if we look at the major pieces of economic legislation over the past half century—the progressive income tax, banking and utility regulation, labor and social security legislation, antitrust laws—it is fairly clear that they were all passed in the teeth of business (including big business) opposition. This is not to comment on the merits of any of these laws, either as they appeared at the time of enactment or in retrospect. But, considered simply as indicators of which class was able to work its will in getting the legislation it wanted, these laws are hard to reconcile with any thesis of increasing power over government by business, particularly big business. A prominent student of constitutional law has noted that

> the view that property itself is the matrix, the seed-bed, which must be conserved if other values are to flourish, has always had expression in American society. . . . [A] concept of property in some form was elevated to first rank by a long line of American figures both influential and unabashed. This strain of thought finds no hospitality in the [Supreme] Court today.[19]

As the dependence of the population on property has decreased, so has its place in the order of values enforced by our legal system. Judged by output criteria, at least, a significant shift in power has occurred.

As for the particular problem of whether larger or smaller business concerns are more successful in getting what they want at the seat of government, this is usually harder to discern because on few public issues is there a clear-cut division. But as one indication we might well consider certain reactions of the general public, for obviously those interests are most powerful (in the output sense) whose striving will arouse the least unfavorable comment. Whether or not Mr. Wilson actually said that what was good for General Motors was good for the country is not clear; but the English language has been permanently enriched by this comment, and the angry reaction to it is well known. Also reasonably familiar is the investigation of automobile marketing practices by a committee of the United States Senate in 1956, and subsequent legislation which provided in effect that the number of automobiles sold in any given local area should be as decided by the manufacturer or the local dealer, whichever number is the *lesser*. (The manufacturer would not ship more than he wished; if he tried to ship more than the dealer wished, this has become "coercion," and actionable at law.) If the measure (and a supporting law passed in 1958 to prevent competition from breaking into local markets by shipments among marketing areas) raises the price of a new automobile by as little as 5 per cent, it will probably cost the consuming public around half a billion dollars per year.[20] The laws passed Congress overwhelmingly despite the disapproval of the antitrust agencies. When the laws were being considered by the appropriate congressional committees, it was repeatedly urged, as an argument in their favor, that automobile dealers wanted them. What was good for the dealer *was* good for the country, and this argument drew nothing but respectful attention.

In the antitrust area, which comes perhaps closest to showing some small-versus-large division, the permanence of the Robinson-Patman Act and the "fair trade" (resale price maintenance) laws do not suggest any success of big-business pressure or failure of small-business pressure, though the division is by no means clear-cut. The federal legitimization of "fair trade" was emasculated by a Supreme Court decision in 1951;[21] within a year Congress had re-enacted it in judge-proof form and more stringent than before. By way of contrast, the 1948 Cement decision destroying basing-point systems[22] was widely protested in part by small but principally by large business interests, and a decade of protests yielded them nothing.

Outside of the antitrust area, it would startle no student of foreign trade policy to be told that the most effective opposition to lower tariffs is from smaller manufacturing enterprises. But perhaps the most striking example is the most small-scale and deconcentrated of all industries, commercial agriculture, which has for two decades been able to secure a government-operated monopoly of certain "basic" farm commodities. Even the (incomplete) budget cost is several billion dollars a year. Protection and other subsidies to the farmers of the advanced industrial nations have not only been an obvious economic waste but also have generated some dangerous reactions in the less developed lands of the non-Soviet world. "Their resentment against the more industrialized countries and their feeling that they are getting a raw deal . . . have been voiced with increasing bitterness. . . ."[23] The governments of the industrialized countries, knowing the situation well enough, have been unable to act. More impressive examples of power (in the output sense) are not easily found.

Looking abroad briefly, the consensus of Lloyd George and Lenin on social stability in France and instability in England has a somewhat odd look today. The countries of polarized labor and capital have been stable; the land of widely diffused ownership of small businesses has been unstable. Nor is the French situation an accident. It is by now trite and obvious that because French property owners are many and small they are politically powerful. Wartime price control and peacetime taxation are widely avoided or evaded; agriculture has been subsidized as in the United States; industry has been carried on by small firms joined into cartels to restrict output and raise prices; the national product has been notably slow to increase (though the last few years offer the hope of a change here); as a scarcely accidental result, the propertyless class is embittered to the point where a fourth of the nation's electorate votes Communist.

SOCIAL MOBILITY

Whether or not individuals in the lower-income groups have more or fewer opportunities for advancement than formerly is not a settled question. Recent research has indicated that the barriers to business success have always been high; business executives of the late nineteenth century were a thoroughly select group, unrepresented of the general population in national origins, place of birth, religious affiliation, and occupation of parents.[24]

With increasing percentages of the population receiving high-school and college educations, one barrier to economic advancement has been lowered.[25] Since ownership of many corporations, and particularly the largest ones, is separated from active management, individuals can and do seek careers where they are qualified, and do not need to hurdle the additional irrelevant barrier of family origin. It comes as no surprise, therefore, that two recent studies indicate, though not conclusively, that within the corporate sphere mobility seems—if anything—on the increase.[26]

For many individuals the prospect of a career in a large concern may be more inviting than the prospect of independent owner-management; for others it may be less attractive. Nobody has suggested how the balance is to be struck; and I suspect it is beyond the powers of either the old or the new welfare economics, or indeed any other discipline. But since the number of independent business firms per thousand employed has not changed much over the last half century, perhaps the increasing mobility within the corporate business sphere has been added to mobility within the whole business universe rather than offsetting any contrary trends. Also, there should be no disagreement that the Great Depression of the 1930's, with its massive unemployment and blocking up of the channels of advancement of any kind, produced more frustration, and of a more dangerous kind, than all the structural economic changes before or since.

BIG BUSINESS AND LABOR UNIONS

The rise of large unions is often ascribed to the concentration of employment in large firms. If by bigness we mean absolute size, then some rough computations—which are all the available statistics permit—indicate a slight positive association between size of plant and degree of unionization as measured by coverage of collective-bargaining agreements. However, if by big business we mean concentration—a large percentage of the industry in the hands of a small number of firms, then there is no association whatever with the degree of unionization.

In addition to the statistics, certain well-known facts support the same conclusion of slight connection between bigness in business and unions. Large unions are characteristic of certain very small-scale industries—e.g., women's garments, the building trades, trucking. Even in the large mass-production industries, effective unions were almost unknown until twenty years ago, which does not confirm the idea of some inherent connection between the two. Finally, European business is smaller (though more concentrated) than American, but European labor was organized into large unions many years before American labor.

In short, the separation of labor from capital seems both a necessary and sufficient condition for unions to exist, and the size or concentration of business is neither. In rejecting the false and sterile dogma that "big business results in big unions" (usually with the definite implication that this is nothing to the credit of big business!) we need not go to the opposite extreme and deny any possible connection at any time. For example, in the garment trades, establishments were very concentrated in space, thousands of workers congregating in a few acres. This, and the unusual homogeneity of their national origins, may well suffice to explain the spread of unions in the industry. At the other extreme, it is plausible that some of the

CIO organization drives in the mid-1930's were deliberately aimed at organizing a few large firms simultaneously because they accounted for the bulk of output, and contracts with them would put the union in a good position to mop up the remaining companies. Thus there may in this instance have been a connection between concentration and unionization. But if so—and only detailed research could settle the matter—it was a specific cause, not a general one. Industry-wide bargaining is a very old phenomenon, long practiced, especially in Europe, in small-scale industries; and in this country not only in the garment trades but most notably in the relatively unconcentrated bituminous coal industry.

Conclusion

In his widely read book,[27] Gunnar Myrdal notes that in the "integrated" societies of the West there has been a redistribution of income and greater equalization of opportunity. Most citizens have acquired a sense of participation in the community, so that the earlier class struggles have lost their significance; and the readiness to share burdens is an index of the nation's cohesion.

It is difficult to dispute Myrdal's conclusion; this essay has tried to relate the result to something more definite than changes in the moral climate, to supply some explanation for varying attitudes shown from one country to another. I doubt that anyone would contend that the French or Italian bourgeois classes are innately more narrow or selfish than the British or American. But they do have more power to avoid the "sharing burdens"—of taxation, or of competition, etc. —than is good for the national product or the peace of society. In the strongholds of small business the social peace is most precarious and the normal disagreements come closer to the mood of class warfare.[28]

Perhaps the generalization which has appealed to a number of venerable figures must—in the light of a hindsight they did not have —be reversed. In the United States particularly, the polarization of capital and labor and the size and fewness of firms have apparently made business enterprises, particularly large enterprises, politically weaker, not stronger. They have been forced to share burdens, and in the end this has perhaps been the price of stability and survival. It may be that the capitalist order is stronger and more stable precisely when there is a very considerable divorce of the population from the means of production.

There is nothing universal about this theory. It presumes a certain degree of literacy and urbanization, and a rising level of income such that the gains of one class need not represent the loss of another. But, if we are to attain any useful knowledge in this area, we shall need to descend from the lofty plane of discussion of "the corporation" or "big business" and instead try to formulate a number of more limited and less sweeping hypotheses.

Notes

[1] Tibor Scitovsky, "A Note on Profit Maximization," *Review of Economic Studies*, Vol. xi, 1943, pp. 57–60.

[2] See Bernard F. Haley, ed., *A Survey of Contemporary Economics*, (Homewood, Ill., Irwin, Inc., 1952), article by Andreas G. Papandreou and comments by Mason and Heflebower, pp. 183–222.

[3] Prepared by Solomon Fabricant on the basis of estimates by Daniel Carson, P. K. Whelpton and A. M. Edwards. See *Studies in Income and Wealth*, Vol. XI (New York: National Bureau of Economic Research, 1949), p. 42.

[4] *Survey of Current Business*, July 1956, pp. 19 and 21, Tables 25 and 28.

[5] Bureau of the Census, *Series P-27*, August 8, 1958. Figures are as of July 1. These are total population, not only gainfully employed.

[6] See Betty C. Churchill, "Size Characteristics of the Business Population," *Survey of Current Business*, May, 1954; and footnote 4 above.

[7] *Federal Reserve Bulletin*, September, 1958, pp. 1032, 1046–1050. This includes only stock sold to the general public, including mutual funds. It excludes stock not publicly traded or held by personal trusts. The former is partly covered in the category "ownership of a business." See later in text paragraph. The data on personal trusts are fragmentary and unsatisfactory. Survey data appear to understate very greatly the *aggregate stock holdings* of consuming units, and their estimates of this variable would in any case be subject to great sampling error for the very reason that stock ownership is infrequent and is also highly concentrated among its relatively few owners. However, there is much less error in the estimate of the *proportion of spending* units owning stock. Indirect holding of corporate stock is more important as a public image than as an economic fact. At the end of 1955 about $354 billion of cor-

porate common stock were outstanding, of which personal trust held about $44 billion, and financial institutions about $26 billion. See Raymond W. Goldsmith and Eli Shapiro, "An Estimate of Bank-Administered Personal Trust Funds," *Journal of Finance*, vol. 14 (1959), Table 2, p. 15. Bank-administered pension funds may amount to as much as $20 billion by 1965. See *New York Times*, May 12, 1959, p. 16.

[8] *Ibid.*, September, 1953, p. 944.

[9] Karl Marx, *Capital*, Vol. I, Part VIII, ch. 32, p. 836 (Chicago, Charles H. Kerr, 1906).

[10] Richard Hofstadter, *The American Political Tradition* (New York, Alfred A. Knopf, 1948), p. 82. And cf. Kenneth Stempp, *The Peculiar Institution* (New York, Alfred A. Knopf, 1956), p. 420.

[11] V. I. Lenin, *Selected Works* (London, Lawrence & Wishart, 1937), Vol. X, p. 124.

[12] *U. S. v. Aluminum Co. of America*, 148 F 2d 416, 427 (C.A. 2, 1945).

[13] *Ibid.*, at 429. Italics added.

[14] Alexis de Tocqueville, *Democracy in America* (New York, Alfred A. Knopf, Bradley ed., 1945), Vol. II, Book 4, ch. 6, p. 311.

[15] *Ibid.*, Book 2, ch. 20, p. 161.

[16] Simon Kuznets, *Share of Upper Income Groups in Income and Savings* (New York: National Bureau of Economic Research, 1953), ch. 2.

[17] *Ibid.*, pp. 37–39.

[18] Cf. "Diminishing Inequality in Personal Income Distribution," *Papers and Proceedings of the American Economic Association*, Vol. XLIV, May, 1954, pp. 236–278.

[19] Paul A. Freund, *On Understanding the Supreme Court* (Boston, Little Brown, 1950), pp. 14, 17. See also pp. 11–12.

[20] New cars and net purchases of used cars in 1955 cost $14.44 billion. (See *Survey of Current Business*, July, 1956.) Were demand absolutely inelastic, revenues would increase by $722 million. The "cost" to the consuming public is of course not only the higher prices but the restricted output, which would exist even if demand were, say, unit-elastic and expenditures unchanged. See also the *Wall Street Journal*, October 10, 1958, p. 1, col. 5, where a salesman is quoted as saying that the 1958 law alone would mean "$100 more profit per car," roughly 5 per cent.

[21] *Schwegmann Bros. v. Seagrams Distillers' Corp.*, 341 U. S. 384 (1951).

[22] *Federal Trade Commission v. Cement Institute et al.*, 334 U. S. 839 (1948).

[23] *The Economist* (London), Oct. 11, 1958, p. 119. See also the Inter-

national Monetary Fund, *International Financial News Survey*, Oct. 31, 1958, pp. 141–142.

[24] William Miller, "American Historians and the Business Elite," *Journal of Economic History*, November 1949; and "The Recruitment of the American Business Elite," *Quarterly Journal of Economics*, May 1950.

[25] Cf. Nelson N. Foote and Paul K. Hatt, "Social Mobility and Economic Advancement," *Papers and Proceedings of the American Economic Association*, Vol. XLIII, May 1953, pp. 375–378.

[26] Mabel Newcomer, *The Big Business Executive* (New York: Harper & Brothers, 1955); and W. Lloyd Warner and James C. Abegglen, *Occupational Mobility in American Business and Industry* (Minneapolis: University of Minnesota Press, 1955), Chaps. 2, 3, 4. The sampling procedure is not fully explained, and large firms are obviously over-represented (see p. 234). Small firms show less occupational mobility than large (p. 35).

[27] Gunnar Myrdal, *An International Economy* (New York: Harper & Brothers, 1956), Chap. III, particularly pp. 17–31.

[28] Cf. *ibid.*, pp. 29–30.

NINE

☆

A DECADE OF
CORPORATE CAPITAL
INVESTMENT: 1946–1955

☆

ELI SHAPIRO
and
MORRIS MENDELSON

Summary

With the cessation of hostilities in 1945 the tempo of corporate capital expenditures increased sharply. In 1946, the first full year of peace, plant and equipment expenditures were almost two and a half times those of 1944, the last full year of war. For fixed investment,[a] the ratio of 1946 to 1944 expenditures exceeded two and a half. And, finally, for total corporate capital expenditures, including changes in inventories,[b] the ratio almost doubles. In the ten years that followed the close of the war corporate capital expenditures amounted to almost $230 billion. The vast bulk of these expenditures was for fixed investment. The annual average change in inventories for the decade was less than $5 billion.

By far the major source of funds used to finance these capital expenditures was internal funds;[c] they constituted almost 83 per cent of the total sources accounted for and over 75 per cent of the total uses. The most important type of external funds[d] was the net issue of securities. This was true of every single year without exception. And, finally, the most important type of security was bonds. Over the decade net working capital increased on the average by slightly less than $5 billion per year.

[a] In addition to new plant and equipment expenditures, fixed investment includes "other capital expenditures," a flow-of-fund concept that covers corporate purchases of residential land and structures, used equipment purchases from the federal government and dealers' margins on new security issues. The term "investment" as used, is not net of depreciation.

[b] Changes in inventories are measured as changes in the book value of inventories after valuation adjustment.

[c] Internal or inside funds, as used here, are defined as the sum of net profits before tax, depreciation, amortization, depletion, insurance benefits, tax refunds, and other internal charges, less the sum of federal and state tax payments, renegotiation payments, dividends, branch profits paid, and bad debt charges.

[d] External funds, as used here, are defined as the sum of net bond and stock issues, net change in mortgage liabilities, net long term borrowing, and net short term borrowing (net of trade credit extended), less the sum of increases in cash, United States and state and local government securities, and other portfolio securities. If all flows were accurately measured, total investment would equal the sum of internal and external funds; since the flows are not accurately measured, the equality seldom holds. The differences are called statistical discrepancy, and there are grounds for believing that the major part of this discrepancy consists of errors of measurement of external funds.

The Depression and War Years

To understand the unusually large demand for funds in the postwar decade, it is necessary to examine the course and direction of private investment during the preceding fifteen years, a period which includes the post-1929 depression through 1940 and the war-induced prosperity beginning in 1941.

From 1929 to 1940 the country experienced a low volume of investment by corporations in plant, equipment, and inventories. There was virtually no net change in the book value of fixed assets of the private nonfinancial corporations. In contrast, from the middle of 1940 through the end of 1941 there was a sharp increase in expenditures for plant, equipment, and inventories by nonfinancial corporations as they responded to the rapid rise in economic activity resulting from the outbreak of hostilities in Europe. The expansion, however, was aborted by the attack on Pearl Harbor and our entry into the war.

As a consequence of the tremendous wartime demands upon our resources, both industrial and human, we shifted to a war program designed to maximize the output of goods and services needed for the successful prosecution of the war. The material allocation system that was introduced to insure the free flow of resources into war and war-related industries left relatively few resources available for private investment in plant, equipment, and inventories. After the early part of 1942 most expenditures on fixed assets were made by the federal government.

The private sector of the United States economy added virtually nothing to fixed plant and equipment during the war. The 70 per cent hike in the Gross National Product from 1941 through 1945 was due mostly to a more extensive use of existing facilities rather than to any proportionate increase in the physical facilities of the country. By the end of 1945 the net book value of the *fixed* assets of all nonfinancial corporations was below the figure for the end of 1941 and about the same as that for the end of 1939.

An integral part of the governmental wartime apparatus for mobilizing the nation's resources was an inventory control system imposed upon business. Essentially, the inventory control froze inventories at a level existing in the early part of the war, and firms had to report their inventory holdings so that the control authority could police the system and insure that goods necessary for the war were not piling up in warehouses. Although the level of inventories was frozen, the volume of sales rose sharply. The net effect was an extremely low ratio of inventories to sales compared with previous experience. This reduced business' need for funds to build up the inventory component of gross working capital.

The inventory freeze had another financial repercussion upon business. Because of the low level of inventories relative to sales, we had the appearance of a seller's market. In a more competitive market situation one obvious form of sales strategy is the extension of trade credit to consummate a sale. However, since there were relatively few goods available then, sellers insisted on more stringent terms of payment and cash sales became more prevalent. Thus the ratio of receivables to sales fell sharply during the war. Since extension of credit on accounts receivable typically gives rise to a need for funds by the credit-granting seller, the decline in receivables also lessened the need for funds by businesses.

The inventory freeze served to reduce business' need for current financing. Moreover, since most of the expenditures on plant and equipment were financed by the government, private business' needs for long-term funds were also minimized.

Between 1939 and 1942 net profits doubled despite the big slice for income and excess-profits tax. After 1942 net profits tended to stabilize. The wartime increase in net worth was substantial, but, as a result of the excess of depreciation and depletion accruals over private expenditures on fixed property, it was exceeded by the increase in working capital. The percentage increase in the net working capital of business corporations from the end of 1939 to 1945 was larger than the increase in either current assets or current liabilities. By far the largest component of the increase in current liabilities consisted of increases in short-term funds owed the federal government in the form of accrued taxes and advances and prepayments on war production contracts.

As a result of all these things, nonfinancial corporations came out of the war with both an unprecedented volume of liquidity and a great need for funds to finance the replacement of war-worn productive facilities with new physical plant and equipment. In addition to replacing physical facilities, it was necessary to augment them in order to handle the enlarged volume of economic activity that characterized the postwar period.

In spite of the relatively high rate of growth of working capital, funds to further increase working capital were needed. After the inventory controls ended at the end of the war and as markets became more competitive, the high and increasing level of sales necessitated increasing inventories. Business had to and did build up its inventory accounts substantially, both absolutely and relative to sales. From the standpoint of the individual business firms, the rise in the price level created a need for additional funds even to preserve the physical size of inventories. With the restoration of a more competitive market, it was also necessary to resort to credit extension as a method of sales competition. Thus the receivable account rose as business reverted to peacetime patterns of sales. Finally, the enlarged payrolls, the increases in wages, and the added expenses associated with the rising price level in the postwar period all compounded the need and demand for additional funds for working capital.

The Flow of Expenditures

The corporate sector is not a decision making organism which responds to changing economic stimuli; rather, it is a composite of decision making units each of which responds in its own way to changing economic forces. A broad group such as the corporate sector is often divisible into subsectors within each of which the degree of similarity is somewhat greater than that between subsectors. The behavior of the whole sector may then be studied in the light of the different behavior of the subsectors and the shift over time of the relative importance of the various subsectors in each type of economic activity.

With this in mind, the corporate sector has been divided into five subsectors:[e] manufacturing and mining; railroads; electric and gas; communications; and trade, service, and miscellaneous.[f]

Our procedure will be to examine each of the major flows in turn to see the extent to which the expansions and contractions of the all-corporate sector were the consequence of relatively uniform be-

[e] For the latter part of the decade corporate flow-of-funds data compiled by David Meiselman and Eli Shapiro for the National Bureau's Postwar Capital Market Study (forthcoming manuscript, *Corporate Sources and Uses of Funds, Annual 1950–1955, Quarterly, 1953–1955*) are available, and for the first half of the decade we have used data compiled by John C. Dawson; *Fluctuations in U.S. Corporate Investment and Finance, 1931–1950.* Ph.D. thesis (unpublished), Cornell University, 1957, Appendix A.
[f] For convenience this sector will be referred to as the trade-service industry.

havior of the component industries and the extent to which they were the result of shifts in activity from one industry to another. A clear-cut separation of these two forces is impossible, but an examination from that point of view is illuminating.

To a certain extent fluctuations in all corporate total capital expenditures are the consequence of changes in the composition of expenditures. By and large, but not without exceptions, the inventory changes are the volatile elements in total capital expenditures. Insofar as this is so, fluctuations in the latter can be explained largely by the shift in importance of inventories in total capital formation. This is not without its implications for the shifts in activity among industries. Changes in inventories are far more important in the manufacturing and mining and trade-service industries. Sharp rises in total capital expenditures which can be traced to changes in inventories can also be traced to the activity of either or both of the latter two groups.

However, the impact of the fluctuations in changes in inventories on fluctuations in total capital expenditures tends to blur the analysis of the industrial composition of expenditures. For this reason we shall deal with fixed investment and changes in inventories separately at first, after which we will examine the behavior of total capital expenditures.

FIXED INVESTMENT

All corporate fixed investment was already rising when the postwar decade opened. The rise slowed down early in the decade, but expenditures continued to drift upward (Chart I). The upward drift was neither even nor uninterrupted, but by 1955 fixed investment was proceeding at the rate of $24.5 billion per year compared with an annual rate of $13.7 billion in 1946.

The first interruption of the upward drift occurred in 1949. In that year fixed investment expenditures fell by $2.4 billion to $17.5 billion. They then rose at varying rates until 1953, by which time they had risen to almost $24.4 billion. The upward drift was again interrupted in 1954, when fixed investment fell by slightly less than $1.0 billion. The last year of the decade was the first since 1948 in which fixed investment by all industries moved in the same direction, or at least in which no industry moved counter to the others. In both the gas and electric and railroad industries fixed investment remained un-

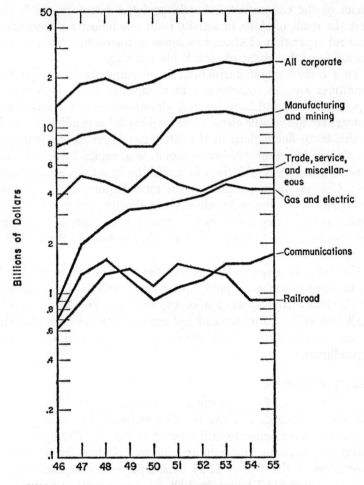

CHART I - CORPORATE FIXED INVESTMENT: BY INDUSTRY

changed at $4.2 and $0.9 billion respectively. In all of the others there was a weak upward movement.

Not all of the subgroups shared in the general upward drift in fixed investment. Only the communications industry reached the decadal peak in fixed investment in 1955. In both manufacturing and mining and the gas and electric industries investment in 1953 exceeded that of 1955 by $0.3 billion each. And, finally, one cannot describe the general movement of railroad fixed investment as an upward drift. The highest level of investment by this subgroup, $1.5 billion, was achieved in 1951. Investment in each subsequent year was either lower or unchanged from the previous year.

CHANGES IN INVENTORIES

The pattern of investment in inventories is quite different from that in durable capital goods. First, there is no discernible upward drift. Second, corporate inventory investment with but minor exception is almost completely dominated by changes in manufacturing and mining inventories (Chart II). Third, the peaks and troughs of

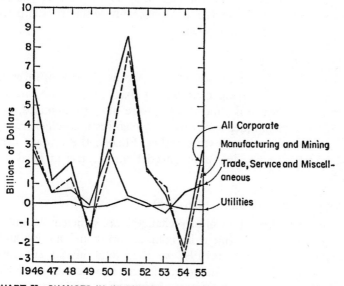

CHART II - CHANGES IN INVENTORY: BY INDUSTRY

changes in inventories do not occur at the same dates as those in fixed investment.

In 1947 inventory investment by manufacturing and mining and the trade-service subsectors were the same. In 1950 the net changes of the latter were larger. In every other year of the decade the net changes of manufacturing and mining inventories were much more pronounced than those of the trade-service industry. That is not to say that the cumulation was greater. As a matter of fact, trade-service investment in inventories rose above that of manufacturing and mining in both 1949 and 1954. In the former year, however, manufacturing and mining decumulated much more than did trade-service, and in the latter year, while the trade-service subsector was adding to its inventories, manufacturing and mining was disinvesting. In 1947 domination of all corporate inventory investment by that of manufacturing and mining was modified but not wiped out. Total corporate inventory changes fell almost twice as fast as those of manufacturing and mining because trade-service inventory investment fell almost as rapidly as that of manufacturing and mining. Again in 1950 the impact of the rapid accumulation by trade-service resulted in all corporate inventory investment rising much faster than that of manufacturing and mining. And, finally, in 1951 the fall in trade-service inventory investment noticeably offset the sharp rise in the all corporate inventory change.

TOTAL INVESTMENT

Total investment, influenced as it was by changes in inventories, followed a more volatile course than fixed investments, its major component. Both peaks and troughs were more pronounced, and in one instance the influence of inventory changes was sufficiently great to shift the peak to two years earlier. Finally, the upward drift in total investment was less pronounced than the rise in fixed investment.

EXPANSION AND RECESSION: 1946–1949

The influence of inventory changes was sufficient to outweigh the rises in fixed investment by manufacturing and mining and the trade-service subsectors in 1947 so that total investment actually fell (see Chart III). The influence of these two sectors, was sufficient to offset the investment activity of the entire utility group so that all corporate investment instead of rising, as fixed investment did (Chart I), actually fell slightly. In 1948 inventories again increased and reinforced the influence of fixed investment, which rose sharply. Thus, in contrast with fixed investment, which rose sharply in 1947 and slowly in 1948, total investment fell slightly in 1947 and rose sharply ($2.4 billion) in 1948. It should be noted, however, that the rise in inventory accumulation by trade-service was not sufficient to offset the fall in the fixed investment of that group. The rise of the all-corporate total investment in 1948 was consequently somewhat dampened by the influence of the trade-service subsector just as was fixed investment.

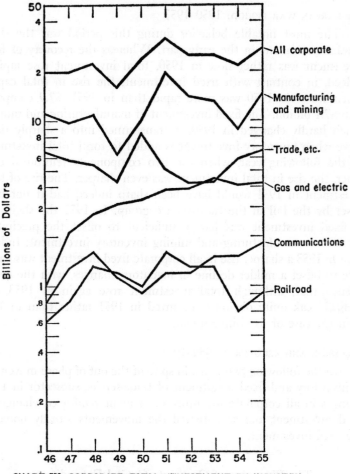

CHART III-CORPORATE TOTAL INVESTMENT BY INDUSTRY

In 1949, since inventory investment did not move countercyclically, the movement of fixed investment was reinforced and accentuated the decline in total investment. The greatest influence of inventory changes, however, is noticeable in the total investment of manufacturing and mining, where a $4.7 billion decline in total investment, augmented as it was by the especially sharp decline in inventory changes, was noticeably more rapid than the fall in fixed investment.

THE KOREAN WAR PERIOD: 1950–1953

The most notable behavior during this period was the sharp upward movement in the early part. Whereas the recovery of fixed investment was rather slow in 1950, total investment rose rapidly. Indeed, in contrast with fixed investment, the rise in total capital expenditures in 1950 was more rapid than in 1951, $7.9 compared with $7.1 billion. The fixed investment of manufacturing and mining, which hardly changed in 1950, is transformed into a sharply rising curve when inventory investment is added to form total investment. In the following year, when the two components reinforced each other, the rise in total investment was even sharper. The rise of total investment in 1951 would have been sharp indeed had it not been offset by the fall in the trade-service group. In 1952 the slight rise in fixed investment was hardly sufficient to offset the precipitous decline of manufacturing and mining inventory investment. Indeed, even in 1953 a sharper rise in all corporate fixed investment was barely able to offset a milder decline in inventory changes, with the consequence that, although total investment rose again in 1953, the cyclical peak quite obviously occurred in 1951 rather than in 1953 as in the case of fixed investment.

RECESSION AND RECOVERY: 1954–1955

In the following two years, in spite of the out-of-phase movement of inventory and fixed investment of trade-service subsector in 1954, changes in all corporate inventory investment reinforced changes in fixed investment and accentuated the movements already noted in the fixed investment.

The Financing of Corporate Capital Expenditures

The association of specific liabilities with specific assets or even specific classes of assets with specific classes of liabilities is at best a hazardous procedure. By their very nature fixed investments are not liquidated for considerable periods of time; sooner or later they must be financed by long-term funds. Some changes in inventory, on the other hand, are expected to be temporary, and the utilization of long-term funds to finance these temporary needs could easily result in the payment of interest on idle funds by the borrowing firm.

Inventories, however, are part of working capital, and net working capital per se is necessarily financed by long-term funds. Since inventory changes are included in both total investment and net working capital changes, the need for long-term funds, it can be argued, is determined by the latter and fixed investment.

In the sections which follow we review the sources of financing of corporate capital formation by examining first the behavior of internal funds and then the changes in volume of patterns of financing in the capital market.

INTERNAL FUNDS

While inside or internal funds are usually considered long-term funds, the first claim on them is the first liability that matures. If an increase in inventories has to be financed, a firm is unlikely to ignore its till cash on the grounds that the recent increase is from inside funds and is therefore part of long-term funds. While comparison of Charts I and IV discloses a certain similarity in the movements of all corporate fixed investment and all corporate internal funds, the similarity is to some extent the result of offsetting industrial movements, as closer examination will show.

The first and most obvious difference between the movements of inside funds and fixed investment is the greater volatility of the former. A relationship between inside funds and fixed investment is more evident in the last three years of the decade than in the preceding seven. The lack of conformity of the first seven years can be interpreted in either of two ways: either no relationship exists, or, more likely, fixed investment is also determined by other variables which, in many instances, are more significant than inside funds. However, except for 1951 and 1952, inverse movements in the flow of inside funds and fixed investment never occurred in more than a minority of industries in any one year. If other variables were relevant, as suggested above, they must have been especially important to specific industries. Otherwise inverse movements would have tended to occur in all industrial subgroups simultaneously.

This observation should be qualified, however. It is quite conceivable that a given factor would have the same absolute influence on all industries, but different relative influences. For example, a rise of $100,000 of inside funds may have the same impact on investment as a fall of ½ per cent in the interest costs. Consequently, if interest rates fell by half a point, industry A would increase fixed investment in spite of a $50,000 fall of inside funds, while industry B would

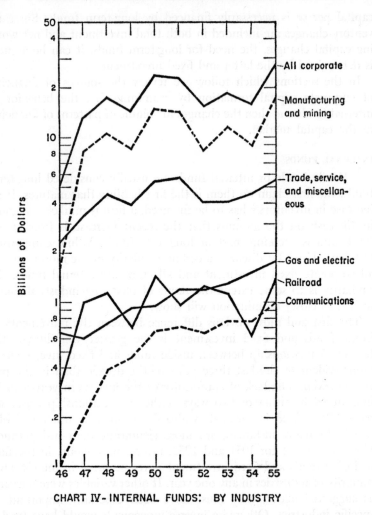

CHART IV- INTERNAL FUNDS: BY INDUSTRY

decrease investment if inside funds fell by more than $100,000. In-
deed, the number of times that the flows of inside funds and fixed
investment moved inversely tended to vary inversely with the relative
importance of inside funds. Over the decade inside funds were
largest relative to fixed investment in the manufacturing and mining
industry and were of decreasing relative importance in the railroad,
trade-service, communications, and gas and electric industries in that
order. There were no inverse movements of flows of inside funds and

fixed investment in the manufacturing and mining industries, while there were one, two, and three such inverse movements in the railroad, trade-service and communications, and gas and electric industries respectively.[g]

Another factor worth noting is that, in spite of the fact that in most instances fixed investment increased, inverse changes in inside funds and fixed investments occurred much more frequently when fixed investment was falling.

In all industries except gas and electric and communications inside funds at one time or another in the decade supplied more funds than were needed for fixed investment. This occurred most frequently in the middle years of the decade and most strikingly in the manufacturing and mining industry. The latter was the only industry in which inside funds exceeded fixed investment for the decade as a whole.

The degree to which fixed investment can be said to be covered by inside funds varied not only between industries but also from year to year. Except for the communications industry in the first half of the decade and the gas and electric industry throughout most of the decade, inside funds tended to exceed 50 per cent of fixed investment. A rough sort of pattern is detectable in most industries. The ratio of inside funds to fixed investment generally rose in the first half of the decade, then tended to decline for the next couple of years, and finally rose again in the last years. To be sure, there are breaks in this pattern, but nevertheless, if the charts were smoothed, this type of pattern would assert itself except in the railroad industry.

In 1946 the dollar volume of inside funds was rather low except in the gas and electric industry. The consequence was a low ratio of inside funds to fixed investment. In the following year the dollar volumes rose to levels more consistent with those of other years, so that the ratios also tended to rise. In the gas and electric industry the opposite happened. While inside funds didn't change much, fixed investment rose rapidly, so that the change in the ratio is quite different from that in other industries.

As was noted, in the first half of the decade the ratio tended to rise. In most industries the rises varied from year to year. In most instances the peak had been passed by 1950. The peak for trade-service, on the other hand, was not reached until 1951.

The date of the subsequent upturns also varies from industry to industry. By 1955 all industry ratios were climbing. In manufacturing

[g] Not counting instances in which one series changed while the other did not.

and mining and trade-service the climb had actually begun in 1953. The gas and electric ratio followed in the next year, 1954.

EXTERNAL FUNDS

The all corporate flow of external funds was almost completely dominated by the flow in the manufacturing and mining industry. Variations in the flows of the other industries modified the impact of

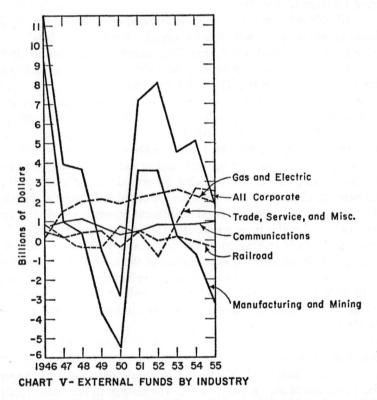

CHART V - EXTERNAL FUNDS BY INDUSTRY

the manufacturing and mining flows, to be sure, but the all corporate and the manufacturing and mining flows had roughly similar movements, (see Chart V). In general, the external fund flows of the other industries did not exhibit the great year-to-year variations that characterized the external fund flow of manufacturing and mining. Before examining this phenomenon more closely, however, a word should be said about the statistical discrepancy. If all flows were accurately measured, total investment would equal the sum of inside and external funds. The flows, however, are not accurately measured, and the equality seldom holds for the estimates. The differences have been called the statistical discrepancy, and there are grounds for believing that a major part of this discrepancy is made up of errors of measurement of external funds. The analysis of external funds is, therefore, subject to some error.

EXPANSION AND RECESSION: 1946–1949

The gap between total investment and inside funds narrowed in general throughout the expansion period, which ended in 1948. It narrowed more rapidly in 1947 than in 1948, but it narrowed nevertheless. The consequence was simple. With each passing year the volume of external funds declined. While accurate as a generalization, the statement is not true of each individual industry. The most noteworthy exception is the gas and electric industry. Total investment in this industry more than doubled in 1947 and almost doubled in 1948. Inside funds, on the other hand, fluctuated within the narrow limits of $0.6 and $0.8 billion; thus external funds rose from a mere $0.2 billion in 1946 to $2.0 billion in 1948.

A similar though not so marked sequence of events took place in the communications industry, where total investment rose sharply in 1947 and less sharply in 1948. In the latter year the $1.6 billion of investment was twice that of 1946. Inside funds rose more rapidly, doubling in each year. However, the level was so low in 1946 that the quadrupled level in 1948 supplied only one-fourth of the needed funds. Thus external funds grew relatively less important, accounting for over 90 per cent of the $0.8 billion of investment in 1946 and for about 75 per cent of total investment in the following two years.

External financing of manufacturing and mining behaved rather differently; in 1946 almost all of its funds came from external sources, and they amounted to $9.2 billion compared with $1.6 billion of internal funds. The situation was rapidly reversed, and in 1947 internal funds were over eight times larger than external funds. In the following three years the decline in the reliance on external funds continued, until in 1950 they amounted to about $–5 billion.

In many respects the trade-service industry behaved very much like the manufacturing and mining group. It will be recalled that the total investment of the trade and service industry declined in this expansive period. Since at the same time inside funds rose, the need for external funds declined. Whereas in 1946 the $0.9 billion of external funds supplied almost one-seventh of the needs, by 1948 this group was actually a supplier of funds by some $0.3 billion.

The most erratic behavior was found in the railroad industry. Between 1946 and 1947 the ratio of external funds to total investment fell from over 0.8 to 0.25. The following year the ratio rose again, though only to slightly over 0.3.

The behavior in the recession year of 1949 was hardly more uniform than in the earlier years. Borrowing by corporate industry as a whole fell rather sharply as external funds dropped from $3.7 billion to $–0.5 billion. The bulk of this change was the consequence of the behavior of the manufacturing and mining industry, which in 1949 *supplied* $3.7 billion of funds. The decline in corporate external funds was reinforced by the decline in the communications industry. The external funds of other industries either rose or, as in the case of the trade-service industry, remained unchanged.

The behavior of the external funds series in the recession is easily explained. In the utilities group variations in inside funds are relatively small. The need for external funds is thus determined by the investment and, more particularly, the fixed investment of the utilities. It will be recalled that both the railroads and the gas and electric companies behaved counter-cyclically in 1949, as their fixed investment actually increased. It was necessary, therefore, for them to resort to a larger volume of external financing than in 1948. The communications industry, on the other hand, experienced a fairly sharp decline in fixed investment, and its need for external funds was consequently diminished. In 1949 the negative changes in manufacturing and mining as well as in trade-service inventories reinforced the declines in fixed investment, thus resulting in sharper declines in total investment than occurred in inside funds. In both cases external funds were negative, $–3.7 and $–0.3 in manufacturing and mining and trade-service respectively.

THE KOREAN WAR PERIOD: 1950–1953

In spite of the fact that this was a period of rather general rapid growth in fixed investment, the fluctuations in external funds were dominated by two factors. On the one hand, there was the erratic behavior of inventories. On the other hand, inside funds reflected the change in the tax structure. 1950 was a year characterized by an unusually high absolute level of profits. Profits before tax rose by over $7.0 billion, the second largest increase in the decade. Primarily because of this, inside funds rose to almost the highest level of the decade. This more than made up for the small rise in fixed investment and the very sharp increase in changes in inventories. The net effect was a continued decline in external funds. External funds of all corporations fell to a decadal low of less than $–2.0 billion. As usual these movements were largely dominated by the manufacturing and mining group. The effect would have been even more marked if the experience of the latter group had been universally shared, but this was not quite the case. Even though the net profits before tax of utilities did rise, and, along with them, inside funds, the latter were relatively so unimportant that external funds remained relatively unaffected. Only the gas and electric industry increased investment in 1950. In each of the utility industries external funds declined somewhat, but only in the railroad industry did it actually become negative. In the trade-service industry the sharp increase in changes in inventories was sufficient to more than offset the rise in inside funds. Since, in addition, fixed investment also increased by more than 25 per cent, external funds rose over $1 billion. This was the only industry in which the flow of external funds did rise.

In 1951 the very sharp increase in manufacturing and mining inventory changes almost completely dominated the investment picture. With the exception of the trade-service group, the tempo of investment increased among all industries. However, the sharp rise in federal income-tax payments more than offset the buoyancy of profits, and inside funds remained substantially unchanged in every industry. Actually, since the declines more than offset the rises, all corporate inside funds fell somewhat. Under the circumstances, it is not surprising that, with the exception of trade-service, the external funds of all industries rose.

In the following year, 1952, profits were not sustained and tax payments continued to grow rapidly. On the other hand, the inventory investment of manufacturing and mining was not sustained. These two effects tended to cancel each other out, and external funds remained relatively unchanged. Only railroads and the trade-service industries experienced actual declines in external funds. Both of these industries, it should be recalled, decreased their fixed investment.

By 1953 the acceleration effect of tax payments was largely spent, and inside funds rose with net profits. On the other hand, only the railroad industry reduced its fixed investment, and only the manufacturing and mining industry reduced its total investment. In the total picture the rise in investment was rather sluggish and the rise in inside funds was sharper. External funds consequently fell. Once again, however, the totals are dominated by manufacturing and mining. While the external funds of the communications industry remained relatively unchanged, those of the other three industries rose, particularly those of trade-service.

RECESSION AND RECOVERY: 1954–1955

In general, the last two years of the decade were ones of declining need for external funds. Investment in inventory and in fixed plant rose in 1954 only in the trade-service group. While inside funds also increased, the use of additional external funds by the trade-service group proved necessary. It was the only industry in which external funds rose. In all the other industries investment fell, and in all but gas and electric inside funds either fell or remained unchanged. Since the decline in inside funds, where such declines occurred, were not as sharp as the declines in investment, the need for external funds also fell. In the gas and electric industry, where inside funds rose, there was a sharper decline in the need for external funds. Not only were the external funds of trade-service out of phase with the other industrial subgroups, but also the magnitude of the difference was sufficient to outweigh the declines in all the other industries put together, with the consequences that all corporate external funds rose.

In the following year every industry increased both total investment and inside funds. The increases in inside funds were greater than the increases in investment, and the external funds of every industry except the communications industry fell. The rise in external funds in the communications industry was trivial, however.

Long-Term Borrowing

Long-term funds were generally a more important source of funds than short-term funds. There were individual years which constituted exceptions to this rule, but by and large the rule held in the postwar decade. This is not particularly surprising. Short-term funds are raised to overcome temporary financial difficulties. These difficulties may result from temporary accumulations of inventories, temporary accumulations of receivables, or temporary stringencies in the capital market which necessitate interim financing. The last is obviously transformed into long-term borrowing sooner or later. Temporary increases in inventories and receivables have a persistent tendency to become permanent in an expanding economy. As plant and equipment expand in response to the need for enlarged output, the level of inventories required also expands, and sooner or later the firm must face the fact that the increase in inventories is a part of that expansion. Also, accounts receivable increase as sales expand and, with a lag, the increase is recognized as the result of an upward trend rather than an erratic increase. The debts incurred to finance them are then generally transformed into long-term form.

A second characteristic of long-term borrowing, at least for the corporate universe in the postwar decade, was that, in spite of its relative importance, it was a relatively more stable source of funds than either net short-term borrowing or decreases in liquid assets. The movements of external funds rarely reflected changes in long-term borrowing. These changes were almost always drowned by the movement of the other two components. By far the most erratic source was decreases in liquid assets.

These characteristics of the corporate universe do not hold without exception for the industrial components. Net long-term borrowing clearly dominated the external funds of the communications and gas and electric industries, not only in terms of levels but also of changes. In the other three industries, the influence of changes of long-term borrowing on fluctuations in external funds is radically reduced.

Borrowing by the various industries rarely expands and contracts in unison. Except for the recession years of 1949 and 1954, at least one industry was out of step with the others in each year of the decade. The amplitude of the fluctuations of all corporate long-term borrowing was consequently somewhat diminished. The most significant changes in long-term borrowing occurred in the maufacturing and mining industry. Except for 1946 and 1947, manufacturing and mining long-term borrowing and all corporate long-term borrowing moved together.

Except for the fact that all corporate long-term borrowing reached a peak in 1952 rather than in 1953, borrowing pretty well followed the pattern of fixed investment, rising from 1946 to 1948, falling in 1949, rising in the next few years, reaching another trough in 1954, and rising again in 1955. The same consistency, however, did not occur in the component industries. The first peak in long-term borrowing of manufacturing and mining occurred only in 1952. Similarly a trough in long-term borrowing occurred in 1949, whereas the trough year for fixed investment was in 1950. In trade-service the first peak and trough occurred in 1948 and 1949 respectively, but fixed investment reached a peak in 1947. Thereafter net long-term borrowing and fixed investment moved up and down together until 1954, when borrowing fell for a year while fixed investment continued to climb through 1955. Whereas fixed investment of the gas and electric industry fell only in 1954 and leveled off in 1955, borrowing leveled off in 1949 and fell in 1950 as well as in 1954 and 1955. Long-term borrowing and fixed investment by the communications industry moved more closely together than even the all corporate group. The only difference in the movements occurred in 1947 when communications' net long-term borrowing declined while its fixed investment continued to rise. Finally, the railroad industry generally increased its borrowing when fixed investment rose and decreased it when fixed investment fell. The only break in this relationship occurred in 1952, when railroad fixed investment fell whereas net long-term borrowing did not decrease until the following year.

One of the noteworthy aspects of net long-term borrowing in this decade is that simultaneously during most of the years cash and portfolio securities were increasing. The trade-service industry, for example, never once decreased its accumulations of cash and securities, and manufacturing and mining resorted to this source of funds only in 1946 and 1954. The communications industry used this source of funds only a little more frequently and over the decade as a whole had significant net increases in cash and securities. The gas and electric and railroad industries were less fortunate and reduced their cash and securities more often than not.

By far the most important financial instrument employed during the decade was the corporate bond. In the manufacturing and mining, railroad, and gas and electric industries, as well as in the all corporate group, net bond issues exceeded issues of both net stocks and mortgages. In many years bond issues by these industries exceeded the issues of stocks and mortgages combined. The communications industry, on the other hand, relied upon stock issues as a source of funds more than it did on bonds after 1948. In a few years funds raised through stock issues by this industry were several times greater than funds raised through bond issues. In trade-service, while bond issues were more important than stock issues, mortgage funds were the most important source of long-term external financing. Net bond issues reached a trough in 1950 rather than 1949 and a mid-decade peak in 1952 rather than 1953. The bond issue behavior of no component industry followed quite this pattern. Bond issues of the communications industry reached the first peak of the decade in 1947 rather than 1948. Trade-service bond issues, on the other hand, did not reach a peak until 1949. No industry reached a trough in 1949. Many hit bottom in 1950, but neither the railroad nor trade-service industries did so until 1951. The all corporate peak of 1952 is due primarily to manufacturing and mining, which issued $2.7 billion of bonds in that year, more than they did in any other year of the decade. The railroad industry was the only other industry that reached a peak in that year. The sharp acceleration of bond issues by trade-service and the lesser increase in issues by the communications industry prevented total bond issues from falling more sharply from the 1952 peak than it actually did. The fall in net bond issues for all corporations in 1953 was only $0.2 billion in comparison with $1.0 billion in 1954. The sharp fall in 1954 was again primarily the consequence of the transactions of the trade-service and communications industries. Bond issues of both of these industries fell rather sharply and more than offset the rise in bond issues by manufacturing and mining and gas and electric. Railroad bond issues declined trivially in 1954 and rose slightly in 1955. For the third successive year the trade-service and communications industries dominated the bond issue field. Their issues rose by about the same amount they had fallen in the previous year, $0.9 and $0.6 billion respectively. While the issues of gas and electric and manufacturing both fell, the fall was not enough to bring the all corporate total down. Issues of the latter rose to $4.2 billion in 1955.

Debt and Equity Financing

In the interest of brevity we shall merely summarize the findings which relate forms of external financing to their relative costs. In an earlier study Hickman noted that the relative volume of new bond and new stock financing conformed closely to changes in the relative costs of these two forms of external financing.[h] In the postwar decade

---

[h] W. Braddock Hickman, *The Volume of Corporate Bond Financing since 1900* (New York: National Bureau of Economic Research, Inc., 1953), pp. 163–179.

the same pattern can be observed. During the first half of the decade bond yields were absolutely low by historical standards, while the costs of external equity funds were as high as they were in the middle 1920's. Thus stock issues accounted for about one-fourth of total external long-term financing. As interest rates rose in the latter part of the decade and the costs of new equity money fell in response to buoyant stock-market prices, both the absolute and relative volume of stock issues rose substantially.

The Suppliers of Funds

In its broadcast sense, all financial flows in a given year are potentially available for investment in corporate securities. The so-called money (short-term financial sectors) markets and capital (long-term financial sectors) markets are linked by changes in relative interest rates, by the simultaneous operations of some financial institutions in both markets, and by the influence of the Federal Reserve System and Treasury operations on all financial markets. Because the capital markets are a major source of funds to finance business expansion, we concentrate our attention on this area through which long-term funds flow.

As can be seen in Table I, the net flow of capital market funds into markets for corporate securities (including term loans), state and municipal government obligations, Treasury issues, and mortgages increased almost without interruption in the ten-year period under consideration. The net capital market flows rose from a low of $9.0 billion in 1946 to a high of $28.5 billion at the end of the decade.

The net flows into corporate securities (including term loans) expressed as a percentage of total net capital market flows averaged about 30 per cent for the period under consideration. There were marked variations in this ratio during the period. Broadly stated, in periods of declining economic activity corporate takings from the capital market fell, while in periods of rising economic activity the reverse held true.

The capital market through which long-term funds are obtained is not a single unified pool into which all borrowers dip. As the economy evolved, specialized institutions developed to service the needs of the major categories of users of funds. A parallel but not necessarily synchronous development took place on the supply side of the market as the savings process became increasingly institutional-ized and individuals resorted more and more to the liabilities of financial intermediaries as outlets for their savings rather than direct investment in the obligations of the ultimate users of funds.

The segment of the capital market from which corporations draw their funds is further divided into a market for bonds and another one for stocks. Both of these are now fairly highly developed.

The development of direct placement of corporate debt instruments with financial intermediaries, mainly life insurance companies, oc-curred along with other developments all of which contributed to a significant redistribution of the holdings of corporate bonds. Before World War II over one-half of all outstanding corporate bonds were held by individuals, personal trust departments of banks, and non-financial institutions. The sharp and continuing increase in personal income-tax rates during and after the war made such securities, whose income was fully subject to tax, very much less attractive than they previously had been to such investors. Life insurance companies, which were taxed at low marginal and average tax rates, and pension funds, whose income is not subject to any federal income tax, had large and growing volumes of funds to invest.

Thus individuals were not only extinguished as suppliers of new funds to the corporate bond market but also on balance drew funds from this market during the postwar decade as they reduced the absolute volume of their holdings. Even commercial banks and fire and casualty insurance companies which were subjected to normal corporate income-tax rates tended to channel their funds into tax-exempt securities and other outlets.

At the opening of the postwar decade individual holdings of corporate bonds had fallen to less than 40 per cent of the total out-standing. Life insurance companies had already become the most important single type of investor in corporate bonds and held more bonds than individuals. The trend toward the concentration of bonds in the portfolios of financial institutions continued well into the postwar decade. Indeed, it received no setback until 1955, when the percentage held by these institutions fell from the peak of the previous year of 82 per cent to 79 per cent. Life insurance companies continued to grow in relative importance as investors in corporate bonds. As early as 1948 they held over half of all corporate bonds outstanding; and, although by 1955 they had slipped about 2 points from their 1954 peak of 56 per cent, they did not hold less than one-

TABLE I

NET FLOW OF FUNDS INTO CAPITAL MARKET SECURITIES
1946–1955
(in billions of dollars)

	(1)* Net Capital Market Flows	(2) Mort-gages	(3) Resi-den-tial	(4) Total Corpo-rate	(5) Corp. Mort-gage	(6) Term Loans	(7) Total Securities	(8) State & Local	(9) Federal
1946	9.0	6.2	4.8	3.6	.8	.6	2.2	-.4	-22.5
1947	14.0	7.2	5.7	6.0	.8	1.0	4.2	1.6	-6.2
1948	16.3	7.3	5.9	7.4	.7	.9	5.8	2.3	-6.8
1949	15.7	6.5	5.3	5.1	.5	-.1	4.6	2.5	2.1
1950	17.0	10.1	8.7	4.2	.6	.2	3.4	3.3	-.3
1951	18.6	9.5	7.8	7.2	.6	.9	5.7	2.5	-.3
1952	25.0	9.1	7.5	9.1	.7	1.2	7.2	3.2	4.3
1953	26.1	9.9	8.2	7.9	.7	.6	6.6	3.8	5.2
1954	24.7	12.5	10.2	6.8	1.0	.4	5.4	4.4	2.0
1955	28.5	16.2	13.4	8.9	1.5	1.1	6.3	3.7	1.2

Source: Federal Reserve Board "Flow of Funds" and National Bureau of Economic Research.
* Col. 1 Sum of Cols. 2, 6, 7, 8 and 9. Negative flows are treated as sources of capital market funds.

half of the bonds outstanding subsequent to the end of 1948. The most rapid growth in holdings was that experienced by non-insured pension funds. These institutions, whose holdings had exceeded 2 per cent of the total outstanding in 1945, held about 11 per cent at the end of 1955 and had become the second largest holder among the financial institutions. This situation resulted in the non-financial corporations having to look to financial intermediaries for the bulk of their long-term debt financing.

The roles of individuals and financial institutions are reversed in the markets for common and preferred stock. Individuals, including personal trust funds, continued to hold about three-fourths of all common stock outstanding in 1945 and 1955 as they did in 1939. Though the legal restraints on institutional investment in equities were relaxed during the decade, financial institutions did not become important holders of common stock. Nevertheless, since financial institutions persistently purchased common stocks in each year of the decade, a small but perceptible decline in the proportion of common stock outstanding held by individuals is evident. The most noteworthy development in the decade is the very rapid growth of and the marked shift in favor of equities by noninsured pension funds. Indeed, in the latter part of the period common stock acquisitions by these funds amounted to approximately one-quarter of the net issues of common stock coming into the market.

Individual holdings of preferred stocks, which accounted for 60 per cent of outstandings in 1945 fell to about 57 per cent by the end of 1955. The pattern of their purchases and sales is noteworthy. They disposed of preferred stock in 1946 and in every recession year and the year thereafter. Their disposals were heaviest both absolutely and relatively in the year immediately following the recession. The most important single type of financial institution in the market for preferred stock was the life insurance companies, with fire and casualty companies a fairly close second. Life companies persistently purchased more than fire and casualty companies, and indeed were sometimes purchasers when the fire and casualty companies were net sellers.

Changes in Financial Structure

In the period under review corporations financed the highest absolute levels of capital formation ever experienced in this country. The manner of financing left its mark on corporate balance sheets.

For all nonfinancial corporations total debt as a per cent of total assets has grown slowly from 39 per cent in 1945, to 46 per cent in 1955. The trend took a slight dip only in 1949, and even less in 1954, but otherwise has been continuing steadily. However, this pattern is not repeated in the breakdown by various sectors.

All sectors, except railroads and possibly communications, have experienced a rise in the ratio of total debt to total assets, the more pronounced rise being among trade-service corporations, and gas and electric corporations. The communications sector experienced a sharp rise in the ratio through 1947, a leveling off and a decline since 1949. Railroads have had a steady decline in the ratio throughout the period.

Considering some sectors individually, it can be seen that manufacturing corporations have a lower total debt to total asset ratio than the ratio for all corporations. This seems to be due to the lower long-term debt to total asset ratio; for the short-term debt to total asset ratio is about equal to the all corporate ratio and has moved in exact conformity with it. As in the ratios for all corporations, the manufacturing corporations' short-term debt ratio dips in 1949 and 1954 due to the cutback in the rate of increase in short-term debt.

Mining corporations have a total debt to total asset ratio that has fluctuated between 30 and 34, but it appears to have hit its peak of 34 in 1952 and has declined subsequently, due to a decrease in both the short-term and long-term ratios.

Railroad corporations have a low short-term debt to total asset ratio which seems to remain stable. The decline in the long-term debt to total asset ratio is the reason for the decline for the total debt ratio in this sector.

Subtracting tax liabilities from short-term debt seems to reduce some of the fluctuations in the short-term debt to total assets ratio. However, it does not seem that it would change any of the trends that appear when tax liabilities are included.

Despite the rise in interest rates, the corporate universe appears to have financed its postwar growth with no signs of financial deterioration. The increase in the debt ratio, while evident, has not put any strain on the capacity of firms in the aggregate to meet interest charges. Rising corporate income has resulted in low interest charge to corporate income ratios.

TEN

☆

INTERNATIONAL TRADE AND UNITED STATES EXPERIENCE: 1870–1955

☆

CHARLES P. KINDLEBERGER

The theory of international trade is of limited use in explaining the course of economic history—and for two reasons. First, it is static, rather than dynamic, explaining still pictures more effectively than a movie plot. Second, we lack a theory of the evolution of a country's economic relations with other trading entities in the course of economic growth which would cover in integrated fashion all aspects of those relations.

The development of a dynamic, integrated theory of international economic intercourse lies beyond the limits of this essay. In its place, the course of United States international trade and commercial policy will be discussed in the light of several partial aspects of the theory, primarily in terms of comparative statics. The trade statistics will be dealt with separately from the politic-economic evolution of commercial policy.

The discussion is limited to the theory of international trade narrowly conceived. It omits any treatment of dollar shortage or any other aspect of the theory of adjustment. There is no mention of capital movements, of the impact of business cycles in the United States on foreign countries, of the evolving role of New York (and Washington) as the world's center for international liquid reserves, of the innovation of international intergovernmental transfers as an adjustment mechanism. Economics possesses, it happens, a relatively crude theory of the evolution of the balance of payments in the process of growth. It is the narrower topic of what happens to comparative advantage and commercial policy in economic development which has by and large been neglected.

The Comparative Statics of United States Foreign Trade

The static theory of international trade is directed to the explanation of what products a country will export and import, under conditions of balanced trade, when tastes, factor endowments, and technology are specified and unalterable. In its purest form, the theory is illustrated with two goods, two countries, two factors, identical technologies in the two countries, perfect competition, no transport costs, and continuous full employment. If factor endowments are broadly the same, trade can be based on differences in taste. Classical theory, however, tended to operate on the assumptions that tastes were more or less similar, but that factor endowments differed substantially. In this circumstance, if one product is usually made with relatively more of one factor, and the other with relatively more of the other, trade is explained by factor endowments. The country rich in land relative to labor will export the land-intensive commodity and import the labor-intensive; and vice versa for the other country with a relatively greater endowment of labor than land. In addition to trade based on tastes, with roughly identical factor endowments, and trade based on factor endowments with similar tastes, it was possible, by introducing external economies, or by relaxing the assumption of perfect competition which excluded internal economies of scale, to have trade starting from a position of two countries with identical tastes and identical factor endowments. Provided each country specialized on a different good, each could cheapen its cost of producing one good relative to the other by taking advantage of increasing returns to scale, or decreasing costs, and be able to export despite identical tastes and factor endowments.

How much of a country's trade at any one time is accounted for by differences in tastes, differences in factor endowments, increasing returns, or any other departure from the classical assumptions has never squarely been studied. In general it has been assumed that differences in taste are quantitatively unimportant as an explanation of trade, and that trade based on this explanation is limited to a few items of luxury consumption such as handicrafts, Paris fashions, Bond street haberdashery, and possibly food specialties.[a] This view neglects the substantial and growing item of tourist expenditure. Rome, Paris, London, and New York are not identical, to be sure; but the tourist trade which makes the resident of each interested in exploring the others may be said to be based on differences in taste and broadly comparable factor endowments.

Tourist trade began to be quantitatively significant after World War I, particularly after the more equal distribution in income in Western European countries and in the United States made it possi-

---

[a] Differences in taste, combined with differences in factor endowments, explain the lack of trade in a vast number of food items. The French drink wine, the Germans beer, the Scandinavians aquavit, the British, Scotch, and Americans bourbon, without trade taking place, until tastes become more identical. In underdeveloped countries one cause of trade, and of loss to the community rather than gain, is the adoption of foreign food habits.

ble for large numbers of people to enjoy foreign travel, which had previously been a prerogative of the aristocracy and the *haute bourgeoisie*. In 1870, however, trade based on differences in taste was unimportant.

Similarly, trade based on increasing returns was probably unimportant in 1870. There is no way to measure this. Increasing returns due to external economies or to imperfections of competition are difficult to distinguish from historically declining costs due to downward shifts of upward-sloping cost curves, such as those which result from discoveries of new resources or technological innovation. Increasing returns are generally considered to be important in manufacturing. The expansion of mass production in the United States came during and after World War I. The expansion of exports of finished manufactures, which rose from 15 per cent of exports by value in 1871–1880 to 31 per cent by 1911–1915 (see Table I) requires another explanation: supply-oriented production in commodities where the materials are subject to weight-losing processes (gasoline and kerosene), or technological innovation in the United States, not yet spread abroad (machinery and automobiles—see Table 2). The first class departs from the theory of comparative advantage in its pure form by introducing transport costs. The second is more significant in implying a change from the assumption of a given state of the arts that is everywhere the same.

Most of the foreign trade of the United States in 1870, however, had its roots in differences in factor endowments between the United States and the rest of the world. Leading exports were cotton, wheat and flour, meat products, including lard, petroleum products, and tobacco. Imports in descending order of importance were sugar, iron and steel manufactures, wool manufactures, coffee, cotton manufactures, and silk manufactures. The United States was a net exporter of a large variety of mineral products ranging from petroleum products to copper, lead, zinc, silver, and gold. Cotton production was based on the existence of large quantities of fertile semitropical land plus a work force of liberated slaves attached to the industry in various ways—plantation settlement, sharecropper, consumption debts. Wheat production was expanding with the resettlement of Civil War veterans in the newly opened Northwest—Minnesota, the Dakotas, Iowa, and Nebraska.

In 1870 the United States had a comparative advantage in land-intensive products, including foodstuffs, agricultural materials, and

TABLE I—PERCENTAGE BREAKDOWN OF UNITED STATES
FOREIGN TRADE BY ECONOMIC CLASSES

	Crude Materials	Crude Foodstuffs	Manufactured Foodstuffs	Semi-Manufactures	Finished Manufactures
			Exports		
1851–1860	62	7	15	4	12
1861–1870	39	16	24	5	16
1871–1880	39	20	22	5	15
1881–1890	36	18	25	5	16
1891–1900	30	18	26	8	18
1901–1910	31	11	20	13	26
1911–1915	31	9	14	15	31
1915–1920*	18	9	18	15	41
1921–1925	28	10	14	13	36
1926–1930	24	6	10	14	45
1931–1935	30	4	9	15	43
1936–1940	19	4	5	19	52
1941–1945	6	2	12	9	72
1946–1950	14	8	10	11	57
1951–1955	13	7	6	12	63
(1956)	(13)	(7)	(7)	(15)	(58)
			Imports		
1851–1860	10	12	15	13	51
1861–1870	13	14	19	14	41
1871–1880	17	16	21	13	33
1881–1890	21	15	18	15	31
1891–1900	26	17	17	14	26
1901–1910	34	12	12	17	25
1911–1915*	35	13	13	17	22
1915–1920	40	12	16	17	14
1921–1925	37	11	13	18	21
1926–1930	37	13	10	19	22
1931–1935	29	16	14	19	23
1936–1940	33	13	14	21	19
1941–1945	33	16	12	21	18
1946–1950	30	19	11	22	17
1951–1955	26	20	10	24	20
(1956)	(25)	(16)	(9)	(24)	(26)

* July 1, 1915 to December 31, 1920.
Source: *Statistical Abstract of the United States, 1957*, p. 898.

TABLE II.—EXPORTS AND IMPORTS—LEADING ARTICLES BY VALUE, 1871–1956
(*in millions of dollars*)

Exports	(1956)	1951–1955	1946–1950	1941–1945	1936–1940	1931–1935	1926–1930	1921–1925	1911–1915	1871–1880
Machinery	(3,796)	2,886	2,074	1,073	495	212	488	320	158	8
Automobiles incl. engines and parts	(1,356)	1,082	820	456	273	146	406	177	36	—
Iron and steel mill products	(1,067)	612	625	543	270	63	171	167	96	1
Wheat and wheat flour	(796)	688	872	104	56	39	230	322	172	108
Petroleum products	(760)	714	559	572	345	232	525	406	137	40
Coal and related fuels	(745)	454	405	164	67	52	122	131	59	3
Cotton unmanufactured	(729)	761	674	151	282	366	766	805	537	195
Tobacco	(333)	315	268	138	110	104	145	165	46	24
Copper and ore and manufactures	(235)	157	74	79	88	40	150	130	120	—

TABLE II (Cont.)—EXPORTS AND IMPORTS—SELECTED LEADING ARTICLES BY VALUE, 1871 TO 1956
(in millions of dollars)

Imports	1871–1880	1911–1915	1921–1925	1925–1930	1931–1935	1936–1940	1941–1945	1946–1950	1951–1955	(1956)
Coffee	49	109	206	282	141	138	266	732	1410	(1,438)
Petroleum products	–	9	92	133	51	48	94	379	782	(1,269)
Paper and manufactures	2	13	105	151	96	124	144	396	616	(750)
Copper incl. ore and manufactures	1	46	78	108	30	48	165	186	388	(501)
Sugar	75	118	295	207	113	138	172	334	411	(436)
Crude rubber	6	83	193	294	75	206	149	311	493	(398)
Machinery	n.a.	8[x]	16	28	11	16	30	87	229	(355)
Automobiles and vehicles	–	3[x]	2	3	1	2	53	25	110	(276)
Wool and mohair	13	43	102	79	19	61	248	291	375	(242)
Cotton manufactures	–	67[x]	86	58	32	39	16	43	80	(154)
Hides and skins	7	103	93	118	40	51	68	92	75	(66)
Raw silk	6	80	348	368	115	109	13	32	27	(32)

Source: Statistical Abstract of the United States.
x=1910–1914.

minerals, with a comparative disadvantage in manufactures. Some considerable volume of manufacturing was maintained with tariff protection in textiles, shoes, iron and steel, and even watches. Much of this industry in the North had matured in the course of the Civil War under the intensified demand for manufactures and because of the interruption of international commerce. But by and large, the classical theory of comparative advantage, as interpreted by Bertil Ohlin in terms of factor endowments, explained the nature of United States foreign trade in the 1870's.

Since 1870 a number of sweeping changes have occurred in the basis for United States foreign trade, not all of them foreseen by the classical explanation. Factor proportions have changed; technology has altered, with a systematic bias in the locus of innovation. Income per capita has risen rapidly, altering the character of demand. The level of transport costs has fallen relative to the prices of commodities —a movement toward the classical assumption. Finally, in the middle of the twentieth century, we see the beginnings of a widening of the economic horizon, which mean that entrepreneurs no longer restrict their calculations to what they can do in their own countries with native land, labor, and capital.

CHANGING FACTOR PROPORTIONS

Land is usually described in acres or square miles; labor in numbers of people; capital in dollars, but occasionally in some such real measure as horsepower. These measures are largely inaccurate. For economic purposes land is not a homogeneous factor which can be added in its totality but consists of hundreds or thousands of so-called noncompeting groups. Qualitative differences are of great importance. Moreover, land is not fixed in amount even if we disregard reclamation and new means of transport. It varies with the discovery of mineral deposits and even more significantly with changes in technology which alter the use of existing land. A device for sintering taconite iron ores or a technique for growing Turkish-type tobacco in North Carolina or flaxseed for oil in Minnesota changes the land endowment of the United States in the same way as the Louisiana Purchase or the first transcontinental railroad or an east Texas oil strike.

Land may decline as well as increase in amount. Depletion, deforestation, the lowering of the water table all reduce available supplies of economic land. A distinction should be made between replaceable and nonreplaceable resources. The first are reduced by poor conservation practices but can be expanded by capital investment—irrigation, seeding, fertilization, purification, etc. This land is indistinguishable from capital. It may increase, remain fixed, or depreciate. Nonreplaceable land, on the other hand, barring new discovery and technological change, can only decline in amount.

The volume and quality of labor and capital have been growing in the United States since 1870. It is likely that the volume of land has also been growing—if one had a satisfactory basis for measurement. Depletion has taken place but at a slower rate than discovery and technological change. Relative to capital and labor, farming land has declined substantially. And with that relative decline, comparative advantage has shifted against the United States in foodstuffs, agricultural raw materials, and especially minerals. Technological change has arrested the change in certain areas, to be discussed presently, but it is a fair statement that the comparative advantage of the United States in land-intensive products which existed in the middle of the nineteenth century has given way a century later to a comparative disadvantage.

Figure 1 sets out a stylized representation of how this has taken place.[1] Land is assumed fixed. The production-possibilities curve of the United States in 1870, A–A, shows resources skewed in favor of the land-intensive and against the labor-and-capital-intensive good. With land fixed, the growth in labor and capital increases capacity each decade in both the land-intensive good and in the other good, but much more in the latter than in the former. By 1950 the production-possibilities curve, B–B, is skewed sharply in the other direction and suggests, although the demand pattern is not given, a comparative advantage in the labor-and-capital-intensive good.

In 1870 the United States production, consumption, and trade patterns are shown by the points P (production) and C (consumption) and the lines X (exports) and M (imports). As skewness in favor of the land-intensive product gives way to skewness against it, the patterns of production, consumption, and trade alter. By 1950 the United States was importing land-intensive products and exporting labor-and-capital type goods. If we designate the 1950 pattern by P', C', X', and M', the dotted lines P–P', and C–C' offer a motion picture in comparative statics, showing how exports of land-intensive products give way to imports.

Table I offers broad support for the picture presented in Figure 1.

Crude materials fall from 62 per cent of exports in 1851-1860 to less than 15 per cent after World War II; and crude foodstuffs from 20 per cent at the peak after 1870 to less than 10 per cent. The fall in manufactured foodstuffs—largely flour and lard—occurred sooner (with a low in 1935-1940) and went further, from 26 per cent in 1890-1900 to 5 per cent.

The picture is not so sharp in imports. Imports of crude materials rose from 10 per cent in 1850-1860 to 40 per cent, but the peak was

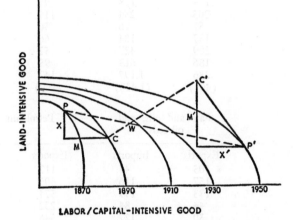

Figure 1. The loss of comparative advantage in land-intensive good through the growth of capital and labor. From Kindleberger, *International Economics*, rev. ed. (Homewood, Ill.: Irwin, 1958), p. 128.

reached during World War I and has been followed by a decline. The upward trend in crude foodstuffs is virtually imperceptible. Some resource commodities, moreover, such as newsprint and refined metals, are included in semimanufactures, which have increased gradually. The only sharply etched evidence is the negative testimony of finished manufactures, which fell by two-thirds from 1851-1860 to 1946-1950 (51 per cent to 17). Half of this fall had been achieved already by 1871-1880, however, and a recovery since 1951, to 26 per cent in 1956, requires another explanation.

The switch from an export to a net import basis occurred at different times in different classes of commodities. This is suggested in Table III, based on secondary sources which do not give extended

TABLE III.—EXPORTS AND IMPORTS OF SELECTED PRIMARY PRODUCTS
BY COMMODITY CLASSES
(*in millions or dollars*)

	Nonferrous metals, except precious metals		Unmanufactured and semi-manufactured wood and paper base stocks	
	Exports	Imports	Exports	Imports
1910–1915	n.a.	n.a.	71	58
1921–1925	173	178	97	177
1926–1930	205	254	119	187
1931–1935	57	96	50	86
1936–1940	137	184	66	120
1941–1945	209	427	52	162
1946–1950	186	613	95	417
1951–1955	286	1,197	147	611
(1956)	(465)	(1,438)	(199)	(678)

	Fats and oils, and oilseeds		Petroleum products	
	Exports	Imports	Exports	Imports
1910–1914	105	45	117	6
1921–1925	157	116	405	91
1926–1930	133	159	524	132
1931–1935	44	84	232	51
1936–1940	30	127	346	48
1941–1945	161	106	573	94
1946–1950	228	228	559	379
1951–1955	432	187	714	782
(1956)	(675)	(166)*	(746)	(1269)

Source: *Statistical Abstract of the United States, 1957.*
   * Includes other edible animal products.

coverage. Non-ferrous metals and raw and semifinished wood products changed from an export to an import basis over the period of World War I with, however, a big increase in the extent of the net deficit relative to exports after World War II. In fats and oils (animals and vegetable, edible and inedible) and oilseeds, an import basis was reached in the second half of the 1920's, but this gave way again to net exports in World War II. The petroleum-products position turned to net imports by value only in 1951–1955. Prior to this period the balance had been in favor of imports for a considerable period, measuring by volume. Imports, however, consisted of crude oil and residual fuel oil, while exported products comprised the more valuable light fractions and lubricating oils.

Sir Donald MacDougall has a chart which shows exports in food-stuffs alone as a percentage of imports declining from 250 per cent in 1900 to approximately 50 per cent in 1955, punctuated by recoveries to 225 per cent after World War I and 150 per cent in and after World War II.[2] But this is a trifle misleading. The decline from 1900 to 1913, 250 to 100, is real and represents in particular the displacement of American animal fat (lard) by tropical vegetable oils in a variety of uses in Europe. Thereafter each substantial devia-tion from 100 has more or less a special explanation: the two wars which drove the percentage up, the 1934–1936 drought which de-pressed it below 50, and the soaring price of imported coffee which lowered it after 1949. Table II shows that the decline in value of exports of wheat and flour from 1946–1950 to 1951–1955 was not substantial. Some wartime exports of prunes, dried eggs, dried milk, and similar high-value food were lost, but a number of these had been new exports beginning in World War II. The Commodity Credit Corporation's program, of first raising domestic prices and then subsidizing exports, makes it impossible to say exactly where comparative advantage now lies in farm products. There is a strong possibility, however, discussed below, that the decline in comparative advantage in wheat and cotton through the growth of labor and capital relative to land has been offset by improvements in tech-nology.

CHANGING TECHNOLOGY

Insofar as foreign trade is concerned, changes in technology divide into two classes: the introduction of new goods, and new and cheaper methods of producing existing goods. The distinction is a loose one; a new good frequently satisfies the need felt by an existing good. The automobile was partly horse-and-buggy, i.e., local trans-port, and partly an entirely new object of consumption. Assuming that an innovation occurs in one country at a time, though it may spread to other countries through investment, sale of technology, or imitation, the development of new goods is likely to lead to ex-ports, whatever factor proportions the goods ultimately favor after the technology has become stabilized and ubiquitous.

New ways of producing existing goods may increase or reduce

foreign trade, depending upon the nature of the innovation. If a country exports capital-intensive goods and imports labor-intensive, a laborsaving innovation will evidently reduce the skewness of the production-possibilities curve, and hence the gains from trade; whereas a capital-saving innovation will increase the skewness. The former is called import-biased; the latter, export-biased.[b]

Figure 2a shows how technology can dominate over factor proportions in determining the direction of trade. Country A with its

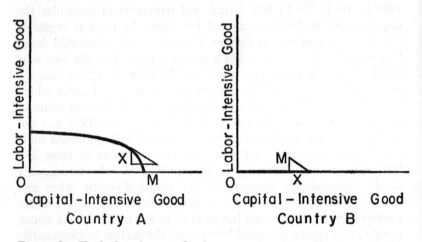

Figure 2a. Trade based on technology: country B unable to make the labor-intensive good.

resources can produce more of the land-and-capital-intensive commodity than of the labor-intensive commodity (using the units chosen); but it exports the labor-intensive commodity because country B cannot make it at all. B's production-possibilities curve lies along the horizontal axis. If it is to trade, it can export this capital-intensive-and-land-intensive commodity only when it has acquired the technology of the other land; and assuming that it has more nearly the appropriate resources, i.e., more labor relative to capital

[b] There is another possibility that an innovation will be so laborsaving as to skew the country the other way and lead it to export the "labor-intensive" commodity and import the "capital-intensive." What will have happened in this case is that the innovation saves so much labor in the previously labor-intensive commodity as to make it capital-intensive relative to the previously capital-intensive commodity. The country will continue to export the truly capital-intensive commodity, but it is now a different good.

and land than A, the direction of trade may change, as illustrated in Figure 2b.

A considerable amount of the trade of the United States is explained by this country's closing the negative technological gap by which Europe lay ahead of it and then opening up a positive gap in the other direction. More recently this technological gap has begun to close again.

The chemical and pharmaceutical industry provides an example of an industry in which this country was technologically backward at the start of World War I. It is true that our factor proportions were

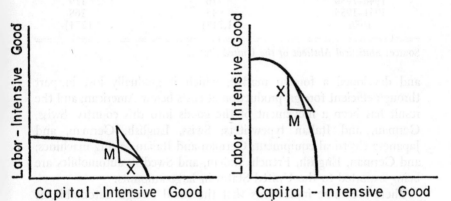

Figure 2b. Trade based on factor endowments after technology has spread from A to B.

not ideal for this capital-intensive industry. And the industry may have an element of decreasing cost in it which meant that entry was impossible without the stimulus provided by the embargo imposed by World War I and the postwar tariff. But World War II found this industry in the United States innovating rapidly and in position to export on a substantial scale, regardless of the factor proportions involved. In some standard chemical products—such as alkalis —the industry was inefficient and survived only with very high rates of protection. But, as Table IV indicates, a positive rate of innovation had led to a large export surplus in the class as a whole.

The opposite of this result is occurring in many fields—office machinery, electrical equipment, sewing machines, and more recently automobiles. These are products in which the United States pioneered

TABLE IV.—UNITED STATES FOREIGN TRADE IN CHEMICALS AND
ALLIED PRODUCTS
(*annual average values in millions of dollars*)

	Exports	Imports
1910–1914	51	88
1921–1925	108	112
1926–1930	135	133
1931–1935	91	66
1936–1940	153	80
1941–1945	400	131
1946–1950	716	119
1951–1955	945	268
1956	(1,248)	(274)

Source: *Statistical Abstract of the United States.*

and developed a foreign market, which it gradually lost in part through efficient foreign production at costs below American; and the result has been a movement of the goods into this country. Swiss, German, and Italian typewriters; Swiss, English, German, and Japanese electrical equipment; German and Italian sewing machines; and German, English, French, Italian, and Swedish automobiles are being exported to the United States in large amounts.

There are some indications that the small foreign automobile is a different commodity from the large American type, and that the import trade is based on comparative advantage due to taste rather than costs of production. But this is not conclusive, and it will not be until an American producer tools up to produce a small car on a large scale at prices which will beat the c.i.f. cost of the imported car. The experience of the Volkswagen company suggests that costs play a significant part. This company contracted to buy an American assembly plant and to import parts. It found, however, that the added labor cost outweighed the saving in transporting the assembled machine. It is also significant that the United States' share of world trade in automobiles, measured in numbers rather than weight or value, has declined from 70 per cent in 1929 to 25 per cent today. It is possible, but improbable, that there has been a taste change all over the world against the larger American models. The more likely explanation is that the technology for producing automobiles is now standardized, and that foreign labor costs give foreign producers an advantage which is not offset by the cheaper capital costs in this country. In important respects, foreigners are even out-stripping United States manufacturers in incorporating significant improvements in automobile design.

Figures 3a, 3b, 3c show cost-reducing innovations in an existing product or products. In Figure 3a the innovation is labor-saving; in Figure 3b it is capital saving; and in Figure 3c there are neutral in-novations (i.e., innovations which increase output of each commodity without changing the proportions of factor inputs). Assuming that the country had a comparative advantage in the capital-and-land-intensive product prior to the innovation, laborsaving innovation

Capital –Intensive Good

Figure 3a
Labor-saving
innovation

Figure 3b
Capital-saving
innovation

Figure 3c
Neutral innovations
in both commodities

reduces imports and possibly converts the industry to an export basis; the capital-saving innovation enlarges exports if the foreign demand is elastic; and the neutral innovation also enlarges exports and reduces the terms of trade.

Import-biased innovations of a land-saving character are outstand-ing in the history of United States foreign trade. These are the synthetics, including synthetic nitrates, synthetic fibers, rubber, detergents, atabrine, etc. Table III shows the sad plight of silk but only the beginnings of the difficulties of wool under attack from dynel and orlon. Rubber might have behaved like coffee had it not been for the role of synthetic in placing a ceiling on the price. The failure of imports of fats and oils to grow like other resource-oriented products (Table III) is ascribable largely to the development of petroleum-based detergents and paint thinners (and partly to the domestic cultivation of linseed for oil). A patent was taken out in December 1957 for a synthetic chocolate.

The analysis of foreign trade becomes complex when two factors work together or in opposite directions. If it be assumed, as the writer believes, that the United States would have a comparative advantage in cotton and wheat if domestic price supports and export subsidies were both removed, this would be the net result of a growth of labor and capital relative to land, which decreases the relative efficiency of the United States in these commodities, more than offset by capital-using and land-saving innovations. These include the application of fertilizer, laborsaving machinery such as the cotton picker, the capital-intensive irrigation of cotton lands in Arizona, New Mexico, Texas, and California, and dry-farming techniques, which are land-intensive in a physical sense but involve the use of previously no-rent land. Professor T. W. Schultz has gone so far as to say that farming in the United States uses more capital than any other factor,[3] although such comparisons can be made, of course, only on an index-number basis.

Another commodity which has changed from land-intensive to capital-intensive (to speak loosely) is coal. Here it is true that depletion has occurred faster in Europe than in the United States, so that a comparative advantage based on land endowments could be said to have opened up. Here also an important contribution to making trade possible has been a decline in transport costs. But the main stimulus has probably been provided by the reduction in production costs brought about by the increasing mechanization of mines, both underground and open-cast. Wages have been rising rapidly owing to the successful efforts of John L. Lewis and his United Mine Workers, but coal prices have fallen. Transatlantic exports, which in the inter-war period were limited to the immediate postwar and the 1926 British strike, have now reached 30 to 40 million tons annually. Japan is importing coal from the United States on a regular basis, across 7,000 miles of ocean. Table V sets out United States coal exports to Canada and Mexico on the one hand and all other destinations on the other. The latter includes small amounts for Latin America, but mainly represents European sales.

An interesting reversal of trade based on technological changes occurred briefly in the radio industry. United States innovations in this field in the 1920's built up a substantial export trade. As the rate

TABLE V.—UNITED STATES EXPORTS OF COAL AND COKE
(*annual average in millions of dollars*)

	Total	Canada and Mexico	Other
1911–1915	59	–	–
1921–1925	131	103	28
1926–1930	122	91	30
1931–1935	52	49	3
1936–1940	67	60	7
1941–1945	164	148	16
1946–1950	405	229	177
1951–1955	454	217	237
(1956)	(745)	(228)	(517)

of innovation slowed down, it became evident that radio assembly was a highly labor-intensive operation, relying upon numbers of dexterous but not very skilled women to wire radio sets. With the spread of the technology to other countries, therefore, factor endowments began to shape the direction of trade more than technology, and imports of radios appeared in the United States market from Germany, the Netherlands, and Britain. Whether independently or partly under the spur of this competition, the United States industry sponsored another substantial and laborsaving innovation—the printed circuit, which eliminated a considerable amount of wiring, and regained its comparative advantage or at least recovered some of the comparative disadvantage. This change was accompanied by the introduction of sets based on transistors, with a new emphasis on small-sized portables. The result was that the foreign invasion of the United States radio market was short-lived.

In industries where the apparent limits of increased efficiency have been reached the basis of trade may reverse itself. Perhaps the clearest example is in heavy electrical generators and transformers, circuit breakers, and similar equipment, where the United States has lost its comparative advantage based on innovation in a product basically requiring large quantities of highly skilled labor particularly expensive in the United States. The United States industry retains a considerable share of the domestic market based on the propensity of public utilities to purchase supplies on a reciprocal basis and to incorporate higher costs into their rate base. This involves a departure from the classic assumption of perfect competition. But where competitive bidding has taken place, under government contracts, foreign suppliers can outdistance their United States competitors.

Current United States expanding lines based on technological innovation are in road-building equipment, high-speed printing equipment, large agricultural machinery, data-processing machinery, and air-conditioning equipment. Machinery has been the pre-eminent United States export category since 1936–1940 (see Table II), when it outstripped petroleum products and cotton. Its lead has widened each subsequent five-year period both absolutely and as a multiple of its nearest challenger. Despite the increase in machinery and vehicle imports since 1945, based upon spreading technology in old lines—sewing machines, typewriters, cash registers, etc.—the rate of innovation appears to be sufficient to keep the total class an area of increasing comparative advantage.

Finally, it is worth noting that technological progress in the United States has whittled away at the input of raw materials required to produce a given output. The Paley Commission report noted that real output per capita (GNP) increased by almost 2½ times from 1900 to 1950 (i.e., from $430 in 1939 purchasing power to $1,022) while primary-product consumption per capita increased by less than 30 per cent over the same period (i.e., from $103 per capita in 1935–1939 purchasing power to $131). If food is excluded, raw-material consumption per capita rises from $43 to $63.[4] This declining trend in total raw-material consumption can be combined with innovations which displace certain imports (silk) and give rise to others (rubber) but the former to a greater extent than the latter. On the basis of the then current trends, the decline in raw-material imports of the United States from 2.7 per cent of GNP in 1929 to 1.6 per cent in 1953[5] is readily explained.

CHANGES IN INCOME

The changing composition of United States export and import trade is also explained in part by the growth in world real income and the consequent more rapid growth in the demand for some kinds of goods than for others. Engel's law states that as income increases the demand for food rises less than proportionately. Its corollary is that demand increases more rapidly for manufactured goods than for foodstuffs, that the demand for manufactured goods grows more rapidly than the derived demand for raw materials, because of the increased degree of manufacture embodied in income-elastic goods. Thus, for example, the income elasticity of demand for food at retail and in restaurants, which embodies a high degree of value added by post-farm services, is higher than for food at the farm; and the demand for products using copper, such as electric equipment, is more income-elastic than the demand for copper.

A country which is a leader in technological innovation is likely to have a high income elasticity of demand for its exports. Insofar as the innovations produce new goods, this is certain to be the case. (Even where the new goods partly replace products of income-inelastic demand, the demand for the replacement good may be said to be income-elastic for the period of re-equipment). Where the innovation consists in a new and cheaper way of making an existing good, however, there is no assurance that it leads to income-elastic demand. The Japanese experience in producing textiles cheaper than Britain is a case in point.

As income continues to increase, income elasticity for a given product declines. Consumers originally anxious to acquire the product have done so. Its use becomes an accustomed part of the level of living. It changes character from a luxury to a necessity, and with this change it becomes income-inelastic instead of elastic. Textiles were highly income-elastic when British exports reached substantial quantities in the 1830's and 1840's. Thereafter this elasticity declined. Automobiles in the United States have moved from a luxury to a necessity until today it is the second automobile, not the first, for which the demand is income-elastic.

Income elasticity of foreign demand for United States products seems to be higher than United States demand for foreign products. T. C. Chang puts the figures at 2.91 and 1.27 respectively;[6] but this is in connection with a cyclical study from which trends have been removed. Another investigation has suggested that an increase of 1 per cent in industrial production abroad is likely to lead to an increase of 1½ per cent in the volume of total United States exports,[7] whereas it is well known from the *United States in the World Economy*[8] that changes in industrial production in the United States in the interwar period led to similar changes in the volume of United States imports. (i.e., 1 per cent and 1 per cent). Finally, Sir Donald MacDougall has calculated that

> while consumption of manufactures outside the United States has increased perhaps tenfold since 1876, the quantity of manufactures imported from the United States has multiplied more than fortyfold.

Eighty years ago the rest of the world took under 1½% of its manufactures from the United States. Now it takes 5-6 per cent.[9]

This is an income elasticity in terms of manufactures of 4. That for United States imports of manufactures runs 1 to 1.5, but applies, of course, to a much smaller base.[10]

If the income elasticity of foreign demand for United States exports is significantly higher than that of United States demand for imports from abroad, the problem of international adjustment is complicated. Adjustment is not impossible; if income grows in the United States faster than abroad, this would offset the bias imparted

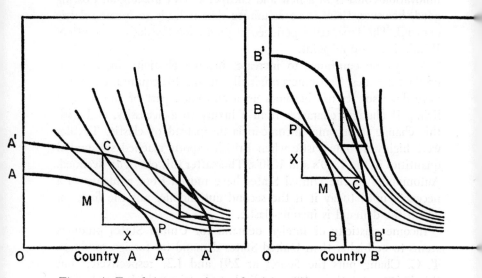

Figure 4. Equal increases in productivity (40 per cent) with income elasticity higher for A's good than for B's.

by income elasticities. Or if Europe were prepared to accept deteriorating terms of trade, and the price elasticities were sufficiently high, adjustment could be brought about in this fashion. In a two-country, two-commodity model, shown in Figure 4, the bias of the income elasticities in favor of A's product and against B's brings it about that, when A and B both grow in productivity, i.e., expand their production-possibilities curves by 40 per cent, the new trade position results in a much more substantial gain for A than for B. This is due less to the change in the terms of trade, although there is some improvement in A's price, than to the fact that output increases in the high value good in A, and in the low value good in B.

THE DECLINE IN TRANSPORT COSTS

Some of the changes described have reduced trade: the change in factor proportions in favor of the imported product, technological innovation economizing the scarce factor, and the shift in demand in favor of the product in which a country has a comparative advantage. But one significant change has taken place in the last eighty years which has widened the basis for specialization and exchange. This is the continued decline in transport costs relative to the costs of commodities.

The movement is not new. The large expansion in world trade after the Civil War was the consequence of the cheapening of overland transport by the railroad and of ocean shipping by the ironclad steam vessel. These developments brought wheat cheaply to Europe from areas of recent settlement. Subsequently the refrigerator ship added meat. But the continued cheapening of tanker and freighter transport since 1929 has meant that the heavy products such as steel, oil, and coal move long distances and across vast oceans, not only where international trade is completely specialized, i.e., from producing countries to those which lack any domestic output of them, but also in competition with domestic producers.

This cheapening of costs is partly a consequence of the subsidization and overproduction of shipping. In the main, however, it follows from technological innovation—the tankers of 45,000, 65,000, and 100,000 tons which can be filled and emptied by pumping so rapidly that turn-around time is determined by the insistence of the crew for shore leave; 30 and 31-inch pipelines laid across the Arabian peninsula from the Persian Gulf to the eastern coast of the Mediterranean; facilities for loading coal at Hampton Roads, which involve dumping in one motion the contents of a trainload of coal cars into hoppers from which the coal can be poured into the ship's hold. Table VI shows the development of European ocean-shipping transport rates since 1900 compared with world prices in international trade. The comparison is extremely rough and ready, and it depends unduly upon the choice of particular years as bases and as measures of price changes. But a more refined measure would support the generalization, unless we insisted on holding the comparison at 1938 for world trade, or at a peak year such as 1946 or 1957 for freights.

TABLE VI
WORLD PRICES COMPARED WITH EUROPEAN OCEAN FREIGHT
RATES, 1900–1955 (1913=100)

World Prices Price index of world trade		European Freight Rates European index of world freight rates	
1900	83	106	
1913	100	100	
1928	139	99	
1938	64	98	
1950	200	154	
(1955)	(222)	(191)	

Source: Prices: Statistisches Bundesamt, *Statistisches Jahrbuch für die Bundesrepublik Deutschland*, 1952, Stuttgart, 1952, p. 60.

Freight rates: C. P. Kindleberger, *The Terms of Trade*, (New York, Technology Press and Wiley, 1956), p. 19.

This relative decline in transport charges has greatly increased international trade in heavy products. Coal and steel are now items of transatlantic commerce. Steel imports into the United States have in fact risen from $38 million in 1929 to $250 million in 1956. In petroleum products the shrinking margin taken by transport costs has meant a more rapid reversal of intercontinental trade than might have been expected.

THE WIDER BASIS FOR TRADE

The two-country, two-commodity, two-factor model assumes perfect competition based on perfect knowledge. In the real world trade moves in grooves dictated by imperfections of knowledge, or perhaps, more accurately, by limitations of the horizon within which producers and consumers exercise their perfect knowledge. One of the most important changes affecting the international trade of the United States and of the world has been the widening of these horizons.

The same phenomenon is familiar in international investment, which flowed in grooves dictated by institutionalized channels of communication. After 1875 the British did their lending largely in the Commonwealth, plus a bit in Latin America, whereas the French loaned in eastern Europe, the Germans in eastern Europe and the Middle East.

Professor Cole has suggested that the entrepreneur can be classified, by his consciousness of the impact of his actions, into community-oriented, industry-conscious, and nation-oriented.[11] In the first of these his horizon of cognition is limited to the local community; in the second he becomes a participant in the affairs of his industry, in trade associations, and in national conventions; in the third stage he is an industrial statesman, interested in such organizations as the CED, the NAM, or the Council of Foreign Relations, or taking a post in government.

A somewhat comparable set of stages can be devised to fit the horizon of awareness of the potentialities of business decision. In the first stage the entrepreneur hires labor and buys material locally, and tends to sell in a local market or, in the case of standardized goods, in the local component of a larger regional or even international market. At a later stage the company grows to national stature. Growth decisions are then not exclusively questions of local expansion but can include the question whether to set up a branch plant in a different location. The national corporation moves capital and supervisory and executive labor freely from location to location within a country and plays an important role in the United States as an institution which assists in the equalization of factor prices and breaking down dual economy within the country. National corporations in the United States have completed moving into the South in search of cheaper labor, cheaper materials, and access to markets. In Italy the same process is just beginning.

The third stage is the internationalization of the corporation. This may begin by the establishment of overseas subsidiaries to produce standardized raw materials or to tunnel a tariff wall by selling domestically produced products in lieu of exports. Its fruition is reached when a corporation is as ready to contemplate expansion abroad as in the home country, not only of standardized products but also of differentiated products and processes and not only for export but also for home distribution. The Arabian-American Oil Company put its accounting offices in Italy to get cheaper clerical help, found Italian clerks expensive because of inefficiency, and then moved its offices to The Hague. A manufacturer of office machines built a subsidiary in Scotland and found it so efficient that it shifted thence its whole production of computers, including those for the American market. The American motion picture industry has become internationalized. Originally turning abroad for backgrounds in an effort to use up blocked currencies accumulated from film rentals, the industry found first that foreign realistic sets lent exotic qualities to motion pictures (a better product) and, second, that labor-intensive pictures (mob scenes) were cheaper. Prior to 1939, the industry's horizon was limited to Hollywood and locations in Arizona and New Mexico. Today the horizon has been broadened to the world.

The movement in reverse is called "demonstration effect" and involves the acquisition, in other countries, of a taste for the products of developed countries, including the United States. But the broadening of the horizon of United States corporations, which is just beginning, promises to expand international trade. A number of companies have moved to or expanded operations in Puerto Rico as a first step. The example of the Nash automobile company (now American Motors) in buying chassis for the Metropolitan from the Austin Company in Britain has been followed by General Motors and Ford in producing small cars for the American market in their British and German subsidiaries. Publishers are importing sheets printed in Britain, the Netherlands, or Japan for binding in the United States. The Hamilton Watch Company is establishing a Japanese subsidiary, ostensibly for meeting Swiss competition in foreign markets. Since the company has not been an exporter for many years, however, it might easily produce parts or whole watches for the American market. A producer of cameras is contemplating buying or building a subsidiary to manufacture shutters in Europe. At least one or two companies are establishing laboratories in Europe where the cost of labor-intensive research is reduced because of the endowment of abundant and cheap Ph.D.'s in science.

There are, of course, drawbacks to shifting manufacturing operations abroad. Transport is more subject to interruption. New tariffs may penalize importation. Dealing with a second government increases the complexity of meeting regulations and raises the chance of diversion to other tasks or confiscation. Domestic labor may object to the loss of custom to foreign competitors. For these reasons many corporations are unready even to contemplate foreign operations, i.e., to include the foreign country in their horizon of knowledge about costs and profitable operations. Despite these obstacles, however, the prospect for international intra-company trade in components and finished goods is one of expansion. The horizon of cognition is broadening from a national to a world (perhaps largely a North Atlantic world) basis.

This trend is too new to reveal itself significantly in the import statistics. Twenty-five per cent of United States imports are produced in subsidiaries of American companies located abroad,[12] but this is mostly in standardized raw materials where the horizon was lifted from the boundaries of the United States to the world as a whole in the early 1920's. The significant post-World War II development is that an increasing number of companies are becoming international to the extent of being prepared to consider foreign production of differentiated products or components for the United States market.

Even in the standardized commodities the process is speeding up. There has been a peculiar competitive position in oil, in which international business was much less competitive than domestic; seven world-wide companies operated internationally, while the domestic producers of crude oil in the United States were many times more numerous. For some years the interests of these two groups have been opposed on the question of imports of crude petroleum into the United States. Since World War II, however, an increasing number of domestic producers have "gone international." Ten companies combined to form the American Independent Oil Company, which obtained a concession in the Neutral Zone of Kuwait. This company has the distinction of drilling more dry holes in the Persian Gulf than any other company until it finally struck oil, and of showing a fine disregard for public relations by bringing its first cargo of oil into the export harbor of Galveston. Other "domestic companies" have entered into long-term contracts to buy foreign crude, have bid on the new concessions auctioned off by Venezuela, and are exploring on concessions all over the world. The line between the internationals and the domestics is blurring.

Something of the sort is taking place throughout American industry above a relatively small size. Business executives lose count of their foreign trips within the year, as they long since have done of journeys between New York and Chicago.

With the internationalization of the manufacturing process, the basis for international trade becomes wider. It seems likely, though it is by no means certain, that the decline in merchandise imports in relation to Gross National Product, which has gone from approximately 7 per cent in 1870 to 2.2 per cent during the war and reconstruction period from 1939 to 1949, and has since recovered only to 2.7 per cent,[13] will come to a halt and perhaps reverse itself.

A widening intellectual horizon may decrease as well as increase trade. Some direct investment replaces exports, whether in market-oriented goods to economize on costs of transportation or because of tariff or quota restrictions. And in a two-factor world complete mobility of capital under appropriate conditions can reduce trade to zero as international goods and factor prices are equalized through factor movements rather than trade.[14]

Given more than two factors, however, one of which, land, cannot move and another of which is largely inhibited in its movement, the net effect of a widening acquisition and knowledge of costs of production in the world is likely to be trade-increasing for the United States. Exports run perhaps 4 per cent of Gross National Product and 7 per cent of the production of movable commodities in gross national product. At the limit, then, exports can decrease by $16 billion if they are replaced in toto by foreign production undertaken by United States entrepreneurs, but imports can increase by $240 billion if foreign production entirely replaces United States production of movable commodities. These limits are unrealistic, of course, but may have some relevance to the question whether a widening cognitive horizon for United States entrepreneurs is likely to narrow or increase the scope of international trade, particularly in connection with the reduction of transport costs just discussed.

United States Commercial Policy

Provided one is allowed to interpret historical facts broadly, the development of commercial policy, and particularly the replacement of protection by freer trade, furnishes an instructive example of the interaction of political and economic forces. This is true both of the repeal of the Corn Laws in Britain in 1846 and of the adoption of the Reciprocal Trade Agreements Act in the United States in 1934. These two parallel courses of action differ in their political origin. In Britain political power shifted from a high-tariff group to a low-tariff group without change in the economic interests of the groups. In the United States political power remained within the control of the same group—broadly conceived, but its economic interest underwent a profound alteration.

The economic analysis which must be brought to the political interpretation is furnished by the Stolper-Samuelson theorem[15] and its inverse. This theorem states that the imposition of a tariff will raise the return to the scarce factor of production and reduce that to the abundant factor. The mechanism is simple. A tariff raises the price of the imported good, in which the country has a comparative disadvantage because it embodies relatively more of the scarce factor. It also lowers the price of the export good, which embodies a relatively large amount of the abundant factor. This change in relative prices induces resources to shift out of the export into the import-competing good. But factors are released from the export industry in a different proportion from that required in the expanding production of import substitutes. Too much of the abundant factor is made available, and too little of the scarce factor. In order to absorb the abundant factor into employment, its price must fall; and in order to economize the employment of the scarce factor, its price must rise. A tariff therefore has the effect of raising the price of the scarce and lowering that of the abundant factor of production. Stolper and Samuelson prove, moreover, that this increase in price of the scarce factor is not only relative but also involves an absolute increase in real income: the loss to the country as a whole from the reduction in trade is levied in its entirety on the abundant factor —and more too.

The simple converse of the Stolper-Samuelson theorem suggests that the abundant factor gains relatively and absolutely, and the scarce factor loses relatively and absolutely, from a reduction in existing tariff barriers. When political power shifts into the hands of the abundant factor, it is to its interest to reduce tariffs; and when a factor of production exercising political power changes from a scarce or intermediate position to one of abundance it gains in economic terms by adopting free trade. This is the operational historical reason which accounts for the movement to freer trade in Great Britain in the 1840's and of the United States in the 1930's, rather than the more optimistic doctrine that these countries changed directions after years of free-trade preaching as a consequence of their intellectual appreciation of the advantages of free trade to the country as a whole.

The application of the theorem to the British case is relatively simple and illuminates the subsequent United States experience. The landlords (wheat farmers) had enjoyed high profits in the Napoleonic period and undertook, since they dominated Parliament, to preserve them by adopting the so-called Corn Laws, a sliding-scale tariff on wheat. The Reform Bill of 1832 represented the successful attempt of the rising commercial and industrial classes to wrest political power from the landed gentry. Shortly thereafter the Corn Laws were repealed. Assisted in timing by the impetus provided by the famine of 1844, which increased the price of food and the cost of living, Sir Robert Peel was slow in recognizing the Whig industrial interest in repeal. And, indeed, the Manchester liberals' agitators, led by Cobden and Bright, put the case in terms of the supply of factors to the manufacturing sector rather than of the demand abroad for exports created by the increase in imports, which is a more modern way to put it.

The difficulties in the way of applying the Stolper-Samuelson theorem in the United States are considerably more imposing. First is the annoyance of having three factors rather than the more convenient two in which the theorem has been demonstrated and is more conveniently understood. A second is the frequent division of the factors, land, labor, and capital, into noncompeting groups, with capital and labor engaged in export industry on one side of the argument and capital and labor in import-competing industry on the other. Another is cultural lag, which has kept certain groups clinging to their ancient advocacies after their interest had fundamentally altered. Still another has been the statistical attempt of Professor Leontief to show, contrary to a vital assumption, that the United States is not capital-abundant but labor-abundant.

In the nineteenth century, certainly through the Civil War and probably up to or after the turn of the century, the abundant factor in the United States was land. This land was not homogeneous. In the 1830's and 1840's the agitation for free trade came from the southern owners of land producing cotton and tobacco. With the decisive defeat of this position in the Civil War, the focus shifted to the Northwest and Midwest, producing corn, lard, and wheat. This area was not undividedly in favor of low tariffs, for reasons which are discussed below. But land was the abundant factor, and capital was scarce (labor was also scarce but possibly less so than capital). Politically in the saddle, and committed to tariff protection, however, were the capital-intensive regions interested in cotton textiles, iron, and steel, and (after 1880) the growing machinery industry. This commitment was not unrestrained; the nature of the democracy in the United States was to limit the repression of the minority by the majority. But it was definite.

With the emergence of mass-production industries in World War I, capital's position as the scarce factor changed. The roots, of course, go further back to the first decade of the century. The export figures for machinery, automobiles, and iron and steel in 1911–1915 (Table II) are strongly influenced by the war in Europe, but they are nonetheless impressive as an indication of an economic transformation in full swing. Within the fraternity of business leaders the mantle of leadership shifted from New England textiles and Pittsburgh steel, to Detroit, Cleveland, Schenectady, Cincinnati, and the Midwest. Farm machinery, automobiles, and electrical equipment were the fastest growing industries, and these were export-oriented rather than import-competing.

Two increases in tariff took place before this economic interest with political power could assert itself and move toward lower duties. In 1919 duties were raised to protect the newly established defense industries in scientific instruments, optical goods, dyestuffs, etc. The Smoot-Hawley Act was formed in 1930 in a measure that began in the spring of 1929 as an attempt to raise the duty on wheat in order to keep out the Australian surplus which threatened to collapse the price structure. In both cases the organization of the Congress, with its practices of logrolling among parochial interests, meant that tariffs were raised not in particular but in general. Only in 1934, in depression, with the border-state leadership of the spiritually committed Cordell Hull, did the midwestern mass-producer interests achieve tariff reduction.

To summarize: in 1850 capital wanted tariffs; land wanted free trade; capital was politically dominant. The United States followed a policy of protection. In 1950 capital wanted free trade; labor wanted tariffs; capital (new capital) was politically dominant. United States policy moved (and drifted through inflation) toward much freer trade.

The division of factors of production into noncompeting groups explains much of the wobble in the historical path. In the nineteenth century abundant land might have been more successful in achieving a lower degree of protection had it not been for the ambivalence of the wheat-growing areas of the Northwest. These were free-trade supporters as they regarded the western European market from which they were excluded by tariffs. Yet over their shoulder to the north lay an even more efficient grain producer in the prairie provinces of Canada which made them disinclined to adopt free trade as a principle. It is idle to speculate under what conditions the midwestern farm bloc would have joined with the South in support of free trade, and the two sections were divided politically on other issues. Canada is perhaps not a fully satisfactory explanation for the absence of the normally impressive political capacity of sections of the United States for ignoring their differences while they focus on areas of agreement. But it is hard to find another explanation why the Middle West voted against, or was lukewarm in defending, its economic interest in exporting.

Noncompeting groups were equally prominent in capital and labor. They divided upon industrial rather than factor lines. Both capital and labor were for tariffs in the small-scale, labor-intensive industries like textiles, gloves, pottery, and glass; and both capital and labor were for freer trade in the mass-production, capital-intensive sector of the economy. To a certain extent capital in each segment organized into different groups. Though they are by no means comparable, the National Association of Manufacturers was the focus of smaller industry and protectionist while the Committee on Economic Development represented larger firms and supported reductions. In similar fashion the American Federation of Labor was largely protectionist while in the mass-production industry Congress of Industrial Organization supported the trade agreements program.

Within the ranks of capital, certain industries, notably iron and steel, started out as protectionist in the nineteenth century but became indifferent rather than opposed to the tariff. Economies of scale converted a number of these from an importing-competing status to an interest in export markets. This phenomenon has been observed in part of the chemical industry. The difficulties faced by the producers of merchant steel, as a consequence of the reduction in freight rates, may encourage that industry, or branches of it, to slip back into its original protectionist frame of mind.

The political shift from protectionism to ostensible support of the trade agreements program within the Republican party, moreover, involved a small shift in the locus of power among the disparate elements of the party. Similarly the low-tariff views of the Democratic party increasingly represented not so much revealed truth or a consensus of view as a narrowly balanced preponderance in favor of lower tariffs from which growing sections of the South dissent because of industrialization.

Not only did noncompeting groups among factors have different interests and hence different political views; differences also occurred between different segments of the same factor in the same industry.

The most complex of these was in oil, where five United States and one foreign oil company of international character were interested in importing while a much larger number of smaller companies within the United States were interested in maintaining prices high. For a time after the war this fundamental division was ignored by the adoption of a meaningless slogan—or rather one which meant different things to the two groups—"Imports to supplement, but not to supplant domestic production." Later the political strength of the independents in Texas, a border state in political terms, was enough to tip the balance in favor of import restrictions, leaving, however, an important and difficult problem whether these should be voluntary, or "voluntary", i.e., imposed informally by government, or formally imposed. The initial line-up after the war, with six international companies on one side and the entire rest of the industry on the other, became gradually modified as one after another refiner found it desirable to sign contracts for and construct new facilities dependent upon imported oil, and as more and more companies "went international," i.e., joined in the search for oil abroad and bid on foreign concessions.

While few industries are divided in this fashion, there is sufficient difference in the size of firms favoring and opposing expanded foreign trade to enable one protectionist to complain that the high-tariff proponents were regarded as vested interests while the supporters of the trade agreements program painted themselves as moved only by the public interest. He suggested that in an earlier day the liberal position had been support for free trade and opposition to monopoly. Today, since the monopolists benefited from expanded exports while small business needed support from abroad, the liberal was obliged, in his view, to defend protection in order to maintain his opposition to monopoly.

Shifts in economic interest and shifts in political doctrine on the tariff issue occur by no means simultaneously. There are cases of business leaders who have shifted their views sharply in response to a change in comparative advantage. Philip Reed of the General Electric Company, long a business statesman of the CED stripe, and interested in free trade, demurred from some CED conclusions on the issue insofar as they might apply to heavy electrical equipment such as transformers, generators, and turbines, and later argued against imports on national defense grounds.[16]

But politicians have a more difficult time in changing position.

Southern political leaders maintained their traditional free-trade stance and in fact served as leaders of the reciprocal trade movement which benefited primarily mass-production industry. This continued until the 1955 renewal of the Trade Agreements Act, in which they entered reservations on the score of textile imports. At the same time, the Middle-west protectionists, such as Senator Taft, who had been nurtured in a Republican tradition which equated tariff reductions in 1894 with the trade depression in 1896 and that of 1913 with a world war, failed to see that the industrial Middle West was becoming the machine shop of the world.

The task of unifying interest and doctrine is always difficult. The CIO, which supports free trade in general, permits some of its member unions engaged in the production of ladies' blouses and men's caps to protest against Japanese imports. They cannot use the rationalization of national defense which has come so handily and naturally to the rescue of honest men interested in finding public justification for a private interest. But the gap between doctrine and interest occurs only because interest is transformed while doctrine remains unaltered.

Finally, the application of the Stolper-Samuelson theorem to the explanation of United States tariff history is disturbed by the controversial findings of Professor Wassily Leontief of Harvard University, who, in two articles,[17] has attempted statistically to undermine the view that the United States after World War II had a comparative advantage in capital-intensive goods and a comparative disadvantage in labor-intensive goods. Using coefficients derived from his input-output studies, he has compared the requirements of capital and labor for producing an additional million dollars' worth of various categories of export- and import-competing goods and found that the capital requirements are slightly higher in import-competing industry and that labor requirements are slightly higher in export industry. These findings, he contends, undermine the widely held view, based on the Heckscher-Ohlin view of the relation between factor endowments and trade, that the United States is capital-abundant relative to the rest of the world and labor-scarce.

Leontief's views have not lacked for criticism.[18] A number of points may be made against his method. The original 1947 figures are hardly representative, since exports were dominated by reconstruction needs and imports had not recovered from the war. The second Leontief article, which uses 1951 trade figures, shows modified statistical results though exports are still labor-intensive relative to import-competing industry and the latter relatively capital-intensive.) The factor proportions of an incremental expansion in output do not necessarily represent the average of an industry as implied by the assumption of fixed coefficients on which the input-output system rests. The measurements from the Census of Manufactures do not adequately distinguish capital from land. Capital requirements in the Leontief articles are extraordinarily high in agriculture, non-ferrous mining, primary lead, copper, and other metals compared to what are normally thought of as capital-intensive industries such as farm equipment, electrical equipment, and motor vehicles (more than twice as high); etc. But the main objection to his conclusion, as pointed out by Robinson, Jones, and Johnson, is that he uses a model based upon an assumption of identical production functions with fixed factors in the trading countries rather than identical production functions with a large amount of room for factor substitution in production functions, or widely divergent and separate production functions.

Except in the case of identical production functions with fixed factor proportions (or a very narrow range of factor substitution), the Heckscher-Ohlin theorem contains an ambiguity. One can compare the capital and labor content of exports and imports of a country (where there is competing domestic of the imported good) using either the factor proportions in the given country or those of its trading partners. The answers will not necessarily be the same, and, like the index-number problem, there is no uniquely correct answer. Assume that the United States imported rice rather than exported it, and that rice is produced in Burma by hand methods of a very labor-intensive method and by capital-intensive means in the United States, including sowing seed by broadcasting it from airplanes. The rice imports use up labor in Burma but economize on capital in the United States. One can regard the imports as labor-saving or capital-saving, depending upon whether one measures by the Burmese standard or the American, but there is clearly no basis for deciding which standard is "correct."

Moreover, it is important to note that the conclusion based on the American standard, that rice imports are capital-saving, is possible only because capital is so abundant and cheap there that it is possible to produce rice in competition with imports by capital-intensive methods. Technological change has operated to substitute abundant capital for scarce labor (and land—that third factor again!). The fact that in this substitution more capital is needed in the import-competing good than in the established industry does not imply that capital is scarce and labor abundant in any fundamental sense. Properly interpreted, then, Leontief's findings, to the extent that they are statistically valid, fail to undermine the view that the United States is capital abundant and labor scarce, and that capital gains from increased exports while labor gains from reduced imports.

The third factor, noncompeting groups, cultural lag, and the use of different production functions in trading countries (or a single production function with a wide range of factor substitution), therefore muddy the application of the Stolper-Samuelson theorem to the interpretation of United States commercial policy though they do not overthrow it. Large-scale research-minded industry using capital *in extenso* benefits from increased imports which put dollars into the hands of the exchange authorities of their foreign customers. Small-scale labor-intensive industry is threatened by imports (and by labor-saving innovation as well.) Two commodities, two countries, two factors of fixed amount and identical production functions with limited room for factor substitutions, perfect knowledge and other simplifying assumptions produce a sharpness of conclusion in international trade theory which cannot be found in the trade returns or in the historical record. Nevertheless, modified to relax these assumptions in the direction of reality, the theory of international trade is still relevant and informing.

Notes

[1] This figure is taken from a thesis by Jaroslav Vanek entitled, *The Natural Resource Content of United States Foreign Trade, 1870–1955* (Mass. Institute of Technology, 1957).

[2] See Donald MacDougall, *The World Dollar Problem* (London: Macmillan & Co., Ltd., 1957), p. 162.

[3] T. W. Schultz, "The Supply of Food in Relation to Economic Development," *Economic Development and Cultural Change,* December 1952, p. 248; see also his *The Economic Organization of Agriculture* (New York: McGraw–Hill Book Co., 1953), p. 125.

[4] *Resources for Freedom,* President's Materials Policy Committee, Washington, Vol. 2, p. 184.

[5] Department of Commerce, "Recent Developments in United States Foreign Trade," in *Foreign Trade Policy*, a compendium of papers collected by the staff of the Subcommittee on Foreign Trade Policy of the Committee on Ways and Means (Washington, D.C.: Government Printing Office 1957). See also the illuminating article by F. H. Klopstock and P. Meek, "Structural Shifts and Recent Trends in United States Trade and Payments," *ibid.*, pp. 317–59.

[6] T. C. Chang, *Cyclical Movements in the Balance of Payments* (Cambridge: Cambridge University Press, 1951), pp. 50, 42.

[7] J. H. Adler, "The Post-War Demand for United States Exports," *Review of Economics and Statistics*, February 1946.

[8] Washington, D.C., Government Printing Office, 1942, p. 39.

[9] Donald MacDougall, *op. cit.*, p. 209.

[10] *Ibid.*, p. 219, n. 1.

[11] A. H. Cole, "A New Set of Stages," *Explorations in Entrepreneurial History*, December 1955, pp. 99–107.

[12] See K. Pizer, *Survey of Current Business*, August 1956.

[13] These figures are not strictly comparable. See Donald MacDougall, *op. cit.*, p. 235.

[14] See Robert A. Mundell, "International Trade and Factor Mobility," *American Economic Review*, June 1957.

[15] W. F. Stolper and P. A. Samuelson, "Protection and Real Wages," *Review of Economic Studies*, 1941, reprinted in American Economic Association, *Readings in the Theory of International Trade* (Philadelphia, Blakiston, 1949).

[16] See his statement "The National Security as Affected by the Importing of Power-producing Equipment," *Foreign Trade Policy, op. cit.*, pp. 663–678.

[17] W. Leontief, "Domestic Production and Foreign Trade: The American Capital Position Re-Examined," *Proceedings* of the American Philosophical Society, September 28, 1953, pp. 332–349; and "Factor Proportions and the Structure of American Trade: Further Theoretical and Empirical Analysis," *Review of Economics and Statistics*, November 1956, pp. 386–407.

[18] R. Robinson, "Factor Endowments and Comparative Advantage," *Quarterly Journal of Economics*, May 1956, pp. 169–192 and August 1956, pp. 346–363; and further papers by Diab, Ellsworth, Hoffmeyer, Johnson, Jones, Swerling.

INDEX

Abegglen, J. C. 123-124, 302
Ackerman, C. S., 176
Adler, J. H., 357
Affluence, future problems of, 24-27
Agricultural implements industry, 237
Agricultural processing industry, 237, 239-243, 279
Agricultural tractor industry, 249-250
Aircraft industry, 237-238, 256, 258, 263
Allen, H., 263
Allied Chemical & Dye, 239, 274-276
Allis-Chalmers, 239, 249-251, 256-257
Aluminum Company of America, 239, 279
American Cyanamid, 270, 277
American Economic Association, 28-29, 48
American economics, applied, 38, 49; derivative character of, 36; doctrinaire character of, 36; earlier, 33-37; institutionalist school of, 37; mathematical, 37, 47; modern, 41-49; "nationalistic" character of, 33; and operations research, 37; "optimistic" character of, 33; present, 47, 50; "pro-business, conservative" character of, 35; professionalization of, 39; "protectionist" character of, 34; statistical, 37; "theological" character of, 34; transition to modern, 37-41; "untheoretical" character of, 35; and work on business cycles, 36; and work on "growth and development," 37
American Federation of Labor, 193, 200, 205-206, 368
AFL-CIO, 212, 220; Ethical Practices Codes, 206-207, 212; Executive Council, 206-207
American Independent Oil Company, 363
American labor, future of, 214-232; role of government in, 197, 211

American labor problems, antecedents to recent past, 192-198; and "cold war," 198; in Great Depression, 198; last quarter century of, 198-214; in New Deal, 198; and postwar boom, 198; and World War, 198
American Motors, 362
American Optical, 259
American society, new forces in, 19-24
American Smelting & Refining, 239, 242
American Tobacco, 239-240, 242
Anaconda Copper, 239
Anti-inflationary moves, 62-64
Antitrust area, 301
Arabian-American Oil, 361
Armco Steel, 239
Armour, 239-240, 279
Arms race, 12
Assembling industries, 243-259, 279
Atherton, H. F., 276
Atlantic Refining, 239, 267-269
Atlas Powder, 277
Austerity, future problems of, 24-27
Austin Company, 362
Auto Workers Union, 210
Automation, 214, 217, 224-226
Automobile, 3, 6; exports to United States, 352; industry, 237, 243, 249, 253-259, 273, 279; marketing practices, 300

Baer, G. F., 194
Bakelite, 273
Bakke, E. W., 200
Baldwin, G. B., 217, 224
Banana industry, 240
Bank reserves, changes in, 61, 65, 69, 72, 77, 78, 84, 86
Banking Act of 1935, 53
Banking and Currency Committee, 155
Barber, B., 95, 107
Bartlett, H. R., 237, 268
Bastiat, 33
Beaton, K., 268

375